LITERATURE IN MOTION

LITERATURE NOW

LITERATURE NOW

Matthew Hart, David James, and Rebecca L. Walkowitz, Series Editors

Literature Now offers a distinct vision of late-twentieth- and early-twenty-first-century literary culture. Addressing contemporary literature and the ways we understand its meaning, the series includes books that are comparative and transnational in scope as well as those that focus on national and regional literary cultures.

Caren Irr, *Toward the Geopolitical Novel: U.S. Fiction in the Twenty-First Century*

Heather Houser, *Ecosickness in Contemporary U.S. Fiction: Environment and Affect*

Mrinalini Chakravorty, *In Stereotype: South Asia in the Global Literary Imaginary*

Héctor Hoyos, *Beyond Bolaño: The Global Latin American Novel*

Rebecca L. Walkowitz, *Born Translated: The Contemporary Novel in an Age of World Literature*

Carol Jacobs, *Sebald's Vision*

Sarah Phillips Casteel, *Calypso Jews: Jewishness in the Caribbean Literary Imagination*

Jeremy Rosen, *Minor Characters Have Their Day: Genre and the Contemporary Literary Marketplace*

Jesse Matz, *Lasting Impressions: The Legacies of Impressionism in Contemporary Culture*

Ashley T. Shelden, *Unmaking Love: The Contemporary Novel and the Impossibility of Union*

Theodore Martin, *Contemporary Drift: Genre, Historicism, and the Problem of the Present*

Zara Dinnen, *The Digital Banal: New Media and American Literature and Culture*

Gloria Fisk, *Orhan Pamuk and the Good of World Literature*

Peter Morey, *Islamophobia and the Novel*

Sarah Chihaya, Merve Emre, Katherine Hill, and Jill Richards, *The Ferrante Letters: An Experiment in Collective Criticism*

Christy Wampole, *Degenerative Realism: Novel and Nation in Twenty-First-Century France*

Heather Houser, *Infowhelm: Environmental Art and Literature in an Age of Data*

Jessica Pressman, *Bookishness: Loving Books in a Digital Age*

Sunny Xiang, *Tonal Intelligence: The Aesthetics of Asian Inscrutability During the Long Cold War*

Thomas Heise, *The Gentrification Plot: New York and the Postindustrial Crime Novel*

Literature in Motion

TRANSLATING MULTILINGUALISM
ACROSS THE AMERICAS

Ellen Jones

Columbia University Press
New York

Columbia University Press
Publishers Since 1893
New York   Chichester, West Sussex
cup.columbia.edu
Copyright © 2022 Ellen Jones
All rights reserved

Library of Congress Cataloging-in-Publication Data
Names: Jones, Ellen, 1989– author.
Title: Literature in motion : translating multilingualism across the Americas / Ellen C. Jones.
Description: New York : Columbia University Press, 2021. | Series: Literature now | Includes bibliographical references and index.
Identifiers: LCCN 2021027192 (print) | LCCN 2021027193 (ebook) | ISBN 9780231203029 (hardback) | ISBN 9780231203036 (trade paperback) | ISBN 9780231554831 (ebook)
Subjects: LCSH: Multilingualism and literature. | Translating and interpreting. | Spanglish literature—History and criticism. | Spanglish literature—Translations—History and criticism. | Portuñol literature—History and criticism. | Portuñol literature—Translations—History and criticism.
Classification: LCC PN171.M93 J66 2021 (print) | LCC PN171.M93 (ebook) | DDC 418/.04—dc23
LC record available at https://lccn.loc.gov/2021027192
LC ebook record available at https://lccn.loc.gov/2021027193

Cover image: *Day Horizon* (2017) © Alex Caminker/Bridgeman Images
Cover design: Chang Jae Lee

For me

Y de repente hablan. Hablan una lengua intermedia con la que Makina simpatiza de inmediato porque es como ella: maleable, deleble, permeable, un gozne entre dos semejantes distantes y luego entre otros dos, y luego entre otros dos, nunca exactamente los mismos, un algo que sirve para poner en relación. Más que un punto medio entre lo paisano y lo gabacho su lengua es una franja difusa entre lo que desaparece y lo que no ha nacido.

—YURI HERRERA

And then they speak. They speak an intermediary tongue that Makina instantly warms to because it's like her: malleable, erasable, permeable: a hinge pivoting between two like but distant souls, and then two more, and then two more, never exactly the same ones; something that serves as a link. More than the midpoint between homegrown and anglo their tongue is a nebulous territory between what is dying out and what is not yet born.

—YURI HERRERA, TRANSLATED BY LISA DILLMAN

La traducción ni traiciona ni sustituye, es una aportación más, un empujón a un texto que ya estaba en movimiento, como cuando alguien se sube a un coche en marcha.

—ANDRÉS NEUMAN

Translation is neither a betrayal nor a substitute, it is another contribution, a further push to something that is already in motion, like when someone jumps into a moving carriage.

—ANDRÉS NEUMAN, TRANSLATED BY NICK CAISTOR AND LORENZA GARCIA

CONTENTS

ACKNOWLEDGMENTS xiii

A NOTE ON TRANSLATIONS xv

Introduction
Translation and Multilingualism in Contemporary
American Literature 1
"Spanglish" and the U.S. English Paradigm 5
"Portunhol" 16
"Frenglish" 20
New Multilingual Writing 22
Translating Multilingualism 26
The Approaches and Structure of This Book 31

Chapter One
"Mi lengua es un palimpsesto": Susana Chávez-Silverman's
Palimpsestuous Writing 36
Part I. Palimpsests in *Killer Crónicas* 40
Linguistic Palimpsests 43
Sonic Palimpsests 45
Textual Palimpsests 50

CONTENTS

    Creative/Critical Palimpsests   54
    A Case Study: "Axolotl Crónica"   58
  Part II. Translating Susana Chávez-Silverman   64
    Calques, False Cognates, and Fake Translations   65
    A Crónica in Translation   68

Chapter Two
Censorship and (Pseudo-)Translation in Junot Díaz's *The Brief Wondrous Life of Oscar Wao*   78
  Part I. Reading the Blanks in *Oscar Wao*   80
    Creolized English and Unexplained References   80
    Blank Texts, Blank Bodies   85
    Narrative Blanks and Fragmentation   87
    Filling in *Oscar Wao*'s Blanks   89
    Authorial Rewritings of *Oscar Wao*   92
  Part II. *Oscar Wao* in Translation   98
    Oscar Wao as Pseudotranslation   98
    Translating a Translation: Achy Obejas's *Oscar Wao*   101
    Filling in *Oscar Wao*'s Blanks   104
    Creating New Blanks   107
    Translation as Palimpsest   113

Chapter Three
"I Want My Closet Back": Queering and Unqueering Language in Giannina Braschi's *Yo-Yo Boing!*   115
  Part I. Queer Language, Queer Texts, Queer Bodies   116
    "A Frustrating Challenge"   116
    Bilingual Difficulty   119
    Queering Language   124
    Policing Language, Gender, and Desire   126
    Queering Eliot   129
    Queer Texts, Queer Bodies   131
  Part II. A Relationship of Equals? Tess O'Dwyer's Translation of *Yo-Yo Boing!*   134
    Approaches to Translation   135
    Increased Accessibility   139

CONTENTS

Unqueering *Yo-Yo Boing!*   141
Translation as Self-Commentary   142
A Queer Textual Relationship?   145

Chapter Four
Fluid Trajectories in Two Versions of Wilson Bueno's
Mar Paraguayo   148
Part I. Border Crossings in *Mar Paraguayo*   150
Linguistic Fluidity   150
Gender and Sexual Fluidity in *Mar Paraguayo*   159
Cultural Hybridity in *Mar Paraguayo*   162
Part II. From South to North: Erín Moure's
Paraguayan Sea   167
Erin, Erín, Eirin: Fluid Borders in Moure's Poetic Oeuvre   168
From *Mar Paraguayo* to *Paraguayan Sea*   173
A Text in Continued Motion   183

Coda
Beyond America: Multilingualism, Translation,
and *Asymptote*   186

NOTES   195

BIBLIOGRAPHY   227

INDEX   245

ACKNOWLEDGMENTS

A version of part of chapter 2 of this book was first published as "'The Página Is Still Blanca': Reading the Blanks in Junot Díaz's *The Brief Wondrous Life of Oscar Wao*," *Hispanic Research Journal* 19, no. 3 (2018): 281–95. A version of chapter 3 was first published as "'I Want My Closet Back': Queering and Unqueering Language in Giannina Braschi's *Yo-Yo Boing!*," *Textual Practice* 34, no. 2 (2020): 283–301. In both instances, I am grateful to Taylor and Francis for their permission to reuse the material here.

I am grateful to the two anonymous readers of this book for their enthusiasm and careful, thought-provoking feedback, which was invaluable in helping me to prepare the best possible version of this manuscript. Thank you also to the series editors at Columbia University Press, David James, Rebecca Walkowitz, and Matthew Hart, and to Philip Leventhal, Monique Briones, Kathryn Jorge, and Adriana Cloud for shepherding the book to publication.

Thanks are due to Hispanic Research Publications at Queen Mary University of London for a subsidy supporting the publication of this book. I am also grateful to Queen Mary for my Principal's Studentship in the Humanities, which enabled me to carry out the research for the first three chapters, and in particular to my two outstanding PhD supervisors there, Rachael Gilmour and Omar García, who have remained cheerleaders for me and my work ever since. In addition, thank you to Sam McBean for her generous feedback; to Zara Dinnen and David Wylot for their encouragement and advice when it came to looking for a publisher; to Peter Howarth, for his kindness and wisdom at a crucial moment; to John London, for his conviction that the book would eventually get published; to Karina Lickorish Quinn, for her insights about multilingualism in the classroom and for allowing me to publish her beautiful essay "Spanglish" in *Asymptote* in 2015; and to John Dunn, Ghazouane Arslane, Samuel Diamond, Andrew Hines, and Shital Pravinchandra, for reading sections of the work at different stages of its development and for sharing their ideas with me.

Thank you to the Institute for Modern Languages Research at the School of Advanced Study for the Open World Research Initiative Fellowship in Languages and Communities, which gave me the time and space to write the final chapter of this book. I was also lucky enough to be able to share work in progress at conferences in locations as diverse as Istanbul, Santiago de Compostela, Oxford, Norwich, and London. Thank you to the conference organizers and to all those who contributed to the conversations that grew out of those presentations.

Thank you to Susana Chávez-Silverman, for all her glorious correspondence over the years (long may it continue to grace my inbox), for agreeing to come all the way to London to read to us, and for permitting me to quote from our interview in 2015; and to Tess O'Dwyer and Erín Moure, for their generous responses to my queries about their work. Thank you also to Erín for permitting me to quote from our email exchange.

Special thanks go to Matthew Kennedy, for encouraging me to do a PhD in the first place; to Katie Da Cunha Lewin for being the other half of my literary brain; to Alexander and Emily Cardona for their enormous generosity in welcoming me into their home for the duration of my studies and making me feel like family; to my actual family for all their support and enthusiasm, and in particular to my mother, a consummate linguist, for always having an etymological dictionary to hand, and for her heroic proofreading efforts, too.

Y por último, gracias a Omar Hernández Martínez, por recordarme que no debo tomarme todo tan en serio y que hay cosas más importantes en la vida que el trabajo.

A NOTE ON TRANSLATIONS

Unless otherwise stated, all translations in parentheses are my own. I recognize their faint absurdity, given the topic of this book.

LITERATURE IN MOTION

INTRODUCTION

Translation and Multilingualism in Contemporary American Literature

In Yuri Herrera's *Señales que precederán al fin del mundo* (*Signs Preceding the End of the World*), from which I have chosen the first epigraph to this book, a young Mexican switchboard operator called Makina crosses the border into the United States hoping to find her brother. Makina is a communicator, an intercessor, a liminal being, and she identifies instantly with the mixture of "anglo" and "homegrown" tongues she hears spoken in the borderlands: a language that is "malleable, erasable, permeable," constantly pivoting between subtly different versions.[1] Like her, it is nebulous, difficult to define, accommodating of contradictions in abundance. And like her, it is in constant movement. This kind of language, and the literary voices that use it, are the subject of this book.

Literature in Motion: Translating Multilingualism Across the Americas is part of an ongoing effort to break down a long-held assumption in institutions of literary study and publication: that literature is fundamentally monolingual. This change in perspective has wide-ranging implications, not only for literary pedagogy and the international publishing industry, but, as this book will demonstrate, also for contemporary translation practices. Translation, I want to show, can be multilingual too. The work of a translator, like the language Makina hears in Herrera's novel, involves constant movement, a repeated pivoting between infinitesimally different versions. In his novel *El viajero del siglo* (*Traveller of the Century*), from where I have taken my second epigraph, Andrés Neuman describes translation as "another contribution, a further push to something that is already in motion."[2] This understanding of translation as movement is not exactly new; it is a commonplace to point out that the word's Latinate etymology, *trans + latus*, means "to carry across." But it is nevertheless an idea to which I will return throughout this study. Movement, I want to show, is something that multilingual writing and translation have in common. Both are fluid, malleable, shifting.

One of this book's main goals is to demonstrate that these two things—multilingual writing and translation—are more similar than is often assumed. Literary multilingualism studies have traditionally focused on the simultaneous presence of multiple languages in a piece of writing, whereas translation studies are concerned with the transfer from one (and it is usually assumed to be just one) language to another. Often, they are described as opposites in this regard. But the readings in this volume demonstrate that it is both arbitrary and unproductive to hold these two literary practices apart from one another. Translation need not—as is often assumed—undermine or eliminate the diversity, complexity, and subversive potential of multilingualism. On the contrary, the two creative practices are closely intertwined, to the extent that translation is always to some extent implied in multilingual writing.

Throughout this book, I understand literary translation as a form of creative versioning, and translators as creative writers in their own right. In the chapters that follow, I read translation both *in* and *of* the work of contemporary multilingual prose writers, attending to the ways different languages shape their writing practices as well as their reception in an increasingly interconnected global literary marketplace. In so doing, this book argues that, when it comes to multilingual literary production, the boundary between writing and translation is often arbitrary and unhelpful. Moreover, it demonstrates that multilingual writing is not so irreducibly specific to particular geographies and communities that it cannot travel; paying sustained attention to the translation of multilingual writing is one means of considering its status as world literature.

The multilingual mixture evoked in Herrera's novel, often referred to as "Spanglish," has a long literary history among writers in the United States and is undoubtedly the best studied of literary multilingualisms

INTRODUCTION

in the American hemisphere. The interplay between these two major languages—Spanish and English—will make up the better part of the analysis in this book: the first three chapters focus on the writing and translation of three U.S. Latinx authors: Susana Chávez-Silverman, Junot Díaz, and Giannina Braschi.[3] However, the oft-maligned "Spanglish" is by no means the only literary multilingualism on the continent, and the final chapter of the book will turn to the work of Brazilian writer Wilson Bueno, whose 1992 novel *Mar Paraguayo* combines Portuguese and Spanish—or "Portunhol"—with the Indigenous American language Guarani, and to the work of his Canadian translator Erín Moure, who recreates Bueno's novel in "Frenglish"—French and English. This final chapter helps to shift the study of literary multilingualism off its United States–centered axis, to broaden it out into the American hemisphere, and into other language constellations. Along with the coda that follows, it seeks to show that the strategies and processes underway in U.S. Latinx writing are by no means restricted to one linguistic community.

Through these readings, the book offers different ways of thinking about multilingual writing and the role of translation in it, including as a palimpsest, as a form of censorship, and as a queer practice. It charts a number of features that often recur in contemporary multilingual texts, which include a commitment to slow, difficult reading; a debt to oral forms; genre and gender fluidity; reflection on the texts' own textuality and circulation; and a sense of being unfinished, or "unfinalizable." In so doing, the book demonstrates that multilingualism and the translational processes it entails are tightly imbricated with other forms of textual and conceptual hybridity, fluidity, and disruption. It also makes clear that these are not minor practices within contemporary American literature; rather, they are crucial to how many writers and translators are engaging with their increasingly globalized, multilingual present.

Far from rejecting translation, all of the writers addressed here in fact give translation a crucial role in their textual composition, whether in the form of playful calques (also called loan translations), pseudotranslations (texts that pretend to be translations), surface translations (where the sounds of one language are translated into the words of another, regardless of the sense they make), or metanarrative devices that anticipate and invite future translation. Translation of their published works for publication in new territories therefore offers a natural creative supplement to processes already underway, one which allows these works to travel beyond their place(s) of inception and to make new connections. Rather than judging the success of these translations, or their degree of fidelity to a source, I examine how they contribute creatively to the work as a whole, which is understood to be a still-evolving entity.

Throughout this book I will use the term "Spanglish" to refer to writing by Díaz, Chávez-Silverman, and Braschi. Although a conflicted term, it remains a useful, widely recognizable shorthand. It is used in the marketing of Braschi's *Yo-Yo Boing!* and of Chávez-Silverman's books (University of Wisconsin Press describes her writing as an "inventive and flamboyant use of Spanglish"),[4] and reviewers and critics often characterize Junot Díaz's writing as "Spanglish," too.[5] All three writers have used the term to talk publicly about their own work, although studying each of them in isolation would undoubtedly lead to three very different definitions of the term. Chávez-Silverman's confident, sustained use of intra-sentential code-switching and highly wrought puns are quite distinct from the anxious inter-sentential code-switching of Braschi's characters, whose English shows signs of ongoing language acquisition.[6] Meanwhile, Díaz uses English much more extensively than either of the two women writers, but it is a "creolized" English, as I argue in chapter 2, structured in part by the syntax and lexis of Spanish. I prefer to think of the term in its plural form: "Spanglishes," in order to emphasize the heterogeneity of language used by these three writers, as well as its continuing motion and evolution as it manifests for each of them in multiple textual versions.

"Portunhol" or "Portuñol" and especially "Frenglish" have less currency than "Spanglish," but I have nevertheless followed the writers themselves in adopting the terms in my readings of their work. Although each of these portmanteau words suggests a too-easy fusion of supposedly sovereign linguistic systems, the chapters of this book discuss at length the idiomatic diversity and structural permeability within each of those systems, and the myriad ways in which each of them manifests in contemporary American literature. At this juncture I want to take a brief look at each of them in turn. I will begin with the term "Spanglish," which is worth discussing at some length, given that it can be applied to the bulk of the literary work to be examined in this book.

"SPANGLISH" AND THE U.S. ENGLISH PARADIGM

First of all, it is important to set the scene here by establishing the norm from which "Spanglish" writing departs. In particular, it is worth outlining the distinct valences of English-language monolingualism, particularly in the United States, where three of the four writers addressed in the chapters of this book are based. A brief survey of recent attitudes toward language there is particularly helpful at the outset of this section.

The 1980s saw the rise of U.S. English and English First, two organizations that sought to establish English as the official language of the U.S. government, on the basis that a common language has an important role in establishing political unity.[7] Although English has long been the de facto national language in the United States, used for legislation, regulations, treaties, and court rulings, historically, unlike many other nation-states, the United States has never had an official language at the federal level. Support for these organizations continued to grow throughout the 1990s, prompted by anti-immigration sentiment directed in particular at newcomers from the country's Spanish-speaking neighbors: mainly Mexico, but also Cuba, the Free Associated State of Puerto Rico, and other parts of Central and South America.[8] Meanwhile monolingualism was further entrenched by a complacent assumption that there was little need to equip the nation with fluent speakers of other languages, because the unprecedented global influence of English meant that others would take on the burden of language learning instead. Brian Lennon points to an Anglophone "flourishing" in the years after the Cold War, between "the vanishing of the old Russian-speaking adversary and the emergence of a new Arabic-speaking one," during which time a survey by the Modern Language Association shows that enrolment in foreign-language instruction declined.[9]

However, the events of September 11, 2001, were a wake-up call that this complacency had been a serious misjudgment. During the United States' occupation of Iraq, its history of Anglocentrism posed a very real political danger, as a dearth of Arabic translators meant that military and intelligence officials were forced to rely on machine translation to convey sensitive information. In the introduction to her book *The Translation Zone*, written during the early part of the conflict in Iraq, Emily Apter characterizes geopolitical relations during the period as being afflicted by failures of understanding at every level, pointing out that translation can be a matter of war and peace.[10] A policy of strict English monolingualism, it became clear, can have serious national security implications. According to Brecht and Rivers, the United States' need for individuals with highly developed competency in languages other than English for use in social economic, diplomatic, and geopolitical arenas had never been higher than in the years following the 9/11 attacks; more than seventy government agencies reported a need for such individuals, where shortages had "adversely affected agency operations and hindered U.S. military, law enforcement, intelligence, counter terrorism, and diplomatic efforts."[11] Around the turn of the century, there was an acknowledgment that the pervasiveness of Anglophone monolingualism was "a serious deficit of educational, economic, and military resources" in the United States, and there was a subsequent revival of support for modern-languages teaching, on the basis that those who speak more than one language are not only intellectual but also political assets.[12] Arabic language teaching and learning in particular drew sudden attention from both the educational community and the federal and local governments, with enrolments in Arabic courses showing rapid growth.[13]

During these years, there was also an intensification of calls within humanities scholarship to understand multilingualism and language acquisition as having equally important roles in national cultural intelligence; as Mary Louise Pratt pointed out in 2003, "language is far too big an issue to be contained by national security issues alone."[14] These years saw a growth in literary scholarship re-evaluating the importance of translation and multilingualism to U.S. literary history and demonstrating the inadequacy of English to tell the stories of U.S. citizens and residents.[15] Werner Sollors in particular, in his edited collection *Multilingual America*, advocated "English plus other languages" and called for a major re-examination of U.S. literary history in the light of multilingualism. Part of a larger project launched at Harvard University by Sollors and Marc Shell, which promoted research on, and the republication of, U.S. literature in languages other than English, Sollors's book is an effort to readjust the national self-imagining in ways that acknowledge the United States to be, and, importantly, to always have been, multilingual.[16] It makes the case that an "English plus" educational policy would both "prepare children for the twenty-first century and preserve the American tradition."[17] Doris Sommer's 2004 book *Bilingual Aesthetics* also argues for the development of a language and literature pedagogy that encourages students to value rather than be ashamed of an aesthetic that results from knowledge of more than one language. Sommer makes the case that society is distinctly better off for being multicultural and multilingual, in ways that go beyond economic and security advantages; she advocates the aesthetic and intellectual stimulation provided by multiple languages, and, in particular, the "democratizing effects of provocation" afforded by "foreignness" or cultural and linguistic difference.[18]

Despite these trends, and despite the relative quiescence of the English-only movement in the 2000s, in 2021 there is a residual, even resurgent Anglocentrism in the United States. Former president Trump's attitudes toward Spanish indicate a measure of retrenchment when it comes to language politics. On the campaign trail, the "nefariously monolingual" Trump resisted buying any Spanish-language television or radio airtime, asserted that immigrants should speak English, not Spanish, and criticized Jeb Bush for speaking Spanish at a rally.[19] In addition to the Trump administration attempting to clamp down on migration and tighten the conditions of citizenship so that it is more difficult for non-English speakers to remain in the United States, the Spanish-language pages of the White House website were removed on Trump's first day in office, not to be restored until Joe Biden was sworn in in January 2021. In the United States, English remains overwhelmingly the language of education and public life, as well as, of course, publishing.

Outside of the United States, English has an important role as a global lingua franca, including in bureaucracy, development, international relations, and big business. In the publishing world, too, it has a corresponding central role in the canon of world literature; Francesca Orsini has shown world literature to be overwhelmingly Anglo-American, while Tim Parks memorably describes it as "dull," in the sense of being excessively homogenous in an attempt to be easily saleable around the world, whether in translation or for an international English readership.[20] Perhaps the most enduring definition of world literature is indisputably monolingual: David Damrosch calls world literature works that "circulate beyond their culture of origin, either in translation or in their original language."[21] As this book will extensively demonstrate, this definition is seriously lacking; it is by no means always possible to assume that a text has either a single "original language" or a single "culture of origin." This United States–dominated, monolingual English literary paradigm is what the writers in the first three chapters of this book are struggling against.

Latinx writers have long resisted English's status as the singular language of value in the United States (and beyond) by registering the presence of Spanish in their writing in both overt and covert ways. Overt uses include its appearance in characters' speech; take this example from Chicano writer Américo Paredes's 1930s novel *George Washington Gómez*, for instance, where readers are told that "an old woman appeared at the threshold screaming angrily at the doctor, '*Viejo cabrón! Pendejo! Ándale!*'" (You old asshole! Idiot! Get a move on!).[22] Covert uses, on the other hand, include the appearance of calques—literal translations of idioms and proverbs—such as, again in *George Washington Gómez*, the exclamation "Mother of mine!" (translated from "Madre mía!"), and the idiom "love from a distance, the love of fools" (translated from the rhyming "amor de lejos, amor de pendejos").[23] These strategies result in the text being read differently by different readers; those who have knowledge of Spanish may feel gratified and included, while those who do not are alienated, because the language of the text is strange or difficult to them.

Paredes's Spanish is, nevertheless, vastly outweighed by the presence of English in his novel, as it has historically been in much Latinx writing. What is more, Spanish words and phrases are often "cushioned," as Lourdes Torres puts it, making them easily understood by nonspeakers of Spanish.[24] For instance, they are often restricted to internationally recognizable items like food and drink (*tortilla, taco*) or family relationships (*mamá, papá*), or to exclamations and expletives, as in the example above ("*Viejo cabrón! Pendejo! Ándale!*"), where the precise meaning of the words is less important than a sense that they are expressed with vehemence, which is sufficiently evident from the punctuation alone.[25] In other instances, Spanish words are explained and translated into English ("'*Tiene usted razón, Hermano,*' he said. 'You are right, Brother.'").[26] This type of glossing can, as Bill Ashcroft, Gareth Griffiths, and Helen Tiffin put it, "impede the movement of plot as the story is forced to drag an explanatory machinery behind it," and is likely to alienate those readers who do have a passing familiarity with Spanish and so must endure redundant repetition.[27]

Since the 1930s, when Paredes was writing, Spanish has come to be mobilized more frequently and more boldly by Chicanxs as a way of validating their experiences in response to the political and cultural exclusions they have long endured in the United States. The Chicanx movement of the 1960s and 1970s saw new university-level courses established across the United States specifically to attend to the cultures and histories of Latinx communities; it was then that "Spanglish" first gained real prominence as a literary style.[28] Many Chicanx writers, including Sandra Cisneros, Ana Castillo, and Rolando Hinojosa, joined Paredes in using Spanish to emphasize themes of identity and marginalization, and as a form of resistance against the dominance of Anglo-American culture. Particularly important is the work of writer and activist Gloria Anzaldúa, a sixth-generation Chicana, born in 1942 close to the border with Mexico. In her *Borderlands/La Frontera: The New Mestiza* (1987), which played a key role in consolidating the academic study of the United States–Mexico border region, she mixes English and Spanish in much more extensive and sustained ways than Paredes does in *George Washington Gómez*. In the preface to the first edition, she asks to be "met halfway"—for readers to engage with all of the text's linguistic demands rather than to rely on translation into English.[29] A key chapter called "How to Tame a Wild Tongue" describes the stigma attached to Chicanx speech, and the concomitant shame it provokes in those who use it. Anzaldúa recalls, for instance, being physically punished for speaking Spanish at school, and being made to take speech classes at university to purge her English of its Mexican accent. Chicanxs, she notes, have also "internalized the belief that we speak poor Spanish. It is illegitimate, a bastard language."[30] Seeking to counter this perception, Anzaldúa argues that Chicanx Spanish is "not incorrect, it is a living language . . . a language with terms that are neither *español ni inglés* [Spanish nor English], but both."[31] She identifies "Tex-Mex" or "Spanglish," whereby she switches "back and forth from English to Spanish in the same sentence or in the same word," as the language that "comes most naturally" to her.[32]

The term "Spanglish" dates as far back as 1933 and usually describes speech in casual or oral registers that combines English and Spanish; for Anzaldúa it is the language she uses with those she knows best: her brother and sister, and her "Chicano *tejano*" (Texan) contemporaries.[33] As she explains, "Spanglish" has long been a derogatory term, used to imply a lesser, impure language variety. Acosta-Belén observes that "speakers of the non-defined mixture of Spanish and/or English are judged as 'different,' or 'sloppy' speakers of Spanish and/or English, and are often labeled verbally deprived, alingual, or deficient bilinguals because supposedly they do not have the ability to speak either English or Spanish well."³⁴ The mixing of English and Spanish in this way is sometimes assumed to be the result of insufficient education, as it is by literary critic Roberto González Echevarría, who, writing in the *New York Times*, suggested that "Spanglish" is mainly used by Latinxs of low socioeconomic status who are illiterate in both languages. For this reason he believes it to be "un grave peligro a la cultura hispánica y al progreso de los hispanos dentro de la corriente mayoritaria norteamericana" (a grave danger to Hispanic culture and to the progress of Hispanics within mainstream North American culture), which "indica marginalización, no liberación" (indicates marginalization, not liberation).³⁵ This association of "Spanglish" with poor language competence is borne out in more recent definitions of the term written by members of the public on the crowd-sourced online site Urban Dictionary, where it is described, to take just one example, as "a hodgepodge of sounds made by people who haven't learned the basics of either Spanish or English."³⁶ Due to this pervasive public perception, linguists often reject the term "Spanglish"; John Lipski has called it "as out of place in promoting Latino language and culture as are the words *crazy, lunatic, crackpot*, or *nut case* in mental health care, or *bum, slob, misfit*, and *loser* in social work."³⁷ Yet Anzaldúa boldly asserts her right to use it, stating: "Until I am free to write bilingually and to switch codes without having always to translate, while I still have to speak English or Spanish when I would rather speak Spanglish, and as long as I have to accommodate the English speakers rather than having them accommodate me, my tongue will be illegitimate."³⁸ "Spanglish" is one way for Anzaldúa to express herself as "a composite being, amalgama de culturas y de lenguas" (amalgam of cultures and languages); but she also writes certain essays and poems in just English, or in just Spanish, and often incorporates words from Nahuatl, too, as a marker of her Indigenous heritage.³⁹ She claims many identity positions, all of which, she argues, are overlapping and mutually informing. Throughout *Borderlands/La Frontera*, the border between the United States and Mexico is established as a metaphor for all types of boundaries and crossings—not just between geographical territories and languages, but also between sexual identities, cultures, ethnicities, and social classes. These crossings are mirrored in the very structure of the book itself, which is ambiguous in terms of genre: the first section is made up of essays that draw on personal experience and Chicanx history, while the second section comprises poems; however, the essays incorporate quotations from poetry, and many of the poems give brutal historical accounts, blurring the boundaries between these two forms.

A closer look at "To live in the Borderlands means you," a poem appearing toward the end of *Borderlands/La Frontera*, demonstrates how "Spanglish" is used to express many of the key aspects of Anzaldúa's border thinking:

Cuando vives en la frontera
people walk through you, the wind steals your voice,
you're a *burra, buey*, scapegoat,
forerunner of a new race,
half and half—both woman and man, neither—
a new gender.[40]

Living in the borderlands denotes much more than being physically between two nation-states. It implies subjection to multiple forms of oppression, including those associated with language, race, class, and sexuality. It can reduce a person, in the eyes of others, to the status of a dumb animal ("*burra, buey*" [she-donkey, ox]), rendering them invisible and silent, their body insubstantial as a ghost, their voice "stolen." Anzaldúa argues in *Borderlands* that different types of marginalization should not be ranked, nor understood to be static, but rather seen as fluid systems that intersect and can take on different forms. She was one of the first Chicanas to publicly claim her lesbianism and to overtly challenge the exclusions of white feminism, insisting instead on the specificity of the multiple prejudices experienced by queer women of color. But there is also hope in these lines: promising "a new race" and "a new gender," they embrace the utopian potential of Anzaldúa's hybrid "new *mestiza* consciousness." We can see in this poem, and across *Borderlands* more widely, a bold claim for the legitimacy of Chicanx experiences, including their speech. There is pride, as well as anger, here, in existing at the crossroads of so many marginalized identity positions.

Anzaldúa's work has been taken up widely in the academy in fields as varied as postcolonial studies, queer studies, and political science, and she remains a powerful figure in the study of Latinx literary bilingualism. We can see the legacy of her intersectional thinking in the work of Braschi and Chávez-Silverman, who explore, for instance, the relationship of "Spanglish" to queerness (see chapters 1 and 3) and reflect on the privileges that accompany membership of a scholarly elite (see chapter 1). However, as I will go on to show, these writers not only replicate but also extend Anzaldúa's strategies of literary multilingualism, demanding more of their readers and engaging more committedly with the exoticization of Latinx identity.

We must remember that Chicanxs, of course, are not the only U.S. writers to have used "Spanglish." The Latinx population of the United States grew by 61 percent between 1970 and 1980, and then again by 53 percent during the following decade, over seven times as fast as the rest of the nation.[41] Many immigrant writers joined Chicanxs in experimenting with a mixture of English and Spanish in their writing, including Dominican Americans like Julia Álvarez and Junot Díaz (whose writing I discuss in chapter 2), and Cuban Americans like Oscar Hijuelos, Cristina García, and Achy Obejas (whose translation work I also examine in chapter 2). The largest population of Latinxs in the United States—after those of Mexican origin, who make up over half—is Puerto Rican. Following a large postwar wave of immigration, particularly to New York, "Nuyoricans" began to use "Spanglish" in their writing as a form of resistance to their marginalization from mainstream Anglophone culture, and as a way of distinguishing themselves from the culture of Puerto Rico itself.[42] Centering on the slam poetry competitions hosted by the Nuyorican Poets Café, Nuyorican literature came to be characterized by oral, bilingual forms used in everyday speech. In an anthology of poetry performed at the café, editor Miguel Algarín described "Spanglish" as "a new language, a new tradition of communication" taking center stage in an emerging poetics of Puerto Rican diaspora.[43] Despite the term's frequently derogatory use, many Nuyoricans and Boricuas (a popular term of self-affirmation in the diaspora, deriving from Borikén, the Taíno word for the island now called Puerto Rico) have claimed "Spanglish" as a positive badge of bicultural identity. For instance, in *Living in Spanglish*, journalist Ed Morales sees "Spanglish" as not just a language but also a powerful new cultural identity and an act of resistance against Anglo-American cultural dominance.[44] The critic Ana Celia Zentella, too, has rebutted the argument against "Spanglish," claiming that the word can be given a more positive meaning, rescued by semantic inversion in a similar way to previously derogatory words like *queer* and *Chicano*.[45] Giannina Braschi, whose novel *Yo-Yo Boing!* I discuss in chapter 3, claims three writing languages, "Spanish, Spanglish, and English," on the jacket of her books, "to explore the three political options of Puerto Rico—nation, colony, or state."[46]

As the Latinx population of the United States has continued to increase (the most recent census data indicates that it has now topped fifty-five million, forty million of whom report speaking Spanish at home), it has become convention for Latinx writers of all kinds to combine English and Spanish in some way.[47] As a result, some have accused them of turning texts into cultural tour guides aimed predominantly at Anglo-American readers. Gustavo Pérez Firmat is among those to point out that in much Latinx writing Spanish is used merely to "bait" readers "with the lure of the exotic," promising safe access via English to a generalized and alluring "latinidad."[48] It is unsurprising that English predominates in Latinx writing, as it does for instance in *George Washington Gómez*, since most writers in the United States have been formally educated in English, and the publishing marketplace there is predominantly Anglophone. But Latinx writers have often written conspicuously for a non-Latinx, English-dominant readership, developing strategies of bilingualism designed for the many non-Spanish-speaking readers who will encounter them. Often, the specific meaning of a Spanish word in a narrative is less important than its ability to signal a vague and unproblematized "latinidad." While historically the idea of a shared pan-Latin American ethnicity has enabled Latin Americans to define themselves against both Spanish colonialism and U.S. imperialism,[49] it also risks erasing the considerable differences between the experiences of, say, a Cuban exile in Miami, a Puerto Rican moving between New York and San Juan, a Salvadoran who fled the civil war, and a Chicanx with a long-standing cultural claim to territory in the Southwest (known as Aztlán).

The global influence of Anglophone culture shapes even the way Anzaldúa accommodates her readers, despite her plea to be "met halfway" when it comes to language. In *Borderlands/La Frontera*, Spanish words appear in italics, marking them as foreign, even in instances where an entire poem is composed exclusively in Spanish; meanwhile, all the English is romanized. In the chapters and passages that combine both languages, Spanish words sometimes appear in glossaries at the bottom of the page, as they do in "To live in the Borderlands means you," the poem discussed above, where readers are told that the words "burra" and "buey" correspond to "donkey" and "oxen."[50] Marlene Hansen Esplin has shown at length how Anzaldúa "compensates for potential unknowns in Spanish by explaining more in English," thus figuring Spanish as "an Other language marked by italics and accounted for by parentheses, footnotes, repetition, context, or other strategies of translation."[51] Graham Huggan has called this phenomenon "strategic exoticism" or "staged marginality," whereby a writer's marginal status is commodified for mainstream readers.[52] It is an aspect of their publishing that Latinx authors have begun to expect and to consciously interact with, in order to reconfigure stereotypical notions of "latinidad" both in their writing itself and in the public presentation of their work.[53] The Latinx writers addressed in this book, for instance, acknowledge the exoticizing potential of their own work, which is by no means a straightforward capitulation to the dominance of Anglo-American culture. Chávez-Silverman, Díaz, and Braschi engage and interact with the expectation that their "latinidad" will be marketed as a commodity to non-Latinx readers, and so comment in complex and knowing ways on their own marginality.[54] Part of the work of this book is to demonstrate how these three Latinx writers break down and subvert long-standing conventions regarding the use of "Spanglish" in published writing. They do it in ways that differ from those of perhaps the most enthusiastic advocate of "Spanglish": Ilan Stavans, a Latinx studies scholar who has positioned himself as the public face of the discipline. Stavans has made many efforts to establish a Latinx literary canon based on the mixing of Spanish and English and has attempted to legitimize and codify "Spanglish" as a literary language. However, while he has undoubtedly helped popularize the term, his uses of written "Spanglish" have not always been well received. As Rachael Gilmour and Tamar Steinitz note in their introduction to a recent collection of essays, multilingualism can "serve dominant visions of the nation-state, or cosmopolitanism, or the effects of global cultural exchange" as well as "unsettle them profoundly."[55] Stavans's attempts to prove the flexibility and depth of "Spanglish" as a literary language by translating into it extracts from canonical works like *Don Quixote* have been criticized for reinforcing the notion that only uneducated people speak "Spanglish,"[56] and for the conservative, colonialist underpinnings of the version of "latinidad" they champion.[57]

It is worth pointing out at this stage that writing in "Spanglish" is not the only means of disrupting the hegemony of U.S. English in literature. For instance, the decision to alternate between publishing in Spanish and in English, thus withholding certain works from monolingual English readers, is transgressive in a quite different way. Peruvian American Daniel Alarcón, for instance, writes extensively in English, but has also chosen to publish a book of short stories, *El rey siempre está por encima del pueblo*, in Spanish.[58] Mexican-born Valeria Luiselli has written both fiction and nonfiction in both English and Spanish, while the Puerto Rican poet Raquel Salas Rivera has published collections in both languages, and in bilingual editions with facing translations. Self-translation, too, has its place in efforts to resist the English paradigm, as of course does the decision to write exclusively in Spanish for Latin Americans and the Spanish-speaking public in the United States.[59] Meanwhile, it should be clear that the decision to publish in "Spanglish" in, say, Mexico—where monolingualism in Spanish (another global lingua franca with a very different imperial history) is assumed but English remains a language of prestige—has a very different valence to publishing in the United States.[60] While it is important to acknowledge that multilingual writing is not the only means Latinx writers have of resisting the cultural dominance of English there, an in-depth discussion of other disruptive action is beyond the scope of this book, which is concerned specifically, as the title suggests, with the relationship between multilingual writing and multilingual translation rather than with attempts to overcome the monolingual paradigm in general.

As will be clear from this discussion, bilingual writing in Spanish and English has been largely studied as a U.S. phenomenon, and much of it is bound up with particular social and cultural histories of that region. This book, however, is committed to thinking about how translation allows "Spanglishes" to circulate more globally, in territories beyond the United States. I begin this in chapter 1, by suggesting that translation into just English allows Chávez-Silverman's writing to be read beyond the U.S. academy, then continue it in chapter 2 with my discussion of Achy Obejas's Spanish translation of Díaz's *The Brief Wondrous Life of Oscar Wao*, and in chapter 3 with my discussion of O'Dwyer's English translation of *Yo-Yo Boing!*. Moreover, given the critical mass and overall influence of U.S. cultural institutions, an American-inflected take on literary multilingualism and on world literature more broadly is becoming hegemonic. By broadening the conversation out from "Spanglish" to discuss the work of Wilson Bueno and Erín Moure, this study attempts to shift that center and remind readers that literary multilingualism is by no means the preserve of the U.S. Latinx population.

"PORTUNHOL"

"Portunhol" or "Portuñol" is neither as commonly used in literary circles nor as widely studied and documented as "Spanglish," in part due to the dominance of the United States in international scholarship, but it remains useful in the discussion of Wilson Bueno's *Mar Paraguayo*, which I examine in chapter 4 of this book. Both spellings have currency, reflecting Spanish and Portuguese orthographic conventions respectively; I use "Portunhol" in this book, following Bueno. Like "Spanglish," "Portunhol" is used to describe a wide range of linguistic phenomena, especially in border regions between Brazil and its neighboring Spanish-speaking territories.[61] It is, like "Spanglish," often said to be undesirable, "the result of laziness, indifference, or lack of respect for the other language and its speakers."[62] Language schools in the region suggest it is the result of ignorance and lack of application, to be remedied by formal language study.[63]

In Brazil, where *Mar Paraguayo* was published, the majority of inhabitants are monolingual in Portuguese, the colonial language, but the country's vision of itself as a linguistically homogenous giant is belied by the 170 surviving Indigenous languages, of which Guarani is one of the more robust. After years of linguistic suppression and language unification, including the prohibition of teaching in any other language, Portuguese is widely used as a lingua franca across Brazil's vast territory.[64] Meanwhile, across the border in Paraguay, Spanish is the de facto language of government and the primary official language, although nearly 90 percent of the largely non-Indigenous population also speaks Guarani.[65] So, although within Brazil Portuguese is undoubtedly the norm, it does not hold anything like the same prestige internationally as English does, and thus the power dynamics at play in "Portunhol" are quite different to those of "Spanglish" used in the border region between the United States and Mexico, or in the Puerto Rican diaspora. As I have already shown, historically, much "Spanglish" literature has subordinated Spanish to English, with which readers are assumed to be comfortable and familiar. English is usually dominant both in terms of quantity and in the extent to which Spanish is translated and explained. This is not consistently the case, however, with either Spanish or Portuguese in "Portunhol" literature. What is more, while Spanish and English are mutually unintelligible, typologically distinct languages (with Romantic and Germanic roots, respectively), Portuguese and Spanish are, on the contrary, highly cognate. They have almost identical syntactic structures, as well as overlapping lexicons, which results in combinations that are qualitatively and quantitatively different from literary combinations of English and Spanish. The enormous similarity between Portuguese and Spanish makes very rapid intersentential code-switching possible, but due to a high proportion of ambiguous elements (that is, elements that are identical in Spanish and Portuguese), separating out the two languages becomes a near impossibility in many cases. John Lipski has demonstrated the difficulty of establishing a "base" or "matrix" language (one language that consistently contributes more words or dictates the order in which they appear) for many "Portunhol" utterances, arguing instead that the combination often produces a "single macro-grammar," as is the case in Bueno's *Mar Paraguayo*.[66]

There is an emergent literature that identifies itself as being written in "Portunhol," although it is not nearly as established as that of "Spanglish." There is, for instance, a reasonably well-documented "Portunhol" literary tradition from the Uruguay-Brazil border; María Jesús Fernández García has discussed the use of border language in dialogue in short stories by Uruguayan writer Saúl Ibargoyen, for example.[67] Many of the same hybrid strategies seen in Bueno's *Mar Paraguayo* can also be found in a series of humorous Brazilian comic books called *Los 3 amigos*, such as the spelling of Spanish-derived words with the grapheme <rr> on the assumption that it will be pronounced with the Brazilian Portuguese velar fricative [x]: writing "rruntar" instead of "juntar," for instance, or "rodidos" instead of "jodidos." Similarly, reliance on Brazilian Portuguese pronunciation of the grapheme <j> is used to achieve the Río de la Plata pronunciation of <ll> as [ž]: writing "mijones" instead of "millones," for instance, and "mijares" instead of "millares." This transcription of words according to the orthographic rules of Portuguese in order to represent the phonetics of Spanish has the effect of alienating some readers and gratifying others, depending on their knowledge of pronunciation rules in certain parts of the Hispanophone world.

There is a prevailing sense that "Portunhol" as a phenomenon remains in its infancy, but that it will continue to grow and develop not only in speech and on the internet, but also in literature. Jesús Fernández García calls it "un producto de futuro, sobre todo en el área de MERCOSUR [the South American trade bloc made up of Brazil, Argentina, Uruguay, and

Paraguay], cuya evolución hoy sólo podemos vislumbrar en la incipiente eclosión de manifestaciones artísticas que reivindican la frontera como seña de identidad"[68] (a product of the future, especially in the MERCOSUR area, whose evolution today we can only glimpse in the fledgling blossoming of artistic expression that defends the border as a marker of identity). This is evident from the recent work of the poet Douglas Diegues, who claims to have been directly inspired by Bueno's *Mar Paraguayo*.[69] Diegues is perhaps today's most vocal advocate of literary "Portunhol." Hailing from the border town of Ponta Porã in Brazil's Paraná state, he published a book of sonnets in 2002 called *Dá gusto andar desnudo por estas selvas: Sonetos salvajes*, written in what he calls "portunhol selvagem," a denomination best explained in his 2008 "Karta manifesto del amor amor em portunhol selvagem" (Manifesto letter of love love in portunhol selvagem). In this "Karta," Diegues paid homage to a savage, rough, or wild mixture of (mainly) Portuguese and Spanish. However, this mixture will make room for any other language too, particularly the Indigenous language Guarani, which is an official language of Paraguay, alongside Spanish.[70] Diegues's open letter was addressed to the then presidents of Paraguay and Brazil, Fernando Lugo and Luiz Inácio Lula da Silva, imploring them to "QUEMAR EL CONTRATO VIGENTE DE LA ITAIPÚ BINACIONAL" (burn the current Itaipú binational contract), the treaty governing the Itaipú dam on the Paraná river, just north of the Iguazú Falls. The letter argues that the existing contract has long hindered cultural and economic relations between the two countries, and asks that a new, fairer, mutually beneficial contract be written in "portunhol selvagem," "la lengua mais hermoza de la triple frontera pues que nel portunhol selvagem cabem todas las lenguas del Brasil y del Paraguay (incluso las ameríndias) y todas las lenguas del mundo" (the most beautiful language of the triple border, because portunhol selvagem fits inside it all the languages of Brazil and Paraguay [including the Amerindian ones] and all the languages of the world).[71] This "triple frontera" describes the region near the Itaipú dam where Argentina, Brazil, and Paraguay meet. There, three national cultures come into additional contact with all the other cultures that tourism and commerce bring to the region, adding new languages to the existing mix of Spanish, Portuguese, and Guarani. The letter was signed by poets and artists from Brazil and Paraguay as well as from Argentina and Portugal.

INTRODUCTION

Diegues's idea of a capacious, democratic, border-crossing literary language that will facilitate international cooperation has proved attractive and has since been adopted by or applied to a number of other writers.[72] It has been described as

> uma língua mestiça, híbrida, nascida espontaneamente do convívio entre falantes do português e do espanhol, que não se deixa domar por regras gramaticais nem se limita a um léxico estruturado. Caracteriza-se pela oscilação entre o português e o espanhol, mantendo-se permanentemente aberta, sem estruturar-se segundo um código previamente estabelecido. Não se pretende uma língua à parte e se reinventa a cada dia.[73]

> (a mixed, hybrid language, born spontaneously from the cohabitation of Portuguese and Spanish speakers, one that is not governed by grammatical rules or limited by a structured vocabulary. It is characterized by the oscillation between Portuguese and Spanish, remaining permanently open, without being structured according to a previously established code. It does not pretend to be a language apart and reinvents itself every day).

In its emphasis on spontaneity and constant change, and its disregard for standardized grammar, this description is highly reminiscent of the Spanglishes used in the work of Chávez-Silverman, Díaz, and Braschi, particularly the "creolized English" of Díaz's *Oscar Wao*, which I discuss in chapter 2.[74] Chapter 4, moreover, will demonstrate how the above description can be applied to Bueno, whose use of language in *Mar Paraguayo* is similarly unruly and unsystematic, incorporating a large amount of vocabulary from Guarani—more contentious still than the combination of Spanish and Portuguese, given the history of Indigenous language suppression in Brazil—as well as occasionally from Italian, French, and English, in addition to its two main languages.

"Portunhol selvagem" can be understood as a symbol of international cooperation and exchange, and of the importance of Indigenous culture in the region. It has special significance today, given the new politics of isolationism and nationalism in Brazil, whose far right president Jair Bolsonaro recently faulted Indigenous peoples for not speaking "our language," Portuguese: "Os índios não falam nossa língua. . . . Como eles conseguem ter 13% do território nacional" (The Indians do not speak our language. . . . How did they manage to get 13 percent of the national territory).[75] Bueno's *Mar Paraguayo* remains a foundational work of "portunhol selvagem," which Diegues continues to hold up as an inspiration for his own writing; it is by far the most sustained and extensive literary use of "portunhol" currently in circulation. Therefore, I retain the term in my discussion of the book in chapter 4.

"FRENGLISH"

Finally, I want to turn to the linguistic mixture that Erín Moure calls "Frenglish" in her 2017 translation of Bueno's *Paraguayan Sea*. The term "Frenglish" is very little used; "Franglais" is more common, a coinage popularized by the French writer René Etiemble in his 1964 volume *Parlez-vous franglais?*, in which he condemned the spread of Anglo culture and language.[76] The idea that French might be influenced by or mixed with English continues to be officially deplored in France, as Philip Thody's book *Le Franglais: Forbidden English, Forbidden American* has shown.[77] Elsewhere in the Francophone/Anglophone world, however, the picture is different. The choice to identify her writing as "Frenglish" (rather than "Franglais") allows Moure to distance herself from the French context and mark her hybrid French-English prose as specifically Canadian, and even more specifically Quebecois.

Moure's hometown of Montreal is unusual among the world's bilingual regions because of the ambiguous relationship between Canada's two official languages. Many multilingual regions with colonial histories are home to one prestigious European language as well as other "local," lower-prestige languages, with native speakers of the latter often required to learn the former in order to participate in business or increase their social status (as is the case, for instance, in the United States and Brazil). In Montreal, however, the situation is different. Canada is officially bilingual in English and French; meanwhile, the state of Quebec is officially unilingual in French. This means that while French may be marginalized within the country as a whole, it is the dominant language of prestige in Quebecois cities like Montreal. (It is important to note that, as languages with colonial histories, both French and English remain "foreign" in terms of First Nation cultures; and that several Indigenous languages are official in Canadian states other than Quebec.) French's status has been bolstered in the region by an exodus of English speakers to predominantly Anglophone parts of Canada and by language policies that aimed to promote French in public spaces and develop a distinct Francophone national identity.[78] Montreal remains the area where knowledge of both official languages is highest: census data shows that in 2016, the English-French bilingualism rate in Canada reached the highest proportion ever at 17.9 percent, with most of the growth of the bilingual population attributable to Quebec.[79]

Although "Frenglish" might not be a term adopted with any regularity by Canadian writers or linguists, in her translation of Bueno's *Mar Paraguayo*, Moure is evidently working in the tradition of avant-garde bilingual Canadian writers who experiment with translation and with the mixing of English and French in their prose. A prominent example is Nicole Brossard, some of whose work Moure has translated.[80] Brossard's 1982 novel *Picture Theory* uses English words in her French text, moving "across languages in its efforts to destabilize identity and meaning," as translator Barbara Godard explains in her preface to the English version, which bears the same title.[81] Godard's translation is itself bilingual; she takes special care over her use of language, because "the meaning of English in a Quebec text and of French in an English text differ greatly in light of the politics of language in Canada."[82] For instance, she uses boldface to indicate the passages that Brossard wrote in English, and introduces French into her translation in order to replicate Brossard's language mixing. This dialogue between languages is identifiable throughout Brossard's career: in 1979, for instance, she edited, in both French and English, an anthology of avant-garde Canadian writing, *Les stratégies du réel*, in which English-Canadian women writers were encouraged to challenge expressive realist discourse and experiment with and problematize language. She was also one of the founding editors of *Tessera*, a bilingual feminist journal established in 1984 that was dedicated to experimental writing, fostered dialogue between Francophone and Anglophone Canadian women writers, and explored the relationships between translation and feminism. Other prominent bilingual works by Canadian women writers include Carole Corbeil's *Voice-Over* (1992) and Lola Lemire Tostevin's *Frog Moon* (1994), and more recently Kathleen Saint-Onge's 2013 autobiography, *Bilingual Being: My Life as a Hyphen*, all written in a mixture of English and French. Many works of Canadian literature continue to be translated from one of the country's official languages to the other, often with the support of public funding, and are sometimes self-translated by the authors themselves (for instance, Nancy Huston's *Plainsong* was also published in the same year as *Cantique des plaines*, in her own translation, and Montreal writer Nathanaël has self-translated many of her own works, in both directions).[83]

In *Paraguayan Sea* and in her other work, Moure is clearly in conversation with this strong tradition of female bilingual Canadian writers. However, despite her engagement with this literary legacy, *Paraguayan Sea* was not published in Canada but rather in the United States, in part, she has explained, because Canadian small literary presses rarely publish translations of works by foreigners, even if translated by Canadians, because they are not able to use their Canada Council funding to offset the cost of publishing and marketing.[84] The choice of "Frenglish" to designate the language of her translation is perhaps appropriate given the book's rebirth in a majority Anglophone environment where English-French language politics have little currency. The second part of chapter 4 of this book will demonstrate that, contrary to what the reductive, flippant term "Frenglish" suggests, Moure's hybrid prose is creative and innovative, interacting with Bueno's source text in ways that enhance and extend it, giving the book new life in the Northern hemisphere.

NEW MULTILINGUAL WRITING

These loose, hybrid designations—"Spanglish," "Portunhol," and "Frenglish"—are useful in the discussion and marketing of the work examined in this book, but I do not want to give the impression that any one of them is a singular, fixed entity. Quite the opposite: they are shifting and multiplicitous, and do not follow rules or precedent with any regularity. The writing discussed in the chapters that follow has, moreover, been chosen specifically because it deviates from and subverts some of the more established language-mixing conventions in literary history. The work examined here advances and innovates on the formal strategies of multilingualism sketched thus far, challenging what Yildiz calls the "monolingual paradigm" in sustained ways.[85] Their multilingualism is extensive and committed, making few concessions to readers who may not be confidently multilingual by assuming a high level of linguistic competence in more than one language. Their hybrid languages allow these writers to articulate a global conscience while being of a distinctly local cultural realm; conscious of their inevitable travel, they remain wary of the ways translation can transform them, and therefore demand that readers remain critical participants in (rather than passive consumers of) their writing. In the work of all four writers, movement between languages is paralleled everywhere by movement between styles, registers, genres, and versions, making textual difficulty crucial to the way they engage their readers.

What is more, these writers have been chosen because they participate in debates that are unique to the contemporary moment. For instance, they acknowledge and question the role of English as the language dominating scholarship and world literature, and respond to the unprecedented interconnectivity, mobility, and digitization of recent decades, advocating slow, careful reading in order to counteract the speed and ease of twenty-first-century reading practices. These writers are conscious of and reflective about their own artistic afterlives, including translational and digital afterlives, which continue to complicate the ways they are read, and they participate in contemporary conversations about disciplinary boundaries in scholarship as well as global language politics.

While it is possible to discern the stylistic and aesthetic legacy of literary modernism here (these writers establish conversations with Julio Cortázar, Jorge Luis Borges, T. S. Eliot, and James Joyce, as the following chapters will demonstrate), the motivations and strategies for language mixing in the early twentieth century are nonetheless very different from those at the turn of the twenty-first. Joshua Miller, Juliette Taylor-Batty, and Laura Lonsdale have demonstrated at length the crucial role of multilingualism in the modernist aesthetic, both in Europe and America, which was concerned with the way technological modernity threatened notions of national and linguistic rootedness.[86] This writing was often concerned, as Viktor Shklovsky argued in his 1971 essay "Art as Device," with making language strange or difficult. Such "difficult, 'laborious,' impeding language" allowed readers to perceive the world anew by making familiar forms and objects seem strange.[87] One important means of achieving this "ostranenie" (variously translated from Russian as "estrangement," "enstrangement," and "defamiliarization") was through multilingualism, as for example in novels like Tolstoy's *War and Peace*, written predominantly in Russian but with a significant use of French. In recent decades, however, globalization, mass migration, and the advent of digital communication have added to the existing linguistic legacies of European colonialism and resulted in new linguistically diverse urban communities. The bilingualism of three of the writers addressed in this book (Braschi, Díaz, and Chávez-Silverman) is the result of U.S. imperial expansion and immigration from Latin America, but all four writers also reflect, in other ways, the increased mobility and transience of late twentieth- and twenty-first-century life: by avoiding narrative linearity, collapsing and distorting narrative time, showing a high tolerance for contradiction and ambivalence, and by participating in the recycling, rewriting, and reshaping of previous cultural forms in ways that emphasize their lack of fixity.

It is also impossible to ignore that much of this writing is actively shaped by (and cognizant of its participation in) a globalized publishing industry dominated by English. Addressing issues of identity and difference in the face of increased global cultural standardization, these writers consciously interact with the interpretation of their own writing, anticipating readerly responses with a mixture of defensiveness and scorn. They show an awareness of their own textuality and incorporate different forms of metalepsis or frame breaking that allow them to respond to aspects of their own publishing, including the use of digital media. These characteristically postmodern techniques enable these writers to reflect on their creative processes and, in particular, to think through how translation is implicated in or inflects those processes. In the following chapters, I focus on layering and open-endedness as defining features of this writing that are everywhere bound up with the processes of translation.

In arguing that literary multilingualism and translation are closely intertwined creative strategies, this book engages with a growing body of world literature criticism valuing writing that obstructs easy access, refuses translation, and escapes comparison. Voices like Tim Parks, Emily Apter, Minae Mizumura, and Brian Lennon figure the global novel as a commodity vulnerable to capitalist modes of production and consumption.[88] According to this argument, as a result of the "McDonaldization of the globe," literature has succumbed to standardization and homogenization, abandoning any political agenda, aesthetic innovation, formal difficulty, and local particularity, all in the name of maximizing readability (and translatability) across cultures and geographies.[89] In response, these critics have begun to valorize "untranslatable" texts that refuse to enter into the market for global literature: Apter calls for new comparative studies that recognize the importance "of non-translation, mistranslation, incomparability and untranslatability," while Lennon proposes increased attentiveness to "idiolectic incommensurability" and for a new discipline of "non-translation studies."[90]

These approaches emerged in the context of a "translational turn" in the humanities, which broadened the horizon of translation into other disciplinary fields, where it has become a metaphor for different forms of global cultural exchange. Within literary studies in particular, critics have highlighted the role of translational processes in the production and circulation of postcolonial and contemporary writing in English, demonstrating how translation can shape a work stylistically, structurally, and thematically, as well as challenging the assumption that languages are self-contained and rooted in particular geographies, rather than mutually informing and transportable. Fiona Doloughan, for instance, emphasizes the potential for enhanced creativity among writers with access to more than one language and culture, arguing that, in much contemporary literature in English, translation functions as a mode of reading as well as of writing.[91] Rebecca Walkowitz, meanwhile, coins the term "born translated" to describe literature that narrates its engagement with more than one language rather than necessarily using them on the page. In "born-translated" writing, "translation functions as a thematic, structural, conceptual, and sometimes even typographical device"; it is *written for translation*, in the hope of being translated, but . . . also often *written as translation*, pretending to take place in a language other than the one in which it has, in fact, been composed."[92]

The work discussed in this book navigates a path between the "idiolectic incommensurability" valued by critics like Apter and Lennon and the "born-translated" literature identified by Walkowitz, demonstrating that they are not mutually exclusive. Writings by Chávez-Silverman, Díaz, Braschi, and Bueno display the linguistic idiosyncrasies and particularities that Lennon argues make a work, at least in a commercial sense, "untranslatable": they mix languages, represent accents or vernacular effects, make references to cultural practices and social customs, use frequent wordplay and rare idioms. However, they also take translation as a prompt for narrative production, thematizing it and anticipating its role in reception. In these ways, they both invite translation and seek to make it difficult.

TRANSLATING MULTILINGUALISM

Given that the recent valorization of "untranslatability" has often included multilingual writing, it has rarely been discussed how multilingual literature might actually be translated.[93] Scholars of literary multilingualism have tended either to distance themselves from translation in order to emphasize the materiality and particularity of multilingual writing, or to restrict discussion of translation to its intratextual rather than intertextual uses.[94] Approaches from within translation studies have tended to be narrowly focused, comparing individual choices made by individual translators,[95] although Reine Meylaerts's and Ranier Grutman's functional descriptive approaches and Meir Sternberg's structuralist model are exceptions.[96] This book combines these approaches, studying not only how translation is involved in multilingual textual production but also how multilingual texts are translated for publication in different editions. Each chapter is structured around a detailed case study that analyses, on the one hand, how the source text deploys strategies of language mixing and translation, and, on the other hand, how its translator deploys similar strategies in their translation. In so doing, I combine a text-oriented approach with a broader view of writing and translation as sociocultural phenomena, reading multiple textual versions in the light of the market demand for writing to be widely readable and saleable, and taking into account the relative power and prestige of the languages in question. In chapter 1, I also combine criticism with the practice of translation, in order to reflect more productively on the phenomenology of reading multilingual writing, and on translation's role as a mode of interpretation.

But it is important to address claims of "untranslatability" before I begin my readings. Such claims tend to mean one of two things. Either they refer to ability, identifying a technical or formal obstacle to translation ("it *can't* be translated") or they refer to responsibility, identifying a theoretical or ethical obstacle to translation ("it *shouldn't* be translated"). When something is said to be "untranslatable" in the former sense, what is usually meant is that translation is difficult rather than impossible. In particular, it often means that translation results in multiple different versions. Barbara Cassin's use of the term "untranslatable" makes this particularly clear. She says, "To speak of untranslatables in no way implies that the terms in question, or the expressions, the syntactical or grammatical turns, are not and cannot be translated: the untranslatable is rather what one keeps on (not) translating. But this indicates that their translation, into one language or another, creates a problem, to the extent of sometimes generating a neologism or imposing a new meaning on an old word."[97] Some words, she argues, require us to keep translating them over and over again, because each translation leaves us wanting to do it again, differently. What Cassin describes is a word that requires continuous, creative translation; a word that is "unable to be finished being translated."[98] Translation of supposedly "untranslatable" words, including those collected in her *Vocabulaire européen des philosophies: Dictionnaire des intraduisibles*, evidently can and does take place, often very successfully, as is evidenced by the above quotation from the English translation of that volume (*Dictionary of Untranslatables: A Philosophical Lexicon*), and of course by the works of Braschi, Chávez-Silverman, Díaz, and Bueno, all four of which exist in translation—in Díaz's case, into as many as twenty-two different languages. This understanding of translation as multiple, moving, and layered is one to which I will return throughout this book.

None of this is to deny that certain structural, stylistic, thematic, and textual features pose greater challenges than others for translators. For instance, texts that attach meaning to one or more specific languages or language varieties are harder to translate, as Walkowitz explains: "[These texts] use proper names whose cultural and historical associations are not easily rendered in a new language. They generate metaphor through homonym, accent, and other vernacular effects. They comment on the relationship between one language and specific other languages, or between one dialect of a language and another. Or they attach ideas to phonological or etymological patterns."[99] This is what lies behind Robert Frost's much-quoted assertion that poetry is what gets lost in translation: the unique connections in poetry between ideas and the forms used to express them are difficult to replicate precisely in other languages, because the sounds, rhythms, and patterns of those languages naturally differ.[100] The same features make the writing addressed in this book difficult to translate. The ideas and commitments that are expressed in part through their form—through their combination of languages, language varieties, registers, and accents—are difficult to replicate using the resources of other languages, or of a single language. These difficulties are not in doubt; however, the idea that multilingual writing is in any literal sense "untranslatable" is wide of the mark. This book will demonstrate at length how translators can represent, in their work, the previous existence of multiple languages and the relationships between them.

The argument that certain texts *shouldn't* be translated, however, can be more compelling than the argument that they can't be. The suggestion in these cases is usually that to translate is to violate a text in some way, or to violate the culture from which it comes. Abdelfattah Kilito, for instance, in a lecture titled "Thou Shalt Not Translate Me," advances the argument that we should safeguard a text's right *not* to be translated, for instance in the case of sacred texts or the private language of prayer.[101] In addition to the technical claim previously outlined—that literary multilingualism is translatable, and in such a way that does not necessarily erase its complexity or subversive potential—this book also ventures a further claim: that multilingualism in literature (whether translated or not) is a politically and culturally progressive force that can help foster critical rigor and disrupt hegemonic cultural regimes including gender, sexuality, and nationality.

In order to demonstrate both these claims, it is helpful to return to Anzaldúa's *Borderlands/La Frontera*, in which the author struggles against the expectation that she will always translate her work—which often depends on the particular relationships between its languages for the way it means—for the benefit of others.[102] It is for this reason, presumably, that *Borderlands/La Frontera* has never been translated, whether into just English, just Spanish, or any other language(s). And yet, for all its challenging the monolingual paradigm, translation remains integral to the structure of the book. For instance, the final poem in the volume, which emphasizes the longevity of Chicanx culture and envisages its continued resilience in the future, appears in two versions, the first called "No se raje Chicanita," the second called "Don't give in, Chicanita." The first version is mainly in Spanish, with a few words and phrases in English, as the following stanza illustrates:

> *Y, cuando los gringos se acaban—*
> *mira como se matan unos a los otros—*
> *aquí vamos a parecer*
> *con los* horned toads *y los lagartijos*
> Survivors *del* First Fire Age, *el Quinto Sol.*[103]

The incursion of English words, coupled with unusual grammatical and lexical choices in Spanish (the indicative "se acaban" rather than the subjunctive "se acaben," and the use of "parecer con"), may be defamiliarizing for many readers of Spanish. Depending on each reader's linguistic competence, the poem will be read in slightly different ways, such that it always has multiple layers. It is then layered again with the appearance of a second version, "Don't give in, Chicanita," which has been "translated by the author" into mainly English, such that the above stanza appears thus:

> And when the Gringos are gone—
> see how they kill one another—
> here we'll still be like the horned toad and the lizard
> relics of an earlier age
> survivors of the First Fire Age—*el Quinto Sol*.[104]

Although the word "translation" is used to describe the second version, this is no straightforward translation. The meaning of the second version sometimes deviates considerably from the first, as in the use of "here we'll still be" for "aquí vamos a parecer," which seems to read "parecer" (to seem, to be like) as "permanecer" (to remain). Anzaldúa edits the poem as she translates, so that the second version has different lineation, and sometimes additional lines, as in the above stanza ("relics of an earlier age"). English and Spanish appear in both versions, but in different ways; although "Don't give in, Chicanita" is mainly in English, the occasional use of Spanish words and phrases makes it at least as bilingual as the first version, with lines like "digging underground / toward that current, that soul of *tierra madre*" (mother earth).[105] In its two versions, this poem illustrates the natural connection between the defamiliarizing aesthetic of multilingual writing and theories of "foreignizing" translation. "Foreignization," a term coined by Lawrence Venuti, describes translation strategies that unsettle and challenge the target readership by surrendering to the forms and ideologies of the source language and culture.[106] The target language is made strange through the influence of the source language, as it is here by the inclusion of the phrase *"tierra madre."* Literary multilingualism, like foreignizing translations, can be "a form of resistance against ethnocentrism and racism, cultural narcissism and imperialism, in the interests of democratic geopolitical relations," as Venuti puts it.[107] It can disrupt the dominance of Anglophone culture, challenging the assumption of a right to "easy reading"—or, as Walkowitz puts it, the right to feel like "native readers" of literature from any given culture,[108] as well as other normative systems like national or sexual identity.

Translational techniques are equally apparent in the first and the second version of Anzaldúa's poem—the source and the target text—demonstrating that translation can defamiliarize and disrupt just as well as bilingual writing can. A translation does not have to be monolingual, nor does it have to erase the subversive potential of its source, but it can be linguistically playful in its own unique ways in order to remind readers of the existence of multiple languages in the version from which it derives. For instance, in her translation of the line "*Esa víbora dormida, la rebeldía, saltará*" as "That sleeping serpent, / rebellion-(r)evolution, will spring up," Anzaldúa uses a neologism to evoke the multiple connotations of a single Spanish word, "*rebeldía.*" The compounding of "rebellion" and "revolution," coupled with the use of parentheses in "(r)evolution," which also accommodates "evolution" (a meaning not immediately evident in the first version of the poem), results in a translation that is unsettling, layered, and provisional; "*rebeldía*" is "untranslatable" in Cassin's sense of engendering multiple, repeated translations. The use of "(r)evolution" in the second version adds something new and unlooked for to the poem as a whole. In this way, "Don't give in, Chicanita" is presented as a natural continuation of the processes already underway in "No se raje, Chicanita."

This poem demonstrates that although Anzaldúa openly rejects the pressure to translate for the benefit of non-Chicanxs, the processes of translation remain integral to her writing. It demonstrates that translation, far from being an annihilation of the complexities of bilingual writing, can open up a work to new readerships while allowing meaning to proliferate in different directions. Although these texts may not, in the first instance, be entirely willing to accommodate semi-fluent and non-fluent readers, in later translational manifestations they are reoriented toward readers with different, sometimes less extensive, linguistic competences. This does not make them capitulations to "McDonaldization," but rather complex responses to the rich contemporary themes of digital communication, globalization, and cultural imperialism. This is writing that actively dramatizes and invites translation, sometimes even collaborating on its own translation (as is the case with Braschi's *Yo-Yo Boing!*), all the while continuing to deflect assumptions of easy equivalence and universal accessibility.

THE APPROACHES AND STRUCTURE OF THIS BOOK

The following chapters draw on theories of post-structuralism in order to advance an understanding of literary translation as an ongoing, unfinishable process. Exploring translation's role in and between different versions of work by Díaz, Braschi, Chávez-Silverman, and Bueno, I turn at different moments to Deleuze and Guattari's concept of the rhizome, a mode of thinking that accommodates multiplicities and resists hierarchy; and to queer theory, which, building on a post-structuralist understanding of identity as a constellation of multiple unstable positions, seeks to disturb or avoid definitions of gender and sexuality. I use these modes of thinking to argue that the open-endedness and seriality of these texts—which derive in part from the role of translation in their inception—means that they are left open to further interpretation and reinscription, including in the form of wholesale translation into new textual versions.

Throughout, I understand literary translation to be a creative practice in its own right, one that can never be entirely faithful to an "original" because an original itself contains no stable or essential meaning. In this I am building on a "creative turn" in translation studies that has sought to redefine literary translation as a creative practice analogous to writing. Most notably, this includes two edited volumes published in 2006 explicitly connecting the work of literary translators with that of creative writers: *The Translator as Writer* and *Translation and Creativity*;[109] and, more recently, Cecilia Rossi's work on the creativity of literary translation and the fluid boundaries between the disciplines of literary translation and creative writing.[110] The active, creative role of the translator is especially apparent in the translation of the contemporary multilingual literature to be examined in this volume. Since this writing is already *about* translation in various ways—it dramatizes translation, invites translation, and deploys translation as a means of defamiliarization—the translators become participants in processes already underway in their source texts. It is telling that the translators of Díaz's *Oscar Wao* (Achy Obejas), Braschi's *Yo-Yo Boing!* (Tess O'Dwyer), and Bueno's *Mar Paraguayo* (Erín Moure), discussed in chapters 2, 3, and 4, respectively, are all writers themselves. Their work illustrates with particular clarity the common ground between multilingual writing and translation.

My analysis builds on a preoccupation in world literature studies with the physicality of the book in an age of digitization—exemplified in calls by David Damrosch and Franco Moretti for emphasis on the "phenomenology" of the work: a book's appearance, circulation, and translation, rather than its "ontology"—combining fine-grained analysis with a consideration of each work as material artefact.[111] For instance, I examine the ways print and digital paratexts (footnotes and epigraphs, but also author interviews and online glossaries) interact with and modify a text itself.[112] By paying attention to multiple textual versions, including translated versions, I am able to examine how this writing circulates in more than one literary and linguistic culture, opening itself up to new readers outside its place(s) of inception.

It is impossible to forget the very different backgrounds of the four writers examined in this book, and the cultural and political histories that have shaped the way they use language. The United States' relationship with Puerto Rico, where Braschi grew up, is not the same as its relationship with the Dominican Republic, where Díaz spent his first seven years, nor indeed with Mexico, where Chávez-Silverman spent the summers during her youth; and none of these relationships is comparable to the relationships between Paraguay and Brazil, or between the different linguistic communities of Canada. Despite beginning in distinct, sometimes multiple locations, and despite being read in varied circumstances, these writings can, as I aim to demonstrate by situating them within a larger evolving argument, be productively brought together—without losing sight of their particularities—to demonstrate a set of shared preoccupations and techniques.

This book is divided into an introduction, four main chapters, and a short coda. Each chapter engages with a different multilingual author-translator pair.[113] Chapter 1 examines Chávez-Silverman's bilingual English-Spanish "crónicas," a unique short form of life writing of which she has published two volumes. It uses the concept of the "palimpsest" to argue that a process of layering is at work not just in the crónicas' language, which embraces rather than rejects inter- and intralingual translation, but also in their genre, modal, geographic, and textual "interstitiality." In the latter part of the chapter, I reflect on my own translation of Chávez-Silverman's "Todo verdor perdurará crónica" for publication in *Asymptote*, detailing a series of challenges and possible solutions, and arguing that ultimately Chávez-Silverman's work opens itself up to experimentation with translation rather than foreclosing it.

Chapter 2 reads Junot Díaz's *The Brief Wondrous Life of Oscar Wao* via its trope of "páginas en blanco"—the partial erasures and rewritings that occur at different stages of its production and reception. It begins by arguing that the novel's creolized language, stylistic devices, and structural organization mimic the experience of reading narratives about or produced under censorship and repression. Positioning *Oscar Wao* as what Roland Barthes calls a "writerly" text, it argues that the novel's linguistic, typographic, and structural blanks demand engaged, active readers (much like Chávez-Silverman's work does) who must translate, explain, and uncensor parts of the novel for themselves. The second part of the chapter considers the role translation plays in both the novel's production and its reception. It argues that translation is subtly incorporated into the novel as a narrative device—pseudotranslation—despite Díaz's apparent policy of non-translation. It then turns to Achy Obejas's translation of *Oscar Wao* into Spanish, considering it as analogous to other paratextual rewritings of the novel, and arguing that her translation responds to processes already underway by partially "uncensoring" the text while also creating new "blanks" of her own.

Chapter 3 examines how anxieties about language, gender fluidity, and queer desire intersect in Giannina Braschi's 1998 bilingual novel *Yo-Yo Boing!*. Identifying the novel's language (particularly the ways in which its English and Spanish interact, transform, and enhance one another) as a key part of its textual difficulty, it argues that this language constitutes a queer practice in its indeterminacy, its resistance to fixity and transparency, and its perception as transgressive. Braschi's language is altered, however, in Tess O'Dwyer's 2011 "translation" of the novel into only English, which I read as a continuation of Braschi's highly self-referential postmodern play. Responding to its own characters' anxieties, O'Dwyer's version "un-queers" their language and thus mitigates the novel's difficulty. Positioning the translation in the context of its publication by AmazonCrossing, which hopes to appeal to a wide readership, this chapter argues that O'Dwyer's problematic translation increases the novel's accessibility and circulation but no longer challenges normative discourse on the standardness and monolingualism of literary language. Nevertheless, I view the two versions of the novel as a complex, contradictory, collaborative whole, one that blurs the lines between production and reception, interpretation and praxis, subverting the traditionally hierarchical relationship between original and translation to instead propose the latter as a condition of textual production.

Chapter 4 extends the work of the previous chapter by tracing the connections between language, gender, and genre fluidity in Brazilian writer Wilson Bueno's hugely popular *Mar Paraguayo* ("Portunhol" and Guarani, 1992) and its recent translation by Canadian poet Erín Moure as *Paraguayan Sea* ("Frenglish" and Guarani, 2017). The first part of the chapter draws connections between Bueno's work and that of the three writers previously addressed in this book, demonstrating that, as in those works of "Spanglish" literature, translational strategies are embedded in Bueno's "Portunhol" in ways that emphasize his work's openness to further reinscription. Exploring the book's connections to the neobaroque and concrete movements, I demonstrate that his multilingual prose incorporates other kinds of textual and conceptual fluidity, as is epitomized by his nameless protagonist, who is a fluid subjectivity in numerous ways: not just as the speaker of more than one language, but also as a Paraguayan at home in Brazil and as a subject in a possibly queer body, with possibly queer desires. The second part of the chapter offers Erín Moure's *Paraguayan Sea* as this book's most powerful example yet of a translation that is multilingual, creative, and fluid, and which interacts with its source text in ways that enhance and extend it. This section examines how Moure reformulates Bueno's multilingual strategies in order to give his work new life in the Northern hemisphere. As with all the writing studied thus far in this book, Moure's *Paraguayan Sea* demonstrates translation to be productive and original, rather than derivative and secondary. I argue that she draws on a tradition of Canadian feminist and queer translation to assert her translator subjectivity in *Paraguayan Sea*, blurring the line between author and translator.

Finally, a brief coda brings together the interests of the previous chapters in an analysis of two special features on multilingual writing that I edited for *Asymptote*, a quarterly online journal of international literature in translation, in July of 2015 and 2016. Two of the texts discussed in this book (extracts from Erín Moure's *Paraguayan Sea* and my translation of Chávez-Silverman's "Todo verdor perdurará crónica") were published for the first time in *Asymptote*'s pages, and the process of compiling the features facilitated the development of this research in numerous ways. The coda argues that the strategies and preoccupations identified in the work of Chávez-Silverman, Díaz, Obejas, Braschi, O'Dwyer, Bueno, and Moure can be traced more broadly across other contemporary multilingual literatures. *Asymptote* gives us a snapshot of writers and translators who, like those addressed in the chapters of this book, are exploring the fertile intersections between languages, as well as the spaces between nations and cultures, speech and writing, gendered identities, and literary genres. The volume and variety of writing submitted to these *Asymptote* features underscore the necessity of cultivating a "postmonolingual condition" (a "struggle *against* the monolingual paradigm," and "multilingual attempts to overcome it") rather than surrendering to a dangerous swing toward monolingualism and the divisive, inward-looking politics with which it goes hand-in-hand.[114] These readings will illustrate the urgency of attending to literature that represents the frictions and paradoxes of multilingual life, especially in a political climate increasingly dominated by border policing and anti-immigrant sentiment.

Chapter One

"MI LENGUA ES UN PALIMPSESTO"
Susana Chávez-Silverman's Palimpsestuous Writing

In the first paragraph of "Glossary Crónica," which opens *Killer Crónicas: Bilingual Memories*, Susana Chávez-Silverman's collection of short autobiographical pieces, the author describes her language as "un palimpsesto" (a palimpsest).[1] The metaphor of the palimpsest, defined as "a parchment or other writing surface on which the original text has been effaced or partially erased, and then overwritten by another; a manuscript in which later writing has been superimposed on earlier (effaced) writing,"[2] aptly explains various, often contradictory, aspects of Chávez-Silverman's writing, beginning with but also extending far beyond her use of language. This chapter argues that Chávez-Silverman's palimpsestuous language lends itself to experimentation with other kinds of layering and fluidity—genre, modal, textual—and opens itself up to translation rather than foreclosing that possibility.

Born to a Mexican American mother and a Jewish American father, Susana Chávez-Silverman lived in Madrid until she was five, when her family moved to California. Until the age of eighteen, she spent every summer with family in Guadalajara in Mexico. As an adult, she has also spent long periods of time in Argentina and in South Africa—two locations that feature prominently in her writing—and she now lives in Southern California, where she is professor of Romance languages at Pomona College. Her work is, perhaps unsurprisingly, thoroughly cross-cultural in its concerns.

It spans the Americas, Europe, Australia, and South Africa, and yet this insistently global perspective intersects at every turn with local, culturally specific, personal concerns, illustrating that, despite the accessibility of a new planetary context for all of our interactions, our lives are shaped by local differences that refuse to be erased by the processes of globalization. This is borne out in her use of language peculiar to certain parts of the world and of references to particular places, events, and people, which give these crónicas intensely specific relevance. Chávez-Silverman writes about her experiences on three different continents, moving constantly and unpredictably between different locations; it is clear that there is no geographical center of her writing, and that she claims any number of places as "hers." Rather, as Ania Spyra reminds us, the crónicas exist in a "weird, cybergeografía" (weird, cyber-geography) (*KC*, 82), forging digital connections via group email correspondence between interlocutors as distant as Oaxaca, Madrid, Pretoria, and Sydney.[3] The crónicas reimagine the global/local relationship without relying on a binaristic assertion of either/or. This chapter will begin to move discussions of "Spanglish" off their conventional U.S. axis, with a view to continuing and expanding this movement later in the book.

Chávez-Silverman has published two volumes of "crónicas," a unique short form of life writing: *Killer Crónicas* and *Scenes from la Cuenca de Los Angeles y otros Natural Disasters*.[4] Each crónica is based around an anecdote or series of anecdotes from the author's life. In many cases they derive from personal correspondence: individual letters and group emails, sent to friends living in other countries, which have been reworked for new readers, while retaining frequent traces of their earlier form. Some, especially in *Scenes*, also include transcribed passages from the author's diaries. They are often digressive, full of interruptions and anecdotes that appear in different forms in multiple crónicas. Their arrangement in the published volumes does not form a chronological narrative; rather, each volume is loosely bound by theme.

It is helpful at this stage to summarize those themes, because in my discussion I will make reference to both published volumes, as well as to some crónicas that are as yet uncollected. The majority of *Killer Crónicas* was written while the author was living in Buenos Aires, and the writing therein dwells in large part on her quest for "authentic" Argentine cultural experiences, and the increasingly apparent futility of such a quest. It also explores the part language has to play in the construction of an "authentic" self. The crónicas in *Scenes*, on the other hand, were written mainly during an artist's residence Chávez-Silverman held in California during the spring of 2008; they often recount her daily experiences of writing and walking in the surrounding landscape, and coalesce around her decision to reread, during the residence, a diary she wrote twenty years earlier while living in South Africa. The diary prompts her to remember a traumatic miscarriage she had in 1982, and to reconnect with her then partner, Howard Montenegro, via email. This volume is less explicitly concerned with cultural and linguistic authenticity than it is with the narrativization of memory and its connection to writing itself.

The aspect of Chávez-Silverman's work that has been most frequently remarked upon by readers, reviewers, and scholars is its use of "Spanglish," which in her case amounts to sustained intrasentential code-switching. Roshawnda Derrick has shown that the crónicas have no identifiable "base" or "matrix" language providing them with a grammatical structure.[5] In this, Chávez-Silverman's work is removed not only from the "cushioned" use of Spanish in writing like that of Paredes, mentioned in the introduction to this book, but also from Anzaldúa's more extensive bilingualism, which still makes some concessions to monolingual Anglophone readers. Nevertheless, I dispute the claim that Chávez-Silverman's work rejects translation, arguing instead that it uses interlingual translation games as a method of creative production, and thus opens itself up to the possibility of being translated.[6]

Yet Chávez-Silverman's work is not only or even primarily "about" language. Rather, bilingualism is one among many "palimpsestuous" aspects of her writing, which has a fragmentary, nonlinear style, is indeterminate in terms of genre, and splices together geographies, temporalities, and textual versions. In her introductory prelude to *Killer Crónicas*, the author invites readers to enter the interstices between conventional categories of knowledge: "dive into este mi texto intersticial. Go on, lánzate. Lance yourself" (*KC*, xxi). She challenges her readers to "lance themselves"—launch themselves—into what is undoubtedly an unfamiliar and often disorienting reading experience by using an expression that relies on a playful mistranslation of the Spanish verb "lanzar" ("to launch"). This bilingual pun, "lance yourself," suggests that readers will encounter in her writing both the freedom and pain of "intersticialidad" (interstitiality). It suggests the puncturing of received ideas and the reduction of bloated complacency; after all, being lanced or drained can be considered a step on the road to healing. It also demonstrates how thinking in the interstices or overlap between languages (and, by implication, between other organizing categories) can be productive and fertile in unexpected ways.

Anzaldúa's intersectional legacy is evident here: as someone for whom displacement is a pervasive ontological condition, Chávez-Silverman is evidently writing in a tradition of literary borderlands conceived as "painful yet potentially transformative spaces where opposites converge, conflict, and transmute."[7] However, Chávez-Silverman's complex transnationalism sets her work apart from that tradition. It is not enough to read it only in the context of Chicana bilingualism; it must be read in broader hemispheric and global contexts. This is rhizomatic work, to use Deleuze and Guattari's term, that reflects in its composition, language, and content the way texts, people, and languages circulate globally in the twenty-first century. Chávez-Silverman mobilizes her "interstitiality" and "palimpsestuousness" in order to inculcate a mode of reading that counters the unprecedented speed and ease of contemporary life, and also to disrupt established disciplinary and linguistic conventions in academic scholarship.

The adjective "palimpsestuous," as Sarah Dillon has noted, suggests a simultaneous relation of intimacy and separation, one that aptly describes the relation between English and Spanish—they are typologically distinct, mutually incomprehensible languages, and yet they have enough in common grammatically, syntactically, and etymologically to allow for the tight intertwining we see in these crónicas.[8] In its proximity to "incestuous," Dillon points out, "palimpsestuous" suggests the strangeness and taboo that results from an *excess* of intimacy, as when two languages are brought into too-close proximity. The word was first used to translate the French "palimpsestueuse," in Channa Newman and Claude Doubinsky's English version of Gérard Genette's work *Palimpsests: Literature in the Second Degree*, in which the concept of the palimpsest is used figuratively to imagine what Genette calls "transtextuality": "all that sets the text in a relationship, whether obvious or concealed, with other texts."[9] These relationships are made very apparent in the crónicas, which flaunt their debt to diary entries, letters, and emails; referring to her personal correspondences, the author has remarked, "I 'palimpsest' them to send to others, I cut and paste."[10] They also flaunt their relationships with work written by other writers, as will become clear in my discussion of "Axolotl Crónica" toward the end of this chapter. The image of the palimpsest is therefore helpful in accounting for the linguistic, genre, modal, geographic, and textual "interstitiality" of Chávez-Silverman's writing, and also in understanding it to be a fluid, social product that can be repeatedly modified, reproduced, and layered.

Part I of this first chapter outlines a set of strategies and preoccupations that Chávez-Silverman has in common with the other writers to be discussed in this book, which include: the mixing of languages, styles, registers, and genres to strategically include and exclude different readers at different moments and therefore encourage them to be active and engaged; the reworking or rewriting of text in ways that emphasize its open-endedness; reflection on the creative process and the ways translation is implicated in or inflects that process; conscious anticipation of how a text will be received; and its continuation in digital and translational afterlives. Chávez-Silverman's work is concerned with other kinds of "experiment" than the strictly linguistic, and in these senses too it can be put productively in conversation with the work of Junot Díaz, Giannina Braschi, Wilson Bueno, and their respective translators. In particular, I examine different kinds of palimpsesting at work in *Killer Crónicas* and *Scenes*, arguing that they contribute to the creation of slow, active readers.

Part II of the chapter takes a more reflective turn as it charts my process of translating one of Chávez-Silverman's crónicas for a new readership, one that has no knowledge, or very little knowledge, of Spanish. Taking as its premise the understanding that my own translation is simply another layer in the crónica's already "palimpsestuous" existence, this section details some of the concerns and challenges arising from translation, and suggests multiple possible solutions, which we will encounter again in the chapters that follow.

PART I. PALIMPSESTS IN *KILLER CRÓNICAS*

The various kinds of layering or "palimpsesting" at work in Chávez-Silverman's writing are both symptom and cause of her reluctance to *explain* her writing. By occupying the interstices between conventional categories, the crónicas demand that we read slowly and carefully, and remain actively engaged. This strategy seems designed to decelerate the pace of modern life and to reverse the newly fragmented modes of reading that have accompanied the advent of the internet. There is a pervasive fear that new technologies are eroding our powers of concentration and shortening our attention span; the sheer scale of material available online today encourages readers to skim quickly and jump from one article to the next in order to find what they are looking for. Meanwhile readers are constantly interrupted by a variety of message notifications, and social media are making them more accustomed to the quick fix of a tweet than to engaging with long texts for an extended period of time. Chávez-Silverman's crónicas, in contrast, go out of their way to make readers slow down and concentrate, if they are to understand and enjoy their reading. They offer a rebuff to recent approaches to the study of world literature, notably Franco Moretti's "distant reading," which puts aside close engagement with texts in favor of aggregating and analyzing large quantities of literary data in order to determine the existence of broad patterns.[11]

Multilingualism has a large role to play in encouraging this slow, active mode of reading. Chávez-Silverman's work represents a challenge to the hegemony of English monolingualism in the United States; she rarely, if ever, makes concessions to readers who do not speak (much) Spanish, and avoids the relative clarity and explanation many readers will have come to expect from writers with "hyphenated" identities (Mexican-American, Cuban-American, etc.). In an interview, she has claimed that "the notion that everything must be clear, transparent, explained is the opposite of what my work is about."[12] She is aware that her "fierce commitment to bilingual writing may confuse, intimidate, frustrate or even put off some readers," but is insistent: "I'm OK with this."[13] In fact, she expects all her readers, even confident English-Spanish bilinguals, to confront a degree of difficulty, and is determined to trouble and disturb U.S. readers often complacent in their assumption that literature will be accessible and easily comprehensible.

Requests from her publisher to explain aspects of her writing in the paratext of her published collections were therefore only reluctantly accepted, and always on her own terms. This is made clear in "Glossary Crónica," which opens *Killer Crónicas*. It is Chávez-Silverman's response to a request from her editor for a glossary to be appended, to help readers navigate her unique use of language. It is customary, of course, for a glossary to follow the main body text, and therefore in some sense be supplementary to it. "Glossary Crónica," however, is positioned at the beginning of the volume, with Roman-numeral pagination as though it is an introduction or a preface. Quite aside from disrupting traditional narrative chronologies and rethinking the boundaries of the book itself, by situating a glossary at the beginning of the text Chávez-Silverman warns readers that a reference work is going to be necessary if they are to proceed. For readers of this work, a glossary is neither optional nor supplementary, but every bit as crucial as an introduction. The irony is that "Glossary Crónica" does not, in the end, fulfil the explanatory function of a glossary ("a list with explanations").[14] Instead, it operates as a crucial framing device, staking out many of the work's key preoccupations in advance: its interest in the written representation of spoken language; a conviction that this unique mixture of English and Spanish is a legitimate language of the United States; a self-consciousness about its own reception, particularly within the academy; and the usefulness of the palimpsest as an analogy for the work's organization. Rather than explaining or defining obscure terms, it is written in the same hermetic mix of languages as the rest of the collection. It even explicitly withholds information, encouraging readers to guess at the origin of some of its playful coinages, like the title of a book she calls "Itchy Scratchy (you guess)" (*KC*, xx).

This partial refusal to explain is also expressed at the opening of her second volume, *Scenes*. When preparing it for publication, Chávez-Silverman was asked to produce an introduction that provided some contextual information for frequently appearing "characters" (friends, family, colleagues), to whom she often refers obliquely or by elaborate nicknames. In response, she wrote "Cartografía Humana/Star Maps Crónica." This introductory piece explains the relationships between her and some of the crónicas' dedicatees, but it also explicitly omits the most important people in her life, including her son. Readers are encouraged to fill in these gaps by doing their own research: "So if you're still curious, pos Facebook 'em, háganles Google, baby! Y si por algún motivo you should come up empty handed, just use the best search engine ever invented: tu imaginación" (So if you're still curious, then Facebook 'em, Google them, baby! And if for some reason you should come up empty handed, just use the best search engine ever invented: your imagination) (*SC*, 9). Like "Glossary Crónica," this invitation troubles the boundaries of the book itself, turning the whole internet into an extended glossary for the text. There is a tension here: although Chávez-Silverman invites the use of digital technology, her invitation is intended to make us engage with her writing more slowly and attentively, as a way of counteracting the speed with which we are increasingly accustomed to reading online. The slower and more carefully we read, the more critical we are able to be, of our own assumptions as well as of others. Doris Sommer has suggested that the value of difficulty and of partial understanding lies precisely in being able to "safeguard the modesty that democracy depends on";[15] a detailed reading of "Axolotl Crónica" later in this chapter will illustrate in more detail how not knowing can enable us to see from multiple perspectives and thereby disrupt normative assumptions. But first, the next section examines the different kinds of linguistic palimpsesting at work in *Killer Crónicas* and *Scenes*.

Linguistic Palimpsests

Bakhtin reminds us in "Discourse in the Novel" that "expropriating [language], forcing it to submit to one's own intentions and accents, is a difficult and complicated process."[16] In "almost every utterance," he explains, "an intense interaction and struggle between one's own and another's word is being waged, a process in which they oppose or dialogically interanimate each other."[17] This combination of conflict and productive dynamism is visible from the outset in *Killer Crónicas*, in which the author attempts to appropriate different kinds of language and explicitly calls into question the authenticity of her own speech. Being Chicana, she says in "Glossary Crónica," it would be more "authentic" if she were to pronounce the consonant at the end of a word like "Madrid" as a voiced interdental "d" (the pronunciation commonly heard on U.S. Spanish-language television), rather than the unvoiced "th" acquired during her early childhood in Spain: "Esa 'd' sería más normal en una hablante *authentically* hispano/hablante, or Chicana, que no?" (That "d" would be more normal in a speaker more *authentically* Hispanophone, or Chicana, right?) (*KC*, xix–xx).[18] Her identity as a Chicana (which already has a long and fraught linguistic history) is further complicated by her connections to Spain. In addition to Peninsular and Chicana varieties of Spanish, she is particularly concerned in *Killer Crónicas* with the written representation of Argentine, specifically Buenos Aires or "porteño," speech—"Glossary Crónica" explains, for instance, how she "began to transcribe an 'h' where the 's' is just a breath, down there. Ehto. Queréh? Ehplicar" (*KC*, xix). She even claims an "honorary Puerto Rican-ness" via her college friends, in her "lexicalization, rapidity of speech, and slight nasalization" (*KC*, xx). In "In My Country Crónica" she decides to make use of the Afrikaans words that have been "insinuat[ing] themselves into [my] head" (*SC*, 53), and peppers her later writing liberally with them. She even appropriates, magpie-like, words from Yiddish, French, Portuguese, and Italian. English and Spanish are evidently insufficient to account fully for her linguistic mixing.

In thinking about the way Chávez-Silverman lays claim to the different kinds of language detailed above, it is helpful to turn to Rey Chow, who, in *Not Like a Native Speaker*, calls for us to abandon the fallacy of the "mother tongue" in preference for an understanding of language as prosthesis: both something *artificial* and something that is *added*. In an extended reading of Derrida's *Monolingualism of the Other; Or, the Prosthesis of Origin*, Chow argues that language is "impermanent, detachable, and (ex)changeable" rather than something that can ever properly belong to us.[19] She suggests that postcolonial subjects have a particularly acute awareness of this. For Chicanxs, for example, whose history involves multiple layers of European colonization and who often lack a single "mother tongue," English and Spanish are both prosthetic because they were imposed. But Chávez-Silverman's language repertoire is more complex still, doubly artificial or "inauthentic" because even her Chicana Spanish is inflected with the sounds of Madrid.

In addition to the mix of languages already discussed, the crónicas involve intralingual stratification and multivocality of the kind Bakhtin describes as "heteroglossia."[20] Take, for example, this passage from "Todo verdor perdurará Crónica":

> Sarita y yo solíamos atarles hilos, like slender kite strings (taught this cruel, irresistible truco por los hermanos López Moreno, Miguel y Alejandro, éste mi dizque boyfriend a los 10 años, till he asked me to hold his watch for him mientras iba a hacer pis behind a tree—pero esa es otra, yuck, muy otra), casting them aloft into the Mexican summer sky[21]

> (Sarita and I would tie threads to them, like slender kite strings [taught this cruel, irresistible trick by the López Moreno brothers, Miguel and Alejandro, the latter my so-called boyfriend aged ten, till he asked me to hold his watch for him while he took a piss behind a tree—but that's another, yuck, a whole other], casting them aloft into the Mexican summer sky).

This sentence begins to give us a sense of the extent to which registers and styles are layered in the crónicas. It begins lyrically, with soft cross-lingual sound repetition ("solíamos atarles hilos, like slender kite strings"), and ends in a similar manner with the high-register formulation "casting them aloft." The parenthetical clauses in the middle of the sentence, however, deviate sharply from the highbrow with "dizque," a contraction of "dice que" used predominantly in spoken discourse; the crude expression "hacer pis"; the childlike exclamation "yuck"; and the informal, abbreviated expression "esa es otra." The abrupt shift in register represents a struggle between two voices: the voice of the adult author, remembering with nostalgia the habitual games of her youth, and the voice of the author as a child, responding with spontaneous repulsion to her boyfriend's request. Elsewhere in her writing, Chávez-Silverman layers the conversational with the scholarly, the confessional, and the dramatic; her multilingualism is far richer and more complex than just movement between English and Spanish, and she adds different voices, accents, and vocabularies to her linguistic repertoire at will.

The construction of language as prosthesis—as layers to be added—disrupts the connection between language and geography, and between language and identity. If language is always prosthetic or inauthentic, then there are no "native" and no "foreign" languages in a given location. As they are acquired, different languages can become part of one's identity, regardless of nationality or ethnicity, just as different languages can become part of a text's identity once it circulates in translation.

Sonic Palimpsests

Chávez-Silverman also pays special attention to the acoustic elements of language. This section will outline her work's representation of and existence in the oral mode, arguing that it results in a double-voicedness that goes above and beyond its playful bilingualism and manipulation of translation strategies.

In the introduction to *Killer Crónicas*, Chávez-Silverman writes: "I can't write sin sentir el latido del corazón (or at least el tecleo de manos on a keyboard), las pulsaciones cerebrales—verbales—de un interlocutor" (I can't write without feeling the heartbeat [or at least the tapping of hands on a keyboard], the cerebral—verbal—pulsations of an interlocutor) (*KC*, xxi).

Many of her crónicas, as I have explained, began as correspondence to friends and family, and most have direct addressees or dedicatees, often more than one—a feature that is made possible by the advent of email replacing handwritten letters. Each of the crónicas begins in medias res, so readers must, as Paul Saint-Amour puts it in his foreword to Chávez-Silverman's second book of crónicas, enter "places and recollections where the writer and addressee seem to have dwelled together for years" (*SC*, ix). Both *Killer Crónicas* and *Scenes* open with invitations to readers to launch themselves into the unknown, to look for, as Chávez-Silverman puts it, "más strange familiars" (more strange familiars) (*SC*, 16). In the introductions to both books, she warns readers that what follows will comprise both intimacy and alienation.

The variety of ways Chávez-Silverman addresses herself to readers allows her to be both public and private—as Saint-Amour puts it, to engage in "daylit veiling" or "encrypting through publicity" (*SC*, x). Sometimes she speaks to a broad nonspecific readership, as when she says, "Luego gente, I swear I don't know what came over me" (Then guys, I swear I don't know what came over me) (*SC*, 31). At other times, she calls out to particular readers: "Te acuerdas Frances? Te acuerdas, Carmen Ivette?" (Do you remember Frances? Do you remember, Carmen Ivette?) (*KC*, 72), and in so doing partly excludes others from sharing in those memories. At other times still, she simply addresses herself to "you," as when she says "Anygüey, you know me" (*SC*, 83). This last one is ostensibly meant for Laura, the author's sister and dedicatee of "South Coast Plaza Crónica," but it draws all readers into a kind of familial intimacy that manages to wrong-foot us—we *don't* know her, after all, at least not in the way we assume her sister does. The use of multiple addressees means that readers move between moments of connection and disconnection, and are continually reminded that different individuals will read the work in different ways.

One important consequence of this origin in personal correspondence is that the tone of the crónicas is often conversational. For instance, we find sentence fragments and sentence-initial conjunctions, and approximations of nonverbal aspects of speech, such as hesitations ("hmm") and other expressive sounds ("uf"). Chávez-Silverman draws on oral forms especially often in *Killer Crónicas*, where she manipulates standardized orthography in order to represent pronunciation, as in the expression "OB-vio (pronunciación porteñísima)" (OB-viously [very Buenos Aires pronunciation])

(*KC*, 41). One consequence of attempting to represent speech sounds in this way is the activation of what Garrett Stewart calls "phonemic reading," in which attention is paid to what readers "hear" in their heads as well as what they see on the page. Readers are warned of this in the introduction to *Killer Crónicas*, where Chávez-Silverman writes: "I can't not write it like I hear it" (*KC*, xix). Phonemic reading pays attention to "not just a phrase's unwritten purposes but also the accidents of audition to which it is prey."[22] The author seems to delight in forcing readers to confront these accidents by drawing attention to homophony. For instance, in "Route 66 Crónica," she describes the image of people jumping from the Twin Towers being "seared into [her] mind's eye/I por siempre jamás" (seared into [her] mind's eye/I forever more) (*KC*, 52). By formulating the homophones "eye/I" thus, the author demonstrates the productive potential of paying attention to how words sound: the layered homophones convey with utmost concision both the distress caused by the image and its lasting effect on her sense of self.

A similar effect is at work in many of the crónicas' titles, which signal, through the use of parentheses, that they might permit double readings. The title of "Un Pico (De)presión Diptych" (*SC*, 64–71), which comprises two crónicas, is itself a diptych of sorts. Through a cross-lexical pun (or what Stewart would call the activation of "transegmental drift") that relies on the similar sounds of "de presión" and "depresión," it suggests the copresence of two titles that we might translate as "A Little Bit of Pressure" and "A Little Bit of Depression," aptly summarizing two crónicas that tell of the pressures and anxieties of motherhood. The full titles of her 2011 book (*Scenes from la Cuenca de Los Angeles y otros Natural Disasters*) and a recent conference presentation ("Vivir [con] la pregunta: Mis crónicas del Sur, y otras hierbas" [Live (with) the question: My crónicas from the south, and suchlike]), with their respective codas ("y otros natural disasters," "y otras hierbas"), warn her audience that what we are about to read or hear will exceed the categories that have been chosen to define it.[23]

Parentheses occur regularly in the main body of the text, too, where again they permit the concise copresence of two simultaneous readings. For instance, in "Hawk Call Crónica," the author refers to herself as "heart(h) bound, more fiercely self-protective than ever" (*SC*, 70), thus simultaneously evoking physical ("hearthbound") and metaphorical ("heartbound") interiority. This device allows the author to project a double-voiced narrative and encourage parallel readings of the same sentence. Garrett Stewart offers a useful description of cross-lexical punning that helps illustrate what it is often like to read these parenthetic formulations: "The double-take, indeed muted double threat—both somatic and linguistic . . . is meant to be in every sense arresting. Grabbed, we are to stop short, go back."[24] The explicit layering of homophones and semi-homophones once again encourages slow, careful rereading.

These processes of layering and supplementing, which have become more and more common in Chávez-Silverman's recent writing, including in her uncollected crónicas, suggest a reluctance to impose a singular description that might guide our reading of the text that follows. It is indicative both of the crónicas' textual indeterminacy and their concern to remain open to different readerly interpretations. It also means that the crónicas lend themselves particularly well to oral performance. An important part of the publisher's marketing strategy for *Killer Crónicas* was to have the author tour university campuses giving performed readings of her work. Each oral performance constitutes a reading of the text; the performer (in this case, Chávez-Silverman herself) makes certain interpretations that can be adjusted or discarded from performance to performance. Each of them differs from the published versions of her crónicas in various ways, as is clear from a comparison of the opening paragraph of the published version of "Glossary Crónica" with an audio recording of a performance, hosted on the publisher's website:

> Me han pedido que (me) explique aquí. I mean, que ehplique mi lengua, my use of language. My odd, oral, transcultural ortografía. My idioma, 'tis of thee. Bueno, mi lengua . . . is a hybrid? Nah! Demasiado PoMo, too Latino Studies (even if it's true). Been there, done that. A verrrrr, mi lengua . . . es un palimpsesto? Sí, eso está mejor. (*KC*, ixx)

> **They've asked me to explain myself here**, I mean, que ehplique mi lengua, my use of language. My odd, oral, transcultural ortografía. My **lengua**, 'tis of thee, **sweet tongue of liberty**. Bueno, mi lengua . . . is a hybrid? Nah! **Too trendy**, too Latino Studies (even if it's true). Been there, done that. A verrrrr, mi lengua es un palimpsesto? Sí, eso está mejor.[25]

The second of these examples is my own transcription of the recording, following the spelling and punctuation in the written version, with added emphasis to indicate changes. We can see that the author has taken advantage of the ephemerality and flexibility of the oral mode. She has said in an interview: "I often change the words as I'm reading to a crowd. I'll look out and if I see it's a very monolingual—in English—audience, I'll change to more English in the middle of the sentence."[26] Changes of the kind she describes are very evident here, as the audio version voices certain phrases in English rather than in Spanish, and so makes manifest some of the phantom alternative-language versions Saint-Amour imagines in his foreword. The oral and written versions complement and complicate one another in interesting ways. The performance recorded by University of Wisconsin Press, for instance, draws attention to an aspect of the written version that may have been overlooked in silent reading. In the oral version the author sings "My lengua, 'tis of thee, sweet tongue of liberty," adding a line that does not appear in the published text and giving it a musical rendering. In doing so, she draws attention to her bilingual rewriting of Reverend Samuel F. Smith's famous patriotic song known as "America," whose opening line usually reads "My country 'tis of thee, sweet land of liberty." In this, Chávez-Silverman foreshadows the controversy over the inclusion of a Spanish version of "The Star-Spangled Banner" ("Nuestro Himno" [Our anthem]) in the 2006 hip-hop album *Somos Americanos* (We are Americans), and over an advertisement for Coca-Cola, televised during major sporting events since 2014, in which "America the Beautiful" is sung in seven different languages, including Spanish.[27] Like these later musical versions of U.S. patriotic anthems, in its opening sentences, Chávez-Silverman's "Glossary Crónica" claims "America" for bilingual Latinxs and asserts her unique mixture of English and Spanish as a legitimate language of the United States. The musical rendering of these lines in her performed version enriches our understanding of the text as a whole by drawing attention to this act of appropriation.

There is a complex mirroring effect at work in the above comparison. Chávez-Silverman's written version (1) is an attempt to record speech sounds using "odd, transcultural ortografía" (odd, transcultural orthography), hence the nonstandard spelling of "ehplique" ("explique") to represent Argentine pronunciation. The audio recording, in turn, is an oral interpretation of that written version. My transcription of the audio recording (2) brings us back to the written mode once again, though my written version deviates, as I have used bold type to indicate, from Chávez-Silverman's previous one. The parallel efforts to represent sound in writing and to interpret writing using speech draw attention to the mutability and ephemerality of both modes. In this juxtaposition, it is possible to conceive of "Glossary Crónica" as involving continual shifting interplay between the oral and written, and as a potentially unfinishable project. This open-endedness manifests in other aspects of the work's composition, as the following section will explain.

Textual Palimpsests

It is useful to turn to Genette in order to think about the composition of the crónicas as a collection of (often self-referential) layered versions that encourage multiple readings and remain open to possible further versioning. In *Palimpsests: Literature in the Second Degree*, Genette puts forward the idea that all writing is rewriting, and that literature, as the title of his book makes clear, is always "in the second degree."[28] He discusses "transtextuality," which encompasses different kinds of relationships between texts, including, among others, "intertextuality," which Genette takes to mean quotation, reference, or allusion to other texts; "metatextuality," by which he means a text's critical commentary on another text; and "hypertextuality," a term describing the relationship of a text B to a previous text A "upon which it is grafted in a manner that is not that of commentary."[29] This latter relationship, which is Genette's main concern in *Palimpsests*, is the result either of direct transformation or of imitation; examples include parody, pastiche, forgery, and continuation. Genette uses the image of the palimpsest to explain the layered nature of hypertextual relations.

According to Genette's model, Chávez-Silverman's work exhibits "autographic hypertextuality" or "auto-hypertextuality."[30] The author gestures toward this in the acknowledgments prefacing *Scenes*, in which she reminds readers that not only has she "performed different versions of these crónicas in many venues during the past four years" (*SC*, xiii–xiv), but that "slightly different versions of various crónicas" have previously appeared in written form, in print and online journals. In interviews, she has admitted that, although they often echo the unstudied sounds and rhythms of speech, the crónicas are actually very carefully curated, the result of an intensive revision process that includes "draft upon draft."[31] As I have already explained, the crónicas often begin their life as texts: "(emails, letters, my hybrid diary entry-epistolary genre, which I often copy over and send, qua letters, etc.) with one or more specific addressees."[32] She even goes so far as to describe her work as "collaborative" in that it is "edited and amended in response to the comments and reactions of [her] interlocutors/dedicatees."[33] This results in frequent commentary on her own previous writing, discussion of her own creative processes, and self-consciousness about her work's likely reception.

This "auto-hypertextuality" is especially apparent in *Scenes*, which, as I have noted, is largely concerned with remembering, and with its own attempt to record memories in writing. It continually refers to the process of its own production, with many crónicas citing the place of writing as "Montalvo Arts Centre, Saratoga, Califas," where the author undertook an artist's residence in the early summer of 2008, and discussing her daily efforts at writing there. In "Solstice/Shamanic Magia Crónica," dated just after the residence, the author refers to the "weeks and *weeks* of thinking, remembering, rereading mi diario, ese Transcript, and scribbling en el diario actual—the 'Momentos Hemorrágicos Crónica,' por ejemplo" (weeks and *weeks* of thinking, remembering, rereading my diary, that Transcript, and scribbling in my current diary—the "Momentos Hemorrágicos Crónica," for example), undertaken at Montalvo (*SC*, 144). This is not the only time Chávez-Silverman makes reference to another crónica in the same volume; *Scenes* frequently draws attention to its own composition and especially to its temporal fragmentation. The memories that surface after her reading her diary from 1982 are the catalyst for many of the book's anecdotes, and the difficulty of capturing the past with any kind of certainty is reflected in the fragmented, fragmenting quality of the crónicas, which often blend into or refer to one another, and in the potential for multiple readings afforded by their bilingualism and attention to speech sounds. These effects are apparent, too, in Díaz's *The Brief Wondrous Life of Oscar Wao*, to be discussed in the following chapter.

It is also in *Scenes* that Chávez-Silverman's process of palimpsesting, or cutting and pasting previous written material, is most apparent. Although the use of email and electronic word processors mean that much of the work of revising and rearranging is rendered invisible to readers, who are presented with a largely continuous published text rather than an obvious collage, the process of palimpsesting does leave some visible traces. All the crónicas make use of features that are common to informal written discourse such as texting or email correspondence: double exclamation marks, frequent capitalization and italicization for emphasis, abbreviations, contractions, acronyms, and regular ellipses—features that evoke the immediacy of speech even as they betray a self-consciousness about their status as writing. There is a contradiction here, in that, although Chávez-Silverman is overtly attempting to counteract the effects of digitization by encouraging readers to slow down, her writing nevertheless already uses precisely the features of electronic communication that facilitate speed.

In "San Francisco Transcript/Diary" (*SC*, 42–52), which flaunts its own convoluted composition, these features are contrasted with the pre-digital in order to highlight the ways digital communication has changed how we use language. The crónica is intertextual from the start, including three epigraphs on the theme of memory and distance. The main body largely comprises the author's diary entries from 1982, in which she describes her miscarriage. "Back then" (*SC*, 43), the diary entries were transcribed longhand and sent as letters to the author's then lover, Howard, who would have been the father of her child. After rereading the diary in 2008, the author types them up and sends them to Howard a second time, via email, to ask whether he remembers. This 2008 email opens the crónica, into which diary entries such as the following are embedded, along with her present-day commentary on them:

28-VI-82

Howard. I have written your name so many times in these past months—five now, exactly, since we met—countless times. Sending you clippings [ah, I still love to do this, snail-mail girl at heart!], wondering what you're doing, if you think of me obsessively in your waking and sleeping hours, as I do? (*SC*, 50–51)

Here square brackets interpolate the voice of Chávez-Silverman in 2008 into the voice of Chávez-Silverman in 1982, giving us temporal layering, as well as a layering of digital correspondence with handwritten letters in a way that highlights how language has changed over time; the expression "snail-mail girl" would not have had currency in 1982, before the advent of electronic communication.

Most of the other crónicas in *Scenes* coalesce around these diary entries, such that certain events or even specific lines from "San Francisco

Transcript/Diary" reappear in different versions, creating a sense of déjà vu. This crónica epitomizes her fragmented mode of writing, which she elsewhere interrupts in order to reflect on her own language use or previous state of mind while writing, signaling these digressions with expressions like "*interruptus*" (*SC*, 125) and "CRÓNICA INTERRUPTA" (*SC*, 80). "Anygüey, esa es otra historia" (or the truncated "esa es otra") becomes a refrain resulting from these frequent digressions that reminds readers of the existence of stories that exceed the present volume. In fact, each of the published volumes has blurred boundaries, as Chávez-Silverman's unique bilingual style bleeds into the books' paratexts (their acknowledgments and the "glossary" in *Killer Crónicas*) and, of course, into her ongoing correspondence, from which further crónicas are being forged: she has referred to emails I exchanged with her in the preparation of this chapter as "mini palimpsestos" (mini palimpsests) and "croniquitas" (little crónicas). Her writing constantly gestures both forward and backward in this way, to previous and future versions, giving an impression of openness and flux. The crónicas exhibit an ongoing process of layering and transformation, which leaves them open to the possibility of further reinscription through translation.

Besides the crónicas' "auto-hypertextuality," there is another form of hypertextuality at work here. By using the term "crónica," Chávez-Silverman consciously writes into, and subverts, a tradition of colonial documentation. Today the word "crónica" denotes a journalistic genre, but it was long ago used by the Spanish to describe encounters with Indigenous peoples in their newly colonized American territories. In their bilingualism, Chávez-Silverman's crónicas recall those written by mestizx and Native American writers themselves. In her classic account of the "contact zone," Mary Louise Pratt details in particular a long letter addressed to King Philip III of Spain, written in a mixture of Quechua and Spanish by an Amerindian by the name of Felipe Guaman Poma de Ayala, which appropriated the crónica form in order to rewrite "the history Christendom to include the indigenous peoples of America."[34]

It is helpful to think about Chávez-Silverman's own crónicas in similar terms. The author shows awareness of the ways her work is likely to be read within dominant Anglo-American culture: as part of the "exotic" culture of the Global South. Furthermore, Chávez-Silverman is mindful of the ways she herself might contribute to that process, especially in the parts of *Killer*

Crónicas that are set in Argentina. She describes herself, for example, as experiencing "el ever-hovering guilt (c)academic of worrying about possibly tropicalizing (o gauchifying) 'lo argentino'" (the ever-hovering crapademic/academic guilt of worrying about possibly tropicalizing [or gauchifying] "the Argentine") (*KC*, 84).[35] Similarly, in "Estragos acuáticos Crónica," describing her own response (as a Chicana) to a Mexican film called *Amores perros*, she remarks, "I essentialized myself. Me tropicalicé, I admit it" (I essentialized myself. I tropicalized myself, I admit it) (*KC*, 63). Beneath this overt preempting of accusations of self-exoticization is the recognition that Anglo-American readers of her crónicas are also likely to read them in a particular way, as the product of an alluringly "other" or foreign culture. Her position as a bilingual Chicana and a tenured U.S. academic makes her, in complicated ways, both culturally dominant and marginalized, and it is this liminality that allows her both to perform and be subjected to the exoticization she describes here.

Creative/Critical Palimpsests

We have already seen the way the crónicas layer different text types: diary entries, emails, and letters. However, they are also situated somewhere between creative and critical styles of writing. In this they beg to be read alongside an expanding body of contemporary writing, particularly by queer and feminist writers, which is loosening the boundaries between the theoretical and the personal, between humanities scholarship and the wider world. Works like Maggie Nelson's *The Argonauts*, Alison Bechdel's *Are You My Mother?*, and Paul B. Preciado's *Testo Junkie* have been described as "autotheory" for the ways they foreground theory's basis in and connection to the lived experience of the theorist.[36] Sara Ahmed's intellectual memoir *Living a Feminist Life* also challenges the erasure of the personal from academic writing by foregrounding how feminist theory is rooted in the experiences of one's everyday life at home and at work.[37] It is possible to trace a trajectory to these writers from a previous generation of feminists including Audre Lorde and, of course, Gloria Anzaldúa, who described her *Borderlands/La Frontera* as "autoteoría-historia" (autotheory-history), "a personal essay that theorizes."[38] Chávez-Silverman, too, fits into this trajectory, as her crónicas recall not only Anzaldúa's bilingualism and intersectional thinking, but also her combination of the theoretical and the personal in *Borderlands*.

The crónicas frequently mobilize theoretical approaches in the humanities, but in ways that encourage readers to attend to how theoretical knowledge is produced by and is applicable to the everyday experiences of the theorist. For instance, Chávez-Silverman describes "a sense of foreboding dogging me, always already (*pace* Derrida) detached, severed from—y anterior a—cualquier fuente reconocible" (a sense of foreboding dogging me, always already [*pace* Derrida] detached, severed from—and preceding—any recognizable source) (SC, 69). Here she evokes the logic of supplementarity (when "a possibility produces that to which it is said to be added on") mobilized in much of Derrida's thinking, in order to describe the nebulous, proleptic nature of her own anxiety.[39] In another instance, she makes a connection between Deleuze and Guattari's thinking and an everyday scenario: in "Diary Inside/Color Local Crónica," she recounts coming across, while walking in the hills near Saratoga, a group of flowers she is unable to identify. The plants "se autopropagan, en un sistema de runners" (self-propagate, on a system of runners) (SC, 15). She asks herself, "¿No serán estos famosos rhizomes, the ones D & G go on about? Oh my god, PoMo culti studies at the grass—o al menos—roots level" (Aren't they those famous rhizomes, the ones D & G go on about? Oh my god, PoMo culti studies at the grass—or at least—roots level) (SC, 15), referring to Deleuze and Guattari's concept of the rhizome, which they used to theorize an approach to interpretation that allows for multiple non-equal entry and exit points.[40] In "Axolotl Crónica," too, theory intersects with lived experience; in it, Chávez-Silverman engages queer theory insofar as it pertains to her own pervasive sense of in-betweenness. Throughout the crónicas more broadly, it is easy to see the influence of poststructuralist thinking about dispersal and nonbinarism, about difference within identity, and about absent presences; the crónicas resist chronology and organization, and their understanding of cultures and languages refuses to admit relationships of hierarchy. In these ways, Chávez-Silverman's personal writing is highly theorized, and it illustrates, as much recent "autotheory" does, the ways theory is rooted in and informed by everyday experiences.

However, the author's somewhat tongue-in-cheek, self-deflating tone also seems to acknowledge and deride the elitism and hermeticism of references such as those above to Derrida and "D & G." In fact, she often parodies the restrictiveness of critical and theoretical writing, including the goals of absolute accountability and comprehensiveness, for instance by including tongue-in-cheek, formal in-text citations for quotations (*KC*, 84). But despite the author's exasperation with scholarly standards, both volumes of crónicas were undoubtedly produced by, and in some senses for, the academy. They are, in very practical ways, scholarly. Individual crónicas have been published in academic journals, such as *Letras Femeninas, Hispamérica*, and *PORTAL: Journal of Multidisciplinary International Studies*, which require readers to have an institutional affiliation in order to access them. Both collections were published with the help of Pomona College, by a press affiliated with the University of Wisconsin. As such, they have been through anonymous peer review, a process unique to academic publishing. This process is discussed in the final crónica in *Scenes*, "(Almost) Milagros Crónica": "Y hablando de eso, what *can* be taking ese second reader so damn long? Van ya casi tres meses que lo entregué.... Quién coño tendrá el condenao librito anygüey? And what do they think about it? ¿Le gustará?" (And speaking of which, what *can* be taking that second reader so damn long? It's already been three months since I submitted it.... Who the hell has the goddamn little book anyway? And what do they think of it? Will they like it?) (*SC*, 147). These lines situate us temporally between the first draft of *Scenes* and the final typeset version, exhibiting the characteristic temporal disjuncture of a palimpsest, inhabited as they so often are by texts from different historical periods. It is a metaleptic moment, in which the possibility of its own reception helps produce the crónica itself, thus reinforcing Chávez-Silverman's repeated view that interlocutors of various kinds are "de donde derivo mi ímpetu. Para escribir" (where I derive my impetus from. To write) (*SC*, 35). Not just her own friends and colleagues, but also anonymous peers within higher education have helped her to refine, improve, and palimpsest the work, and even give her material for new writing.

As well as being produced within a scholarly context, the crónicas are also in large part consumed by the academy, rather than by readers more broadly. Part of University of Wisconsin Press's series Writing in Latinidad, the two collections are marketed largely to those teaching and learning in Latinx studies courses. *Scenes*, in particular, also makes itself attractive to teachers designing linguistics courses; it includes an afterword, written in English by Michael Shelton, a linguist at Occidental College, titled "Linguistic Perspectives on Code-Switching" (*SC*, 155–59), which provides a framework for students of linguistics to study the book's use of code-switching between English and Spanish. The crónicas encourage the close attention and concentration usually demanded of readers in higher education; students will be rewarded for having familiarity with a range of philosophical thinkers, which enables them to grapple with the complex ideas that often underpin and illuminate otherwise trivial-seeming anecdotes. As a scholar of Argentine literature herself, Chávez-Silverman refers often to the work of Jorge Luis Borges and Julio Cortázar, who are similarly noted for expecting readers to engage with conceptual difficulty; in *Scenes* she even explicitly compares her crónicas to Cortázar's 1963 novel *Rayuela*.[41] It is clear that the crónicas are critical and theoretical as well as literary and creative.

Despite being both produced and read primarily within universities, *Killer Crónicas* and *Scenes* are evidently not conventional critical discourse, nor are they marketed as such, but rather as a form of life writing, albeit one that frequently engages theoretical work. In "Montalvo Diary," the author expresses some of the anxiety she feels when dedicating time to writing crónicas rather than more conventional academic genres (*SC*, 22). Yet, despite that perceived divide, in truth there is a continuum between the different kinds of writing Chávez-Silverman produces: her emails, interviews, conference presentations, and published work have a continuity of style, taking the same playful, irreverent approach to language, mixing languages and registers, and drawing often on puns and nonstandard spelling. Despite the anxiety expressed in *Scenes*, her position as a tenured professor has given her the authority to begin to trouble the boundaries of acceptable or appropriate written registers within the academy proper. Given the increasing precarity of academic labor today, bilingual writing and indeed different species of "autotheory" are kinds of writing that remain the preserve of senior, tenured academics, because, despite fewer and fewer opportunities for publishing, the monograph remains the condition for promotion and tenure in most humanities departments in U.S. universities.[42]

Since she received tenure in 2005, Chávez-Silverman has been able to allow crónicas to entirely dominate her publishing output. By doing so, she responds to Walter Mignolo's lament that "hybrid" languages like that of Gloria Anzaldúa cannot become "languages of scholarship."[43] As in other parts of the publishing industry, monograph publishing tends to abide by the convention that a piece of writing should be in a single language (as this book does, with its parenthetical translations of all non-English text). This is certainly the case with University of Wisconsin Press: the press releases and website content they provide is exclusively in English, as is the paratext of Chávez-Silverman's books—the jacket copy, foreword, afterword, title page, and table of contents. But Chávez-Silverman brings her personal voice—a hybrid, bilingual voice—into the domain of the critical, thereby resisting the division between the critical and the creative, and also mounting a firm challenge to the predominance of English monolingualism in literary-critical discourse, both in the United States and internationally (a challenge that helps to dispel the perception that "Spanglish" is the preserve of the poorly educated). Ironically, it is a challenge that would not have been possible without institutional support from the U.S. university system itself.

A Case Study: "Axolotl Crónica"

Before moving on to discuss strategies for translating Chávez-Silverman's work, I'd like to focus in detail on one crónica from *Killer Crónicas* that demonstrates with particular clarity many of the features I consider to be fundamental to Chávez-Silverman's writing, and to the other writing discussed in this book. "Axolotl Crónica" recounts the author's discovery of a tank of axolotls—a kind of amphibious salamander native to Mexico—in a bar in Buenos Aires, days before she was to leave the city to move back to the United States. Like many of her crónicas, it is concerned with ways of reading; it evokes both intimacy and estrangement through its assumption of multiple interlocutors; it anchors itself in multiple territories (Buenos Aires, Paris, Mexico); it is written and then rewritten in a different version; it has a hypertextual relationship with work by a different writer (Julio Cortázar); and it signals the author's complex attitudes to the scholarly by using queer theory both to criticize and implicate herself in problematic ways of seeing. It also suggests we might read Chávez-Silverman's work via the notion of queerness, a concept I will explore more extensively in chapters 3 and 4. This crónica relies on an understanding of writing as an ongoing process of versioning that closely resembles the process of translation.

"Axolotl Crónica" centers on a discussion of the "male gaze," which the author finds herself guilty of enacting. The tank she discovers in the Buenos Aires bar contains three axolotls, one black and two white. The author is fascinated by them and reminded of Julio Cortázar's short story "Axolotl" about a man who becomes obsessed by one of the rare creatures in the Jardin des Plantes in Paris.[44] At first she assumes the black one is male, and uses stereotyped images of masculinity to describe it: "Como boxeador. Like an outclassed middle-weight against the ropes. O un toro acorralado entre picador y banderilleros" (Like a boxer. Like an outclassed middle-weight against the ropes. Or a bull trapped between picador and banderilleros) (*KC*, 102–3). She imposes, tongue firmly in cheek, equally stereotyped characteristics on the white "female" axolotls, who are imagined to be his girlfriends: "Esas rubias, calladas criaturas femeninas. Raised up on their fragile, transparent forearms. Parece que rezan. Meditan en el más ashá" (Those blonde, silent feminine creatures. Raised up on their fragile, transparent forearms. It looks like they're praying. Meditating on the afterlife) (*KC*, 103). They are silent, devout, delicate, and otherworldly. The crónica then breaks, and we are presented with a subtitle, "Axolota: versión #2." What follows is a rewriting of the crónica so far, in which the author realizes she has been identifying with the "lector macho" discussed in the previous crónica and asks herself whether the black axolotl might in fact be a pregnant female (hence the feminine suffix in the subtitle, "Axolota"). Just as elsewhere she accuses herself of (self-)exoticization, here too Chávez-Silverman implicates herself in the practices she is criticizing.

"Axolotl Crónica" is a conscious engagement with Cortázar's short story "Axolotl" from his 1956 collection *Final del juego*.[45] That story, like Chávez-Silverman's crónica, is also about a gaze: the mesmerizing gaze of an axolotl in a tank, which bewitches the narrator until he spends hours every day staring into its eyes. He says, "Los ojos de los axolotl me decían de la presencia de una vida diferente, de otra manera de mirar" (The axolotl's eyes spoke to me of the presence of a different life, of another way of seeing), and indeed the story ends with the narrator switching places with the axolotl and becoming trapped in its body inside the tank.[46] Like Cortázar, Chávez-Silverman draws our attention in "Axolotl Crónica" to the relativity of the gaze and to different ways of seeing. She does this not only by breaking the crónica into two versions, but also by addressing at least three different specific readers: two dedicatees (including Cortázar himself, or

"JC") and the axolotls of the crónica's title, all directly addressed as "tú" (you) and "ustedes" (you, plural). The crónica thus reminds us that each reader will read the crónica in a particular way, and that other readings may differ considerably from our own.

In rewriting Cortázar's story, Chávez-Silverman proposes further "maneras de mirar" (ways of seeing) that the Argentine author does not make room for, either in "Axolotl" or elsewhere in his work. Realizing that she has made stereotypical assumptions about the black axolotl's gender, Chávez-Silverman rejects, in exaggerated self-loathing, the "lector MACHO" (MALE reader). But she also rejects what she refers to as the "dreaded *lector hembra*" (dreaded *female reader*), assumed to be "insípida, irracional" (insipid, irrational) (*KC*, 104). Chávez-Silverman is specifically referring to Cortázar's "lector-hembra," one half of a dichotomy established in his 1963 novel *Rayuela*. In the novel, a character named Morelli describes two kinds of reader: the discerning, active "lector-cómplice" (reader-accomplice) who is both "copartícipe" (partner) and "copadeciente" (fellow sufferer) for the author, and the shallow, passive "lector-hembra" (reader-female), who "no quiere problemas sino soluciones, o falsos problemas ajenos que le permiten sufrir cómodamente sentado en su sillón, sin comprometerse en el drama que también debería ser el suyo" (doesn't want problems but rather solutions, or false problems belonging to others that allow them to suffer comfortably seated in their armchair, without engaging in the drama that should also be theirs).[47] Chávez-Silverman, like Cortázar, values active readers who will look beyond the work's "fachada ... bonita" (pretty façade).[48] Nevertheless, she baulks at the association of female gender with passivity, irrationality, and even base animality in the term "lector-hembra."

Her sardonic use of typography in "lector MACHO" and "*lector hembra*" reifies the stereotypical attributes of each gender—man's size and strength (uppercase) and woman's elegance and beauty (italics)—and signals a desire to move beyond this basic binary understanding. She and the bar's owners agree that "*no se sabe*" (nobody knows) (*KC*, 104) how to read the axolotls' gender, so they settle on something in-between. It's worth noting that what might otherwise have been a problematic association between blackness and male aggression or atavism when the black axolotl is compared to a boxer and a caged bull is nuanced by more feminized comparisons: the "black beauty" is likened, in its movements, to a hula dancer (*KC*, 102). Chávez-Silverman rejects the choice between Cortázar's two ways of reading, and proposes instead "ambas lecturas" (both readings), or even "todas" (all) (*KC*, 104). To describe this queer reading, she borrows the expression "*lectora macho*" from Rosemary Geisdorfer Feal, one of the crónica's dedicatees, whose "Queer Cortázar and the Lectora Macho" appears in Chávez-Silverman's own edited collection of essays on queer Latinx sexualities.[49]

To be sure, some aspects of Chávez-Silverman's writing chime with conventional notions of the feminine; its genre and linguistic fluidity, for instance, and its inability to be contained within neat typologies recall the "écriture feminine" outlined in works of French feminist theory.[50] Like these crónicas, women's writing was imagined to be limitless and diffuse, with the potential to disrupt and resist hegemonic power structures in much the same way Chávez-Silverman resists Anglophone monolingualism in the United States. But rather than aligning herself with theorists like Hélène Cixous and Luce Irigaray, in "Axolotl Crónica" Chávez-Silverman explicitly rejects *both* male *and* female, identifying herself with the genderqueer black axolotl. In this way gender queerness is added to the many other forms of in-betweenness and ambiguity the author uses to position herself as both insider and outsider, privileged and marginalized, dominant and subordinate.

The characteristics the author says she and the axolotl have in common are ones that indicate a poor fit with identity categories of various kinds. The voice identifies with the axolotl because of its dynamism, its contradictions, and discomfort with its environment: "Sos como yo. Animal oximorónico, fronterizo, incómodo, desesperado. En constante movimiento" (You're like me. Oxymoronic, border-dwelling, uncomfortable, desperate animal. In constant movement) (*KC*, 103). These are all traits that can be identified in Chávez-Silverman's self-portrayal, and in her writing, where the trope of the border dweller appears in various other guises, such as a coyote stalking the edge of the city, half-tame and half-wild (*SC*, 153). The black axolotl's "constante movimiento" (constant movement) is of course apparent in her continual switching between English and Spanish, creative and critical, public and private.

It's also worth pointing out here that the author's identification with the black rather than the white axolotls is in keeping with her racial self-representation elsewhere in her writing. In an essay that is "at once self-representational and critical"—a contribution to a volume examining how

U.S. universities are structured by and for white men—the author embraces and theorizes her own biracial and culturally hybrid identity, defining herself oxymoronically as "pura bicultural" (pure biculturality).[51] White and green-eyed, with Russian and Romanian roots but a strong sense of Mexican and Chicana identity (a "white-skinned, Jewish, brown Mexi-girl," as she memorably describes herself in *Scenes*, 55), she reflects on how she has always been seen as "too Mexican for the Jews, too *güera* [white] for the Mexicans and too *algo*, something unidentifiably, disconcertingly exotic, for the Anglos."[52] Embracing her ambiguous racial heritage has helped her to establish a teaching practice that is boundary-blurring and interdisciplinary, one that puts students' curiosity at its center, deferring closure and celebrating ambiguity. In her recent book *Heartthrob*, her poor fit with established racial categories is exaggerated amid the very different racial dynamics of apartheid South Africa, where the word "Chicana" has no currency: "en la paranoia taxonómica del apartheid no había modo de leer a una Chicana" (in the taxonomic paranoia of apartheid, there was no way of reading a Chicana) (*SC*, 55). There, the problems of thinking within the old black-white binary are thrown into sharp relief and her U.S.-formed racial paradigms are challenged. The version of Chávez-Silverman who narrates *Heartthrob* repeatedly identifies with the black and Afrikaner populations rather than with her boyfriend's exclusively white social circle: after feeling like "a stranger in alien territory" for many weeks, she confesses she felt sort of "at home . . . happier, more alive" in the predominantly black neighborhood of Soweto.[53] Although her "Raza roots come out al sol" (in the sun), there they see her as "una mujer blanca [a white woman] (or, well, white-looking)"; someone who is "bien paleface."[54] In contrast, her boyfriend's white sisters fetishize her curly hair, and her mother-in-law, she reflects, is rather scandalized by it: "Le parecerá too 'ethnic,' supongo" (She'll find it too "ethnic," I suppose).[55] Chávez-Silverman seems to suggest that she exceeds established racial categories not only in the United States, but also in a part of the world with a very different history of race relations, and her identification, in "Axolotl Crónica," with the "black beauty" is in keeping with that self-presentation.

Chapter 3 will discuss at length the intersection between gender, sexuality, and other facets of identity, but for now, it is enough to suggest that by associating herself with the black axolotl that may or may not be male, Chávez-Silverman becomes not just the performer but also the potential subject of queer ways of seeing. Eve Kosofsky Sedgwick defines "queer" as "the open mesh of possibilities, gaps, overlaps, dissonances and resonances, lapses and excesses of meaning when the constituent elements of anyone's gender, of anyone's sexuality aren't made (or *can't be* made) to signify monolithically."[56] The openness she identifies with queer is evident throughout Chávez-Silverman's work, in its layered, palimpsestuous structure. The structure of "Axolotl Crónica," for instance, involves interruptions, doubling back, and rewriting from a different perspective. Ultimately the author allows multiple versions to coexist rather than choosing between them: the axolotl can be either male or female; it can also be both, or neither. The crónica also includes a "coda"—conventionally a supplement to the basic structure of a piece of music—that reiterates her reluctance to impose finality on the text or to close down the conversation. Its presence here reminds us that there is always more to Chávez-Silverman's writing; it is never quite finished, but rather left open to further reinscription. In the final lines of the coda, she laments having to leave Buenos Aires, saying, "No me iré. I'll be back" (*KC*, 105), reassuring herself of the provisionality of her absence, and her readers of the provisionality of the text itself. This provisionality is reiterated yet again by a later version of "Axolotl Crónica," published in *PORTAL* in 2012, which includes further layering, editing, and reorienting toward new readers, as is evident from the title and dedication:

Axolotl/Bichos Raros Crónica
Susana Chávez-Silverman, Pomona College
Buenos Aires/Los Angeles
29 julio, 2001/25 mayo, 2010
Para Julio Cortázar y Alejandra Pizarnik, in memoriam
And for Wim Lindeque and James Zike, for (y)our way of seeing.[57]

Here we can see Chávez-Silverman's characteristic parentheses and forward slashes, which permit a new doubling of the title, a new temporal and spatial disjuncture, and the introduction of new interlocutors for the text. The various versions of "Axolotl Crónica" are summed up particularly well in this description: "En su escritura, la autora no busca la clausura ni la resolución sino al revés: la apertura radical, para ella misma y para sus lectores" (In her work, the author does not look for closure nor resolution, but rather the opposite: radical openness, for herself and for her readers).[58] If queer is an "open mesh," something that cannot be made to "signify monolithically," then by definition it avoids the closure and resolution described here. Reading Chávez-Silverman's work as queer means attending to its radical openness, its fluidity and provisionality. It means escaping simplified taxonomies by "lancing" ourselves into the interstices.

PART II. TRANSLATING SUSANA CHÁVEZ-SILVERMAN

Part II of this chapter will consider the role translation plays in both the production and reception of Chávez-Silverman's work. First, I want to demonstrate how translation is embedded in both the writing and the reading of it. Saint-Amour, in his foreword to *Scenes*, describes its layering thus: "One can hear the unchosen codes ghosting like an overtone series, in every 'question' a phantom 'pregunta.' In the aggregate, these branching choices open out on something larger: other itineraries that a life, lived in many places and through many codes, might have taken" (*SC*, xi). For Saint-Amour, each expression in English suggests, or contains within it, parallel expressions in Spanish (and vice versa), such that each crónica is haunted by a host of alternative versions. The act of reading Chávez-Silverman's bilingual writing therefore involves (or, at least, entertains the possibility of) translation. This idea has gained traction among recent critics of multilingual and translational literature; Brian Lennon, for instance, suggests that "reading a text written in more than one language is, itself, already an act of something like translation, in the cognitive comparative 'processing' of different languages."[59] Reading Chávez-Silverman's writing resembles the act of translating more than most reading does: it requires reading slowly, rereading, looking up unfamiliar words and ideas, then reading again, in much the same way as a translator would do.

Translation is conventionally a means of enabling communication or facilitating access, a way of clarifying—often by domesticating—something otherwise "foreign" or "other." When Ania Spyra contends that in *Killer Crónicas* Chávez-Silverman rejects translation, she is correct to the extent that translation is not used as a means of explaining and elucidating for the benefit of monolingual Anglophone readers, as we saw in the examples from Paredes discussed in the introduction to this book.[60] But translation is nevertheless central both to narrative production and narrative organization in Chávez-Silverman's writing, giving it a double voice and implying that it is an unfinished, perhaps unfinishable project. It is simply that she does not champion the kind of translation that facilitates communication, but rather the kind of translation that slows it down. She uses translation to defamiliarize words and objects such that they are perceived in new ways. This has the effect of lengthening perception, forcing even confident English-Spanish bilingual readers to read slowly and attentively before they can interpret, thus "deautomatizing" our reading processes in order to counteract the contemporary compulsion to skim or "consume" text rather than engage with it in depth.[61] As Haun Saussy puts it, with delayed interpretation, "our forms become valuable since we no longer see them as mere vehicles for transmitting what is already known."[62]

Calques, False Cognates, and Fake Translations

Chávez-Silverman achieves this by flagrantly, playfully transgressing widely accepted conventions in translational practice. For example, translators usually consciously sidestep the literal translation of idioms and other figurative expressions and instead attempt to find target-language idioms expressing a similar idea. Chávez-Silverman is not interested in finding those alternatives. Instead, she creates calques, whereby an idiom is translated literally. Calques are especially palimpsestuous in that they give the impression of one language having been partially effaced by another, with the first in some measure still discernible. Indeed, the word's etymology, from the French "calquer" meaning "to trace," gives credence to the idea that calques undertake a kind of palimpsestuous work, recalling as it does layered sheets through which an underlying design can be dimly discerned.[63] It reminds us too that words do not have a fixed reference to some kind of transcendental signified, but are—to use Derrida's term— "traces" of other words that rely upon their differences from one another in order to signify.

Take, for instance, the calqued title of *Killer Crónicas*, which flaunts the volume's ongoing delight in the often unexpected productivity of poor translational practice. First, as Maria Lauret points out, the title is a "killer" joke, suggesting that the crónicas are hilarious, impressive, excellent.[64] It is also (as "Glossary Crónica" explains) a reference to Esteban Echeverría's *El matadero*, a foundational early nineteenth-century Argentine prose work.⁶⁵ The "matadero" of the novella's title refers most obviously to the slaughter yard in which its action takes place, but also more obliquely to the "killer" characteristics of those in the service of dictator Juan Manuel de Rosas ("matadero" is related etymologically to the verb "matar," "to kill"). Echeverría's anti-dictatorial narrative recounts the slaughter of fifty bullocks to feed the starving citizens of Buenos Aires in order to explore the division between barbarism (exemplified by state-sanctioned terrorism) and civilization (symbolized by the "unitarios" who resisted it). By choosing the calque "killer" rather than "slaughteryard" (the word chosen by Norman Thomas di Giovanni and Susan Ashe for their English translation of *El matadero*), Chávez-Silverman suggests that her work shares Echeverría's preoccupation with oppression and repression.⁶⁶ She also acknowledges the possibility that these crónicas will be considered barbarous in comparison with normative, Anglophone modes of writing. The use of "Spanglish," as I explained in my introduction, is often assumed to indicate poor command of both English and Spanish and is associated mainly with informal conversation; Chávez-Silverman's enormous erudition, as revealed in both *Killer Crónicas* and *Scenes*, upturns that assumption as thoroughly as *El matadero* upturns assumptions about barbarism and civilization in de Rosas's Buenos Aires. The title of *Killer Crónicas* also signals its preoccupation with Mataderos, an area on the outskirts of the city that was historically a hub for the province's meat industry and which served as a crossroads between rural and urban Buenos Aires. Now a tourist destination because of its seasonal Feria de Mataderos—a folk market and traditional gaucho show—it features a number of times in *Killer Crónicas* as part of the author's fruitless search for "authentic" Argentine culture. The volume's calqued title, in sum, concisely anticipates the complex linguistic layering to come, highlighting the productive potential of inauthentic or "fake" translations (*KC*, xx).

Other calques from Spanish into English that frequently appear in Chávez-Silverman's work include the phrases "EYE" and "LITTLE EYE" (often capitalized thus, these are literal translations of the Spanish expression "ojo" and its diminutive "ojito," meaning "watch out" or "take care"), "fixate yourself" (fíjate) (*SC*, 78), "results that" (resulta que) (*SC*, 41), and "as God commands" (como Dios manda) (*SC*, 18). Examples of calques from English into Spanish include "the abeja's rodillas" (the bee's knees) (*KC*, 67) and "en la espuela del momento" (on the spur of the moment) (*SC*, 58). In both directions, they can be unexpectedly pertinent and evocative: for instance, the author describes encountering a "(trout) blonde duo ... una de ellas covered in diamonds, huge as huevos" (one of them covered in diamonds, huge as eggs) with "surgery and 'buttery-blonde' reflejos" (surgery and "buttery-blonde" reflections) in an expensive California restaurant (*SC*, 137). Here Chávez-Silverman trades one sense of the word "trucha" for another, replacing its colloquial Argentine meaning, "fake," for its better-established meaning, "trout." Its use describes the two women's dyed-blonde hair and also evokes an image of trout-like, surgery-enhanced lips. Their appearance is prosthetic or fake, but so is the translation—one of her "*faux traducciones*," as the author puts it (*KC*, 143).

Just as Chávez-Silverman delights in fake translations, she also often uses false cognates, which involve making sonic rather than semantic connections between words in different languages. Exemplifying, as Garrett Stewart puts it, "what the wrong spelling can get right," Chávez-Silverman refers to a friend who is "jubilating this month from UC–Irvine" (*SC*, 127)—"jubilar" means "to retire" in Spanish, but her version brings out the joy many people feel at knowing they will never have to work again.[67] She also avoids the Spanish word for "tenure" ("permanencia") because the false cognate "ternura"—meaning "tenderness"—is "such a more gorgeous word" than "la permanencia" (*KC*, 45).

Chávez-Silverman tends to use translation in contexts where it is usually avoided. Unlike with idioms, we do not usually interpret or translate proper names but simply transpose or transcribe them from one language context to another, assuming that their "meaning" inheres in the person or thing they designate rather than being properly semantic. Hence Plaza de Mayo will usually remain thus in English translations, rather than appearing as May Square. Chávez-Silverman, however, treats names as though they have the same semantic value as any other word; rather than transcribing them, she interprets and then translates them. For her, Avenida Las Heras is The Hairs (*KC*, 13), bell hooks is campanita ganchos (*KC*, 53), Antonio Banderas is Tony Flags (*KC*, 11), and the Mexican poet Amado Nervo is Beloved Nerve (*KC*, xx). In this way, the author tears down the assumption that a word, even a proper name, can ever have a single fixed referent, or that there could ever be a one-to-one equivalence between words in different languages. She draws readers' attention to the multiple possible signifieds each signifier might gesture toward, and makes an irreverent game out of destabilizing language, humorously exploiting the various ways meaning shifts from context to context.

Where translators see calques and false cognates as pitfalls to be avoided, Chávez-Silverman draws out their value and often their humor, using them to renew and rejuvenate tired clichés. In this she takes up a suggestion made by Doris Sommer, who, in her two volumes *Bilingual Games* and *Bilingual Aesthetics*, argues that we should allow linguistic "errors" to stimulate new ways of thinking.[68] An interlingual game such as "lance yourself" (*KC*, xxi) aptly illustrates the way in which puns can be both amusing and disturbing, because they estrange language and make meaning proliferate. Their potential for derailing direct expression and comprehension is in line with the provocative nature of Chávez-Silverman's writing, which seeks to obstruct globalization's values of speed and commensurability. Moreover, it shows that translation does not necessarily have the effect of explaining, elucidating, or making reading easier; it can add complicating layers to an existing palimpsest.

A Crónica in Translation

In this final section, I offer some quasi-critical, quasi-personal reflections on my experience translating Chávez-Silverman's "Todo verdor perdurará Crónica" for a readership that was assumed to speak only English. The crónica and my English version of it, "All Green Will Endure Chrónicle," were both published for the first time in the online journal *Asymptote* in July 2015.[69] My analysis and conclusions will be personal, suggestive, and provisional, because this approach is in keeping not only with Chávez-Silverman's depiction of the creative process, but also with my own understanding, explored at length in this book, of translation as a practice that is open to reflection and reinscription.

I have already argued that Chávez-Silverman does not reject translation, but rather relies on it (and often revels in it) as a means of creative production. I have also suggested that translation is necessarily involved in the reception of her work, as readers are required to translate calques, false cognates, and names in order to process and interpret them. Given these characteristics, and given that versioning is an important element of the crónicas' narrative organization, as both an intratextual *and* an intertextual process, her work does not foreclose the possibility of being translated by another. Rather, I think of my own translation as one among many layers in an already palimpsestuous work. To return to Rey Chow, if language is always prosthetic or inauthentic, then a translation is only as inauthentic or as derivative as its "original"; it is a supplement that can potentially enrich and extend the work itself. Like any translation, it is, of course, provisional, and in the following pages I offer a number of possible alternatives to the choices that were published in 2015.

Umberto Eco argued that James Joyce's *Finnegans Wake*, often considered a limit case for translatability, is "by the very fact of being theoretically untranslatable... also, of all texts, the easiest to translate, since it allows a maximum of inventive liberty and does not impose obligations of fidelity that are in any way fixed or calculable."[70] His argument is borne out, at least to some degree, by there being at least enough translations of *Finnegans Wake* to be the subject of a whole critical monograph.[71] Radically multilingual texts might on the surface appear impossible to translate, but, as Rosenwald points out, "impossibility of one sort or another is the ground of every translation and of all translational renown," in that it involves striving toward a goal that can never fully be reached—something Barbara Cassin also acknowledges when she terms concepts that require multiple, repeated translation "untranslatables."[72] In the case of Chávez-Silverman's crónicas, the features most often said to be difficult to translate are precisely those the author appears to take the greatest delight in: proper names, especially those with complex cultural associations; metaphor through homonym or etymology; the representation of accents and other vernacular effects; comments on the relationships between specific languages; idioms.[73] As I have already noted, Chávez-Silverman often translates these forms herself, drawing on the productive possibilities of flouting translators' conventions. Her writing does not reject translation or assume its inadequacy; rather, it illustrates a persistent curiosity about the multiple possible ways a given word might be understood and rendered in another language and enjoys the humor that can result from choosing an unconventional translation. In my view, the crónicas repeatedly open up the possibilities for translation rather than closing them down. I propose to follow the advice of one perceptive reviewer of *Killer Crónicas*, who points out that "el Spanglish es tan traducible como cualquier otro idioma" (Spanglish is just as translatable as any other language).[74]

One advantage of publishing in *Asymptote* is that it allowed for greater interactivity between different modes and media than print would have done. The online journal enabled multiple versions of the crónica to be published simultaneously: the translated version links easily to the bilingual version, and a translator's note encourages readers to consider the two side by side. It also adds a third layer, with a link to an audio recording of the author giving a bilingual reading of the crónica that differs in small ways from the bilingual written version. The illustration by Cody Cobb makes the publication even more multimodal. This tripartite publishing strategy magnifies tendencies already at work in the crónica itself, which is a story of avatars, versions of memories, and uncanny connections: the author encounters a hummingbird in her garden and is reminded that she dreamed of precisely such an encounter the previous night, only to also remember a similar encounter with a flying beetle many years before. Publishing digitally in a journal of international literature also seems especially apt for a writer who uses email correspondence as a means of bringing together diverse interlocutors living all over the globe, allowing what is sometimes a very local work to have global reach. The author has said that as she "palimpsests," she will "experiment and negotiate with different levels of intimacy and privacy" in order "to strategically open originally private texts out to more readers."[75] This translation can be conceived as a different kind of "opening out," to new readers with different language abilities, and with little connection to U.S. higher education. It is important, though, that it remains a *strategic* opening out, given the author's insistence that her work not be "clarified or explained."[76] A major challenge was to translate in a way that would still encourage slow and careful reading, but that would strategically manage the degree of difficulty imposed on readers.

The first decision was that, unlike the source text, my target text would have a clear base or matrix language: English. This, however, would make it difficult to convey aesthetic effects comparable to those produced by the contrast between the two languages in the source text.[77] María García Vizcaíno has discussed various strategies for replicating the effects of that contrast, including retaining some words from the source language, and introducing different varieties or registers of the target language; I will discuss both of these foreignizing translation techniques, among others.[78]

I decided quickly that I would retain *some* of Chávez-Silverman's Spanish, in much the same way that Gloria Anzaldúa does when she translates her poem "No se raje, Chicanita" as "Don't give up, Chicanita."[79] This meant it was necessary to find a way of illustrating that the degree of bilingualism was greater in the source than it was in the target text.

One way of visually indicating the bilingualism of the source text would be to use italics and regular font to distinguish between passages that appear in different languages. This would produce something along the following lines:

Source text: Me puse a barrer los fallen pine needles y stray eucalyptus leaves que se me caen, badgeringly, de los giant trees al otro lado del fence.

Option 1: *I started to sweep up the* pine needles *and* stray eucalyptus leaves *that fall,* badgeringly, *from the* giant trees *on the other side of the* fence.

Option 2: I started to sweep up the *pine needles* and *stray eucalyptus leaves* that fall, *badgeringly*, from the *giant trees* on the other side of the *fence.*

This technique leaves a typographical trace of the language mixing in the source text and replicates some of its visual complexity. However, as I have already mentioned, prevailing editorial convention in Anglophone publishing is that non-English words appear in italics in order to mark them as foreign. The use of italics in a translation would therefore imply a hierarchical relationship between the two languages, something that is resolutely avoided by the author. Besides, Chávez-Silverman uses italics liberally for other purposes: for emphasis, to indicate direct speech, or to mark out words from languages other than English and Spanish—functions that would have to be borne by other typographical means.

Another possibility would have been to replace italics with typefaces that are not associated with foreignness in Anglophone publishing, such as boldface, underlining, or fonts of different sizes. This is one of many strategies chosen by Susanna Nied in her recent English translation of poems by the Danish poet Naja Marie Aidt:

      I went back to
the kitchen, where I was going to bake Swedish *juleboller* but the flour
was vitamin enriched, the yeast extra strong, the whole batch tasted too
swollen and sweet, we gave up and once more got a glimpse of the old

blodmand, the bloodman who stood starting into the window with a horribly
wolfish smile, a spindly finger pointing, "Is it me that he wants?" asked the child in her eighth year, who isn't the *least bit* afraid.[80]

In this translation, regular font represents what appeared in Danish in the source text, while underlined words, words in larger font size, and words in italics indicate the previous presence of words in Greenlandic, Swedish, English, and French. This strategy results in translations that are visually very diverse and hectic looking, and although this seems appropriate for a text that, like Aidt's poem, is full of digressions and blends a number of different text types, I decided it was too exhausting on the eye to be a feasible strategy for a prose text rather than a poem, and given the extent of Chávez-Silverman's bilingualism.

Having abandoned both these possibilities, I experimented with diacritics as a way of foreignizing certain English words. Spanish makes heavy use of acute accents, and I experimented with positioning them on English words. This had the undesirable effect of sometimes implying that those words required an unusual pronunciation (as with the vowel sound in "wéaring" or "yéars") or emphasis (as with "attentión"), and thus often distorted the sonic and rhythmic life of the text. In certain instances, however, the accents reiterated the natural rhythms and stresses of the author's voice, as in the phrase "I knów it sounds crazy" or "So then (and ónly then)"; in these instances, I decided to keep them, as I liked the way they made readers stop short and question whether or not they were reading words in English. I also retained Hispanophone punctuation conventions where they differ from Anglophone ones, resulting in forms such as in the phrases "¡Fuck me, she almost took my eye out!" and "¿And his message?"

I decided to reuse Spanish words that share Latinate roots with English ones, such as "presencia," "aprehensión," and "simultáneamente," as well as some very common Spanish words likely to be familiar to readers from exposure to Anglo-American popular culture, such as "casa," "amor," and "corazón." On reflection, I might also have left "clase," "sucinto," and "distancias" in Spanish. What is more, some probably less well-known Spanish words are repeated in the original numerous times, alongside their "equivalents" in English—for example "colibrí" and "hummingbird." I decided to leave these in Spanish in the translation for readers to work out their meaning from the context. I also retained the convention of referring to individuals using the definite article, as with "la Joanna" and "la Leslie." Finally, I chose to translate "checando," the present continuous form of the verb "checar" (a variant of "chequear" used in Mexico), as "comprobing." "Checar" derives, according to the *Real Academia Española*, from the English "to check."[81] In an attempt to mirror that language contact, "comprobing" is a neologism formed by adding an English suffix to the more common Spanish verb "comprobar," also meaning "to check." I hoped that these various strategies of visual estrangement would disconcert monolingual Anglophone readers and prolong their perception in ways that echo Chávez-Silverman's own writing.

As I discussed earlier in this chapter, Chávez-Silverman's work often employs forms specific to a particular regional or national variety of a language, and this "crónica" is no exception. Expressions unique to Mexican, Chilean, and Argentine varieties of Spanish appear alongside more global or "standard" Spanish. One option would have been to render these forms into different registers of English in an attempt to echo some of their diversity, but this ran the risk of being lost in the text's existing cross-lingual register variation. For this reason, I decided to choose expressions in English that had specific regional associations in an attempt to replicate the scale of the different geographies covered by the original. In line with the author's largely Americanized English, I chose spellings like "realized" and "internalized" over "realised" and "internalised," and hoped that other Englishes would stand out against this norm.

For example, the word "pendejo" is used to mean "idiot," "fool," or "asshole" in various Latin American Spanishes but not Peninsular Spanish; I chose the broadly British "like a bit of a prick" to translate "medio pendejamente," to try to recreate some transatlantic distance, this time between the United States and Britain.[82] Similarly, I chose to render the Mexican expression "pos órale" as "awrite then," an informal spelling of "alright then" often used to indicate Scottish pronunciation. Likewise, "Eso: un heartbeat alado" became "Aye: a winged heartbeat." It might be objected that "eso" can be considered "standard" Spanish and does not demand a region-specific form in English. However, there were many places where I was obliged, reluctantly, to efface diversity, and so where possible I took advantage of other opportunities to create it, a strategy often called "compensation" in translation studies.[83] The expression "al tiro," which appears twice in this "crónica," means "right away," "as soon as possible," or "immediately." It is very common in Chile, although also used in other South and Central American and Caribbean varieties of Spanish.[84] Only able to find global or "standard" English expressions with similar connotations, in the end I opted for "tout de suite," which—although not specific to any one variety of English—being a loan expression from French, it at least sounds sufficiently strange to Anglophone readers as to replicate the foreignness of "al tiro" to certain readers of Spanish. I hoped that shifting the text into new Anglophone geographies in this way would have the effect of simultaneously globalizing and localizing the language, replicating a tension already at work in the original. Although the author expresses no personal connection to either Scotland or England, her understanding of language as prosthetic—available to be appropriated at will—makes this strategy in some senses fitting: it allows me to layer my own linguistic affiliations onto hers.

Two of the greatest challenges in translating "Todo verdor perdurará Crónica" were deciding how to translate the calque "little eye," and the hybrid word "anygüey." The former is, of course, already in English, although in order to process it a reader requires comprehension of the Spanish idiom "ojito." I considered three options: (1) leaving it as "little eye"; (2) translating it back into Spanish as "ojito," which had the advantage of foreignizing the target text with a Spanish word, but the disadvantage of effacing the playful bilingual game; or (3) creating a new calque. I landed on the phrase "reloj fuera," which can translate very literally as "watch out," a more or less accurate interpretive translation of "ojito." This version is by no means perfect; although in other contexts "watch out" works perfectly well for "ojito," in the context of Chávez-Silverman's sentence ("LITTLE EYE: even if I suck at putting a number on distance, tengo aguda consciencia de cómo medir el tiempo" [RELOJ FUERA: even if I suck at putting a number on distance, I have an acute conciencia of how to measure time]), a more appropriate rendering might be "take heed," "take note," or even "Don't be fooled," none of which can be calqued as easily or interestingly as "watch out." Moreover, there's a distinct possibility "reloj fuera" would be read as "clock out," which would make even less sense. Translating "anygüey," which relies on knowledge of Spanish spelling conventions in order to be pronounced like the English word "anyway" (/ɛnɪweɪ/), involved similar translational compromises. "Anyway" is usually rendered in Spanish as "de todas formas," "de todas maneras," or "de todos modos." Unlike with "watch out," I could think of no interesting calqued version of any of these expressions. I was also reluctant to keep "anygüey" because English speakers would not hear it as "anyway." I opted instead for "anywáy," the acute accent giving the word a touch of foreignization but not indicating any important change in pronunciation.

Another key decision was how to translate the title. "Todo verdor perdurará" alludes to Isaiah 15:6 and also to a 1943 novel by the Argentine writer Eduardo Mallea, *Todo verdor perecerá*. Chávez-Silverman has played on the sound connection between "perdurará" and "perecerá" to recast the phrase as a positive statement. Mallea's novel includes the Isaiah quotation as an epigraph, which in the King James Version of the Bible reads, "For the waters of Nimrim shall be desolate: for the hay is withered away, the grass faileth, there is no green thing."[85] I would have needed to give the crónica the awkward title "There Is a Green Thing" if I had wanted to retain the biblical allusion (most other versions echo the King James's "there is no green thing"). John B. Hughes translates the title of Mallea's novel as *All Green Shall Perish*, and I chose "All Green Will Endure" to translate Chávez-Silverman's "Todo verdor perdurará."[86] This is more idiomatic in English, although undoubtedly a compromise in more ways than one. Common translations of the word "crónica" into English include "article," "chronicle," and "column"; I chose "chronicle," to retain the connection to historical accounts of European explorations in Latin America, but added an acute accent, "chrónicle," to bring the word slightly closer to "crónica."

Some of these strategies—the use of diacritics on English words, for example—may be too unusual and alienating for regular use in a full-length translation; we will see in the following two chapters that the translators of Díaz's, Braschi's, and Bueno's bilingual work have taken quite different approaches to the ones I settled on here. But for a writer so determined that her work be difficult to read, and who is already so playful with orthography, I found them appropriate for a short publication as part of a feature on experimental works of multilingual writing.

In her book *The Palimpsest*, Sarah Dillon considers the way in which "writing about the palimpsest becomes an act of palimpsesting: any new text about the palimpsest erases, superimposes itself upon, and yet is still haunted by, the other texts in the palimpsest's history."[87] This is true not only of the present chapter, but also of a translation, which can be considered another layer to the palimpsest—another version of an already multivalent, multimodal crónica. In fact, translation, according to Genette, is paradigmatic of transposition—the process by which a hypertext is created from a hypotext.[88] It follows that in order for the palimpsest to be a useful analogy for Chávez-Silverman's work, we must remain open to the possibility of its further reinscription. Besides, although her work takes an important stance against the hegemony of English in global publishing and academic institutions, there is nevertheless an overwhelmingly playful character to her language. Her delight in multilingualism and curiosity about the productive possibilities of translation recall the bilingual games collected by Doris Sommer.[89] While arguing that multilingualism is good for democracy and rouses readers from a state of intellectual torpor, Sommer insists, too, on its ability to surprise and amuse. Genette likewise pointed out the playful nature of the hypertext, which he conceived of as a game; he considered "light" hypertexts such as pastiche and parody to be paradigmatic of the genre; "using and processing a (hypo)text for purposes foreign to its initial program is . . . a way of playing with it, of having fun with it and making fun of it."[90] Without wanting to "make fun" of Chávez-Silverman's text, translating it is certainly one way of continuing the disruptive playfulness evident in her own language games. Although there are, of course, many compromises to be made, translation offers opportunities for creativity in new directions. Chávez-Silverman has demonstrated that translation can make meaning proliferate rather than closing it down, and, with this in mind, I have viewed the translation as a hypertext, another layer in an already palimpsestuous work. As Lawrence Rosenwald perceptively notes, translation "is necessary for readers, but also for the life and growth of the works themselves."[91]

What we can also learn from thinking about the crónicas as a palimpsest is that, for Chávez-Silverman, there is a continuum between the acts of writing, reading, and translating, as all three are overlapping processes than can never be entirely finished. In particular, I have shown that translation—as a set of processes that both move through and structure a text, keeping it in motion—remains crucially important both to the production and the reading of these crónicas. Chávez-Silverman presents her work as a collection of fluid, shifting versions that can—and should—be read in multiple ways, and that remain open to reinscription, including in the form of translation itself. To some degree this palimpsestuousness is not unique to these collections but is a feature of all the writing considered in this book. We see the features described here, to different degrees, in Giannina Braschi's *Yo-Yo Boing!* and Junot Díaz's *Oscar Wao*, and in Wilson Bueno's *Mar Paraguayo*, as I will argue in the chapters that follow.

Chapter Two

CENSORSHIP AND (PSEUDO-)TRANSLATION IN JUNOT DÍAZ'S *THE BRIEF WONDROUS LIFE OF OSCAR WAO*

Junot Díaz's *The Brief Wondrous Life of Oscar Wao* is one among a number of recent English-language dictatorship novels by writers in the United States that offer second-generation perspectives on repressive Latin American regimes and their afterlives.[1] The novel is one character's frustrated attempt to recuperate a narrative in the aftermath of the "Trujillato," the period between 1930 and 1961, when, as Díaz explains in *Oscar Wao*'s first footnote, Rafael Leonidas Trujillo Molina held absolute power in the Dominican Republic (2). The narrator and fictional author, Yunior, attempts to trace a curse, or "fukú," back through three generations of Oscar de León's family history: Oscar and his sister, Lola, who grew up in New Jersey in the 1980s and '90s; their mother, Beli, who spent her teenage years in Santo Domingo; and their grandfather Abelard, who is thought to have brought the fukú on his family by somehow angering Trujillo. In the course of his narration, Yunior returns repeatedly to the trope of "páginas en blanco," blank pages: "Considered our national 'genius,' Joaquín Balaguer was a Negrophobe, an apologist to genocide, an election thief, and a killer of people who wrote better than himself, famously ordering the death of journalist Orlando Martínez. Later, when he wrote his memoirs, he claimed he knew who had done the foul deed (not him, of course) and left a blank page, a página en blanco, in the text to be filled in with the truth upon his death. (Can you say impunity?) Balaguer died in 2002. The página is still blanca" (90). The blank pages indicate the lack of accountability for members of the regime (Balaguer was a close counsellor to Trujillo, and his successor) and also the censorship it perpetuated. Blank pages and other kinds of blanks appear throughout the novel as metaphors for the epistemological uncertainty produced during and after a repressive dictatorship.

This chapter is concerned with tracing *Oscar Wao*'s own "páginas en blanco." It argues that, in addition to blanks in Dominican history, there are blanks in the novel's language and in its structural organization, and that these linguistic and textual blanks limit readers' access to information in order to mimic the experience of reading a text that has been partially excised by a censor. Part I begins by focusing on the blanks created by Díaz's "Spanglish," which I argue actually constitutes a "creolization" of English, whereby Spanish is incorporated into it. By mixing languages in this way, Díaz positions the novel in a tradition of Caribbean creole writing that values opacity, and creates intermittent blanks in comprehension for a range of readers. Further blanks in comprehension are created by the novel's enormous range of reference, by its multiple addressees, and by its omission of certain proper names for Dominican characters, places, and institutions. What is more, the novel's fragmented and open-ended structure demonstrates that Yunior (as fictional author) struggles to present a "full story" (243) of the de León family, which has long been entangled with a repressive political regime. This fragmentation, along with the sometimes opaque language, makes manifest the novel's concern with the inevitable presence of unreadable blanks in narratives, particularly those written about or during dictatorships.

The chapter will then argue that the novel's various blanks invite active participation from readers. Drawing on Judith Butler's argument that censorship can be productive as well as restrictive, it explores how *Oscar Wao*'s blanks, far from simply closing meaning down, leave it open to further rewriting. Reading *Oscar Wao* necessarily involves translating, explaining, and uncensoring, activities that amount to filling in blanks or "writing" parts of the novel for oneself, making it, in Roland Barthes's terms, a "writerly" text. In order to interrogate a claim Díaz has made repeatedly (in interviews and in the novel itself) about writers—that, like dictators, they are wielders of absolute power—I will pay attention to some of the novel's authorial paratexts, in which Díaz makes a playful show of "filling in" *Oscar Wao*'s blanks and silences while actually demonstrating the futility of such a task. This excessively shifting, fragmented, and expansive novel, written about and in the wake of a repressive regime, illustrates with special clarity the inability of an author to ever write a "full story."

Part II of this chapter will consider the role translation plays in both the novel's production and its reception. It will argue that, despite Díaz's apparent policy of non-translation, translation is actually intimately involved in *Oscar Wao*'s narrative structure. It is written as a partial pseudotranslation—a fictional translation without an original—and shares many aesthetic similarities with so-called genuine translations. Since the novel is already in part written as a translation, translation of *Oscar Wao* for new target readerships continues many of the processes already underway in the source text. Focusing in particular on Achy Obejas's translation of the novel into Spanish, I consider how it is analogous to the paratexts already discussed, demonstrating how it elucidates, explains, and fills in some of the novel's blanks, while also creating new blanks of its own. Taken as a whole, the different versions of this novel constitute a shifting, palimpsestuous work whose meaning is continually being constructed in acts of (re-)writing and of reading.

PART I. READING THE BLANKS IN *OSCAR WAO*

Creolized English and Unexplained References

The first "blanks" I want to address are those produced by Díaz's language. Díaz is fluent in Spanish and incorporates it consistently into his work, but he does not compose in Spanish, as Braschi and Chávez-Silverman do. He has never published a text (or even a substantial part of a text) in just Spanish. His "Spanglish," too, is a quite different beast from that of Chávez-Silverman. As already explained, this loose designation, "Spanglish," should not be taken to indicate a fixed entity; rather, it manifests differently in the work of each of the three Latinx writers addressed here. In Díaz's case, I want to argue, his "Spanglish" is better understood as a creolization of English.

It is important to note that, unlike Chávez-Silverman's, Díaz's writing does have a matrix language, which is very clearly English. Yet, in *Oscar Wao*, English becomes a marker of the arrogance and complacency of readers in the United States, tainted by its association with imperialism and foreign intervention. Díaz uses Spanish as one way to disrupt that complacency; as in Paredes's work, Spanish words and phrases appear intermittently in Díaz's English, although, unlike Paredes, Díaz does not incorporate contextual explanations or translations. Nor does *Oscar Wao* include a glossary of Spanish terms, which he was obliged to do by his publisher in his earlier collection of short stories, *Drown*.[2] Spanish remains almost without exception both untranslated and unexplained.

Créolité, or Creoleness, is a literary aesthetic based on Creole language and culture that celebrates the cultural and linguistic heterogeneity of the so-called Francophone Caribbean.[3] In *Oscar Wao*, Díaz creates a new version of Creole orality within English, which produces intermittent unfamiliarity and partial incomprehension—a series of blanks in understanding—for a range of different readers. In one interview, Díaz emphasized the importance of linguistic mixing to the expression of Caribbean ideas and narratives: "There is not a single word nor a piece of history that does not have some relation to the Caribbean. For me, writing a novel about the Caribbean was like an invitation to use all the words, every part of history that I know. I don't think there's anything that's foreign to the Caribbean.... The person who tries to speak about Santo Domingo only in Spanish is going to have a lot of problems. It's better to use five or six languages."[4] In saying this, Díaz closely echoes the arguments of Patrick Chamoiseau, Jean Bernabé, and Raphaël Confiant, whose manifesto, *Éloge de la créolité* ("In Praise of Creoleness"), sought to reconfigure Caribbean identity along the lines of Créolité.[5] Creole language and culture are heterogeneous, plural, and open-ended, and the authors proposed a new literary aesthetic to express them. They declared that "Creoleness is not monolingual. Nor is its multilingualism divided into isolated compartments. Its field is language. Its appetite: all the languages of the world," a sentiment Díaz echoes when he states that Santo Domingo is best expressed in "five or six languages" (*Oscar Wao* also includes words in French and Urdu, and of Taíno origin).[6] For them, Créolité is about claiming and using the interlectal, the disruptive and chaotic contact zone between acrolectal French and basilectal Creole, emphasizing the oral qualities of the latter, which is primarily a spoken language, and moving toward a literary aesthetic thoroughly permeated and continually motivated by its lexis and syntax.

Díaz has explicitly aligned himself with Caribbean literary models rather than U.S. ones, and often cites Martiniquan writer Patrick Chamoiseau as a particular source of inspiration.[7] Chamoiseau's novel *Texaco* incorporates Creole into its French; its strategies of creolization include the transcription of French words according to Creole pronunciation, the suffixation or truncation of French words and distortion of French syntactical structures according to Creole rules, and the use of oral features such as contractions and sentence fragments.[8] These strategies overlap considerably with those used in *Oscar Wao*. Just as Chamoiseau uses Creole to structure his French, sociolinguistic studies of *Oscar Wao* have shown that Díaz allows the syntax and lexis of Spanish to structure his English, through techniques such as "focus preposing" and elision of the pronominal subject, both of which are common in Spanish but not English.[9] What is more, Díaz does not simply use "standard" written English and Spanish, but moves between different varieties, registers, and orthographies in each of those languages in order to create a sense of orality. For instance, he often uses demotic English that relies on features common in speech and employs vocabulary from a number of different varieties including, prominently, African American Vernacular English. Just as Chávez-Silverman's stay in apartheid South Africa forced her to confront the relativity of racial paradigms, Dominican (and indeed other Afro-Latinx) immigrants to the United States find themselves subject to a different kind of racial categorization: they are often assumed to be African American—Black—even where they may previously have been considered white in an island context. The characters Oscar and his sister, Lola, find that they fit into neither black nor white America. Oscar's lack of interest in hiding his afro means he is not included in white society; but he is also, as Carpio puts it, "a character so outside the stereotypes of blackness and brownness," with his bookishness and total lack of machismo, that he is rejected by Dominicans and African Americans, too. Lola, for her part, is considered something of a freak as a goth—a subculture famous, of course, for the use of white foundation—because of her dark skin (they call her "Blacula," 54); but then, on the other hand, she is rejected by other "morenas" for her "thin nose and straightish hair" (15). Meanwhile their mother, Beli, despite being born to a well-to-do, white-passing Dominican family, has skin that is "*black* black: kongoblack, shangoblack, kaliblack, zapotecblack, rekhablack" (248). In this way she is linked not only with Africans brought to the Caribbean as slaves, but also with dark-skinned Asians and Indigenous Americans. She and her children escape or exceed categories of blackness in the parts of the world where they reside.

One way that Díaz signals the racial ambiguity of Afro-Latinxs is by having his United States–based Dominican characters—particularly Yunior—use African American slang alongside Caribbean Spanish. As critics like Glenda R. Carpio, Rachel Norman, and Daniel Arrieta Domínguez have noted, he uses phrases such as "I got jumped," "let me steal on her ass," "them two were tight," and, of course, perhaps the most fraught word in the English language: the N-word.[10] Taking a lead from Toni Morrison, who, he argues, wrote specifically for an African diaspora readership,[11] Díaz has Yunior racialize his reader by referring, for instance, to "us niggers," thus creating a sense of community and inclusivity with readers who are able to use that word as a term of endearment or affiliation, while leaving aside readers who cannot.[12]

Like his English, Díaz's Spanish, too, is flexible and "nonstandard," using spellings—such as "pa' 'fuera" ("para afuera," outside) (22), "buenmoso" ("buenmozo," handsome) (24), and "urikáan" ("huracán," hurricane) (25)—that evoke spoken forms by reflecting pronunciation; playing on the "j"/"y" confusion frequently experienced by Hispanophone speakers of English with phrases like "una puta major" (standard spelling would be "una puta mayor," meaning "a bigger whore") (103) and names like "Yunior" (Junior); and inventing evocative punning neologisms such as "Truji-lío" (a pun on "Trujillo" and "lío" meaning "fling," "affair," or "trouble") (152). The flexibility of his English and Spanish means they include and exclude certain readers to different degrees at different moments.

These techniques of creolization are compounded by Díaz's refusal to visually signal the appearance of non-English words with italics or quotation marks, a strategy that led to a change in editorial policy at the *New Yorker*, where a number of extracts from his work were originally published, and which encouraged many other Latinx writers to follow suit. They are also compounded by the frequent omission of diacritics on words such as "que" ("qué," what) and "mas" ("más," more) and in the abandonment of Spanish orthographic conventions such as the use of "¡" and "¿" to introduce exclamations and questions. These will appear strange not only to speakers of Spanish; to readers expecting to see only English, these words may appear at first glance to be familiar, because there are no overt typographical indications of "foreignness," but, when read more closely, turn out to be unexpectedly strange, producing partial blanks in comprehension.

This semi-communicability is something Díaz's language has in common with the Creole aesthetic proposed by Chamoiseau and his contemporaries. The authors of *Éloge de la créolité* argue that a certain amount of incomprehensibility is essential to their literature. They claim that Creoleness will not be "completely communicable. It will not go without its opaqueness," and that readers shall "live its discomfort as a mystery to be accepted."[13] The use of creolized language creates gaps and silences in reader comprehension, as unfamiliar words and phrases become mere inscriptions on the page, or, when voiced, mere sounds. The result is a series of shifting semantic blanks that echo throughout the novel thematically, structurally, and typographically.

Another way of strategically including and excluding different readers at different points in the narrative—thus creating intermittent blanks in their comprehension—is to imply a readership that is extremely heterogeneous. Yunior often speaks directly, and personally, to an individual addressee (or sometimes addressees), but one that shifts and changes. Sometimes his interlocutor is assumed to be black ("Negro," "us niggers"). Sometimes they are male ("players"), sometimes female ("sisters"). Sometimes they are from the United States, sometimes from the Dominican Republic ("plataneros" [banana growers]). Sometimes they are a member of the academic community; sometimes they share Oscar and Yunior's taste in speculative genres.

These shifting and heterogeneous addressees allow Díaz to swing frequently from high- to lowbrow references, from the *Fantastic Four* to Derek Walcott, from *Lord of the Rings* to Edouard Glissant, without stopping to contextualize or explain, in much the same way he refuses to translate Spanish words into English. For instance, he asks questions such as, "You ever seen that Sargent portrait, Madame X? Of course you have" (181), which validate some readers' knowledge while making others feel ignorant or excluded. The result is that all readers will identify with or understand some allusions and references, but none are likely to understand all of them, because the novel establishes such an enormous referential framework that no single reader can bring to it an exhaustive understanding. Scholarship long assumed that literary texts were intended for a specific group of competent readers who were in an ideal position to understand them, but *Oscar Wao* demonstrates with particular clarity how a text can have multiple targets; how some readers may be the target of confusion or alienation, as well as of confidence and inclusion; and how these effects may be performed on the same readers at different points in the same work. Like the text's creolized language, encounters with unfamiliar, unexplained cultural references create shifting, intermittent blanks in comprehension, preventing any reader from taking for granted that the text should be in some proprietary way *theirs* simply because of the dominant language they speak or the prestigious culture they recognize. When combined with typographical blanks such as "the —— Academy" (71), "the Blessed B——í clan" (100), "Officer ——" (318), which clearly evoke the restrictive discursive practices of a repressive regime, these more subtle moments of opacity create echoes of the epistemological uncertainty that prevails during and after a period of censorship. As the following section will demonstrate, the novel's linguistic and textual blanks are intimately bound up with historical and contemporary structures of oppression at work in the Caribbean.

Blank Texts, Blank Bodies

The blanks in comprehension produced by *Oscar Wao*'s creolized English and wide referential framework serve not only to unsettle and frustrate readers accustomed to feeling at home in their reading; they are also thematically pertinent to a novel largely concerned with the ways Trujillo's erosion of civil liberties thwarts, even many years later, any attempt to narrativize and explain events of that period. They mimic the experience of encountering the historical silences that are part of the legacy of a repressive regime.

The novel recounts how Trujillo attempted to destroy any information—especially printed documentation—that might undermine his authority. For instance, a footnote describes a historical figure called Jesús de Galíndez, a Columbia University doctoral candidate from Spain (96–97). Galíndez's dissertation was titled *La era de Trujillo: Tesis doctoral sobre la brutal tiranía* (The Trujillo era: Doctoral thesis about the brutal tyranny).[14] Having tried and failed to buy the document, Trujillo allegedly kidnapped Galíndez in New York, flew him to the Dominican Republic, and had him tortured and killed; his body was never found. The fictional character Abelard is treated similarly on account of his half-written book reportedly describing Trujillo's "supernatural" abilities. When Abelard is arrested, the book also disappears: "Every paper he had in his house was confiscated and reportedly burned . . . not a single example of his handwriting remains" (246). He dies not in 1953, as his family are told, but after fourteen years' incarceration in Nigua prison. He is tortured until he loses all mental faculties and is buried in an unmarked grave.

Disappeared books are thus repeatedly linked with the disappeared bodies of their victims, and are underscored by the appearance in the novel of both textual and bodily "blanks." The so-called Man Without a Face, for instance, appears repeatedly as a harbinger of the de León family fukú. Beli and Oscar both see him immediately before being the subjects of near-fatal state-sanctioned violence, and his blank face points to the perpetrators' anonymity. Elsewhere it is victims—those "brief, nameless lives" in the novel's epigraph from *Fantastic Four*—who are faceless. Terrifying dreams in which Oscar wears a "wrathful mask" and sometimes "has no face" betray Yunior's fear that Oscar will disappear in the same way his grandfather Abelard did (325). Readers of *Drown* (1996) will also be reminded of two stories in that collection that feature a boy whose face was mutilated by a pig as a small child. In "No Face," wearing a mask grants the boy anonymity and the confidence to imagine a powerfully hypermasculine identity for himself based on the supernatural abilities of comic-book heroes. In "Ysrael," however, we see him unmasked and vulnerable. Despite talk of doctors and facial surgery, Rafa's tired conviction that "they aren't going to do shit to him" tells us that Ysrael will likely remain "faceless"—a forgotten nobody.[15] Yunior's fear is that the same will happen to Oscar. In the dream, Oscar has a similarly impressive "wrathful" demeanor when he appears masked; unmasked, however, he is not only vulnerable but also disturbing, because he lacks that most fundamental marker of identity: a face. His "seamless" hands, moreover, are holding a blank book (325), meaning that both bodily and textual markers of identity—face, fingerprints, handwriting, the lifelines on his palms—are rendered illegible.

The erasure of written texts is therefore bound up with the comprehensive erasure of individuals' identities and suggests that the violence of Trujillo's regime (and its aftermath) is in some way *beyond language*: beyond representability in words. Yunior describes Beli's beating, after all, as being "the end of language" (147). This notion is reinforced, perhaps counterintuitively, by Díaz's creolized English. Despite its capaciousness and exuberance, its willingness to borrow so generously from different languages and varieties, and the multiple ways it is able to signify, it does not, as the

CENSORSHIP AND (PSEUDO-)TRANSLATION

authors of *Éloge de la créolité* put it, "go without its opaqueness," but produces semantic blanks at different moments for different readers.[16] These moments of linguistic emptiness work in tandem with the trope of "páginas en blanco" to reify the notion that there are inevitable narrative blanks in the history of the Dominican Republic. We can see this particularly clearly in a passage about Beli. Following a traumatic childhood as a restavek, during which time she acquired an enormous scar on her back from boiling-hot oil, Beli uses silence as a way to forget and to "forge herself anew" (260):[17] "Of those nine years (and of the Burning) Beli did not speak ... for *forty years* she never leaked word one about that period of her life. ... Even today La Inca rarely saying anything more than *Casi la acabaron*" (258). The phrase "*Casi la acabaron*" (They nearly finished her off) neatly illustrates the way Díaz uses language to reify the historical silences he describes, by denying non-Spanish speakers access even to La Inca's single terse comment about Beli's childhood. In instances like this one, the semantic "silence" produced by unfamiliar words is more powerful and pertinent than any actively signifying language.

Narrative Blanks and Fragmentation

The silences imposed by the dictatorship, as well as those clung to by victims as self-preservation tactics, make attempts to reconstruct narratives from this period extremely difficult, as is apparent in the presence of blanks in the story of Oscar's family itself.[18] Yunior characterizes himself as a wielder of absolute power when he notes the frequent conflict between writers and dictators: "Dictators, in my opinion, just know competition when they see it. Same with writers. *Like, after all, recognizes like*" (97, emphasis in original). The suggestion here is that authors have total, exclusive control over their narrative material. Yet, despite this supposedly authoritarian hold over the story, Yunior is candid about the limitations imposed on his task. He remarks: "What's certain is that nothing's certain. We are trawling in silences here. Trujillo and Company didn't leave a paper trail—they didn't share their German contemporaries' lust for documentation" (243). Faced with only vague half knowledge, his attempts to reconstruct de León family history, entwined as it is with the Trujillato, repeatedly come up blank. Unable to impose a single, dictatorial narrative, he must instead offer multiple possible versions of events that take the place of a "full story" (243).

For instance, Abelard's arrest: "On all matters related to Abelard's imprisonment and the subsequent destruction of the clan there is within the family a silence that stands monument to the generations, that sphinxes all attempts at narrative reconstruction. A whisper here and there, but nothing more" (243). This arrest—which, because it was perpetrated by the Trujillo regime, is considered the origin of the family fukú—is explained in a number of ways: it might have resulted from Abelard's refusal to offer his daughter to the dictator as a sexual partner, from a misjudged joke, or from the contents of the book he was writing. Readers are explicitly told "you will have to decide for yourself" (243).

The novel Yunior offers us is therefore structured according to partial silences and repeated rewritings, in which episodes of family history are replaced with new stories that are simultaneously distant from previous ones and intimately connected to them. The most powerful of these rewritings is central to the novel's plot: Beli falls in love with "the Gangster," which brings her to the attention of the Trujillo family; she is taken to a cane field and violently beaten. She forces herself to forget—to erase her own history—and start a new life. Decades later, her son Oscar falls in love with Ybón, which brings him to the attention of the military police; he is taken to a cane field and violently beaten, twice. On the second occasion, at the moment of Oscar's death, when his attackers hold a gun to his head and say, "Listen, we'll let you go if you tell us what *fuego* means in English" (322), Díaz links this single act of violence with some of the most abhorrent in Dominican history: the Haitian genocide under Trujillo. That Oscar's death is ultimately triggered by his ability to understand a word and pronounce it in English, "fire," enters it into a cycle of violence that stretches back at least as far as the so-called parsley massacre in 1937, in which a shibboleth, the Spanish word "perejil" (parsley), was purportedly used to separate Francophone Haitians from Hispanophone Dominicans.[19] Oscar's act of translation allows us to glimpse the violence hidden behind *Oscar Wao*'s other blanks and silences.

As the narrative draws to a close, it fragments into shorter and shorter sections that signal the approach of the end: "The Final Voyage," "The Last Days of Oscar Wao," "The End of the Story," "On a Super Final Note," and "The Final Letter." Yunior's difficulty in providing a conclusion to the plot suggests that the novel cannot end, but rather will continue to repeat itself. Its cyclical patterning undermines his supposed role as writer-dictator because it requires him to offer multiple versions rather than a single, indisputable narrative. Yunior can never be "Trujillo with a different mask," as Díaz has suggested in interview; rather, he is unable to gain full authority over his narrative because the repressive culture it represents produces blanks and silences that readers themselves must fill in.[20]

Filling in *Oscar Wao*'s Blanks

In an essay on censorship and silencing, Judith Butler posits a deconstructive understanding of censorship as a technique by which discursive practices are maintained. Given that our social interactions consist largely of such discursive practices, it follows that censorship is the norm rather than the exception. Understood in this way, censorship is not only restrictive and privative, but also formative and productive; it is an everyday part of our expression and establishes the behaviors that define us as social subjects. Censorship "precedes the text," in which Butler includes speech and other cultural expressions, "and is in some sense responsible for its production."[21] This insight reminds us that *Oscar Wao*'s various "páginas en blanco" can spur the production of speech as well as enact its suppression, because a blank space maintains "the promise of full representation heralded by silence," which is to say that it keeps all possible understandings and interpretations simultaneously in play rather than choosing only one.[22] I have already suggested that Chávez-Silverman's translation games require readers to become translators, looking words up and thinking about their literal and figurative meanings in both English and Spanish in order to grasp the author's wordplay. A related phenomenon is at work in *Oscar Wao*: precisely because of the blanks they contain, Díaz's language and structure are open and expansive, inviting active participation from readers who must translate, explain, or even "write" parts of the text themselves.

The idea that readers can (or should) also be writers of a text is set out in Roland Barthes's *S/Z*.[23] Barthes argues that the goal of literature is "to make the reader no longer a consumer, but a producer of the text."[24] Reading should therefore be work, a "labor of language," and readers should be active.[25] Texts that are uncomfortable or even partially unreadable, that challenge our expectations and require us in some sense to write as we read them, he terms "writerly" texts, in contradistinction to "readerly" texts, which neglect to challenge the reader's subject position, allowing them to remain largely passive. He speaks of "an attempt to abolish (or at least to diminish) the distance between writing and reading . . . by linking the two together into one and the same signifying practice."[26] There is continuity here with Cortázar's "lector cómplice" and "lector hembra" as imagined in *Rayuela*, discussed in the previous chapter, although Barthes takes the concept further by suggesting that there are texts that actively demand a certain kind of reader.

When Maria Lauret observes that "really reading Díaz is *work*," involving careful research and taking notes on every page, she is recognizing *Oscar Wao*'s "writerly" characteristics.[27] The blanks I have described turn the act of reading into a concerted, active effort. They also allow us to position *Oscar Wao* alongside other self-consciously "writerly" texts that use blanks and silences to stimulate active reading, such as *Skriv selv* [Write it yourself] by the Danish writer of concrete poetry Vagn Steen, which consists—other than the front and back covers—entirely of blank pages, inviting readers quite literally to write the poems themselves.[28] *Oscar Wao*'s relationship with a work such as this is most apparent in Yunior's insistence that readers must "decide for themselves" about certain aspects of de León family history, and in the typographical blanks (such as "Officer ——") that beg to be written over. However, the novel's use of creolized language is "writerly," too; in order to overcome the semantic blanks produced by unfamiliar words, readers are forced to become translators (and translators are perhaps the paradigmatic active readers) who, like those who encounter Steen's book, must by necessity write parts of the text for themselves in language they understand. *Skriv selv* may be a radical attempt to turn readers into writers, but it is nevertheless helpful in understanding the way Díaz's own blanks and silences encourage a dynamic and active relationship between reader and text. By assuming different kinds of knowledge and experience, and refusing to explain, the novel encourages readers to research its wide range of cultural and linguistic references.

Readers have expressed anxiety about the noticeably incomplete nature of their understanding of *Oscar Wao*, and often resist that incomprehension very strongly; Sonja S. Burrows's ethnographic study of reader reviews (which are almost exclusively written in English) found that readers react vehemently and often negatively to the novel's use of Spanish.[29] That the novel invites thorough exegesis is evidenced by the considerable critical attention it has attracted both from the media and the academy, and by the number of scholars who attempt to identify the reading that will provide the most comprehensive explanation. Burrows herself, for example, claims that "the text [of *Oscar Wao*] is *fully comprehensible* only to the bilingual."[30] Others believe the key to understanding lies not in the novel's use of Spanish, but in its intertextual references, with Tim Lanzendörfer arguing that "the novel offers a sweeping reinterpretation of Caribbean history in a way that is *completely intelligible* only if one understands the relevance of its primary fantasy intertext, *The Lord of the Rings*."[31]

One reader's response helps us see particularly clearly how the novel's blanks and silences provoke active reading in order to dispel incomprehension. The Annotated Oscar Wao is a website compiled by a non-Spanish-speaking reader who identifies herself as Kim."[32] After relying on multiple internet resources to avoid "miss[ing] out on half of the story" when reading the novel, Kim amassed a total of 813 annotations to *Oscar Wao*, striving to collect as much information as possible. The list was crowd-sourced over time as other readers contributed their own suggestions, explanations, and translations. The annotations cover cultural references like food and drink, dance, historical figures, places, and references to books, films, comics, music, and art. They translate terms from Spanish into English and define high-register English words such as "apotheosis," "milieu," and "diaspora," drawing on free online encyclopedias, dictionaries, books, and articles, as well as anecdotal evidence from other readers. One of the very first entries "explains" the Dominican Republic by including a link to the Wikipedia entry on the nation.

In her comprehensive examination of *Oscar Wao*'s numerous paratextual "portals," Ellen McCracken explores how paratexts—defined by Gérard Genette as material that is both part of a text and separate from it, in the "'undefined zone' between the inside and the outside" of a text—affect the way readers navigate the novel and shape their understanding of it.[33] She rightly notes that Kim's Annotated Oscar Wao has "help[ed] to change the interpretive strategies of thousands of the novel's readers" by filling in the semantic blanks produced by its creolized language and unexplained references.[34] McCracken is interested in the provisional and shifting nature of digital paratexts like Kim's, which lack fixity and authority and therefore contribute to the novel's sense of openness. For this reason, she admires Kim's admission of "lack of control over the literary text, gaps in knowledge, and inadequate cultural competence in certain areas."[35] I would contend, however, that Kim's annotations are driven precisely by a desire to gain control over the text and fill in its gaps. The endless task of listing and defining reveals a desire to establish authoritative, stable meanings for the novel's many references and allusions. In some instances, a definition appears on the list even if it offers nothing that cannot be gleaned from the novel itself: "Café Atlántico," for instance, is glossed as "from context, a club." Its appearance in an ordered, dictionary-style list gives this entirely self-evident reading the appearance of authority and credibility.

The research Kim compiles is an attempt to "uncensor" the novel. But if we understand censorship in Butler's deconstructive sense, as a normal and constitutive part of speech and a prerequisite for social interaction, it follows that this task will always necessarily be incomplete. As Butler puts it, "no text can remain a text—that is, remain readable—without first being subjected to some kind of censorship," because "every text or expression is in part structured through a process of selection that is determined in part by the decision of an author (or, speaker) and in part by the language in which one expresses oneself."[36] If all expression is "always already censored to some degree," this applies to Kim's explanations as much as to Díaz's novel. What is more, Kim's attempts to explain and "uncensor" *Oscar Wao* through meticulous documentation can only ever be partial: "It makes no sense to try to oppose censorship: to oppose censorship fully is to oppose the conditions of intelligibility."[37]

Kim takes very literally one kind of reading *Oscar Wao* invites: a reading that involves active research. But her project completely ignores another kind of reading it also demands: one that admits the impossibility of a quest for full, definitive meaning. The experience of partial incomprehension persists despite all her annotations, because no amount of thorough research will deliver an all-encompassing understanding, or what Yunior calls a "full story" (243). This is especially true, of course, of a novel explicitly concerned with the difficulties of narrating a period of history in which information was destroyed and victims kept silent to protect themselves.

Authorial Rewritings of *Oscar Wao*

Oscar Wao's authorial paratexts add to the novel's already multiple and incomplete layers, overspilling the boundaries of the main printed text.[38]

They also, importantly, allow Díaz to respond tongue-in-cheek to readers' desire for clarity; as I discussed in the introduction, critics have identified a trend in recent literature to abandon formal difficulty and local particularity in favor of increasing readability and translatability across different territories, against which Díaz, like the other authors discussed in this book, pushes.[39] Paratext allows him to playfully write over *Oscar Wao*'s textual blanks as a way of highlighting the need for readers' ongoing participation in the construction of textual meaning.

Díaz is not shy about explaining his work, though in doing so he often adopts an attitude of condescension toward readers and draws attention to the inadequacy of their frames of reference. This is apparent in his many interviews, but also in *Oscar Wao* itself, in which he preempts and parodies the kind of reading identifiable in Kim's Annotated Oscar Wao by including his own thirty-three footnotes. Footnotes give the impression of scholarly rigor; they purport to fill in the blanks in readers' cultural knowledge by explaining aspects of Dominican history, culture, and geography and giving brief biographies of historical figures related to the Trujillo regime. The explanations, however, are always offered in such a way that they chastise readers for their ignorance; their tone is deeply sarcastic, and they are especially contemptuous of U.S. readers' naivete about—and complicity in—their nation's interventions in the Dominican Republic: "(You didn't know we were occupied twice in the twentieth century? Don't worry, when you have kids they won't know the U.S. occupied Iraq either.)" (19). In this respect, Díaz is among numerous contemporary postcolonial authors who, as Sarah Brouillette has argued, consciously interact with the interpretation and reception of their texts, "indulging, resisting, and critiquing its imagined consumption" and often making attempts to "reorient or re-educate an unsophisticated reader."[40] The footnotes are in fact as likely to frustrate as they are to elucidate, entering readers into a secondary discourse that has as many blanks to be filled in as the main narrative. For instance, rather than translating Spanish passages for non-Spanish-speaking readers, they incorporate further Spanish and draw attention to readers' inadequate language skills, as when one footnote quotes from a book in Spanish in order to illustrate the dire conditions of the Dominican Republic's Nigua prison: "As Juan Isidro Jiménez Grullón said in his book *Una gestapo en América*, 'es mejor tener cien niguas en un pie que un pie en Nigüa [sic]'" (it is better to have a hundred parasites on a single foot than a single foot in

Nigua) (250)—a joke that is entirely lost on non-Spanish speakers.[41] Parodying the scholarly standards of objectivity and comprehensiveness in much the same way as Chávez-Silverman does in her crónicas, the footnotes adopt formulae common to academic writing such as "it should be noted that" (87), "end quote" (235), and "see the 1966 election in the DR" (90). And yet they often obfuscate instead of clarifying, and rely on speculation, anecdote, and dubious authorities. In an ironic nod to readers' frequent desire for certainty and legitimacy, one note even refers us to an imaginary "Dictionary of Dominican Things" (20), undermining the authority presumed to inhere in scholarly apparatus. Overall, the notes contest the assumptions readers are likely to make about their function: that they are there to aid understanding, guide interpretation, or improve readability. Shari Benstock's assessment of the way footnotes function in a series of other "writerly" texts—*Tom Jones*, *Tristram Shandy*, and *Finnegans Wake*—is helpful here. She says, "the notion that the notes are somehow an 'aid' to reading, already a translation for the benefit of readers, is purposely inverted: the notes become a stumbling block, a barrier to understanding."[42] The use of features common to scholarly writing is a way of increasing the hermeticism of the work, just as Chávez-Silverman's references to Derrida and Deleuze and Guattari are.

In interviews, Díaz again teases readers searching for a key to understanding his novel. On a number of occasions, he has referred to aspects of his work that are "easily missed," before proceeding to explain them, tempting readers to trust his authority and read the novel exclusively in the ways he suggests.[43] This strategy is especially striking in an interview with Paula M. L. Moya, in which Díaz appears to clarify certain aspects of *Oscar Wao* that are ambiguous. Referring to the curse on the de León family, he claims, "For me, the family *fukú* is rape. The rape culture of the European colonization of the New World—which becomes the rape culture of the Trujillato."[44] This much can be understood from Yunior's narration, which makes very clear the link between the Dominican Republic's colonization by the Spanish (from which fukú is said originally to derive) and Trujillo's sexual predation. However, Díaz goes on: "I always wrote Yunior as being a survivor of sexual abuse. He has been raped too. The hint of this rape is something that's present in *Drown* and it is one of the great silences in *Oscar Wao*. This is what Yunior can't admit, his very own *página en blanco*. So, when he has that line in the novel: 'I'd finally try to say the words that could have saved us. / —— —— ——,' what he couldn't say to Lola was that 'I too have been molested.'"⁴⁵ Here we see Díaz quite literally filling in his own blanks, giving readers of the interview a very specific interpretation of his most developed character as well as reminding us of the suggestion, made elsewhere in the novel, that violence, including sexual violence, is somehow beyond textual representation.[46] That this reading is not made explicit in the novel is clear from the interviewer's reaction:

PAULA: Right. Now, am I just a bad reader? Or . . .
JUNOT: No.
PAULA: . . . is it that silenced?
JUNOT: It's that silenced; that elliptical. Perhaps it's too great a silence, which is to say, it's probably too small a trace to be read.[47]

There is an irony in the author providing readers with details too subtle to be read without his retrospective intervention. By telling us that Yunior was raped, he appears to offer a key that will allow us to read the text more profoundly or to grasp a fuller meaning, whereas in reality, as he admits, the only thing to be found in the novel is silence. He has remarked: "I've almost never read an adult book where I didn't have to pick up a dictionary. I guess I participate more in my readings and expect the same out of my readership. I want people to research, to ask each other, to question. But also I want there to be an element of incomprehension. What's language without incomprehension? What's art?"[48] Díaz's model for reading is therefore twofold: he encourages readers to work hard at engaging with the text in order to be rewarded with a better understanding of it, while at the same time acknowledging that that understanding will always be partial.

An extract from *Oscar Wao* published online in 2013 allows us to see especially clearly the way Díaz plays with readers' desire for further information about the novel, and with the frequent trust placed in an author's commentary on their own work. It appeared on a website called Genius, which describes itself as "a conversation built around texts and the interpretations of those texts."[49] It operates on similar principles to Wikipedia, allowing—as the Annotated Oscar Wao does, but in more interactive fashion—readers to give their own explanations of a text, sometimes alongside and in dialogue with "verified" authors' commentary, too. The site hosts an excerpt from *Oscar Wao*, comprising three lines and a long footnote that describes "Outer Azua," a fictional location in the Dominican Republic where Beli spent her childhood.[50] The extract is accompanied by twenty-three of Díaz's previously unpublished "author-verified" annotations of that footnote.

The extract appears to indulge the powerful desire for explication that drove the Annotated Oscar Wao project: many of the annotations provide sources for the novel's references to science fiction books and films, quoting from them and sometimes including images of book jackets or authors. Díaz himself takes center stage as the primary authority on the novel: each annotation is accompanied by his name, a photograph of his face, and a green tick next to the word "author." Many are anecdotal and personal, concerned with his creative process and the way aspects of the novel are rooted in his own life, thus seeming to perpetuate the idea that an understanding of fiction is dependent on knowledge about the author's biography.

It seems unlikely that, having written a novel so concerned with the irrecoverability of historical narratives and the always partial nature of understanding, Díaz would encourage reading practices premised on belief in a dictatorial, "author-verified" meaning, a transcendental signified waiting to be revealed. A closer look at the annotations shows him to be playing a more complicated game. For one thing, the voice of the annotations is similar enough to Yunior's voice—it takes the same patronizing tone toward readers ("in case you didn't know")—to warn that, like the novel's own footnotes, they are unlikely to be straightforwardly helpful. Sure enough, they do not solve any textual problem; instead of conclusively filling in the blanks, they open up a whole new line of discourse and raise a new series of questions, continuing to make readers work at comprehension. A rhetorical "get it?" following a punning reference to two different fantasy intertexts, "Oz" and "Zardoz," and the introduction of new Spanish phrases make clear that these annotations, just like the novel's original footnotes, serve at least in part to draw attention to readers' ignorance, making a show of furnishing them with information while simultaneously withholding it. Díaz is mocking a desire for authority, clarity, and comprehensiveness, and the assumption that hidden meanings can be uncovered by careful research.

It is telling that the excerpt is accompanied by a fifteen-minute audio file of an interview between Díaz and an editor at Faber and Faber, publisher of *Oscar Wao*. In it, the author discusses Yunior's role in assembling Oscar's story, but concludes that the reader "is the only person who can add the final piece."⁵¹ On a page where authorial commentary is ostensibly given so much weight, we hear Díaz saying, on the contrary, that only the reader can provide the most important, final part of the story—and indeed, readers themselves are able to add their own annotations to the extract alongside the author's.

Díaz uses paratexts to play at being author-dictator and at filling in the novel's blanks. Ultimately, though, like the novel itself, the Genius extract acknowledges the futility of trying to create a singular, all-encompassing narrative in a textual work. As a continuation and purported explanation of *Oscar Wao*, it draws attention to the novel's already fragmented, layered, and open-ended structure, and reminds us that its "páginas en blanco" render it impossible to complete.

This chapter began by arguing that Díaz's creolization of English and unexplained references create a series of semantic blanks that shift depending on readers' linguistic and cultural competence. These moments where language is emptied of signification recall the information vacuums produced by a culture of censorship and chime with the appearance in the novel of blank bodies, blank texts, and silences.

But blanks in their various guises do not simply close meaning down; rather, they also keep multiple possible understandings simultaneously in play. Díaz foregrounds rather than hides the relativity of access resulting from his creolized language, making it serve as a model for the kind of reading he values: one that does not assume the right to an easy understanding, but rather accepts discomfort and unfamiliarity as incentives to engage actively in the construction of textual meaning. The openness afforded by the inclusion of "páginas en blanco" is evident not only in the main text, but also in its authorial paratexts—notably the footnotes and the continuation on Genius—each of which declines to translate, explain, or fill in the novel's blanks with any degree of seriousness, and instead invites further continuation and rewriting.

Given the layered characteristics of the numerous paratexts discussed in this chapter, we might picture *Oscar Wao*, like Susana Chávez-Silverman's crónicas, as a palimpsest. Like a palimpsest, it contains blanks and erasures; like a palimpsest, it consists of multiple layers; like a palimpsest, it invites repeated reinscription, and, like many palimpsests, it incorporates different languages, such that parts of it remain partially illegible to different readers. As well as encouraging a particular mode of reading, the partial erasures and repeated rewritings characteristic of a palimpsest serve, in *Oscar Wao*, to illustrate that narratives produced about or under conditions of domination will, more than most, always contain certain unreadable blanks.

PART II. *OSCAR WAO* IN TRANSLATION

I have suggested that *Oscar Wao* encourages readers to become translators or even "writers" by making them actively fill in its blanks and silences. I have also suggested that the novel, made up as it is of repeated, circular narratives, leaves itself open to further rewritings—of which translation is one important manifestation not yet considered in any detail here. Part II of this chapter will focus on translation's role in multiple versions of *Oscar Wao*, arguing that translation is intimately involved in its narrative construction, and even that the novel is already written as a translation. For these reasons, I argue, translating *Oscar Wao* into other languages continues many of the processes already underway in the source text.

Oscar Wao as Pseudotranslation

In the previous chapter I argued that Chávez-Silverman, while appearing to reject translation, actually incorporates it into her bilingual play. We can observe a similar role for translation in *Oscar Wao*. The novel appears to adopt a policy of unapologetic non-translation, incorporating Spanish words and phrases into its English rather than translating them, thus creating intermittent unfamiliarity and partial incomprehension for a range of readers. It appears to reject not only interlingual translation, but also other kinds of "translation" understood more broadly as a form of elucidation, as Díaz declines to explain cultural and historical references or allusions to literary texts, films, comics, and games of various kinds. I have argued that it avoids accommodating readers who do not share Díaz's own cultural and linguistic repertoire and instead leaves blanks for readers to fill in. However, this apparent policy of non-translation is not so hard and fast. As soon as the decision was made to narrate predominantly in English events that took place, or are imagined to take place, in a different linguistic context—one in which Spanish is used much more extensively than it is in the text—translation became an essential part of *Oscar Wao*'s narrative makeup. We understand that in many of the novel's conversations characters are speaking in Spanish, especially in the chapters that follow Oscar's mother and grandfather, Beli and Abelard, who live in the Dominican Republic. Parts of the novel are written *as a translation*, purporting to take place in a language (Spanish) other than the one in which they have, in fact, been composed (English). The novel is therefore in part what Gideon Toury calls a "pseudotranslation." Although Toury's definition refers in the main to published texts that, in their entirety, are taken by their reading public to be translations, parts of *Oscar Wao* nevertheless meet his definition of pseudotranslation, also known as "fictitious translation," "original translation," and "supposed translation": a text that is presented as a translation but has "never had a corresponding source text in any other language."[52]

This becomes clear when we consider the way Yunior filters and patches together a series of different voices as he writes the de León family history, including an entire chapter narrated by Lola, whose addressee ("you"), it gradually becomes apparent, is Yunior himself. Many of these voices, we understand, he has "translated" from Spanish into English. He translates, for instance, testimony from Oscar's adopted grandmother, La Inca, who speaks directly (if briefly) toward the end of the novel, and from Oscar's love interest, Ybón, incorporating their accounts into his version of the family history. He also translates the final interaction between Oscar and his Dominican murderers, in which the line "We'll let you go if you tell us what *fuego* means in English" (322) is, of course, we understand, uttered in Spanish. In this way, much of the novel's dialogue, despite being narrated primarily in English, is understood to have been expressed in Spanish. Parts of the novel are therefore already in translation; but it is a translation with no original. Toury points out that "due to the practice of embedding features in fictitious translations which have come to be associated with genuine translations, it is sometimes possible to 'reconstruct' from a fictitious translation bits and pieces of a text in another language as a kind of 'possible source text'—one that never enjoyed any textual reality, to be sure."[53]

One of the features of what Toury here calls "genuine" translations is the retention of occasional words from the source language, often culturally specific terms that have the effect of reminding readers they are reading a translation. This foreignizing technique is analogous to the defamiliarizing creolization of English in *Oscar Wao*, in which words and sentences from varieties of Spanish are incorporated into a predominantly English narrative. They have the same function of suggesting synecdochically that the text is a translation from Spanish into English.

Another feature of "genuine" translations, one that is often criticized and avoided, is the use of calques, whereby a metaphorical expression in the source language is rendered literally in the target language despite that metaphor not being in common use. For instance, we are told that in Oscar's early adolescence a fellow pupil called Olga insults him by calling him "a *cake eater*" (17). This is an awkward and uncommon slur in English, although its meaning is very apparent, given that we know Oscar is overweight. Despite its unusualness, it is possible to reconstruct Olga's "original" words in Spanish: "cometortas," a light insult used in Mexico to mean "fool" or someone who is especially gluttonous. Another example of a calque appears when Yunior describes early signs of the de León family fukú: "The family claims the first sign was that Abelard's third and final daughter, *given the light* early on in her father's capsulization, was born black" (248, my emphasis). The expression "given the light" is uncommon in English but we can "reconstruct," as Toury puts it, a more natural-sounding Spanish "original": "dar a luz" ("to give birth," literally "to give to light").

Yunior does not call attention to the "translated" nature of *Oscar Wao*'s narrative; in fact, the novel never explicitly discusses the challenges or opportunities of translation, nor do its characters display much self-consciousness about their movement between languages. Yet despite this attitude, due to the presence of "translational" features such as those described above, the narrative gives the impression of having been translated from a series of "original" sources to which readers do not have access. The novel's status as a partial pseudotranslation adds a further layer of epistemological uncertainty to Yunior's narration, highlighting the impossibility of establishing a historical narrative that can make any kind of claim to stability or completeness; as I have argued, Yunior draws attention to his own unreliability and expresses doubt about the knowability of the past and its representation in literary form. The partially "translated" nature of the narrative only emphasizes its openness to revision and rewriting. It also reveals that, despite Yunior's apparent rejection of translation in favor of multilingualism, translation can in fact play an important role in textual production.

Translating a Translation: Achy Obejas's *Oscar Wao*

If *Oscar Wao* itself is already in some respect a translation, what does it mean for the novel to be translated wholesale into another language for a different reading public? Unlike in the case of Chávez-Silverman, Díaz's enormous acclaim has resulted in *Oscar Wao* being translated into twenty-two different languages. These include two editions in Spanish, translated by the Cuban American writer Achy Obejas, to which I will pay attention in the remainder of this chapter. I argue that *Oscar Wao* and its many paratexts, including its Spanish translation, can be productively regarded as constituting a single and coherent object of study. Rather than judging the success or otherwise of Obejas's translation, or its degree of fidelity to the source text, I examine how it contributes creatively to the novel, which I consider to be a still-evolving entity. Like the annotated footnote published on Genius, this translation is a creative supplement to the novel itself.

Translating *Oscar Wao* into Spanish in some senses constitutes a back-translation, or what another Cuban novelist, Cristina García, has called a "restoration."[54] Obejas's task is often one of reaching toward (or "reconstructing," in Toury's terms) an imagined but nonexistent Spanish original. When, for example, La Inca says to Lola, "Your mother was a diosa. But so cabeza dura. . . . She was cabeza dura and I was . . . exigente" (75) (Your mother was a goddess. But so headstrong. . . . She was headstrong and I was . . . demanding), the Spanish words ("diosa," "cabeza dura," and "exigente") signal that we are to understand the entire conversation to have taken place in Spanish. When, therefore, Obejas translates this as, "Tu madre era una diosa. Pero tan cabeza dura. . . . Ella era cabeza dura y yo era . . . exigente" (Vintage Español, 80), she is writing an imagined "original" to Yunior's foreignizing "translation." I do not mean to suggest that substantial portions of the novel are in any sense "reversible," nor that Díaz could even necessarily have written the novel in Spanish; only that the reader is given to understand translation to play a key role in the fictional writer-narrator's—Yunior's—composition, and that any translator of *Oscar Wao* would need to be sensitive to that fact.

Translating pseudotranslation is problematic, as Leo Tak-Hung Chan points out. Referring to works that are, like *Oscar Wao*, bi- or multilingual, he remarks that "it is a commonplace belief among translation scholars that all translations invariably signal foreignness in one way or another, but that view is not entirely accurate when applied to original texts which are already 'translated' (in part or in full)."[55] This is because what is likely to be alien to many readers of the original turns out to be familiar in the translation, while what is more likely to be familiar becomes that which is "alienated or alienating."[56] For instance, whereas in Díaz's version of *Oscar Wao* the use of Spanish words and phrases serves a number of specific purposes (to signal that a whole conversation is taking place in Spanish, or to alienate a particular group of readers, for example), in Obejas's version it need not mean anything at all; Spanish is simply a neutral medium of communication; what was foreign has become familiar. The risk is that, in circumstances where the target language is also one of the source languages, the translation ends up being linguistically homogeneous, with none of the shock effects produced by the contrasts between languages in the source text.

The scale of the task facing Achy Obejas when she was hired to translate *Oscar Wao*, then, was already daunting, but it was exacerbated by the fact that readers—including Díaz himself—had found serious fault with the first translation of his earlier collection of short stories, *Drown*.[57] *Los boys*, published in Spain by Mondadori and translated by Miguel Martínez-Lage, was oriented firmly toward a peninsular Spanish readership and written in peninsular Spanish; Karen Cresci has demonstrated how Castilian vocabulary like "gilipollas" for "assholes" removes readers entirely from the Dominican-American setting.[58] Obejas describes how Martínez-Lage made Díaz's "New Jersey homeboys sound like . . . well, Toni Morrison characters speaking in Irish brogue, or a Cockney accent. It was that dissonant."[59] Díaz himself suggested that the erasure of regional language in Martínez-Lage's translation revealed underlying assumptions about the cultural supremacy of Spain and the greater legitimacy of an "imperial castellano" (imperial Castilian), saying that "las editoriales españolas ni siquiera cuestionarían esto, y este sería el tipo de traducción que considerarían adecuada" (the Spanish publishing houses wouldn't even question it, and it would be the kind of translation they would consider to be adequate).[60] And *Drown*, as Anna María D'Amore has pointed out, is just one among many works by U.S. Latinxs to have been translated by publishers in Spain who are reluctant to recognize the linguistic heterogeneity of Spanish as a global language.[61]

A second version of *Drown* by Eduardo Lago as *Negocios* for Vintage Español in the United States aimed at a U.S. Spanish-speaking readership.[62]

Lago understood that, in order to achieve this, his Spanish needed to be flexible and capacious, given all the different varieties of that language spoken in that country. Nonetheless, he also wanted to maintain a particular emphasis on Dominican Spanish, as he has suggested in an interview,[63] and this desire is borne out in the translation itself, which Karen Cresci has shown to be quite closely aligned with that particular variety (and as such more linguistically homogenous in general than Díaz's original collection is).[64]

The example of Martinez-Lage's translation in particular illustrates the risks when translating literature from historically marginalized populations for readers in the Western world. As Gayatri Spivak puts it with reference to the translation of Asian women writers into English, "there can be a betrayal of the democratic ideal into the law of the strongest," whereby "all the literature of the Third World gets translated into a sort of with-it translatese, so that the literature by a woman in Palestine begins to resemble, in the feel of its prose, something by a man in Taiwan."[65] The politics of difference are smoothed over in the name of "readability" rather than brought to the fore. However, as Spivak points out, if only the translator "surrender[s] herself to the linguistic rhetoricity of the original text," "attend[s] to the author's stylistic experiments," and considers the status of the source language in the world, the result can be a different kind of translation.[66] It was important for Obejas, as it was for Eduardo Lago, to take into account the relationship not only between English and Spanish, but also those between U.S. Spanish, Caribbean Spanish, and Peninsular Spanish in her translation of *Oscar Wao*.

Obejas is a journalist, translator, and writer of fiction and poetry whose relationships to the Caribbean and to the United States are comparable in some ways to those of Díaz himself. Born in Cuba, she moved with her family to the United States at the age of six (Díaz moved from the Dominican Republic aged seven). Like Díaz, she incorporates Spanish into her predominantly English writing (although, unlike Díaz, she has also composed texts entirely in Spanish). In her poem "Sugarcane," for instance, she evokes spoken Caribbean Spanishes alongside English by omitting consonants in ways that are suggestive of Cuban pronunciation ("pue'e" [puede, can] and "azuca'" [azúcar, sugar]).[67] As Annabel Cox has shown, the poem draws on African American Vernacular English and Afro-Caribbean cultural forms, and employs the Indigenous Taíno names for the Dominican Republic and Puerto Rico ("quisqueya" and "borinquen," respectively) in order to represent the racial and ethnic heterogeneity of the United States' Hispanophone Caribbean diaspora.[68] Obejas's other publications span both the Hispanophone and Anglophone markets; although she writes predominantly in English, her volume *Aguas y otros cuentos* was published in Spanish in Cuba, and comprises eight short stories, six of which have been translated from English.[69] Like Díaz, she has gone through a process of normalizing the use of Spanish in her English writing: her first collection of stories, *We Came All the Way from Cuba So You Could Dress Like This?*, italicized Spanish words appearing in the narrative and included a glossary of Spanish terms, while her more recent writing does not.[70]

Obejas translated *Oscar Wao* into Caribbean Spanish. Despite never having visited the Dominican Republic herself, she sought to use as many Dominican features as possible, working with a Dominican editor, María Teresa Ortega, to avoid replicating Martínez-Lage's tendencies to replace the Dominican Spanish in *Drown* with more widely recognizable "standard" Spanish forms.[71] The translation was well received by critics; reviewer Alejandro Gándara wrote in *El Mundo*: "A pesar de ser una traducción del inglés, suena inusitadamente libre en español: mezcla jergas, mezcla idiomas, mezcla tonos, mezcla vulgarismos y cultismos, arcaísmos y corrupciones . . .; en suma, uno recibe el ruido de la calle" (Despite being a translation from English, it sounds uncharacteristically free in Spanish: it mixes slangs, it mixes languages, it mixes tones, it mixes lowbrow with highbrow, archaisms and corruptions . . .; in sum, we get the sound of the street).[72] The translation was produced in close collaboration with Díaz himself, who reviewed the work in stages, allowing Obejas to approach the kind of "intimacy" Spivak argues is necessary in order to replicate the "rhetoricity" of the source text.[73] Considering her translation as a paratexual rewriting analogous to those already discussed, the following sections will demonstrate how Obejas continues and supplements translational processes already at work in Díaz's novel. She responds to his invitation to fill in the blanks, gaps, and silences in his narrative, but also creates blanks of her own for certain Spanish-language readers.

Filling in *Oscar Wao*'s Blanks

Because translation rights are sold on the basis of language and territory, Obejas's translation exists in two editions, both published under Random

House (now Penguin Random House) imprints. The first, from Mondadori in Barcelona, is distributed in Latin America and Spain and is called *La maravillosa vida breve de Óscar Wao*.⁷⁴ The second, from Vintage Español in New York, is for the Spanish-speaking North American market and is titled *La breve y maravillosa vida de Óscar Wao*.⁷⁵ The main text in each of the two editions is almost identical, as Boyden and Goethals have demonstrated in a thorough comparison.⁷⁶ However, there are some important differences of editing and of paratext, as I will explain.

Translation into Spanish cannot help but fill in many of the blanks that are so conspicuous in the source text, especially since, as readers are told in a translator's note in the Vintage Español's edition, Obejas retains Díaz's own Spanish "lo más posible" (as much as possible). Returning to a previous example will help illustrate this: "Your mother was a diosa. But so cabeza dura. . . . She was cabeza dura and I was . . . exigente" (75). In these lines from the original, all the character-defining content words are in Spanish, meaning that the relationship between the two women being described—the beautiful ("diosa") but headstrong ("cabeza dura") Beli and the demanding ("exigente") La Inca—is hard for non-Spanish-speaking readers to grasp. For those readers, the Spanish words are devoid of sense; there is a semantic silence surrounding the relationship between mother and daughter. Obejas's translation, "Tu madre era una diosa. Pero tan cabeza dura. . . . Ella era cabeza dura y yo era . . . exigente" (Vintage Español, 80), transparent to *all* readers of that version, not just some of them, voices the silences in the source text, creating presence and signification where before there were only evacuated words and empty sounds. Translation into Spanish necessarily risks erasing the politics of "creolization" and its emphasis on the value of opacity.⁷⁷

As many of Díaz's references are to Anglo-American culture, Obejas often embeds explanations of those references into her translation. For instance, in her translation of a reference to the Watcher, a figure from the Marvel comic book series the *Fantastic Four*, whose persona Yunior appropriates in his role as storyteller, she integrates an explanation (absent in the original) of the Watcher's provenance and role. Díaz's reference to "another Watcher, the one who lamps on the Blue Side of the Moon" (20) is translated as "otro Vigilante, [e]l super-ser del universo Marvel que está del Lado Azul de la Luna *y mira y mira, pero jamás interviene*" (and watches and watches, but never intervenes) (Vintage Español, 22; Mondadori, 32;

emphasis added). Obejas also translates abbreviations and acronyms into full expressions, such that they are more transparent in the target text. For example, she translates the sentence "Oscar sat in the back of the class, behind his DM's screen" (23) as "Óscar se sentaba en el fondo del aula, detrás de la pantalla *en la que coordinaba los juegos de Dungeons and Dragons*" (on which he was coordinating his games of Dungeons and Dragons) (Vintage Español, 25; Mondadori, 35; emphasis added), explaining an abbreviated reference to a dungeon master's screen used in the role-play game Dungeons and Dragons. In a third example, she explains Díaz's oblique reference to off-track betting in a description of a man as "paunchier than an OTB regular" (93) by rendering it as "más panzudo que *los tipos que apostaban a los caballos en el barrio*" (the local guys who bet on horses) (Vintage Español, 100; Mondadori, 103; emphasis added).

Additionally, the Vintage Español edition also fills in some of the blanks in Díaz's text by including 131 translator's footnotes in addition to the existing 33. It is not entirely uncommon for footnotes to appear in translations in order to allow the translator to explain a choice or to elaborate on some complexity in the original. However, the main purpose of the additional footnotes in the Vintage Español edition of *Oscar Wao* is not to explain any translational difficulties or to compensate for the loss of polysemy by providing access to the original text.[78] Rather, their main function is to provide additional information not available in Díaz's version. Obejas explains: "It was Junot who suggested the Spanish version have translator's footnotes—a counterpart to the extensive footnotes in the original—explain concepts that Latin American readers might not be familiar with. He'd seen the practice in Patrick Chamoiseau's novel *Texaco* and thought this would be a good way of shorthanding some references."[79] In this interview, Obejas identifies a translational model—Rose-Myriam Réjouis and Val Vinokurov's translation of Chamoiseau's *Texaco*—that is open about wanting to be more *readable* than its comparatively opaque original.[80] In her translator's note, Réjouis remarks: "Some would say . . . that if you can read Patrick Chamoiseau's *Texaco*, maybe we overtranslated it. . . . Have we then as translators betrayed the original book by actually making it readable when it can strike so many as opaque? We of course don't think so."[81] Réjouis and Vinokurov translate passages of Creole into English where Chamoiseau did not translate them into French. They offer additional translations where the author's own deviate considerably from the literal meaning, and include a glossary of Creole terms at the back of the novel. This is a model that understands the task of the translator to involve elucidation, explanation, or even "uncensoring."[82] Obejas follows this model, borrowing some of Réjouis and Vinokurov's strategies to make her version of *Oscar Wao* more readable than Díaz's. The majority of her footnotes, which, like Réjouis and Vinurokov's, are distinguished from the author's by square brackets but are not numbered separately, are mainly used to explain references and allusions to science fiction and fantasy, or to history, culture, and geography. A smaller number translate English words that have been retained from the source.

As Ellen McCracken has pointed out, Díaz's own footnotes are an integral part of the fiction, echoing in their first-person style the rhythms, syntax, and diction of the main narrative.[83] They highlight the novel's own inaccuracies and silences, privileging anecdote and speculation over factual documentation. Obejas's footnotes, in contrast, are written in a largely detached, third-person voice, and offer a degree of stability and reliability that is notably absent from Díaz's footnotes. Unlike the latter, Obejas's notes offer up authorities for their explanations and quotations and provide information willingly rather than begrudgingly.[84] These footnotes are Obejas's response to Díaz's invitation to fill in the blanks in his text, and in doing so she shows herself to be the paradigmatic active reader. Like Kim's Annotated Oscar Wao, the translation responds to Díaz's insistent refusals to explain and elucidate by researching all areas of Díaz's cultural repertoire thoroughly.

Creating New Blanks

Nevertheless, Obejas's translation strikes a balance between "filling in" the blanks in Díaz's novel and creating blanks of its own. Maria Tymoczko has noted that "in trying to adapt the multiple layers of information in a text to a new reception environment, a translator will almost inevitably produce a longer text. Even that eventuality does not result in a full capture and transposition of all the coded information . . . no text can ever be fully translated in all its aspects: perfect homology is impossible between translation and source."[85] Obejas's translation is, as Tymoczko suggests is the norm, longer than its source text, notably in the Vintage Español edition, due to the inclusion of the extra 133 footnotes. However, even with the footnotes, the translation is by no means a complete explanation or "uncensoring" of Díaz's novel any more than Kim's Annotated Oscar Wao is. Returning to Butler's notion of censorship as a constitutive part of every discursive practice, we are reminded that all texts are "always already censored to some degree" and that to completely uncensor them would render them unintelligible.[86] Obejas's text has its own blanks to be filled in, explained, or "written" by its new target readers. Just as I hoped to achieve in my translation of Chávez-Silverman's "Todo verdor perdurará Crónica," this is a *strategic* opening out to new readers.

One of the ways Obejas achieves this is through the use of English. In an attempt to counteract the erasure of opacity that necessarily results from translating into one of the novel's source languages, and from the need to explain some of the Anglo-American cultural references, Obejas includes much more English in her version of *Oscar Wao* than either of the translators used in their Spanish versions of *Drown* (although the incidence of English remains considerably lower in Obejas's translation than the incidence of Spanish in the source text). Obejas sometimes employs the same strategies used by writers like Américo Paredes and Gloria Anzaldúa whereby the minority language (in this instance, English) is "cushioned" through translation and contextualization, as in the following example: "Whether I believe in what many have described as the Great American Doom is not really the point" (5); "Que yo crea o no en lo que muchos han llamado **The Great American Doom—La Gran Perdición Americana**—no viene al caso" (Vintage Español, 5; Mondadori, 17; emphasis added). In this example, the appearance of English ("The Great American Doom") estranges the text for readers of the translation, but their understanding is not compromised, because a Spanish translation appears shortly afterward, embedded in the same sentence ("La Gran Perdición Americana"). In other instances, however, Obejas keeps an English expression but offers a more oblique appositional gloss in Spanish. We can see this, for instance, in the insult frequently directed at Lola after she starts dressing as a Goth during her teenage years: "They just called me devil-bitch. Yo, devil-bitch, yo, *yo!*" (54); "Terminaron llamándome **devil-bitch**. ¡Oye, **Cerbero**, oye tú, *oye!*" (Vintage Español, 58; Mondadori, 65; emphasis added). Obejas's translation of "devil-bitch" as "Cerbero" (Cerberus) is more inventive than her translation of the "Great American Doom." It requires knowledge that this is the name of a three-headed dog said to guard the gates to

CENSORSHIP AND (PSEUDO-)TRANSLATION

the underworld in Greek mythology. Readers will be unable to grasp the basis on which the insult is made unless they have knowledge of the myth, and unless they appreciate that in English "bitch" refers to a female dog as well as being an offensive word for a woman. In this instance, retention of an English phrase is an opportunity for Obejas to add a further layer of complexity to Díaz's narrative, in which readers are asked to do extra work in order to make connections.

Obejas also incorporates English into her Spanish in ways that recall how Díaz's English is "creolized" by Spanish. In her translation, there is a small number of words with Hispanic-looking orthographies but which derive from English, such as "fókin" and "bróder" ("fucking" and "brother"). Comparable to "que" and "mas," which appear in the source text normalized according to English orthographic conventions (they lack the requisite Spanish diacritics), "fókin" and "bróder" look like Spanish words, because the acute accents mark them as such, but may remain strange for readers if they have no knowledge of the English words from which they derive.[87] This foreignizing technique reminds us once again of the similarities between the aesthetics of multilingual writing and translation. As in Anzaldúa's poem "No se raje, Chicanita," here similar strategies are being used in Obejas's version of *Oscar Wao* and in Díaz's version. Translating multilingual writing involves continuing certain processes and replicating certain effects that are already apparent in the source text.

It is worth noting that the Mondadori edition (published in Spain and Latin America) excises some of Obejas's English. While in the Vintage Español edition the titles of English-language films, books, comics, and games, plus certain references to fantasy and science fiction, remain in English, in the Mondadori edition they are translated into Spanish. For instance, where Vintage Español prints "ghetto," Mondadori prints "gueto" throughout; where Vintage Español keeps "the Brotherhood of Evil Mutants," a collection of characters from the Marvel Comics Universe (Vintage Español, 103), Mondadori prefers to translate this as "la Fraternidad de Mutantes Malvados" (Mondadori, 106). This greater excision of English in an edition published in Spain and Latin America (territories in which Spanish is the dominant language) reflects an anxiety about language purity long associated with the Real Academia Española and its numerous subsidiaries in the Americas, which today aim to ensure "el buen uso y la unidad de una lengua en permanente evolución y expansión" (the good use and unity of a language in permanent evolution and expansion).[88] While any translation into Spanish cannot help but downplay the importance of creolization to the novel's portrayal of Caribbean diaspora, Mondadori's use of English is more conservative than Vintage Español's, making it less successful in replicating Díaz's redress of the unequal hierarchical relationships between languages spoken in the Caribbean and the United States.

Another way Obejas creates new blanks for Spanish-language readers is through the use of Caribbean Spanishes. The combination of widely used forms and Caribbean localisms allows her to compensate for the lesser degree of bilingualism in the translation than in the source; this kind of "intralingual variation," Boyden and Goethals note, "offsets on a lexical level what gets lost on a syntactic level."[89] It creates a sense of alienation and confusion for speakers of varieties of Spanish from outside the Caribbean that is comparable to the confusion felt by all non-Spanish speakers reading Díaz's original; in other words, the translation creates its own blanks, too. A closer look at the following passage illustrates how this works:

> Once on the **bus** Olga had called Oscar a *cake eater*, and he'd almost said, Look who's talking, <u>puerca</u>, but he was afraid that she would rear back and trample him; his **cool-index**, already low, couldn't have survived that kind of a <u>paliza</u>, would have put him on par with the handicapped kids and with Joe Locorotundo, who was famous for masturbating in public.
> (17, BOLD AND UNDERLINING ADDED)

> Una vez en la **guagua**, Olga le había dicho a Óscar que no era más que un *cometortas*, y él por poco le contesta: Mira quién está hablando, <u>puerca</u>, pero le dio miedo que ella se levantara y le entrara a golpes; su reputación de **papichulo**, ya por el piso, no hubiera aguantado semejante <u>paliza</u>, lo habría puesto al mismo nivel que los muchachos lisiados y junto a Joe Locorotundo, famoso por masturbarse en público.
> (VINTAGE ESPAÑOL, 18; MONDADORI, 29; BOLD AND UNDERLINING ADDED)

Díaz's version of this passage uses two Spanish words, "puerca" and "paliza." Obejas keeps them in her translation, rather than choosing English words, but mimics the effects of the original—the sense of unfamiliarity many readers will experience when they encounter the Spanish terms—by using regional vocabulary that will not be known to all speakers of Spanish. Here, "bus" and "cool," both common in many varieties of English across the globe, are translated respectively as "guagua" (rather than with the more widespread "autobús") and "papichulo," both of which are words common in some Caribbean Spanishes but not necessarily in widespread use elsewhere (in fact, in many Spanish-speaking territories "guagua" is used to mean a baby rather than a bus, therefore this lexical choice will be particularly strange for some readers).[90] This strategy succeeds in recreating for non-Caribbean Hispanophone readers—particularly Peninsular readers—some of the alienation felt by many predominantly Anglophone readers of the source text. Obejas thus subverts the processes observable in a translation like Martínez-Lage's version of *Drown*, which erases aspects of a "marginal" culture for the ease and comfort of European readers.

It is also worth noting that Obejas's footnotes do not of course explain *all* the novel's cultural and historical references. The footnote appearing in the Genius extract illustrates this: it is described by Díaz as his most expansive, where he simply goes "buckwild" with obscure allusions.[91] On Genius, he adds as many as twenty-four annotations explaining the footnote's references to science fiction and translating its uses of Spanish, while Obejas includes not a single footnote. Like Díaz's own, then, Obejas's notes are always partial, invitations for readers to learn more by doing their own research.

In fact, an important part of the footnotes' role is simply to remind readers that what they are reading is a translation. In the Vintage Español edition, in particular, the role of the translator is highly visible in the text. Obejas makes her presence immediately known in the first pages of the novel by including a translator's note, followed by three footnotes to Díaz's own first footnote. The rest of her notes are interspersed evenly throughout the novel (Díaz's cluster in chapters that discuss the Trujillo dictatorship), reminding readers at regular intervals that what they are reading is already a processed text, filtered through another reader's interpretation and rewriting. Far from being invisible, Obejas willingly advertises her own creative contributions to the novel, adding another layer of unreliability to a narrative voice whose ability to tell the story with any degree of authority is already in question.

In certain footnotes, Obejas draws particular attention to the limitations of translation and encourages readers to be critical of it. For instance, in one of the very first notes, she explains the English word "fly," which appears in both her version and Díaz's: "Pronunciado *fla-i-*: Chévere, volao, bárbaro, macanudo, estupendo" (Vintage Español, 11). By offering multiple possible translations for this word—some unique to parts of Latin America ("chévere," "bárbaro") and others more widely recognized; some very colloquial, some more formal in register—it begins to resemble what Cassin calls an "untranslatable": a word or concept that requires repeated, continual translation. It draws attention to what translation cannot immediately or succinctly convey, and encourages readers to be critical of and alert to translational processes at work elsewhere in the novel.

Importantly, Obejas's footnotes continue the work of the source text by increasing the degree to which it (self-)exoticizes. Like Díaz's own, they are reminiscent of the extensive anthropological footnotes appearing in many colonial translations into European languages, which sought to explain colonial cultures and languages to European readers. While Díaz's footnotes use a sarcastic tone, dubious authorities, and opaque references in order to expose and subvert this tradition, Obejas takes a different approach. Her footnotes (which, we must remember, appear only in the version sold in North America) "explain," objectify, and exoticize U.S. and European culture as often as they do Caribbean culture. Díaz's footnotes focus primarily on aspects of Dominican history unlikely to be familiar to Anglophone readers, but Obejas's footnotes are attached indiscriminately to references to cultures from all around the world. For instance, she explains Díaz's reference to the "Hija de Liborio" (Vintage Español, 57), an early twentieth-century Dominican revolutionary who became a kind of messiah, and her own use of Caribbean terms such as "baro" (Vintage Español, 26) and "yola" (Vintage Español, 28). However, she also explains the use of words in Urdu (Vintage Español, 99) and Japanese (Vintage Español, 115), a reference to a Persian god (Vintage Español, 96), a British pop band (Vintage Español, 58), and an Irish singer (Vintage Español, 40). She also turns the imperial, exoticizing gaze on U.S. culture at least as often as she does on any other part of the world, explaining references to the work of U.S. authors Edgar Rice Burroughs and Stephen King, and U.S. television programs *Fractured Fairy Tales* and *Planet of the Apes* in the first twenty pages alone. She offers what will be, for many, redundant explanations of things that have currency even outside of the United States, thanks to the dominance of U.S. culture globally, such as a reference to the Kennedy family: "La Maldición de los Kennedy es una referencia a una serie de lamentables sucesos ocurridos en la famosa familia de Kennedy. Various miembros de la familia han muerto en circunstancias extraordinarias: los hermanos John y Robert fueron asesinados y John, Jr. murió in 1999 en un accidente aéreo" (Vintage Español, 4) (The Curse of the Kennedys is a reference to a series of tragic events affecting the famous Kennedy family. Various members of the family have died in extraordinary circumstances: the brothers John and Robert were assassinated, and John Jr. died in 1999 in a plane crash). Like Díaz's footnotes about Trujillo, which explain important aspects of Dominican history for readers presumed to be unfamiliar with it, this footnote about the Kennedys ironically constructs, in the novel's very first pages, an implied North American reader who is ignorant of major aspects of U.S. culture and history.

Obejas's explanations have a democratizing effect, giving supposedly "marginal" cultures an equal footing with more powerful ones. They are also an indication of the diversity of the audience the publisher hopes to reach; just as Díaz himself assumes different kinds of knowledge and implies different kinds of readers at different points in the narrative, Obejas, too, seems to keep in mind readers from diverse backgrounds.

Translation as Palimpsest

Obejas's translation of *Oscar Wao* knowingly supplements processes that are already underway in the novel itself. It is analogous to the novel's other paratexts—Díaz's own footnotes, the annotations on Genius, and the many published interviews with the author—in that it attempts to fill in some of the novel's many blanks. Such a comparison casts translation and writing as analogous processes, even as overlapping sections of a continuum. The Spanish translation necessarily creates its own blanks, which pose new questions for readers, in similar ways to the novel's other paratexts. The translation, too, is in its own right a "writerly" text, which perpetuates the novel's palimpsestuous structure. Its existence in more than one version, each offering a quite distinct reading experience, is the most obvious indication of this: the two versions remind us of translation's infinite potential for revision and reworking. The Vintage Español edition in particular contributes to *Oscar Wao*'s open structure. It does this by emphasizing the novel's existence on multiple textual levels, both through the sheer number of footnotes and by appending notes to existing notes (see, for example, Vintage Español, 3) in much the same way that annotations are appended to a footnote in the online Genius extract. In these ways the translation increases the degree to which the narrative overspills its conventional boundaries, escaping the printed book and looking out to further paratexual reinscriptions.

As in Chávez-Silverman's writing, and in Braschi's, to be discussed in the next chapter, in *Oscar Wao*, Díaz's engagement with translation as a means of narrative production (its having been written as a partial pseudotranslation) and of reception (the requirement that readers translate and "uncensor" parts of the text for themselves as they read) means that the novel is already conspicuously in motion, unfixed. Obejas's translation into Spanish succeeds in perpetuating that motion by projecting the work into circulation outside the Anglophone world, where it will engender new and unexpected readings and "rewritings."

Chapter Three

"I WANT MY CLOSET BACK"

Queering and Unqueering Language in Giannina Braschi's *Yo-Yo Boing!*

Exasperating, confusing, utterly frustrating: these are frequent criticisms of Giannina Braschi's 1998 novel *Yo-Yo Boing!*. The "doubled sign" of the title—or tripled or even quadrupled sign—flags the novel's difficulty from the outset.[1] The phrase "Yo-Yo Boing!" signifies in multiple ways, so much so that Doris Sommer and Alexandra Vega-Merino, who authored the introduction to the novel's first edition, felt obliged to explain it, though they were unable to agree on the best way to do so. Vega-Merino identifies a reference to a popular Puerto Rican television comedian known as "Yo-Yo Boing," while Sommer believes it to be a reference to Julia Álvarez's character "Yolanda" ("Yo") from her novel *How the García Girls Lost Their Accents*.[2] These allusions aside, in its repetition of the Spanish term for the first person, "yo," it describes the novel's own split subjectivity and the dizzying energy of its bilingual middle section, which bounces from one idea and one language to another, comprising lively dialogue in both English and Spanish between an indeterminate number of characters in New York City. Difficulty has been the overriding criticism of *Yo-Yo Boing!* by readers and reviewers, and is said to derive largely from the book's use of two languages; unlike Junot Díaz's *The Brief Wondrous Life of Oscar Wao*, Braschi's novel is not written mainly in English, but combines it throughout with words, sentences, long passages, and even whole chapters in Spanish. Persephone Braham suggests the novel's readership will be restricted to a "small, bilingual circle of New York academics" as only they will be able to "decode" it.[3] A reviewer for *Publishers Weekly* calls the novel "a frustrating challenge," arguing it will be of interest "only to the most literary-minded of bilingualists."[4] Even Sommer and Vega-Merino admit that "readers may feel the strain of [Braschi's] demanding freedom."[5]

Braschi's use of language is evidently a source of unease for these readers, as it is for many characters in *Yo-Yo Boing!* itself. The anxiety it produces means that, in the novel, language is policed in the same ways that queer desires and gender practices are. Part I of this chapter examines how anxieties about language, gender fluidity, and queer desire intersect in *Yo-Yo Boing!*. Bearing in mind that Braschi's language has in common with queer subjectivities a degree of difficulty in making itself intelligible, I will argue that her use of language constitutes a queer practice. Part II then examines Tess O'Dwyer's 2011 "translation" of *Yo-Yo Boing!* into English only, arguing that it is an integral part of the novel's postmodern self-commentary; in responding to characters' anxieties, it "un-queers" their language and thus mitigates the novel's difficulty as part of an appeal to a wider readership. Viewing the two versions as a complex, contradictory, collaborative whole, this chapter will demonstrate that *Yo-Yo Boing!* blurs the lines between production and reception, interpretation and praxis, subverting the traditionally hierarchical relationship between original and translation and instead proposing a model of textual production that accepts translation, in Rebecca Walkowitz's words, as "medium and origin rather than as afterthought."[6]

PART I. QUEER LANGUAGE, QUEER TEXTS, QUEER BODIES

"A Frustrating Challenge"

Like Susana Chávez-Silverman and Junot Díaz, Braschi is committed to alienating and challenging her readers. The strategies of estrangement, defamiliarization, or "ostranenie" she uses in order to make poetic language difficult, laborious, and "foreign to the reader, even to the point of semi-comprehensibility" have been enacted most conspicuously in canonical texts of high modernism such as T. S. Eliot's *The Waste Land*, which Braschi cites and rewrites at some length in *Yo-Yo Boing!* (the protagonist claims, "Este poema va a ser parte de mi vida" [This poem is going to be part of my life] [*YYB*, 222]).[7] The two works have in common extreme forms of intertextuality (by which I mean frequent use of quotations from and references to other sources), polyphony, abrupt transitions of speaker, setting, and time, and the use of more than one language.[8] "Blow Up," the long middle section of *Yo-Yo Boing!*, comprises conversations that revolve around an author (eventually named "Giannina Braschi") suffering from writer's block. Her halting literary output bears some resemblance to *Yo-Yo Boing!* itself, and her characterization draws on aspects of Braschi's own life, making the novel a self-conscious work of metafiction. Many of the protagonist's conversations are with a male live-in partner who is also her editor, translator, and transcriber, and with whom she has a turbulent personal and artistic relationship; but there are also other voices, often nameless and always unannounced. Mixing highbrow culture with lowbrow humor, characters move seamlessly from childish ditties to scatological jokes and references to popular culture, then on to fast-paced discussions of narrative form or multiculturalism.

The novel contains abundant allusions to art, music, film, philosophy, and literature from across the Americas and Europe, such that readers may struggle to follow the thread of certain conversations if they are not familiar with the works being mentioned. This is illustrated by a passage of dialogue in which the protagonist is trying to decide whether she would prefer her partner to buy her some takeout nachos or spare ribs:

> —You'll starve to death if you don't decide.
> —Par délicatesse, j'ai perdu ma vie.
> —You're Buridan's ass, not Rimbaud.
> —Don't explain, okay. I don't need your explanation, I prefer to listen to the words. Think them. If I can apply them to my life, then I understand and I'm happy. Fetch me ribs.
> —I would prefer not to.
> —Bartleby.
> —Don't cite your references.
> —The owl of Minerva beats its wings at dusk!
>
> (*YYB*, 89–90)

What should be the most prosaic of exchanges instead sparks, in the space of fewer than ten lines, references to a philosophical paradox about free will, a poem by Arthur Rimbaud, Herman Melville's short story "Bartleby, the Scrivener," and the German philosopher Hegel's allusion to the mythological owl of Minerva. Passages such as this are as densely allusive and intertextual as, for example, Joyce's *Ulysses* or Eliot's *The Waste Land*. Braschi does not apologize for their difficulty, but rather uses one of her characters to make the case, much like Díaz and Chávez-Silverman do, for a reading experience characterized by incomplete understanding. We see this when, shortly after this exchange, one of the characters is criticized for misinterpreting a literary allusion; the other responds: "I don't always get it like everybody else gets it, but I get it. There's always an understanding in misunderstanding" (*YYB*, 90), suggesting that the reinterpretation of texts in new contexts encourages critical thinking and creativity.

The above passage demonstrates Braschi's refusal to distinguish among anonymous speakers, which disrupts readers' ability to identify the views of a particular character or to follow their development. In the first half of "Blow Up," the protagonist and her partner each display such fickleness of opinion that they often appear to be one another's alter egos rather than discrete characters (this is exacerbated by the use of nicknames differentiated only by gendered suffixes: "kiko" and "kika," "chipo" and "chipa"). During this dialogue, new anonymous voices frequently intervene in the form of reported speech, as the couple recount for one another episodes from their past, dreams, and ideas for books and films. Tags such as "she said" are rare, quotation marks are never used, and imagined or remembered scenes are often spliced together with conversations in the narrative present in such a way that, even without the abrupt and unannounced shifts in topic of conversation, time, and setting, readers would lose track of who is speaking. Alongside the text's use of multiple languages, these features contribute to the difficulty experienced by the novel's readers and reviewers. Braschi is writing in a tradition of modernist and postmodernist dialogue novels in which "narrative action is constituted almost entirely by character speech."[9] Even in Sommer and Vega-Merino's introduction, what starts out as a unified voice splits into conversation, mimicking the dialogic nature of "Blow Up," the middle section of *Yo-Yo Boing!*. Dialogue novels often experiment with narrative structures based on repetition and miscommunication rather than causal logic and linear progression, and, as Matthew Badura reminds us, are frequently characterized as "difficult."[10]

This difficulty can be explained by the degree to which they demand that readers be active.

Theories of active readership, such as that expressed by Roland Barthes in *S/Z*, which I discussed in the previous chapter in relation to the "blanks" in Díaz's *Oscar Wao*, are applicable to *Yo-Yo Boing!*, too. This is partly because its heavy reliance on dialogue means readers are offered no narrative context save for the utterances of characters themselves, making the text open to many potential realizations. It is also partly because its variety of cultural references, like *Oscar Wao*'s, is vast, ranging from Fellini films to Golden Age Spanish poetry, to twentieth-century Russian novels, to U.S. television series from the 1980s, such that many readers will be familiar with some references but none is likely to be familiar with all. It is also, of course—as in the work of Díaz and Chávez-Silverman—because of its bilingualism, which makes *Yo-Yo Boing!*, as so many reviewers have complained, in Barthes's words "a labor of language."[11]

Bilingual Difficulty

Much of the difficulty ascribed to *Yo-Yo Boing!* undoubtedly derives from its uncompromising assumption of bilingual competence in its readers. *Yo-Yo Boing!* was written at a time when debates about the use of English and Spanish were having considerable impact on both U.S. and Puerto Rican politics. The 1980s had seen the rise of the Official English movement, and, according to the U.S. Census Bureau, in March 1998, when *Yo-Yo Boing!* was published, "Hispanics" in the United States (excluding Puerto Rico) numbered around 30.8 million and accounted for 11.4 percent of the country's total population (269 million). In only eight years, their total number had risen by 48 percent, up from 20.8 million in March 1990.[12]

Although people of Mexican origin make up the majority (64.5 percent) of those immigrants, Puerto Rico has been an obstacle to Official English becoming law in the United States because of the two territories' unique relationship. The status of the island, of which the United States took possession in 1898 as part of its spoils from the Spanish-American War, has long been that of "estado libre asociado" (associated free state). During the 1990s, Puerto Ricans debated repeatedly whether to abandon their commonwealth status in favor of becoming the fifty-first state of America. As

Braschi writes in *Yo-Yo Boing!*, "Los puertoriqueños son puntos y comas. No pueden decidirse o por el punto o por la coma" (Puerto Ricans are semicolons. They can't decide between a full stop and a comma) (*YYB*, 214–15). They voted to retain the status quo by a slim margin in a plebiscite in 1993, and again in 1998, with 50.5 percent voting for no change and 46.6 percent for statehood, and only a very small proportion voting in favor of independence.[13] Some, such as Puerto Rican writer Rosario Ferré, saw the multicultural United States' large and rapidly expanding Latinx population as a reason to embrace statehood, arguing in the *New York Times* that Puerto Rican culture and language could no longer "be disappeared" on the mainland.[14] Others disagreed fervently, like her contemporary Ana Lydia Vega, who, in an open letter, accused Ferré of putting forward "una tan triste apología de la asimilación" (a very sad defense of assimilation).[15]

Because of the dominance of Spanish in Puerto Rico, the possibility of it gaining U.S. statehood is therefore a threat to the Official English movement. The island has been officially bilingual since 1898 (barring two short interludes during which Spanish was the only official language), although in practice the Puerto Rican government has functioned in Spanish throughout the twentieth century and beyond. Puerto Ricans from both sides of the political spectrum agree that Spanish is indispensable to their national identity. This means that, in contrast to the Latinx writers addressed so far in this book, Braschi's bilingualism is a challenge not only to English-language monolingualism in the United States but also to some more conservative aspects of Spanish-language Puerto Rican culture, as a number of critics have argued. Maritza Stanchich, for instance, shows how Braschi's writing "levels the playing field of power dynamics between English and Spanish," seeking to forge parity between two powerful imperial languages.[16] He shows Braschi's work to be a break not only with the hegemony of English but also with Puerto Rico's insular cultural nationalist discourse, which sees Spanish as the lynchpin of modern island identity. In challenging this latter linguistic regime, Stanchich argues, Braschi does not "reinscribe colonial US English imposition but, rather, interrogates what such prescriptions have hidden, as well as in whose interests they have been made."[17] While she makes this point convincingly, I find myself wondering how different the ethico-political gesture of resistance might have been had *Yo-Yo Boing!* been published in Puerto Rico rather than the United

States. José L. Torres-Padilla, too, has argued that Braschi's work "undermines the essentialist perceptions of literature and purity in language held by the island's cultural elite."[18] Unlike Stanchich, however, he also cautions us to be mindful of bringing too much idealism to a linguistic analysis of Braschi's work. Relying on language alone "as a stance of resistance against imperialism and hegemony," he argues, promotes an idealism that "supports the continuing colonial status of Puerto Rico and undermines any desire for self-determination that might effect real change."[19] Torres-Padilla thus reminds us that there are limits, both in Braschi's work and in the work of other writers addressed in this book, to the transgressive potential of multilingual writing.

Yo-Yo Boing! was written against the backdrop of these debates and is set in New York—long home to the mainland's largest number of Puerto Ricans, who have established a community with customs and literary practices distinct from those of the island itself. In her 1988 essay "La vida es un Spanglish disparatero: Bilingualism in Nuyorican Poetry," Frances Aparicio divided writers of Puerto Rican origin into two groups. On the one hand, she identified writers educated in Puerto Rico who share "an intellectual, highly stylized—and politically committed—literary production" in Spanish.[20] On the other hand, there were "Nuyorican" writers, born and raised in New York, whose creative and original response to this is to "write in English or in Spanglish, and strive to create an oral, bilingual context which reflects the popular culture and the social conditions of the puertorriqueños in El Barrio."[21] This latter kind of writing, Aparicio claims, is "based on popular language, on the everyday speech of *la gente*" in New York.[22] The term "Nuyorican" came to be synonymous not just with New York Puerto Ricans but specifically with the literary community centered around the Nuyorican Poets Café, founded in 1971 and famous for hosting highly publicized and interactive slam poetry competitions. *Nuyorican Poetry: An Anthology of Puerto Rican Words and Feelings* collected many of the poems performed at the café, and contained a manifesto-like introduction in which its founder, Miguel Algarín, placed "Spanglish"—"a new language, a new tradition of communication"—at the center of an emerging poetics of Puerto Rican diaspora, and helped establish Nuyorican poetry as part of an emerging Latinx literary canon.[23] As Ed Morales puts it, the writing collected in *Nuyorican Poetry* and in a later volume, *Aloud: Voices from the*

Nuyorican Poets Cafe, comprises "a bilingual literature from the streets," characterized overwhelmingly by its orality and by popular forms.[24]

Although Braschi performed at the café during the 1980s, *Yo-Yo Boing!* sits comfortably in neither of Aparicio's categories of Puerto Rican literature. The novel recalls "Nuyorican" writing in its dialogic character and "aggressively performative" bilingualism in its use of popular rhymes and its lowbrow humor.[25] However, as we have seen, *Yo-Yo Boing!* combines its popular intertexts with many more that are unabashedly academic; its characters debate topics ranging from Western philosophy to immigration and poetic form. Moreover, it makes much more extensive use of Spanish than the poems collected in the café's anthologies. Unlike Díaz, who "creolizes" his English by incorporating Spanish forms, Braschi uses the two languages more or less equally, including long opening and closing chapters entirely in Spanish. Like Díaz, though, and Chávez-Silverman too, Braschi does not capitulate to market pressures to translate her use of Spanish for the benefit of non-Hispanophone readers.[26] Rather, the speakers in "Blow Up" move back and forth between the two languages in quick succession with no attempt to gloss or explain. Once again, this defamiliarized language disabuses readers of any assumption that a text should be easy to access, or that they should be entitled to a full understanding.

It is also important to note that Braschi's idiosyncratic English suggests non-native usage, but in such a way that it emphasizes the creative potential of writing in a language one is not entirely comfortable with. For example, in one scene, the accusation "you obliviated the Indians" (*YYB*, 135) is leveled at a British character, recovering an archaic verb to suggest the way Native Americans were both obliterated and consigned to oblivion. In another instance, the protagonist gives a bilingual performance at a literary salon, during which an audience member complains: "What am I doing here, listening to a Rican who can't spick English or Spanish" (*YYB*, 164). The nonstandard spelling of "speak" satirizes the Hispanic accent and makes a pun on "spic," an offensive term for a Spanish-speaking person from Central or South America or the Caribbean. In a final example, one character erroneously explains an English idiom: "Son of a beach—she explained—son las putas americanas [the american whores] who come to Puerto Rico and have sex on the beach, and sus bastardos [their bastards] are called: son of a beach" (*YYB*, 221). The pun, which arises from difficulty hearing and pronouncing the distinction between "bitch" and "beach," makes us laugh but also satirizes the relationship between the United States and Puerto Rico.

The above examples demonstrate that, as well as obstructing communication and encouraging active reading, semi-fluency can be a surprisingly expressive resource. In its combination of English and Spanish, its calques, overcorrections, and false cognates, *Yo-Yo Boing!* makes a claim for the creative potential of writing in a nondominant language. Not only do these examples make us laugh, they also allow us to see from different perspectives. This is what Doris Sommer explores at length in her *Bilingual Aesthetics*, arguing that language "mistakes" can be pleasurable while also challenging the status quo. She argues that they provide both aesthetic and intellectual stimulation, evoking a combination of laughter and discomfort.[27] Turning to Viktor Shklovsky's "ostranenie," she makes the connection between humor and the unease produced by defamiliarized language: "What [Shklovsky] doesn't say is that this organized confusion [of estrangement] makes you laugh. In other cases, it might make you shudder or otherwise feel 'funny,' because good jokes have that tragicomic, double-dealing quality that sends you coming and going between disturbing effects."[28] Braschi does not resort to oft-used, semi-codified "Spanglish" terms, but rather terms that "aspire to a signature originality," as Sommer and Vega-Merino put it, therefore assuring their capacity for estrangement.[29] The language "mistakes" in *Yo-Yo Boing!* often manifest as nonstandard orthography (like "spick"), which has a long history of functioning both as a form of defamiliarization and as comic device in literature, especially when it is used to represent dialectal variation linked to class and educational background, or to represent non-native speech.[30] They also manifest as puns (like "son of a beach") that disturb our assumption of linguistic stability by placing multiple word meanings, whether within or between languages, in competition with one another, often making them as unsettling as they are amusing. This combination of the transgressive and the humorous is crucial to the way Braschi engages her readers. In the following section, I connect these funny but disturbing language "mistakes" to other acts of social transgression in *Yo-Yo Boing!* and to the equally unsettling effects they have on characters who encounter them, working toward the claim that Braschi's language can be read as a queer practice.

Queering Language

Debates about bilingualism in the United States in the years leading up to the publication of *Yo-Yo Boing!* were in important ways bound up with contemporary thinking about gender and sexuality. Braschi is writing in a tradition of intersectional thinking begun by Chicana "third-world" feminists Gloria Anzaldúa and Cherríe Moraga, whose edited volume *This Bridge Called My Back* was dedicated to exploring the intersecting oppressions of women of color.[31] Third-world feminists held that a person has different overlapping social identities according to their race, class, gender, sexuality, or language, which must all be equally accounted for and acknowledged as being inextricably linked. Dissatisfied both by the predominantly white mainstream feminist movement and by the sexist Chicano movement, they sought a feminism that would not require them to isolate or privilege one part of their identity but could accept that each part is in constant dialogue with the others. Anzaldúa, in particular, explores the way her identity as a Chicana and as a speaker of multiple languages intersects with her identity as a woman attracted to women. As Sandra K. Soto notes, Anzaldúa's essay "To(o) Queer the Writer—Loca, escritora y chicana" included an early critical evaluation of the usefulness of the term "queer" to Chicana identity. In it, Anzaldúa explains her dislike of the word "lesbian," likening it to "Hispanic," another identity category imposed by others with which she does not identify, and indeed "queer," which she says has been appropriated by the academy. This avoidance of labels goes to the heart of the concept of queer, which holds that it is not possible for individuals to identify or label themselves queer, since the very idea of queer is to disturb or avoid definitions and categorizations (although in practice it is used as an inclusive term to refer to myriad nonbinary gender identities and sexual orientations).[32] Anzaldúa and third-world feminism had a considerable impact on the development of queer studies; José Esteban Muñoz, for example, in his exploration of the performance, activism, and survival of queer people of color, consciously examines the "critical, cultural, and political legacy" of *This Bridge Called My Back*, which he describes as an example of "disidentification": a partial disavowal of dominant cultural forms that involves working to restructure them from within.[33]

Although *Yo-Yo Boing!* is in some respects distant from Anzaldúa and Moraga's work—it does not explicitly take part in social protest, for example, and readers will argue over what values the novel upholds—positioning it in this tradition is nonetheless productive. It allows us to see the way the novel's thinking about language and ethnicity is entwined with its thinking about gender and sexuality. Its characters are in-between, fluid subjectivities in numerous ways: as Puerto Ricans caught between statehood and independence, as speakers of more than one American language, as creative minds caught between the roles of translator and writer, and as subjects in queer bodies or with queer desires. What's more, there is an insistence on the overlapping, mutually constitutive nature of different social identities, which encourages readers to think about the ways a person's linguistic identity, especially the act of speaking and writing in a language that isn't their "mother tongue," might intersect with their queer desires and practices.

Eve Kosofsky Sedgwick defines "queer" as "the open mesh of possibilities, gaps, overlaps, dissonances and resonances, lapses and excesses of meaning when the constituent elements of anyone's gender, of anyone's sexuality aren't made (or *can't be* made) to signify monolithically."[34] I find this definition particularly useful in thinking about *Yo-Yo Boing!*'s characters, who identify and disidentify at different moments with different genders and sexualities. Moreover, although "queer" has been associated primarily with the deconstruction of two powerful binarisms in lesbian and gay studies—female/male and heterosexual/homosexual—I find Sedgwick's "open mesh" a useful way of thinking about Braschi's language, too. Here is another practice that "cannot be made to signify monolithically," whose relationship to dominant linguistic norms is complex and in flux, and whose "lapses and excesses of meaning" will vary depending on each reader's own linguistic competence. Although Sedgwick recognizes the danger of removing "same-sex sexual expression" from queer's "definitional center," she also sees enormous value in work that "spins the term outward along dimensions that can't be subsumed under gender and sexuality at all" and acknowledges that this sort of work "deepens and shifts" the "gravity (I mean the *gravitas*, the meaning, but also the *center* of gravity)" of the term itself.[35] Braschi's language is queer in the sense that it does not conform to convention or expectations; however, I will also demonstrate that it is associated in the novel with culturally marginalized sexual identities.

The disruption, defamiliarization, and complexity of Braschi's prose style are easily legible in relation to challenges of queer representation, with their frequent undecidability and indeterminacy, their resistance to fixity and transparency, and their appropriation of the transgressive. There is some precedent for readings such as this. Heiko Motschenbacher has seen a parallel between the way genital surgery affirms physical gender binarism and the way "purist" approaches to language, such as those advanced by the Académie Française, attempt to make language conform to the dominant discourse, implying therefore that deviations from "standard" language, such as those at work in Braschi's novel, constitute a queer linguistic practice.[36] Lawrence La Fountain-Stokes, too, reads "Spanglish" alongside queer identities on the grounds that both have been linked to notions of impurity, deviance, or degradation. His article "La política queer del espanglish" (The queer politics of Spanglish) argues that code-switching "tiene mucho que ver con lo queer en su sentido de transgresión sexual, cultural y social" (has much in common with queer in the sense of sexual, cultural, and social transgression), and makes the case for "Spanglish" as a queer literary praxis.[37] In a separate article, he recognizes Braschi's debt to intersectional thinking when he argues that, for characters in *Yo-Yo Boing!*, refutation of lesbianism constantly overlaps with "the shame of the colonial subject—in other words, the shame of being Puerto Rican."[38] What he does not say is that it also overlaps with the shame of speaking "imperfect" English, or of mixing English with Spanish. Bilingualism and non-native language use in this novel are everywhere bound up with queer subjectivity, and in many cases are derided by others as a transgression of social norms.[39]

Policing Language, Gender, and Desire

A number of key passages in *Yo-Yo Boing!* reveal linguistic and gender and sexual marginality to be policed in strikingly similar ways. To begin with the latter, we often find characters reacting negatively to those who do not conform to conventional notions of masculinity and femininity. For instance, the protagonist's partner, envious of a castrato singer's voice, laughs unkindly at him for being insufficiently masculine (*YYB*, 92). Later, a gay couple accuse a woman of being a lesbian because she does not wear skirts to work (*YYB*, 136–37), and a friend implies the protagonist is not behaving in a manner suitable to her gender when he criticizes her for being a writer rather than a mother, as though the two were mutually exclusive. In the latter role, he says, she would have been "much, much better" (*YYB*, 184). Gender norms are portrayed as a source of anxiety for her, too, when, during a dream about menstruation and motherhood, she is asked to sign an exam paper not with her name but with the words "El Niño" ("The Boy") if she wants to ensure it will receive "una A definitiva" ("a definitive A") (*YYB*, 189). Her sexuality is also brought into question: after she calls her cousin's wife a lesbian, she is accused of defining herself "by projecting her sins onto others" (*YYB*, 198). Her response is a firm (if hypocritical) insistence that no one but she can determine her sexuality: "Well, I am not [a lesbian] if you think so. I am if I think so. Only, if I think so. . . . And I don't think so" (*YYB*, 199), and the vehemence of her refutation leads us to doubt her sincerity. In fact, in all these examples of characters policing one another's behavior, we suspect that the maker of the accusations, as much as the recipient, feels a degree of discomfort and conflict about their sexuality or gender.

The same argument can be made about language. The novel's protagonist, though more comfortable in Spanish, writes predominantly in English, and attention is frequently drawn to her perceived infelicities in that language. She relies on her partner, more confident in his English, to edit and translate her work, telling him "my book needs your English" (*YYB*, 33). However, he further undermines her confidence by highlighting linguistic "mistakes" in her speech and writing:

> —I want my orange juice. Juicy red with its pepas [seeds].
> —Seeds.
> —And I want fresh squeezed. I don't want chocolate. It gives me grains.
> —Pimples.[40]
>
> (*YYB*, 26)

Here he corrects her interspersing of Spanish words into her English ("pepas") and her use of calques ("grain" is a false cognate with "grano," which means "pimple" in Spanish). The irony is that he too occasionally falters with language, as in the following lines: "I rolled my tongue again—**oops**—frenó en el paladar—déjame parar—a ver si para—**oops**—frenó en el paladar—la lengua montada en la cólera de su frenillo" (I rolled my tongue again—**oops**—it braked on my palate—let me stop—let's see if it stops—**oops**—it braked on my palate—my tongue riding its frenulum furiously) (*YYB*, 100, emphasis in original). Here his frustration at the difficulty he has rolling his "r"s is described in terms of his tongue being angry at his "frenillo" or frenulum—the membrane connecting the tongue to the floor of the mouth—for acting, as its etymology suggests it should, as a brake. His stuttering demonstrates that the physical act of pronunciation (in this case of sounds common to Spanish) can be fraught with difficulty and suggests that he assuages his anxiety about his own language by dictating how others should use it. Throughout the novel, other characters do the same, passing judgment on one another's pronunciation in comments such as "I can understand Spanish but I can't understand Puerto Ricans" (*YYB*, 164), "I know you'll say it wrong" (*YYB*, 132), and "Repeat after me: *thunder*. The tongue behind your teeth: *Th-under*" (*YYB*, 126).

These two causes of anxiety—language, and gender and sexuality—come together in a pivotal scene in which the protagonist performs at a literary salon. Importantly, the poems she chooses to perform are written almost exclusively in English, her nondominant language and one that is associated, as we have seen, with much unease. It is an idiosyncratic English, notable for its inverted word order, awkward expressions, neologisms strung together on the basis of sound association, and for being peppered with occasional Spanish ("immobility, immortability, tran / quility, morbality, morbidity, mortability, / murámonos moribundos," *YYB*, 168). In her nervousness before going on, she complains to her partner: "Why did you made [*sic*] me wear this Mao Tse Tung outfit? It doesn't fit me. I don't belong here. I'm scared. Why did you take me out of my closet. . . . I want my closet back. Close my doors. Do you think they really want to know who I am?" (*YYB*, 165). The fear, discomfort, and shame associated with performing work largely written in her nondominant language are linked here with uncertainty about sexuality and gender. Sexuality, because she describes herself as reluctantly out of the closet; gender, because she is in cross-dress, and also because immediately before going on stage she imagines herself as "un niño perdido entre el gentío" (a *boy* lost in the crowd) (*YYB*, 166, emphasis added). Immediately after the performance, she has a panicked response to the audience's laughter. Her unwillingness to be labelled "funny" reminds us that the word can describe something strange, suspicious, or unpleasant—connotations it shares, of course, with the word "queer."[41] Her strident rejection of the audience's laughter can therefore be read as a thinly veiled denial of queer identity: "You're imposing your laughter on me. . . . And you think I'm funny. It's really insulting. I don't have a sense of humor. Respect my wishes" (*YYB*, 173). This disproportionate response conveys a fear that her writing in non-native English will be interpreted as an expression of queerness.

Queering Eliot

It is in the final conversations in "Blow Up" that Braschi's "Spanglish" is presented most clearly as a queer practice. These conversations consist of repeated (mis)quotation from literary texts by William Blake, Charles Baudelaire, and eventually, extensively, from T. S. Eliot's *The Waste Land*. Eliot's ability to use multiple languages—German, French, Italian, Hindi, Latin—is held up as the standard to which Braschi's speakers should aspire, and they repeatedly accuse one another of falling short of it. As the characters quote lines from the poem in its many different languages, one asks anxiously, "What does it mean?" (*YYB*, 219). She is subsequently ridiculed for not understanding, even though none of her companions is able to offer her an adequate translation (instead, as a way of distracting, they quote different lines from the poem, in English). Moreover, they continue to police one another's pronunciation; when one of them quotes a passage in German, another asks "¿Cómo es su pronunciación?" (How is her pronunciation?), to which the response is "fatal" (awful) (*YYB*, 219). They eventually rewrite *The Waste Land*'s multilingualism, rendering lines in Spanish and re-rendering them in "Spanglish," as an expression of Eliot's frustrated homosexual desire, which they perceive in the poem's references to Eastern and Western asceticism: the Fire Sermon and St. Augustine's *Confessions*. It is worth quoting this passage at length in order to illustrate the peculiar workings of Braschi's dialogue, which withholds not only explanatory narrative but also speech markers:

> —I never liked Eliot. So unsensual, unappealing, repressed. I mean, being in the closet is alright, if you come out, someday. But he never came out. And then he wrote:
> > *Burning burning burning burning*
> > *O Lord Thou pluckest me out . . .*
> —What does pluckest mean?
> —Oh, Dios, por que me desplumas. Dios lo desplumó, y por eso se hizo religioso. [Oh, God, why are you plucking out my quills. God plucked his

quills, and because of this he became religious.] His sexual desire was so repressed hasta que Dios le quitó todas sus plumas. Pero qué es un poeta sin plumas? Es como un vampiro sin dientes. O una bruja sin escoba. [. . . until God plucked out all his quills. But what is a poet without quills? He is like a vampire without teeth. Or a witch without a broomstick.]

—I would never have written:

> Do I dare to eat a peach? Shall I part my hair
> in the middle?

I would have eaten the peach. I have eaten plenty. And why is it so difficult to part your hair in the middle. Scardy [sic] cat, pussycat, pusilánime [cowardly].

—O Lord thou pluckest meeoowt.

—Meowt. O Lord thou pluckest meeoowt. Oh Dios, me estás pluckeando del closet [Oh God, you are plucking me out of the closet].

(*YYB*, 219–20)

Viewed through the lens of popular genre literature as a comically incapacitated vampire or witch, Eliot is emphatically dethroned from his vaulted position at the pinnacle of elitist modernism. More importantly, he is positioned in a queer space in a number of ways.[42] Here, as in so many other instances in this novel, characters impose a sexual identity onto another person, and find fault with them for it. The insult "pussycat" (the characters seem to be mocking him for his "Old Possum's Book of Practical Cats," the poem on which the musical *Cats* was based) casts him as a cowardly, closeted homosexual, but also as a woman, through its association with female genitalia.[43] In an unexpected cross-phonological leap, Eliot is made, literally, to "meow," as the vowel sounds in "me out" are elongated until their referential function dissolves in an animal cry, thus making the poet transgress the human/nonhuman border in addition to the male/female border. That "meow" is understood to be an expression of Eliot's queer desire. It also highlights the opaque materiality of foreign words, their semiotic blankness for readers without the requisite language skills (in this instance, for a character with incomplete understanding of Eliot's English), and the creative ways they can be repurposed. The characters in this conversation worry that their linguistic skills are insufficient, but then demonstrate precisely the expressive and innovative potential of uncertain, fluid, queer forms resulting from partial knowledge and from language contact.

"I WANT MY CLOSET BACK"

Queer Texts, Queer Bodies

Braschi's representation of "Spanglish" as a queer practice is also articulated through her engagement with feminist narratives of the female body as a maker of textual meaning. Foregrounding the body as the site of language production (we have already seen how she demonstrates the physicality of speech by making her characters stutter and stammer), she disrupts and rewrites these narratives from a queer perspective.

Yo-Yo Boing!'s opening section, "Close Up," comprises a detailed third-person account of a woman's intimate bathroom rituals that imagines the text as body as well as the body as text. This section dwells on the physicality of the female body, refusing to shy away from its various excretions and secretions. The woman in the bathroom takes fascinated pleasure in the abject: her own feces, a scab, pus, plucked hairs. In this, as La Fountain-Stokes has pointed out, it recalls Monique Wittig's *The Lesbian Body*.[44] Just as, in Wittig's text, the graphic "splitting" of personal pronouns and the exploration of the insides as well as the outsides of bodies suggest that no subject is coherent or self-contained, in *Yo-Yo Boing!* Braschi depicts the female body visibly growing and transforming, in exchange with its environment, suggesting that it is in an ongoing state of flux, rather than a fixed entity with definable boundaries. Language is portrayed as being integral to these bodily processes. A vocal warm-up is described in autoerotic terms, the careful articulation of each vowel sound engaging the woman's entire body and culminating in the orgasmic exclamation "**OH-OH!**" (*YYB*, 17, emphasis in original). She takes physical pleasure in the way the vowels "han ejercitado sus músculos, han escuchado la contracción de sus tripas, el sonido quisquilloso de sus costillas, las nucas y las astillas de los dedos, los pelos de las axilas" (have exercised her muscles, have listened to the contraction of her guts, the fussy sound of her ribs, the nape of her neck and the splinters in her fingers, her underarm hair) (*YYB*, 17). What is more, language itself is embodied: the vowels are lovers, "parejas ubérrimas" (fertile couples), with hips and heads and toes (*YYB*, 17).

"Close Up" sets the scene for the novel to depict women's bodies as makers of meaning and sources of literary inspiration. Later passages recall feminist narratives of the female body as text, and as the site of a specifically female literary production, such as Hélène Cixous's "The Laugh of the Medusa" and Luce Irigaray's "When Our Lips Speak Together."[45] For instance, Braschi turns repeatedly to the image of the tongue as both sexual trope and a tool of language production. In a much longed-for flourishing of writing activity, the protagonist says, "I'm writing it while I'm screaming it.... It gives my tongue an orgasm" (*YYB*, 49), an image that gestures toward Cixous's idea of female masturbation as "a veritable aesthetic activity, each stage of rapture a composition, something beautiful."[46] However, Braschi not only recalls but also disrupts these narratives, much criticized for their focus on sexual difference, and rewrites them from a queer perspective.[47] We see this in the frequent depiction of literary inspiration as a somatic phenomenon. For example, the protagonist's partner recounts a dream in which he acts as her muse, making her literally pregnant with inspiration: "Yo estaba echándole viento a tu ano, y tu barriga se inflaba, y tú te elevabas de la cama, te elevabas, chocando contra el techo y rebotando contra el suelo.... *Es la inspiración, negrita mía, es la inspiración*" (I was blowing wind into your anus, and your belly was inflating, and you were rising up off the bed, you were rising up, bumping against the ceiling, and bouncing off the floor.... *It's inspiration, darling, it's inspiration*) (*YYB*, 104–5). Here the narrative of female body as a maker of meaning is queered, not only by the association with anal sex, but also because the relationship between the habitually masculinized writer (the female protagonist) and the habitually feminized translator/muse (her male partner) has been subverted, such that the translator is the source of literary inspiration and the writer merely the vehicle for it. This subversion of creative hierarchy and its queer potential will be explored further in part II of this chapter, but for now it is sufficient to point out that, in imagining creativity in these terms, Braschi queers both the processes of bodily reproduction and the (bilingual) text that is "conceived."

This image of pregnancy as inspiration is not the only depiction in *Yo-Yo Boing!* of the maternal body as a vehicle for textual production. Perhaps Braschi's most visceral description of literary creativity recalls Cixous's suggestion that when a woman speaks, she "physically materializes what she's thinking; she signifies it with her body."[48] Repeating the image of the mouth-as-vagina, the protagonist dreams she is giving birth through her mouth to a puppy. This dream, too, is interpreted by her partner as a sign of inspiration: "You're giving birth through your mouth, through your tongue to another fragment" (*YYB*, 52). Like the previous dream, this is no conventional narrative of motherhood; rather, I would suggest that the act of literary production is queered by its transgression of the human/nonhuman border.

Braschi frequently associates her literary creativity with animals, particularly hybrid ones. For instance, at one point in the novel the protagonist's work is described as "a new creature, half feathers, half fur" (*YYB*, 101). "Pelos en la lengua," a short piece she published in *Hopscotch* in 2001, helps us to understand that, for Braschi, the animalistic quality of her writing derives from its bilingualism. In it, she compares her mixture of English and Spanish to "un perro realengo" (a stray dog), saying "aúlla como un perro al infinito" (it howls like a dog into the infinite).[49] But as well as depicting her bilingual writing as an animal, Braschi also repeatedly sexualizes the process of creation: there is a recurring link in *Yo-Yo Boing!* between images of tails and tongues, the former standing in for animals, the latter for both language and desire. In the protagonist's dream, the puppy's birth is depicted as a quasi-sexual experience; far from her being "in agony" (*YYB*, 52), the birth unexpectedly evokes pleasure and sensuality, almost desire: "Movía su colita como hélice chocando con mi paladar y mis encías. Me hacía tanto y tanto cosquilla en la boca. [He moved his little tail like a propeller bumping against my palate and my gums. It was so, so ticklish in my mouth.] Almost a feast" (*YYB*, 51). Its description recalls another scene, one that has undeniably erotic overtones, in which the protagonist remembers being aroused by a former boyfriend during a kiss characterized as an extended dance between their tongues: "La lengua de él y la mía se acariciaban, y se tocaban las colas, bajando y subiendo" (His tongue and mine caressed each other, and they touched tails, falling and rising) (*YYB*, 59).

In this dream, the fragments of literary text being "born" (which, like *Yo-Yo Boing!* itself, are written in a unique, transformative mixture of English and Spanish) are imagined as the offspring of cross-species desire. Writing bilingually is depicted as a transgression of the supposedly "natural" divide between species, which is analogous to a transgression of the "natural" boundary between genders and the desires they are expected to feel (we might also recall here the depiction of a sexually frustrated homosexual T. S. Eliot as a cat). In the protagonist's dream, human and nonhuman animals alike are able to slip out of their categorical distinctions and biological determinations in a way that resonates strongly with Sedgwick's understanding of "queer" as an "open mesh of possibilities," and which epitomizes Braschi's ability to think across and between conventional taxonomies.[50]

Part I of this chapter has focused on Braschi's representation of bilingual writing and writing in a nondominant language as a queer practice. In its ability to defamiliarize or estrange, her language is "funny"—both in the sense of making people laugh and in the sense that it is perceived as strange, disturbing, or even unnatural. The following section will explore how that difficult, funny, queer language fares in translation.

PART II. A RELATIONSHIP OF EQUALS? TESS O'DWYER'S TRANSLATION OF *YO-YO BOING!*

In 2011, thirteen years after its original publication by Latin American Literary Review Press, *Yo-Yo Boing!* was published in a new edition by AmazonCrossing. This stripped the novel of the exclusivity of expensive scholarly publishing and massively expanded its potential reach. Latin American Literary Review Press is a small press linked with an academic journal, which focuses on translation and bilingual writing. The publishers there are likely to have assumed a small readership for *Yo-Yo Boing!*, but one that would endure, as the book continued to be read by researchers and students working in the fields of postmodern and postcolonial literature, translation studies, Latin American studies, and beyond. AmazonCrossing, in contrast, in just over ten years has become the United States' most prolific publisher of translations into English, with three times as many translated titles as its largest competitor, Dalkey Archive Press. Its reliance on ebooks and on paperback publishing via print-on-demand means its books are available globally and priced affordably, as these technologies minimize warehouse and distribution costs, and waste from unsold titles. Amazon's publishing strategy is simply to reach the greatest number of readers possible.[51]

It makes sense, therefore, that alongside the reedition of the bilingual novel, they also published a monolingual edition in English, "translated" by Tess O'Dwyer. O'Dwyer is the acclaimed translator of Braschi's earlier collection of poems, *Empire of Dreams*.[52] The pair has a close personal relationship, habitually doing joint readings. O'Dwyer even has her own fictional counterpart in the novel in a character called "Tess." She takes an interventionist approach, revising the text extensively, and the result is an English version that reduces the novel's difficulty. As I will demonstrate, it is more fluent and musical than the bilingual version, which, as we have seen, employs many strategies of disruption and opacity. In ways that recall some of Achy Obejas's strategies in her translation of Díaz's *Oscar Wao*, O'Dwyer goes beyond simply translating all the passages originally appearing in Spanish, such that she clarifies and standardizes Braschi's language in a number of ways. In this sense, the new version complements Amazon-Crossing's publishing strategy, increasing the novel's accessibility and circulation but no longer challenging normative discourse on the standardness and monolingualism of literary language.

However, O'Dwyer's version is not merely a capitulation to the global dominance of Anglophone monolingualism, embodied by transnational corporations like Amazon. The changes it incorporates respond to the anxieties (particularly about language, but also about gender and sexuality) expressed by Braschi's characters, and thus bring to life a translation as it is imagined in the novel itself: one that calms the author-protagonist's fears that her text, because of its language, might be "queer." Examining some examples will help illustrate these claims and demonstrate how O'Dwyer's seemingly controversial approach to "translation" is in many ways an extension of the work's self-commentary. But first it is helpful to view O'Dwyer's version in the context of postcolonial, feminist, and queer approaches to translation.

Approaches to Translation

Translators and theorists of translation have often advocated a foreignizing translation strategy as a means of resisting dominant ideologies. The concept of "foreignization," elaborated by Lawrence Venuti in contradistinction to "domestication" or "assimilation" in his book *The Translator's Invisibility*, is understood here to refer to a translation that make readers continually aware of its having originated in a different linguistic culture.[53] A foreignizing translation shows greater loyalty to its source language than to its readers, whom it challenges and unsettles, and from whom it requires active participation. Postcolonial theorists such as Gayatri Spivak and Venuti himself have argued that foreignization is particularly necessary in translations from non-European into European languages, as a way of emphasizing cultural difference, of foregrounding and empowering colonized voices, and of counteracting a homogenizing appropriation of the dominant source culture by the target culture.[54]

Feminist translators, too, have used foreignizing strategies to give women a voice as a way of combating patriarchal hegemony. The conventionally hierarchical relationship between author and translator has often been sexualized, with the "derivative" work of the translator cast as passive, reproductive, and feminine, bound by fidelity to the author's "original," which in turn is considered active, productive, and masculine.[55] Taking their cue from post-structuralist theories of language that debunk the concept of a single, recoverable textual original, feminist translators see translation as a creative practice in its own right, one that is productive rather than reproductive.[56] They challenge the traditional understanding of authority in translation, and engage with texts as "literary activists."[57] Luise von Flotow has identified three key strategies of interventionist feminist translation: *supplementing*, which is to say, the use of wordplay, nonstandard typography, and graphics as creative ways of expressing the multiple meanings connoted by words or phrases in the source text; *prefacing and footnoting*; and *hijacking*.[58] The last strategy involves "correcting" a text on political grounds, in order to undermine the patriarchal language of the original, and is often criticized for being "unfaithful." Canadian translators such as Barbara Godard, Susanne de Lotbinière-Harwood, and Suzanne Jill Levine have used wordplay, nonstandard typography, and graphics to make themselves—and the female subject more broadly—visible in translation. This "womanhandling" of the source text, as Godard calls it, as with many postcolonial translations, is often buttressed by a preface and extensive notes in which the translators willingly advertise their interventionism.[59] Feminist translation developed in direct response to the avant-garde work of feminist writers adopting a highly experimental, difficult style, and has found "its most felicitous applications [in] texts which are themselves innovative writing practices," including multilingual writing practices.[60] We might suspect that an innovative text like Braschi's *Yo-Yo Boing!*, which values difficulty and experiments with abrupt and unpredictable combinations of languages, genres, registers, and voices, might inspire a translation that draws on foreignizing, interventionist strategies in an attempt to replicate the radical nature of the original.

Another reason we might expect a translation of *Yo-Yo Boing!* to make use of foreignizing strategies is that there is an emerging field of queer translation that is drawing on similar techniques to postcolonial and feminist translators, but as a means of resisting heteronormativity. William Burton, for instance, has suggested borrowing the techniques of supplementation, prefacing, footnoting, and hijacking in order to call attention to an author's heterosexist or homophobic views, describing this as a process of "inverting" the text, which is to say, turning it against itself in order to reveal the "hidden power relations of heterosexism."[61] Elizabeth Sara Lewis, for her part, has demonstrated how similar strategies can be used to call attention to an author's existing queer perspective and "maintain or sometimes strengthen queer elements in texts."[62] In her study of subtitling, she proposes techniques such as nonstandard word order, increased formality, and the use of ellipsis in order to give subtle emphasis to queer relationships.[63]

Just as feminist translators have seen a parallel between the conventionally hierarchical male/female and original/translation binaries, and have sought to disrupt those relationships by giving women and translators increased agency and visibility, queer translation theorists see queerness as an appropriate metaphor for translation, in its frequent invisibility, its performativity, and its endless deferral of meaning.[64] The two are, in B. J. Epstein's words, "comparably indeterminate and similarly imbricated with issues of gender and sexuality, playfulness and power."[65] Drawing a parallel between Judith Butler's non-essentialist conception of gender—as produced and maintained by political and cultural contexts and discourses—and a post-structuralist understanding of signification as infinitely deferred, William Spurlin conceives of translation, much like gender, as "a performative act that is always already influenced by culture and not reducible to a textual body alone."[66] Christopher Larkosh understands translation in similar terms as a "transcultural practice that calls into question any and all claims to one's own or others' centrally fixed identity."[67]

However, while there are certain aspects of queer and feminist translation practices discernible in the English-only version of *Yo-Yo Boing!*, O'Dwyer also deviates from them in significant ways. Although the two translation practices have in common an interventionist approach, their effects are, perhaps surprisingly, in important ways directly opposed; in fact, O'Dwyer goes a considerable way toward contradicting von Flotow's observation, in reference to the foreignizing strategies of feminist translators in particular, that "the modest, self-effacing translator who produces a smooth, readable target language version of the original has become a thing of the past."[68]

O'Dwyer does not mark, either typographically or linguistically, where Braschi moves from one language to another, neither does she rely on foreignizing strategies more generally. Instead, she uses what Meir Sternberg calls "homogenizing convention."[69] In his framework for understanding the different methods available to translators for conveying the presence of more than one language in a source text, "homogenizing convention" is the strategy of ignoring the fact that the language presumably spoken by characters differs from the language in which the action is being represented. Here no attempt is made, as Sternberg puts it, to "rise to the mimetic challenge" of indicating that the language being represented differs from the language doing the representing.[70] So, even though certain characters in O'Dwyer's version of *Yo-Yo Boing!* might tell us they are speaking Spanish, their conversations are nevertheless recounted in English. Besides the occasional use of swear words, exclamations, or terms of endearment in Spanish, there is little suggestion at all that, in a different textual version, this is a bilingual novel. Unlike in the Spanish version of *Oscar Wao*, which advertises the translator's presence heavily, there is no preface or translator's note outlining O'Dwyer's aims and approach, nor explaining her decisions. Even the endorsements printed on the jacket of the English-only edition are the same ones that appear on the back of the bilingual version, only they have been edited to remove all references to the novel's bilingualism. For example, Jean Franco's quotation in the original reads: "The best demonstration yet of Braschi's extraordinary virtuosity, her command of many different registers, her dizzying ability to switch between English and Spanish. It is also a very funny novel" (*YYB*). But in the English-only edition, it has been edited thus: "The best demonstration yet of Braschi's extraordinary virtuosity... It is also a very funny novel" (*YYB*, TO). These edits to the book jacket blurb tally with a "translation" that does not draw attention to the bilingualism of the source text, but rather commits to being thoroughly English.

This is not to say, however, that O'Dwyer's approach is not interventionist. It is just that O'Dwyer's interventions cannot be aligned with the practices of supplementation, prefacing and footnoting, and hijacking developed by feminist translators, and appropriated by queer translators. O'Dwyer's interventions do not "foreignize" the text; they do not alert readers to its status as translation, nor do they call attention to queer perspectives. On the contrary, they make the text more familiar to, and easily accessible for, the target (English-speaking) readership, and consequently also downplay some of the text's queer elements. These strategies allow O'Dwyer to respond to the anxieties expressed by Braschi's characters, making manifest a translation as imagined in the novel: one that not only has the power to attract a greater number of readers, but that also standardizes its linguistic idiosyncrasies and reduces its protagonist's fear that her writing is in some way queer.

Increased Accessibility

Since O'Dwyer does not compensate for her version's lack of interlingual variation with, for example, intralingual variation (in contrast to Achy Obejas's shifts between different varieties of Spanish), the abrupt transitions so prevalent in the bilingual version of *Yo-Yo Boing!* are necessarily fewer. What is more, as well as translating Braschi's Spanish, O'Dwyer makes extensive edits to her English (unlike Achy Obejas, who retains Díaz's Spanish "lo más posible" [as much as possible]), the result of which is that the language of the English-only version is considerably less defamiliarizing than that of the bilingual version: less self-consciously awkward, more conventional in its word order and orthography. For example, where the bilingual version reads "you obliviated the Indians" (*YYB*, 135), in the English-only version the expression is returned to its standard form: "you obliterated the Indians" (*YYB*, TO, 130). Similarly, in the bilingual version, during the protagonist's performance an audience member asks: "What am I doing here, listening to a Rican who can't spick English or Spanish" (*YYB*, 164), while in the English-only version they ask: "What am I doing here, listening to a Rican who can't speak English or Spanish" (*YYB*, TO, 159). Characters do not stutter or mispronounce in the English-only version, a consequence of which is that the novel is less linguistically innovative. Changing "obliviated" to "obliterated" removes the pertinent association with oblivion and forgetting, while changing "spick" to "speak" takes some of the sting out of the criticism, and also some of the humor; the irony in the bilingual version lies in the fact that, despite criticizing the pronunciation of the "Rican" giving the performance, the audience member themselves seems to speak English with a Hispanic accent.

Another example, from a scene in which the protagonist, inspired by a popular rhyme, is composing aloud, and her partner is transcribing for her, illustrates the greater musicality of O'Dwyer's version:

> Rocka my baby
>   on the tri tad
>   when the come baby
>   cris o wind blow
>   I feel the wind swagging me away, away, away.
>
> (*YYB*, 118)

> Rock-a-bye baby
>   On the tree top,
>   When the wind blows
>   The cradle will rock.
>   I feel the wind swaying me away, away, away.
>
> (*YYB*, TO, 113)

In the bilingual version, the Anglophone lullaby is distorted as though memorized incorrectly by a non-native speaker with perhaps only partial understanding of the content, rendering the words humorous but also unfamiliar, unsettling, and discordant—funny in both senses. The translation, however, restores musicality and diminishes the humor by including the lullaby in its standard form, with standardized punctuation and formatting. The violent term "swagging" (seemingly a blend between "swaying" and "dragging") is replaced by the gentler form "swaying," the introduction of rhyme (between "sway" and "away") making the line milder and more reminiscent of a lullaby. Without even *translating* anything in the traditional sense of transferring content from one discrete language to another, O'Dwyer has significantly reduced the degree to which the language in this passage defamiliarizes.

In place of unusual and creative distortions of English, O'Dwyer introduces more conventionalized deviations from the standard: forms like "ain't," "'n," "c'mon," "ya," and "nah" are repeatedly introduced where standard forms previously existed. These features have a directly opposite effect to the distortions in the bilingual version. They index colloquiality and a confident familiarity with English rather than an English acquired late in life and spoken anxiously with Hispanic pronunciation and unusual lexis. Non-native speakers of English have increased confidence and authority in the English version; where in the bilingual version orthography and word choice mark linguistic infelicities associated with having learned English late in life, in the English version these same characters instead appear calmly in control of their language.

The reduction of difficulty is also visible in O'Dwyer's subtle changes to formatting and layout. The English-only version often marks off interjections using italics, centering, line breaks, and introductory em dashes, helping readers to follow Braschi's chaotic dialogue. Tags are inserted into blocks of speech, making it easier to keep track of which character is voicing which opinion, as we can see from a comparison of the two versions:

>   —What happened? We were fantastic.
>   —You were fantastic. I loved when you gave the vuelos the e-e-elos. You were the only one who understood.
>   (*YYB*, 200)

>   —What happened?—**she asked**. We were fantastic.
>   —You were fantastic—**I said**. I loved when you gave the heys and the ho's. You were the only one who understood.
>   (*YYB, TO*, 194, EMPHASIS ADDED)

Elsewhere still, statements are changed to questions to make it more obvious that they are eliciting a response, and that the next line of text is not, therefore, uttered by the same speaker. These changes may be subtle, but they are nevertheless important, because they assume a reader less willing to *work* at following the dialogue, one with less patience, who is less willing to be discomfited by unfamiliar forms, and because they impose a degree of certainty where ambiguity previously reigned.

Unqueering *Yo-Yo Boing!*

O'Dwyer's changes help realign the novel with what is considered standard or normative, not only in terms of language but also in terms of characters' gender and sexuality. In this sense O'Dwyer takes the opposite approach to that proposed by scholars of queer translation such as Burton and Lewis:

weakening rather than strengthening the queer elements in the text.[71] This is especially evident in the scene of the protagonist's poetry performance. Importantly, the English of the poems is re-familiarized in O'Dwyer's version, which forces unusual coinages back into codified forms. Word order is standardized, so "stinking my breath / of immortality" (*YYB*, 167) becomes "my breath stinking of immortality" (*YYB*, TO, 162), and the playful blends are edited back to recognizable forms, so "in mutinity–in / mutility–immotivated" (*YYB*, 167) becomes "in mutiny— / in futility—unmotivated" (*YYB*, TO, 162). As I have observed, the poems in the bilingual version are written predominantly in English, despite the protagonist being more comfortable in Spanish, and her nervous cries of "I want my closet back" (*YYB*, 165) before going on stage suggest that, for her, performing in her nondominant language is an exposure akin to coming out as queer. In O'Dwyer's English-only version, readers may still be reminded of the performativity of gender, but the association between non-native writing and queerness is dissolved; the protagonist's nervousness appears to stem only from regular stage fright. O'Dwyer also translates the protagonist's description of herself in this scene—"un niño perdido entre el gentío"—as "a child lost in the crowd" (*YYB*, TO, 161); although in Spanish masculine suffixes are often used in the plural to collectively denote subjects of both male and female gender, the choice to translate the singular "niño" as "child" rather than "boy" here is unusual, and seems designed to remove the gender ambiguity the protagonist shows in the bilingual version, in which she imagines herself as both woman and boy. Moreover, O'Dwyer deletes in its entirety the passage in which the protagonist takes offence at the audience's laughter during her performance, appearing to interpret the label "funny" as a euphemism for "queer" (*YYB*, 173; *YYB*, TO, 167).[72] Like the other edits to Braschi's English, this deletion prevents the suggestion (which provokes such anxiety in the novel's characters) that the protagonist and her language might be queer.

Translation as Self-Commentary

These translational interventions may appear out of sync with Braschi's apparent concern to challenge readers and make them active by pushing against the restrictive categories of language, sexuality, and gender. However, as I have already suggested, I read the "translation" of *Yo-Yo Boing!* as a highly self-aware continuation of the novel itself. In an extract from *Yo-Yo Boing!* published on her personal website, Braschi engages playfully with the tension between the bilingual text's undeniable difficulty and its subsequent reorientation toward comprehensibility and accessibility in O'Dwyer's version. The extract, taken from the bilingual edition, includes illustrations and hyperlinks to resources purporting to explain certain literary, philosophical, and cultural references.[73] It appears to do similar work to O'Dwyer's English-only version—helping to guide readers through the narrative—but is actually tongue-in-cheek. The hyperlinks are reminiscent of the "explanatory" notes belatedly appended to *The Waste Land* when it was published in book form, which perplexed readers intent on engaging in scholarly exegesis of its references and allusions in the belief that the notes offered a key to understanding the poem. Far from offering explanations that will "unlock" the passage's meaning and overcome its fragmentation, the links on Braschi's website lead to resources that are vague and unscholarly, and the images, uncaptioned, do little to aid interpretation. Besides, the resources provided are conspicuously partial. There is an image of Garcilaso de la Vega, but not of the three other writers of the same period mentioned in the same sentence; a link introducing Socrates, but not Alcibiades, the lesser-known figure. As in Díaz's annotated extract from *Oscar Wao* published on the Genius website, here Braschi seems to be toying with readers' desire for clarity and implying the futility of attempting to follow up each of the novel's allusions.[74] In this extract, she anticipates resistance to her novel's inaccessibility but does not apologize for it. Rather, she points to the impossibility and unnecessariness of complete understanding.

The extract also gives us a blueprint for reading O'Dwyer's translation as part of the novel's own ludic self-commentary. This reading is possible because *Yo-Yo Boing!* is largely about the experience of writing (or trying to write) a work like *Yo-Yo Boing!*. It is highly self-aware, continually anticipating readerly resistance to its methods and perspectives in what Mark Currie has called "rhetorical prolepsis."[75] These include its heavy use of dialogue, its lack of explicit political engagement, and especially its bilingualism; one character, for instance, says to the protagonist, "You must realize that you're limiting your audience by writing in both languages" (*YYB*, 162). The novel looks forward to its reception: not just criticism of the kind quoted in the introduction to this chapter, but also translation. Early on in the novel, the protagonist, haltingly producing fragments of writing, demands of her partner, "You should already be translating this work" (*YYB*, 33).

The fictional translation anticipated in *Yo-Yo Boing!* is made manifest in O'Dwyer's real English-only version of it. The novel depicts two translators (like so many other things in this novel, the translator figure is double: a man dominates the early part of "Blow Up" before mostly giving way to "Tess"), both of whom are highly interventionist. The fictional translators are accorded an unusual degree of authority over the protagonist's writing, which they edit and transcribe as well as translate, and both are also authors in their own right. The male translator "transforms" the protagonist's words, as he explains, by "editing your repetition, your mispronunciation" (*YYB*, 122). This of course recalls the way O'Dwyer, in her real translation, standardizes Braschi's hybrid neologisms and orthography. "Tess," for her part, is described as "the power behind the throne" (*YYB*, 197) and is said to be able to guarantee the protagonist's success. This reminds us that it was O'Dwyer's award-winning translation that led to the publication of Braschi's collected poems in English as *Empire of Dreams*, inaugurating the Yale Library of World Literature in Translation.[76] The conventionally hierarchical author-translator relationship is transformed in the novel into one of collaboration between equals (remember, it is the translator who "inspires" the writer by blowing into her anus in the dream), and this reflects the real relationship between Braschi and O'Dwyer, which is, in the latter's own words, "symbiotic."[77] Like the fictional translators, O'Dwyer herself is a published writer, and is undoubtedly *Yo-Yo Boing!*'s editor as well as its translator. If O'Dwyer's translator's note to *Empire of Dreams* is anything to go by ("We collaborated. . . . Together we reinstated lines and poems and rearranged the sequence"), theirs is a relationship of reciprocal influence.[78] Although O'Dwyer may not employ interventionist strategies in the same ways that postcolonial, feminist, and queer translators have done, what her version of *Yo-Yo Boing!* does have in common with those approaches is a view of translation as a creative project in its own right, and of the translator as active and authoritative.

The relationship between the two versions of *Yo-Yo Boing!* involves a kind of metalepsis, whereby the text and its own reception or interpretation (translation) are often inseparable. Neither version of the novel is fixed or self-contained, but includes within itself aspects of the other. There is what

Currie has called, borrowing Derrida's vocabulary, "a relation of supplementarity" between the two.[79] The bilingual version contains within it the mark of what is to come; in other words, although the "translation" does appear, chronologically speaking, after the bilingual version, the former is nevertheless portrayed as being a condition of the latter's very production. The possibility of the translation in some sense "produces" the novel, to which it is said to be a supplement. It is easy to see how characters' anticipation of the novel's reception produces their self-consciousness about language, for instance. Imagining future criticism of her decision to incorporate English into the novel, Braschi writes language anxiety into her dialogues as a form of preemptive self-criticism, and, anticipating the eventual desire for an English translation, even imagines what kind of translation that might be: a collaborative one in which her bilingualism and linguistic infelicities are erased. In turn, O'Dwyer's English-only "translation" responds to characters' anxieties about language, gender, and sexuality by realigning them with standard or normative practice. We can therefore perceive careful irony rather than a lack of sensitivity in the way O'Dwyer's version smooths out some of the characters' linguistic idiosyncrasies, their gender fluidity, and their queer sexualities, recognizing that it responds not only to reviewers who disparage the novel as frustrating and difficult, but also to the novel's own theorizing of translation.

A Queer Textual Relationship?

The inadequacy of the terms "original" and "translation" to describe the relationship between the two versions of *Yo-Yo Boing!* should by now be abundantly clear. Rather than dividing them into these opposing categories, I have instead referred throughout this section to textual "versions" in order to avoid the imposition of a hierarchical relationship between the two. I want to suggest that it is possible to imagine the relationship between those two versions as a queer one, insofar as it seeks to disturb or avoid binary definitions. In so doing, I do not mean to risk evacuating the word "queer" of its meaning by untethering it entirely from questions of sexuality and gender and using it as a stand-in for ambiguity, complexity, or transgressiveness. Rather, the comparison rests on the previously mentioned long-standing historical tradition of sexualizing the original-translation relationship, with the translation being figured as feminine. The most persistent of these tropes is "les belles infidèles," in which translations, like women, are said to be incapable of being both beautiful and faithful.

Translators have in common with women and with homosexuals a history of being articulated through tropes of secondariness or belatedness, and in this sequential organization—heterosexual/homosexual, male/female, and original/translation as first and second, respectively—there is an assumption that chronology is hierarchy. Women have long been constructed as "the second sex," other to the male self and articulated only by, through, and in relation to men; likewise, homosexuality has been considered a secondary and inferior identity position in relation to heterosexuality.[80] In a similar way, translation is conventionally understood to be belated or secondary in relation to a primary original. Despite translation conventionally appearing as "part of literature's second act," in *Born Translated* Rebecca Walkowitz demonstrates how contemporary writers are reversing and subverting that sequence by approaching practices conventionally understood as secondary (translation, but also reading and editing) as sources of production.[81] She gives the name "born translated" to literature that treats translation "as medium and origin rather than as afterthought," and, although she primarily focuses on writing in English that narrates its engagement with other languages rather than actually using them, the term is in many ways applicable to *Yo-Yo Boing!*.[82] Here, translation is simultaneous with writing, playing an integral role in its creativity and innovation.

Yo-Yo Boing! reminds us that this subversion of sequence is a queer move. Just as theorists have found the concept of queer a helpful way of understanding gender and sexual identities that do not fit into the conventional hierarchies of male and female or heterosexual and homosexual, it can also be helpful in understanding these two texts—versions—that defy the usual sequence of textual development and composition, that exist outside of or between the poles of original and translation. Like the language of the bilingual version, which occupies the spaces between English and Spanish, and like its characters, who move between normative gender binaries and the desires conventionally attached to them, the two versions of *Yo-Yo Boing!* occupy a queer space between first and second, original and translation, production and reception. Braschi's queering of language may to a large degree be undone in the English-only version of *Yo-Yo Boing!*, but left in its place is a queering of textual production itself. Not only does the book remind us, in its voracious citation and reshaping of other texts, that all writing is at least partially derivative (as evidenced by the following exchange: "That's not your thought, it was Mona's and before it was Mona's it was Hannah Arendt's.... Mona took it from Hannah Arendt, and Arendt took it from Borges" [*YYB*, 89–90]), thus undermining the idea of the "original," but it also claims to be the product of equal, generative—we might say "same-sex" or "androgynous"—collaboration rather than to exist in hierarchical relationship with a secondary, derivative—historically imagined as "feminine"—translation. Even the physical appearance of the two versions underscores this point: in their AmazonCrossing editions they are virtually indistinguishable, with the same title and the same jacket design; only a small gold circle on the front cover that reads "English translation by Tess O'Dwyer" distinguishes one from the other.

Studying the versions of *Yo-Yo Boing!* together reveals that, while translation is not an uncomplicated cure for the difficulty of bilingualism—it results in crucial changes not only to style but also to perspective—neither does it necessarily deaden creativity, as Sommer and Vega-Merino claim in their introduction to the 1998 edition; as is clear from the introduction's title, "Choose and Lose," which is the same as that of the first chapter of Sommer's *Bilingual Aesthetics*, they argue that multilingualism is quashed at the expense of complexity, richness, and creativity.[83] The English-only version of *Yo-Yo Boing!* shows that this is not the case. The two versions of the novel are in conversation in precisely complex, rich, and creative ways. Taken together, the different textual manifestations of *Yo-Yo Boing!* accommodate a degree of ambiguity that allows fictional subjects to escape simplified taxonomies: to intermittently hide and reveal their sexualities, to express shifting views on language practice, and to be ambivalent about different forms of artistic collaboration. They playfully queer and unqueer their own language use and creative processes, successfully resisting attempts to make either of them "signify monolithically."

Chapter Four

FLUID TRAJECTORIES IN TWO VERSIONS OF WILSON BUENO'S *MAR PARAGUAYO*

In an editorial note to one of the first editions of the Brazilian journal *Nicolau*, its founding editor, Wilson Bueno, describes the journal's aims: to transcend all geographical, cultural, political, and artistic boundaries, dedicating itself to the "múltiplos estratos imigrantes que, ao longo dos anos, moldaram a nossa cara e o nosso caráter" (the multiple layers of immigrants who, over the years, have shaped our [Brazil's] face and our character).[1] This is an apt summary of the concerns of Bueno's oeuvre, which is permeated by hybridity and movement, and of his book *Mar Paraguayo*, fragments of which first appeared in *Nicolau* in December 1978.[2] Bueno was a writer, journalist, and editor from the state of Paraná in Brazil, born in 1949 and sadly murdered in 2010. *Mar Paraguayo*, which will be the main subject of this final chapter, was by far his most successful work, gaining him both national and international recognition after it was published in 1992.[3] The focus of this book thus begins to broaden, turning away from the various "Spanglishes" of United States–based writers toward a more hemispheric view of American literary multilingualism.

Somewhere between short fiction and prose poetry in terms of genre, *Mar Paraguayo* is a confessional narrative spoken by a woman (apparently) from rural Paraguay, who moved to the capital, Asunción, and later to Guaratuba, a Brazilian coastal town often referred to as the Paraguayan Sea because so many middle-class Paraguayans flock there for their summer holidays. In Asunción, she met the "viejo," an old man who encouraged her into prostitution, and to whom she remained tightly bound in a sexual relationship that was sometimes pleasurable, sometimes not, until his recent death, possibly at her own hands. The principal aim of her narrative seems to be to convince readers or listeners of her innocence.

This speaker has fluid national, cultural, linguistic, and gender identity. She is Paraguayan but lives in Brazil, and expresses herself in a mixture of three languages: Spanish, Portuguese, and Guarani, the three main languages of the border region between those two countries. Although she is coded female, at times she appears not to be a woman but rather a gay man adopting female pronouns, someone who is sexually attracted both to conventionally masculine and to more feminine physical attributes. She calls herself a "marafona," a word that can refer to a type of rag doll with no facial features, to a transvestite, and, more commonly, to a prostitute. She thus characterizes herself as a trickster, a performer, and an enigma: a blank space waiting to be filled in. The first part of this chapter will draw connections between Bueno's work and that of the three writers previously addressed in this book, demonstrating that, as in those works of "Spanglish" literature, translational strategies are embedded in Bueno's multilingualism in ways that emphasize his work's openness to further reinscription. Exploring his work's connections to the neobaroque and concrete movements, I demonstrate that his multilingual prose lends itself easily to other kinds of textual and conceptual fluidity.

Although Bueno's other writing has been translated into Spanish, English, and French, and published in Argentina, Chile, Mexico, the United States, and Canada, *Mar Paraguayo* remained untouched by translators for many years, until Canadian poet and translator Erín Moure's *Paraguayan Sea* was published in 2017.[4] The second part of this chapter will position *Paraguayan Sea* in the context of Moure's previous work and examine the creative ways in which it responds to, extends, and complements Bueno's *Mar Paraguayo*. I demonstrate the extent to which this 2018 Best Translated Book Award longlisted translation is multilingual, playful, and challenging to readers, opening up Bueno's writing to new geographies while posing as many questions as it answers.

The main thrust of my argument in this book—namely, that multilingualism and translation are closely intertwined creative strategies through which other forms of textual and conceptual hybridity are explored—is borne out extensively in both *Mar Paraguayo* and *Paraguayan Sea*. Both versions of the book are expressed in a hybrid mixture of languages, and both versions disrupt conventional understandings of nationality, culture, genre, gender, and sexuality. The importance of taxonomical fluidity is signaled in their titles: the sea, and water more broadly, is one of their major recurring themes, and is important in articulating their various border crossings. The phrase "mar Paraguayo" or "Paraguayan sea" is of course a contradiction in terms, given that Paraguay has never possessed a sea coast. Instead, its "coast" is formed, to the south, by the powerful Paraná river, a fluid border with both Argentina and Brazil that acts as Paraguay's route to the sea. The word "mar," which already straddles a linguistic border because it can be read in both Spanish and Portuguese, is frequently employed by Bueno to convey enormity, incoherence, or the erasure of boundaries. Moreover, a large part of the marafona's characterization is achieved via identification with the sea: "Mi mar? Mi mar soy yo. Ĩyá" (My sea? I am my sea. Ĩyá), she tells us (*MP*, 77). She is Ĩyá, a Guarani aquatic god or water spirit, as well as the sea itself, in all its enormity and fluidity. The sea is hers, but it is also *her*—flowing and nebulous, in linguistic, cultural, but also sexual and gender terms. The infinite fluidity implied in this identification reminds us of the shifting, unfixed, unfinishable nature of multilingual writing, and its openness, as this chapter will show, to reinscription in different versions.

PART I: BORDER CROSSINGS IN *MAR PARAGUAYO*

Linguistic Fluidity

In the introduction to this volume, I discussed Douglas Diegues's idea of a capacious, democratic, border-crossing literary language he calls "portunhol selvagem," described as

> uma língua mestiça, híbrida, nascida espontaneamente do convívio entre falantes do português e do espanhol, que não se deixa domar por regras gramaticais nem se limita a um léxico estruturado. Caracteriza-se pela oscilação entre o português e o espanhol, mantendo-se permanentemente aberta, sem estruturar-se segundo um código previamente estabelecido. Não se pretende uma língua à parte e se reinventa a cada dia[5]

(a mixed, hybrid language, born spontaneously from the cohabitation of Portuguese and Spanish speakers, one that is not governed by grammatical rules or limited by a structured vocabulary. It is characterized by the oscillation between Portuguese and Spanish, remaining permanently open, without being structured according to a previously established code. It does not pretend to be a language apart, and reinvents itself every day).

In its emphasis on spontaneity and constant change, and its disregard for standardized grammar, this description suggests "portunhol selvagem" has much in common with the language used by Chávez-Silverman, Díaz, and Braschi, particularly the "creolized English" of Díaz's *Oscar Wao*, discussed in chapter 2. Diegues continues to hold up Bueno's work as foundational in the development of "portunhol selvagem"; indeed, it is easy to see how the above description can be applied to *Mar Paraguayo*, whose use of language is similarly unruly and unsystematic, borrowing occasional words from Italian, French, and English, in addition to its three main languages. Bueno doesn't follow the grammar or syntax of any language consistently; in his own words, "a língua não tenha nenhuma lei" (the language [of the book] has no law).[6] In the novel's very first paragraph, readers are told to expect "vertigem de linguagem," a feeling of vertigo or dizziness with regard to language. Bueno's novel is not set on the "triple frontera," but rather in Guaratuba, Brazil, and yet it can be understood—and is obviously understood by Diegues—as a representation of the meeting of cultures and languages in that part of the world.

The novel's first sentence (the opening line of the preface, "Notícia"), which functions as a metatextual and metalinguistic warning, gives us a sense of how Bueno's language operates: "Un aviso: el guarani es tan essencial en nesto relato quanto el vuelo del párraro, lo cisco en la ventana, los arrulhos del português ô los derramados nerudas en cascata num solo só suicidio de palabras anchas" (A warning: Guarani is as essential to this tale as the flight of the bird, the speck of dust on the window, the cooing of Portuguese or the cascade of spilt nerudas in a single lonely suicide of wide words) (*MP*, 17). We can see that languages are as closely combined here as they are in Chávez-Silverman's crónicas, but the greater typological proximity of Bueno's Spanish and Portuguese (in comparison to her English and Spanish) means that here it is often more difficult to identify which language is being used at any given moment. For instance, some words here are clearly Portuguese, identifiable by their spelling or use of diacritics: *guaraní, essencial, quanto, cisco, arrulhos, português, cascata, num, só, suicídio, outra*. About the same number are clearly Spanish: *un, el, es, tan, vuelo, del, lo, en, ventana, solo, palabras, anchas, una, error*. But a handful could be read in either language: *aviso, relato, derramados, nerudas* (this last word, referring to Pablo Neruda, functions as synecdoche for the Spanish language). And that still leaves us with three words: *nesto, párraro*, and *dela*, which belong to neither Spanish nor Portuguese, but are nevertheless comprehensible to readers of either language. This pattern is typical of the rest of the novel, where alongside "standard" words in Spanish and Portuguese we also find creative hybrids like "esquierda" (between "izquierda" and "esquerda"), "ferviendo" (in-between "hirviendo" and "fervendo"), and "morcielago" (in-between "murciélago" and "morcego").

In addition to these hybrid coinages, Bueno frequently translates between each of his three languages in the body of the narrative. We can see this in the following sentences, in which the marafona is describing the inevitability of solitude, and of old age, which for her represent a kind of hell: "Uno se va, criolo vagabundo de los caminhos, rufión ô gigolô, e acá se pone de nuevo, de nuevo, de novo el infierno. Añareta" (You go, creole vagabond from the streets, ruffian or gigolo, and here hell shows up again, again, again. Hell) (*MP*, 25). Translation does not function here in order to explicate or explain, as it often does in less committedly multilingual writing. Knowledge of both Spanish and Portuguese is assumed by the writer. Instead, translation is employed as a key strategy to achieve emphasis and rhythm. We encounter the phrase "de nuervo," which belongs to none of Bueno's languages but recalls the anxious energy of the word "nerve" ("nervo," "nervio"), before it is translated into Spanish ("de nuevo") and Portuguese ("de novo"), both meaning "again." Intratextual translations such as these contribute to the novel's rhythmic, repetitive style. Bueno then translates the word "hell" from Spanish ("infierno") into Guarani ("añareta").

Unlike with Portuguese and Spanish, knowledge of Guarani is not assumed by the writer, who provides an "elucidário" (from "elucidar," to elucidate), a glossary, which, in the original Iluminuras edition, offers translations of Guarani words into Portuguese.[7] Guarani words often appear, as they do in the passage quoted above, at the ends of sentences and paragraphs, translating a key idea or word from the preceding lines and acting as a sort of summary. This reiterates the claim made in the opening line of the novel that Guarani is crucial to the book's composition, and just as important as the much more frequently used Portuguese and Spanish. Guarani is an official language of Paraguay, where it is spoken by the majority of the population. It is also spoken, to a much lesser extent, in parts of Brazil, Argentina, and Bolivia. First codified and written by Jesuit priests in the early to mid-seventeenth century, it remains one of the most widely spoken languages in the Americas, with just over six million speakers.[8] It is also the only indigenous American language whose speakers include a large proportion of nonindigenous people. Yet, despite being so widely used in Paraguay, it only achieved official-language status alongside Spanish in 1992, the same year that *Mar Paraguayo* was first published, and it remains associated with poor education and a humble existence. Indeed, Guarani is what is considered to be "selvagem"—savage, rough, uncivilized—about Diegues's "portunhol selvagem." Bueno's protagonist associates it with "ñemomirĩ. Ñemomirĩhá"—"humility. Humiliation" (*MP*, 23).

Nevertheless, Bueno claims that it is equally as important in *Mar Paraguayo* as Spanish ("los derramados nerudas" [the spilt nerudas]) and Portuguese, which, quantitatively speaking, make up a much greater part of the text. Despite its relatively infrequent appearance, Guarani's highly inflected, agglutinative structure is used effectively by Bueno to build rhythm and repetition into his prose. Extra morphemes are added to root words in order to modify their meaning, as above with "ñemomirĩ. Ñemomirĩhá" or the oft-used "añareta. Añaretameguá" ("Hell. Hellish"). This allows Bueno to be playful and punning; patterns of sound and meaning are easy to create by adding extra syllables.

Guarani functions in a very different way to Portuguese and Spanish in *Mar Paraguayo*. It does not form part of the narrative's syntax, but rather contributes key vocabulary, expressing the novel's most important ideas. A quick glance through the glossary confirms that all the novel's key themes are articulated through Guarani words: animals, water, the sea, language, mortality, the divine. It also retains a crucial defamiliarizing function; as it is a less widely spoken language on a regional and global level than Portuguese and Spanish, more readers are likely to find Guarani words strange and empty of signification. Its presence demonstrates Bueno's refusal to allow the Indigenous aspects of Brazilian and Paraguayan culture to be eclipsed by those deriving from Europe, as well as his commitment to unsettling his readers and making them work actively to understand the narrative.

Nevertheless, the inclusion of a glossary is an acknowledgment that this language has many fewer speakers globally than either Portuguese or Spanish, and that, being typologically very distinct from those two closely related European languages, it would be difficult for speakers with no familiarity with it to glean any meaning from Guarani words. The use of Guarani in *Mar Paraguayo* is therefore in tension: on the one hand, it contributes to many readers' experience of defamiliarization; on the other hand, if Guarani expresses many of the narrative's most important themes, readers need to be able to understand them, and the glossary provides the necessary entry point—a countermovement of familiarization. It is a sign that, while *Mar Paraguayo* is meant to be difficult, it is not meant to be impenetrable.

The glossary also demonstrates the degree to which Bueno engages with rather than rejects translation. In chapter 2, I showed that translation can function as a form of elucidation, explanation, or even uncensoring, opening up parts of the text that were opaque in the source. We see this function of translation in Bueno's glossary, too, in the way it helps mitigate reader incomprehension. The author goes as far as to explain aspects of Guarani grammar and its implications for the book's content; included alongside a glossary entry for an extremely long Guarani word is the following note:

> *Obs.*: tamanha aglutinação de sufixos diminutivos acoplados ao nome próprio, Brinks, realiza em guarani o que só pode ser visto através de um microscópio, tornando a coisa diminuída, algo (quase) invisível; na sugestão do texto, o que não se pode ver ou o que efetivamente, no caso, *não existe*[9]

> (NOTE: The endless agglutination of diminutive suffixes coupled to a name, Brinks, creates in Guarani something so miniscule that it can only be seen through a microscope. It's been turned into something so tiny, almost invisible, that the very text suggests it's something that can't be seen or that, effectively, in this case, *does not exist*).
> (PS, 72)

The note refers to the name of the narrator's dog, which she calls Brinks, Brinks'i, Brinks'imi, Brinks'michĩ, Brinks'michĩmi, Brinks'michĩmíra'ymi, and finally Brinks'michīmíra'ytotekemi, with each diminutive suffix reducing the dog in size. This aspect of Guarani—its ability to create words whose increasing length on the page denote decreasing size—is one that readers who do not speak the language are unlikely to appreciate without this authorial note. The inclusion of the glossary means, as Bueno has said in an interview, that "any high school student can decipher [the book's] weft, even if it holds keys, 'traps,' and 'citations' that only obsessive readers manage to grasp."[10] This is a readable text, but one that encourages active research from its readers.

The glossary is evidence of the degree to which Bueno encourages readers to appreciate translation as a creative process. His renderings of Guarani words highlight the extent to which translations are multiple and shifting, also open to rewriting; they are multiple rather than singular, offering a series of synonyms or definitions rather than just one. For instance, the word "ne'ẽ" is translated as "palabra; vocáblo; língua; idioma; voz; comunicação, comunicar-se; falar; conversar."[11] Here we have a perfect demonstration of translation as multiple, moving, and layered; readers will recall Barbara Cassin's definition of "untranslatability" not as that which cannot be translated but as that which one continues endlessly to translate, as that which is "unable to finish being translated".[12] "To speak of untranslatables in no way implies that the terms in question, or the expressions, the syntactical or grammatical turns, are not and cannot be translated: the untranslatable is rather what one keeps on (not) translating."[13] Bueno thus draws attention to what translation cannot immediately or succinctly convey, and encourages readers to be critical of and alert to translational processes at work elsewhere in the book.

If we are to examine the linguistic heterogeneity of *Mar Paraguayo*, it is important to understand the ways Bueno's writing is in conversation with the concrete movement, especially the work of the Brazilian Noigandres poets. We have already seen the continuities between Díaz's work and other more self-consciously "writerly" authors, including the concrete poet Vagn Steen. The connections between Bueno and the concrete movement are stronger still. It was a diffuse movement, with strands developing simultaneously in Europe and Latin America, but it had a strong foothold in Brazil, where three poets from São Paulo—Décio Pignatari and the brothers Haroldo and Augusto de Campos—founded the magazine *Noigandres* and first coined the term "concrete poetry." The movement was united in treating language as raw visual or auditive material in order to create a "tensão de palavras-coisas no espaço-tempo" (tension of thing-words in space-time), as Augusto de Campo put it.[14] Aural and visual or typographical effects were often as important as, or even more important than, semantics.

Bueno himself drew attention to the shared trajectory between his work and that of the de Campos brothers and the wider concrete movement via an interest in the linguistic multiplicity of James Joyce's *Finnegans Wake*. I have mentioned in previous chapters linguistic multiplicity's centrality to modernist forms of defamiliarization in that it allowed writers to reflect and challenge notions of national and linguistic rootedness. For the Noigandres poets, Joyce's famously multilingual novel was fundamental to the development of their work, its linguistic creativity providing a stimulus for their own poetical experiments. According to Augusto de Campos, the very idea of concrete poetry grew out of a term from *Finnegans Wake*: "verbivocovisual poetry," which the Noigandres poets interpreted as a "radical form of poetry that emphasizes the materiality of the word—both its visual and sound dimensions, related to its meaning."[15] In an essay titled "Fronteiras: Nos entrecéus da linguagem," Bueno too makes a clear connection between his own work and Joyce's novel when he says, "O guarani é um elemento autóctone no possível 'pan*a*roma' de *Mar Paraguayo*" (Guarani is the autochthonous element in the possible "pan*a*roma" of *Mar Paraguayo*).[16] In *Finnegans Wake*, Joyce refers to the "panaroma of all flores of speech," a playful, synaesthetic image that describes linguistic variety as an olfactory feast—an aromatic panorama.[17] Bueno's use of the word not only draws attention to the rich linguistic variety of *Mar Paraguayo*, it also makes a firm connection between his own work, Joyce's, and that of the concrete poets—who borrowed the term "panaroma" for a book of their own, *Panaroma de Finnegans Wake*, a collection of Portuguese translations and "transcreations" of fragments from Joyce's novel, accompanied by interpretive notes.

Multilingualism was an important way in which the concrete poets achieved a radical disassociation between sound and sense. In poems like Augusto de Campos's "Lygia fingers," from his 1953 collection *Poetamenos*, they found sonic resonances across different linguistic systems. "Lygia fingers" contains words in Portuguese, English, Italian, German, and Latin, cut up into sections or syllables in different colors, and juxtaposed with other fragments of words such that they offer multiple ways of reading.[18]

The extreme defamiliarization resulting from reading a poem with this many languages has the effect of encouraging readers to pay attention to sound and visual elements instead of sense. A poem such as this might be described, in his brother Haroldo de Campos's terms, an "open work of art": a porous and mobile work that invites readers to take an active and creative role in its completion.[19]

As a multilingual text, *Mar Paraguayo* is in obvious conversation with this kind of poetry, but we find particularly strong echoes of the concrete poets' strategies in certain passages. One such passage is this long paragraph that begins a new section in medias res, and which showcases Bueno's extraordinarily inventive cross-lingual playfulness with sound: "Como um juego de jugar: pimpirrota, piribela floral, loculho sierva, cincinati, abrolhos, carmencinda, madressilva, pirilampos, antanas bástitas, casamarilha, locos complutos, boludo lorgo, lacalheseda, amarelinhas, esconde-atrás, noclins ereiras, marcha adelante, los cantantes jugos de ruedas, teresinas-de-jesus, las teresinas, entrançada gaucha, guapa glauchas, catatéicos, constreros, filíciquis, rosaes, oscuro mistério de fábula original, las tranças, las troupas, helicáreos rans, duncans, vitrinas, duendes, vagaus, pilvos conscentes, broquílides silfos, lunfens de lérias, lunfens vivaces, como un juego-de-jugar" (*MP*, 29). Here we have a colorful list of semi-sensical hybrid words that seem to denote comically distorted children's games, nicknames, plants, flowers, places, ailments, and more, playfully linked together according to sonic and rhythmic patterns rather than semantic connection or any established grammar. Like the concrete poets, here Bueno concentrates on the material from which text is made: language. In passages like these, *Mar Paraguayo* is not so much "an instrumental text"; it is "not about declarative prose," as Erín Moure puts it, but rather, to a large extent, about language itself.[20] Bueno offers a bare linguistic framework that acts as a kind of mental play area for the reader, inviting them to use their poetic imagination—like readers of Junot Díaz's fiction—to fill in the blanks, navigating their way between Portuguese and Spanish to tease out the multiple nuances of each word. It is an "open work of art," in Haroldo de Campos's terms, a fact of which the marafona herself reminds us: "Los confidencio, a vos, lectores inventivos, más invenctivos que la invención de mi alma cautiva" (I confide in you, inventive readers, more invenctive than the invention of my captive soul) (*MP*, 27; my spelling of "invenctive" echoes Bueno's "invenctivo").

At other moments in *Mar Paraguayo*, the text's appearance recalls concrete poetry's determination to fuse text and image, and to exploit the visual as well as semantic and phonetic elements of language. In a long section in which the marafona is embroidering traditional Paraguayan lace called ñanduti, Bueno uses colons to visually reproduce the needle's repeated entry and exit points on the cloth: "nudo: trança: laçada: lançada: nudo: trança" (*MP*, 50) (knot: twist: loop: loop: knot: twist) (*PS*, 40). Although *Mar Paraguayo* is ostensibly a prose work, written in long paragraphs that take up multiple pages, in instances like these it comes closer to resembling poetry, as the marafona's narrative is broken down by the colons into short statements, forcing the reader to pause in much the same way as would division into poetic lines.

The concrete poets always extolled the practice of translation, which was often incorporated into their writing. For instance, "surface translations" were an important way in which they aimed to create "thing-words in space time," separating the visual and acoustic properties of words from their meaning. Also referred to as "homophonic translation," this strategy involves rendering the sounds of a poem into another language, using whichever words create the nearest approximation to the poem's sounds, regardless of their meaning. This famous surface translation of a nursery rhyme is illustrative:

Un petit d'un petit	Humpty Dumpty
S'étonne aux Halles	Sat on a wall
Un petit d'un petit	Humpty Dumpty
Ah! degrés te fallent	Had a great fall
Indolent qui ne sort cesse	All the King's horses
Indolent qui ne se mène	And all the King's men
Qu'importe un petit d'un petit	Couldn't put Humpty
Tout Gai de Reguennes.	Together again.[21]

In this example, the "translator" has largely ignored the semantics of the nursery rhyme, leaving it up to the reader to exercise their imagination and make sense of the "translated" text in whatever way they can; the meaning of the French version bears little resemblance to the English.

This is an extreme example of a strategy that Bueno approximates at certain moments in *Mar Paraguayo*. If we take, for example, the word "párraro," which appears in the book's first line, we can see how Bueno excels at making words written in one language reflect the oral life of another language. In this instance, in order to understand the skill at work, we need to know that the Portuguese word for "bird" is "pássaro," while the Spanish word is "pájaro." By spelling the word "párraro," Bueno has taken advantage of the frequent Brazilian pronunciation of the grapheme /rr/ as a voiceless velar fricative [x]. Brazilian Portuguese speakers are likely to pronounce "párraro" as /ˈpaxaɾo/, which sounds like the Spanish word for bird, "pájaro." A Spanish word is thus hidden in an estranged spelling, available only, ironically, to speakers of Portuguese. Take another example: the word "jenas." Its spelling reflects the porteño pronunciation of the grapheme /ll/ in the Mar de Plata region of Argentina, because it is written in such a way that only Portuguese speakers, for whom /j/ is [ʒ], will pronounce the word how it sounds in that variety of Spanish: "llenas" [ʒenas]. In short, Bueno transcribes words according to the rules of Portuguese in order to represent the phonetics of Spanish, much as concrete poets were doing in their "surface translations." The effect is to remind readers of the marafona's foreignness in Guaratuba, to intermittently include and exclude different readers at different moments in the narrative, and to playfully explore the particularities of different linguistic varieties in ways that are highly reminiscent, for instance, of the oral register of Chávez-Silverman's crónicas.[22] Moreover, it has the effect of lengthening perception, forcing even confident bilingual readers to read slowly and attentively before they can interpret, thus "deautomatizing" our reading processes.[23]

As in the work of the other writers addressed in this book, translational strategies are already implied in Bueno's multilingualism, which has the effect of keeping readers active and making them accustomed to experiencing a degree of partial incomprehension. However, as in the work of Chávez-Silverman, Díaz, and Braschi, this linguistic fluidity is accompanied by other forms of in-betweenness, hybridity, and movement, including, as the next section will show, gender and sexual fluidity.

Gender and Sexual Fluidity in *Mar Paraguayo*

The marafona's gender remains unknown in the preface, "Notícia," but as soon as the main part of the novel—"Ne'e"—begins, we have a statement of identity: "Yo soy la marafona del balneário" (I am the marafona of the beach resort) (*MP*, 19). While this seems at first glance an unambiguous statement of female gender identity—"marafona" is a feminine word and is preceded by a feminine pronoun—it turns out to not be so simple. Although most of the speaker's self-referential pronouns are feminine, there are clues in the text that the marafona might be understood to be a transvestite or a gay man adopting female pronouns.

The word "marafona" can mean a prostitute (in its etymology, it refers to a deceitful woman, a trickster), but it can also refer to a man who dresses up as a woman at carnival time. We know that the speaker is a performer who covers herself in "rouge y batom" (blush and lipstick) (*MP*, 30) and wears a "ráfia peruca" (raffia wig) (*MP*, 44), and her constant preoccupation with ageing and appearances suggests a taste for costume and performance. Elsewhere she describes herself as a "mariposa," a butterfly: the symbol of metamorphosis, transformation, and transgender pride.

As well as her gender, the speaker's sexuality is also changeable. She expresses sexual desire for multiple men (although their gender too is sometimes fluid) as well as a woman. At numerous moments in the narrative, the Brazilian actress, model, and international celebrity Sônia Braga emerges as a figure of sexual desire for the narrator as the marafona watches her in a telenovela ("sus ancas que me ponen en arrepios toda la vez que aparecen en el video como se fuera la derradera disposición de una vida" [her buttocks give me goosebumps whenever she appears on screen, as though she's the ultimate aim of a life] [*MP*, 21]), and she begins to dream of her "más y más" (more and more) (*MP*, 22). Meanwhile the main narrative describes the marafona's sexual relationships with two men: an old man whose presence she resented but whom she ultimately mourns, and a youth with whom she has a steamy affair (or at least appears to, as there is a suggestion that the affair is largely imagined). Although her relationship with the old man was a professional one—she was bound to him through a form of sex work—he nevertheless brought her a degree of sexual pleasure, and she remembers him for his "língua sútil a explotar-me con gusto, gozo, y orgasmo" (subtle tongue exploiting/exploding me with enjoyment, pleasure, and orgasm) (*MP*, 22).

In particular, the marafona's intense sexual relationship with the young boy is repeatedly characterized as queer. The way she describes their coupling places her sometimes in the role of a man: "Soy la que enrraba los menores de diecisiete años, señora!, soy yo, soy yo, la marafona de Guaratuba" (I'm the one who bums boys under the age of seventeen, señora! It's me, it's me, the marafona of Guaratuba) (*MP*, 64). Here she positions herself as an older man taking advantage of a minor, given that the verb "enrabar" refers to the act of anal penetration. Moreover, sometimes she seems attracted to the boy for his conventionally masculine strength—his "duros muslos cavalo—la fuerza inventada del hombre en sus ombros" (hard stallion muscles—the invented strength of man in his shoulders) (*MP*, 17)—and at other times for his androgynous beauty: he is a "muchacho de buço" (boy with a downy upper lip) (*MP*, 33) with "agilidad felina" (feline agility) (*MP*, 64) who wears a "tanga" (thong/G-string) (*MP*, 60) and rides a bicycle "con los colores del arco-iris" (in the colors of the rainbow) (*MP*, 59). The reference to "su gusto de concha y sal" (his taste of conch shell/cunt and salt) (*MP*, 52) is ambiguous—he tastes of the sea, but also, euphemistically, of female genitalia, though it is unclear whose.

Both the marafona and the young boy are associated with the sea in ways that underscore the fluidity of their desires and gender identifications. Each is depicted walking proudly into the water; first the boy, "el que imponente marcha: dirección del mar" (he who marches magnificently: towards the sea) (*MP*, 52), after they have sex, and later the marafona, who, having lost hope of his return, describes herself walking drunk, naked, into the sea, under a leaden sky that augurs a storm. In this scene and elsewhere, water is linked repeatedly with sex and desire—swimming is depicted as an almost orgasmic experience as the marafona weeps for the boy and his desired body. The boy is described as "aquel otro mar—el niño" (that other sea—the boy) (*MP*, 69), who tastes of salt, and whose cobra blue-green eyes look like "el propio abismo en el mar" (the sea's own abyss) (*MP*, 31).

The boy's eyes, his "dos ojos verdes, mboihovi" (two green eyes, mboihovi) (*MP*, 31), are an important way in which his genderqueerness is highlighted. In Guarani, the word "mboihovi" refers to the blue-green color of a cobra; as Erín Moure puts it, it is "really a bluish green or greenish blue, in European culture" (*PS*, 73). The boy's repeated association with cobras and serpents more generally ("sus muslos y músculos, su verde en los ojos, la serpiente, la serpiente, la serpiente" [his thighs and muscles, the green in his eyes, the snake, the snake, the snake] [*MP*, 70]) might seem simply to underscore his virility, the snake's length recalling as it does the male sexual organ. However, as Florentino has demonstrated, serpents, including the Ouroboros—an ancient image of a serpent or dragon biting its own tail—appear frequently in Bueno's work in association with movement, continuity, infinitude, and gender ambiguity.[24] In his later collection *Jardim zoológico* (1999), for instance, there appears a story about the yarará, a species of pit snake endemic to southern Brazil, Paraguay, and northern Argentina that transitions repeatedly between male and female. His connection to snakes therefore suggests that the boy is not uncomplicatedly masculine. Animals, and, more specifically, the boundaries between humans and nonhumans, become a greater preoccupation in Bueno's later work; he went on to publish four bestiaries: *Manual de Zoofilia* (1991), *Jardim Zoológico* (1999), *Cachorros de Céu* (2005), and *Os chuvosos* (2007), but animals both real and imaginary appear in *Mar Paraguayo*, too. The narrative is populated with birds, snakes, spiders, dogs, scorpions, and insects, as well as hybrid creatures, part human, part nonhuman, such as the siren (half bird, half woman). The marafona herself identifies as a sphinx (*MP*, 51), a famously hybrid, deceitful, and potentially dangerous mythological creature with the head of a human and the body of a lion. We saw in chapter 2 how Giannina Braschi associates her literary creativity with animals, particularly hybrid ones. There, writing bilingually is depicted as a transgression of the supposedly "natural" divide between species, which is analogous to a transgression of the "natural" boundary between genders and the desires they are expected to feel. In Bueno's book too, human and nonhuman animals identify with one another, seeming to slip out of their categorical distinctions and biological determinations in ways that mirror how the prose slips out of one language and into the next, and how the "marafona" and her lovers slip in and out of conventional gender definitions.

Cultural Hybridity in *Mar Paraguayo*

Mar Paraguayo's linguistic, genre, and gender fluidity is accompanied by a diverse mixture of cultural reference points. In addition to his self-conscious connections to the concrete movement, Bueno is writing in the tradition of the neobaroque—the twentieth-century resuscitation of the baroque by writers and theorists in the Americas.[25] The term is generally said to have been coined by the Cuban writer Severo Sarduy, whose 1972 essay "El barroco y el neobarroco" ("The Baroque and the Neobaroque") describes this style of writing as being characterized by extreme artifice, linguistic dynamism, heterogeneity, excess, and transgression.[26] In many ways it involves an aesthetics of recycling—Sarduy points out that processes of mixing and borrowing, especially quotation and "reminiscence" ("in which the foreign text melds indistinguishably with the original"), are essential to the neobaroque style—allowing writers to say something new by remaking old forms.[27] In contrast with the historical baroque movement, which was often synonymous with political conservatism, the neobaroque has been appropriated and reformulated for anti-colonial purposes, often displaying a complex interplay of European and Indigenous elements. As Monica Kaup has argued, the neobaroque "refuses to regard culture as a fixed, 'self-contained system,' the property of discrete, segregated social groups. Rather, the baroque is an 'antiproprietary' expression that brings together seemingly disparate writers and artists."[28]

For Haroldo de Campos, the baroque and neobaroque were central instruments of the Brazilian anti-colonial tradition of anthropophagy.[29] The "movimento antropófago" or cannibalist movement was initiated by Oswald de Andrade in his "Manifesto Antropófago" ("Cannibalist Manifesto"), published in 1928, which became a central text of Brazilian modernism and anti-colonial primitivism.[30] Written in poetic, telegraphic prose, the manifesto uses the idea of cannibalism in order to subvert the European perception of Indigenous Americans as savage and primitive. It draws on Montaigne's essay "Des cannibales" ("On the Cannibals"), in which he argued that the ritual cannibalism of the Indigenous Brazilian Tupi people was far less barbaric than many "civilized" European customs, in order to suggest that Brazil's ability to "cannibalize" other cultures is actually its greatest strength, and central to its national identity.[31] Through this metaphor, Andrade aimed to reverse the perception that there was a one-directional flow of artistic influence between Brazil and Europe, figuring cannibalism as a process by which other cultures are chewed and digested in order to be transformed into something new. He describes European colonizers, for instance, as "fugitives from a civilization we are eating, because we are strong and vindictive like the Jabuti"—the jabuti being a tortoise from northern Brazil, known in local culture as an astute trickster figure.[32] Perhaps the most oft-cited example of this "cannibalist" style, in which elements of European cultures are transformed via Indigenous ones, is the phrase (originally written in English) "Tupy or not Tupy, that is the question," in which Andrade transforms the famous line from Shakespeare's *Hamlet* into a reference to the Tupi people.[33]

"Anthropophagous reason," according to Haroldo de Campos, refers to the "critical devouring of universal cultural heritage as a way of becoming authentically Brazilian and American"; but it also conveys our global contemporary condition: "To write, today, in both Europe and Latin America will mean, more and more, to rewrite, to rechew."[34] The aesthetics of recycling and reprocessing that is central to neobaroque writing is, in the cannibalist movement, understood via a metaphor of digestion. The foreign is deconstructed via the processes of chewing and swallowing, giving rise to interchange and new relationships. In "The Rule of Anthropophagy: Europe Under the Sign of Devoration," Haroldo de Campos describes anthropophagy as a process involving "appropriation and expropriation, dehierarchization, deconstruction ... all suggestions, after being broken down and mixed, are prepared for a new remastication, a complicated chemistry in which it is no longer possible to distinguish the assimilating organism from the assimilated material."[35] It is easy to identify aspects of neobaroque and anthropophagous thinking in Bueno's writing, with its linguistic pyrotechnics and its references to cultural production from across Europe and the Americas, including Indigenous cultures. Bueno cites (explicitly or implicitly) literary figures from across Latin America (Adélia Prado, Gabriel García Márquez, Pablo Neruda) and Europe (Gertrude Stein, Rainer Maria Rilke, Stéphane Mallarmé, Federico García Lorca), combining these at every turn with references to popular culture (the Brazilian model and actress Sônia Braga, the famous bolero "Quizás, quizás, quizás," or the Cuban rumba "Corazón de melon"), moving fluidly between what are conventionally understood as "high" and "low" culture in much the same way as the other writers addressed in this book. As the author himself said of *Mar Paraguayo* in an interview, "It's all in there—from Greek mythology to Yoruban Candomblé animism, from hillbilly dress-up to soap-operative guesses, from Verlaine to Baudelaire, with the Brazilian Parnassian poets and 'pulp literature' thrown in" (*PS*, 96). One work with which Bueno's writing has a particularly obvious engagement is Mario de Andrade's *Macunaíma*, the foundational text of Brazilian modernism first published in 1928, whose shapeshifting protagonist, representation of multicultural

Brazil, and play with different linguistic varieties give it obvious parallels with *Mar Paraguayo*. The protagonist, Macunaíma, is described in the title of the book as "o heroi sem nenhum caráter," "the hero without a character."[36] In his lack of a fixed identity, he represents the amalgamation of Brazil's different ethnic and cultural groups, suspending, as Haroldo de Campos puts it, "the dogmatic investiture of a single, unique character to be ultimately found."[37] In this sense he is similar to the marafona, with her fluid linguistic, national, cultural, and gender identity. She imagines herself as an "inmensa madona macunaima, índia, pajé, tupã" (*MP*, 70) ("immense Macunaimian Madonna, Indian, pajé-shaman-prophet, Tupã" [*PS*, 61]). This Madonna is "Macunaimian" in that she is dark-skinned, Indigenous, imbued with the powers of the supreme god "Tupã," according to the Guarani creation myth, and yet still Mary, the mother of Jesus in the Christian faith. She is a racial, cultural, and religious hybrid that could well be described as being "sem nenhum caráter" herself.

In the sense that it is profoundly intertextual and heterogeneous, then, not to mention in the way it "rechews" words from different languages to create new hybrid words, *Mar Paraguayo* belongs firmly to the neobaroque tradition. However, the intertwining of Indigenous and European cultures in *Mar Paraguayo* goes much deeper than single references such as the one to *Macunaíma* mentioned above, a fact that becomes particularly evident in a long passage in the middle of the novel in which the marafona describes her work with the traditional Paraguayan embroidered lace, ñanduti. In this section, the marafona occupies an authorial, quasi-godlike position, one that includes aspects of both Guarani and Western cultural traditions. Near the beginning of the passage, she muses on the tale she is telling, saying, "esto relato solo quer y desea sê-lo un juego-de-jugar: como los dioses en el principio, en el tupã-karai" (this story only wants and desires to be a game of make believe: like the gods in the beginning, in the tupã-karai) (*MP*, 39). She imagines herself like the Guarani deities of fire and water playing at manipulating the humans in her power, before going on to position herself as a spider weaving a web in ways that recall aspects of Greek mythology. In Guarani, the word "ñanduti" refers not just to traditional lace embroidery, but also to a spider web, because it denotes a weave so fine as to be almost invisible. As the marafona weaves, the passage becomes more surreal; she imagines releasing millions of eggs to populate the room with miniscule venomous spiders. She appears to manipulate the other characters in her tale, like a god manipulates humans: her web is a trap for the young boy she desires, her needle a lethal weapon to kill the old man with whom she lives. The scene recalls not only the myth of Arachne, who, in Ovid's *Metamorphoses*, challenged the goddess Athena to a weaving competition and as punishment for overreaching was transformed into a spider, but also the three Fates who spun and cut the threads of human destiny. The marafona is the hybrid Indigenous-European author of her own tale, weaving the fates of the characters who occupy it. This passage constitutes a rewriting or "rechewing" of ancient European myths via Indigenous American cultural traditions. In its own repurposing of previous narratives in this way, *Mar Paraguayo* reminds us of the extent to which texts, in their multiple versions, are in constant conversation with other texts.

Mar Paraguayo is full of contradictions and ambiguities and refuses to be easily categorized. Like the other writing addressed in this book, its multilingualism and translational strategies coexist with many other forms of hybridity or fluidity, creating a border-crossing, intersectional space of difference, innovation, and possibility. Bueno moves repeatedly and seamlessly between languages and cultural reference points, alienating and accommodating different readers at different moments in the text, so that no reader feels entirely at ease. He commits to making readers work hard at understanding his narrative, while never abandoning readability entirely. The book's preoccupation with that which is moving, unidentifiable, or unfinishable—the vast and uncontainable sea, animals that shift and transform, the invisible or even nonexistent dog Brinks, for instance—coupled with the way it appropriates, reuses, and repurposes cultural references and narratives from around the world are all signs of its openness to reinscription in new versions, including translated versions. As is clear from his punning biography printed in the Nightboat Books edition of *Paraguayan Sea*, Wilson Bueno was supportive of Erín Moure's translation project: "Bueno himself encouraged Moure to translate his book, as he wished to send it on a journey through the northern Americas and other English shores, not this time in its original wangling but in the mixelated accents of Quebec, moure-or-less, as *Paraguayan Sea*" (PS, 116).

The second part of this chapter will examine Moure's playful, multilingual, challenging new version of *Mar Paraguayo*, demonstrating the many ways it complements and extends Bueno's work.

PART II. FROM SOUTH TO NORTH: ERÍN MOURE'S *PARAGUAYAN SEA*

The recent translation of Wilson Bueno's *Mar Paraguayo* by Erín Moure, who is herself a renowned poet, exemplifies my argument, put forward throughout this volume, that translation need not erase the difficulty or ingenuity of multilingual writing; it, too, can be linguistically playful and challenging, a creative practice to be valued in the same way as any other writing. Published in the United States by Nightboat Books, an independent publisher committed to supporting work that "resists convention and transcends boundaries," Moure's *Paraguayan Sea* was longlisted for the Best Translated Poetry Award in 2018.[38] In many ways her translation of Bueno's work is an obvious extension of Moure's previous oeuvre, both as a poet and a translator, the two roles being often indistinguishable in her work. A fourth-generation descendent of Galician emigrants to Canada and resident of the bilingual city of Montreal, Moure has consistently sought to explore transnational themes in her writing, to challenge standards of accessibility, and to experiment with the use of multiple languages. The very first statement on her personal website is a multilingual one: "It's about poetry. Falamos poesía. Je suis poète et traductrice et éditeure" (Let's talk poetry. I am a poet and a translator and an editor).[39] She remains committed, as these lines demonstrate, to the contiguity and intertwining of multiple languages, including in her translation work. Like Bueno's own, Moure's work is deeply intertextual, often cerebral, and pays detailed attention to the sound and shape of language as well as to its semantic value.

Paraguayan Sea is this book's most powerful example yet of a translation that is multilingual, creative, and fluid, that interacts with its source text in ways that enhance and extend it. This section examines how Moure creatively reformulates Bueno's multilingual strategies in order to give his work new life in the Northern hemisphere. As with all the writing studied thus far in this book, Moure's *Paraguayan Sea* demonstrates translation to be productive and original, rather than derivative and secondary. I argue that she draws on a tradition of Canadian feminist and queer translation to assert her translator subjectivity in *Paraguayan Sea*, blurring the line between author and translator.

Erin, Erín, Eirin: Fluid Borders in Moure's Poetic Oeuvre

As is the case with Braschi's writing, Moure's work has been intermittently dismissed by both literary critics and academic scholars as difficult or even unintelligible.[40] One Canadian reviewer of Moure's *Little Theatres* claims to have given up on the work entirely because their "obfuscometer [was] reading off the charts."[41] This "difficulty," like Braschi's, comes in part from her writing's dense intertextuality. Although she has mainly produced work outside academic institutions, she is in constant conversation with theorists, philosophers, and cultural critics; for instance, her self-consciously cerebral work *O Cidadán* engages a raft of interlocutors including Lyotard, Levinas, Lispector, Derrida, Bloch, and Butler, recalling the way Susana Chávez-Silverman often uses literary and critical material as catalysts for her own crónicas. In this sense Moure's work is often theoretical as well as literary, refusing easy distinctions between critical and creative writing. Like all the other writing addressed in this book, it is committed to challenging and sometimes alienating readers, making way for a reading experience characterized by close engagement and partial confusion.

However, again like Braschi's, another important reason why Moure's writing is described as "difficult" is its frequent multilingualism. Since the 1970s, when she began writing, Moure has worked across English, French, Galician, Portuguese, and Spanish, translating from one to another but also writing poems that code-switch at the level of the line or the word, and that incorporate, as Shannon Maguire puts it, "outlandish puns," "roiling syntax and audacious neologisms" that delight in being cross-lingual.[42]

In chapter 1, I worked through Rey Chow's contention that we ought to abandon the fallacy of the mother tongue and instead understand language as prosthesis, as acquired and always artificial rather than something that can ever properly belong to us. If language is always prosthetic or inauthentic, I argued, then there is no "native" or "foreign" language in any given situation; as individuals use or acquire languages, those languages become part of their identity, regardless of nationality or ethnicity. We have seen this reflected in Chamoiseau, Bernabé, and Confiant's argument that creoleness has as its appetite "all the languages of the world" (see chapter 2), and in Diegues's contention that "portunhol selvagem" contains "todas las lenguas del Brasil y del Paraguay (incluso las ameríndias) y todas las lenguas del mundo" (all the languages of Brazil and Paraguay [including the Amerindian ones] and all the languages of the world), and in the way Díaz, Chávez-Silverman, and Bueno appropriate multiple linguistic varieties in their writing.[43] Like these other writers, Moure understands language to be both capacious and prosthetic: "It seems natural to me to use in poetry all the words, or any of them," she has said.[44] And also: "I never saw the sense in writing in only one language. When my body expresses itself in more languages, why present a thought in only one? Why shut down the forces that are at work in the poems? Why restrict thought's possibilities in the poem, sound's possibilities?"[45] *Search Procedures* (1996) contains some of Moure's more multilingual poems, which in many ways resemble her translational style in *Paraguayan Sea*. The poems in this collection are, as Skoulding puts it, "a feminist articulation of frontiers, boundaries, and the process of locating oneself":[46]

> Interpretative relax. Hormone
> exigence parfois aimerait
> cut-up laughing. You're
> symbolise rien coulait ce que
> physis empathetic impetus of
> Honte. Amertume légère de son
> madness, dance of spout lineal
> fusion du possible. Espérons
> interpretive gleam. Side view
> boîte ouvrante très proche à
> collaborative drive. Edge visible
> ôtez le « je ». Interpellant
> literal land layer, adverbial
> poudre, saurons donc respirer
>
> "literal land layer," as if layered in the head, words lined by dint of
>   "interpretation," each layer oscillating, ignites cortical screens or paths

unavailable to the expulsive reader who dismisses "absolute" a piece where so little "actually" fits together, there is no palpable image or whole.[47]

This enigmatic poem (only partially reproduced here) is a multilingual exploration of fluid subjectivity, of a search for identity via physical layers of language that build up like sediment (as "adverbial poudre" [powder]). Moure explores the interpretive possibilities of language mixing as well as the madness, shame ("honte"), and bitterness ("amertume") associated with it. She employs many cognate words that can be read in either English or French ("exigence," "dance," "fusion," "possible," "visible"), a strategy that, as we will see, features strongly in her translation of Wilson Bueno, and which makes possible multiple different phonemic readings. The fluidity between languages in this poem ties in with Moure's exploration, throughout *Search Procedures*, of fluid borders between bodies and between texts. A series of poems in tightly intertwined English and French, which comprise seemingly self-contained stanzas surrounded by white space, are actually linked together by a line of prose that runs from one page to the next (only part of the prose line quoted above appears on the same page as the stanza that precedes it), in which readers are told that "so little 'actually' fits together, there is no palpable image or whole," and are invited to let "each layer oscillate."[48] These lines invite us to rethink the boundaries between textual versions in ways that recall Chávez-Silverman's palimpsestuous writing, in which she layers interconnected versions of her crónicas. They remind us not only that any given text is in a relationship, whether obvious or concealed, with other texts, but also that a text itself may be fluid and shifting.

For both Bueno and Moure, sound is critical. As Skoulding puts it, "the main action of Moure's poems is in language, and their main emphasis is on linguistic encounter."[49] Moure has traced this interest back to a conference she attended in 1983, where she met many feminist writers, including fellow Canadian Nicole Brossard, and began to think about "the poetic felicity of non-mimetic language."[50] We see this, for instance, in a piece titled "Sovereign body39 (vis-á-vis)," from *O Cidadán*, which explicitly invites readers to pay attention to the sounds of words in different languages, rather than to their meanings:

What if we listen to the noise and not the signal?
tor = tower
blé = wheat

visi (vis-á-vis) = a relation, also: isi—a certain symmetry of i's around a curved channel.⁵¹

Here Moure pushes past meaning and pays attention to the sound associations arising from a given word: in "visi," she doesn't just see meaning, she also sees the shape of the letters, the patterns they create. In this sense she shares concrete poetry's interest in the radical disassociation of sound and sense. For this reason, noise was chosen as the central organizing concept in the recent anthology of her work, *Planetary Noise*, edited by Shannon Maguire.⁵²

Moure's writing also engages consistently with translation in ways that blur its boundaries with other forms of textual work; she describes translation as being "part of her poetic practice."⁵³ One of the most obvious examples of this is *Sheep's Vigil by a Fervent Person*, her "transelation" of *O Guardador de rebanhos* by Portuguese writer Fernando Pessoa. Pessoa published the book under the name Alberto Caeiro, and Moure writes her English version under a pseudonym of her own, Eirin Moure, Eirin being the old Galician version of her name. In her "transelation"—a term chosen in order to convey the *elation* she felt at working on Caeiro's text, her "readerly happiness at Caeiro's wit"—she transports early twentieth-century rural Portugal to early twenty-first-century Toronto.⁵⁴ The earnest male speaker in Pessoa's poem becomes a Canadian woman, sheep become stray cats, and Caeiro's pastoral landscape becomes an urban world that still bears traces of the rural. The term "transelation" is also a way of advertising Moure's presence in this text, of signaling that this is no straightforward translation but something extra. In addition to language, content has been translated—carried across from one location and one moment in time to another. The resulting style is chatty and irreverent, full of interpolated asides from Moure that are all the more visible thanks to the work's publication in a bilingual edition, Caeiro's Portuguese on the verso, Moure's English on the recto page. In her choice of title, *Sheep's Vigil by a Fervent Person*, we get a glimpse of her playful attitude toward the Portuguese original, which functions for her as "remnant, text, or score" rather than something to be revered or privileged.[55] Like Chávez-Silverman, she takes delight in "faux translations,"[56] false cognates, and unlikely transcriptions: the author's name is hidden in the translated title. "Pessoa" means "person" in Portuguese, while "Fernando" becomes "fervent," both through sonic similarity and the fervent way the speaker scorns poets and philosophers who invest the natural world with mystical meaning.

Sheep's Vigil is just one example of Moure's ability to "unseat ... translation and any standard notion of its reliance on an original."[57] Her work has been described by Sherry Simon as "unoriginal writing"[58] (a reference to Marjorie Perloff's book of a similar name),[59] in which "ludic exercises" are triggered by other "original" texts, like Pessoa's *O Guardador de Rebanhos*. What is more, these "ludic exercises" leak into paratexual apparatus—the title page and book jacket—in ways designed to destabilize the coherence and integrity of their authorial voice. Like Pessoa, who had three fully-fledged heteronyms and as many as seventy other names under which he wrote, Moure's authorship is multiple rather than singular. The linguistic multiplicity of the texts she produces is reflected in the way her authorial name shifts between several variants across publications: Erin Moure, Erin Mouré, Erín Moure, Eirin Moure. These are not pseudonyms as such—they are not intended to hide her identity. Rather, each orthographical variant suggests the transposition from one language context to another and serves to confound readers' ability to pronounce her name aloud. They suggest a fluid authorial/translatorial identity that resonates strongly with the kinds of texts she works on, including *Paraguayan Sea*, as the next section will demonstrate.

As well as employing multiple languages in her writing and translations, Moure experiments with genre and textual boundaries. In *O Cidadán* (2002), via a heterogeneous mixture of documents—"Georgettes," "catalogues of harms," and "aleatory" poems that comprise, among other things, diagrams, calculations, film scripts, and photographs—Moure examines the nature of national and regional but also linguistic and textual borders, weaving Spanish, Portuguese, and Galician into her English.[60] Among the various documents are a series of meditations on the life and work of De Sousa Mendes, a Portuguese consul general who "in 1940 in Bordeaux, France, issued 30,000 visas to refugee Jews, admitting them to Portugal in direct defiance of instructions," and was punished harshly for his actions.[61] These prompt reflections on citizenship and national boundaries, and ultimately argue, as Moure herself puts it, "for a notion of frontier or border as a line that admits filtrations, that leaks. A notion of leaky borders. Not rigid, not sealed, not marking strict limits of 'outside' and 'inside' when dealing with identity."[62]

A public epistolary exchange between Moure and another multilingual poet, Caroline Bergvall, called "O YES" mimics and extends the work of *O Cidadán*, which, as Bergvall points out, "makes visible its contact with others' work,"[63] resulting in a collection that is fractured, self-consciously intertextual, linguistically and visually heterogeneous. As an overt collaboration between two authorial voices, "O YES" works on multiple temporal levels, interspersing into a main text comments from a future moment of writing, much like Chávez-Silverman does in *Scenes from la Cuenca de Los Angeles*. For instance, Bergvall writes, incorporating Moure's contributions to their conversation: "I work outside fixed institutional frameworks and defend the idea that thinking can take place in interstices. You say, I don't like the word margins, for it cannot dislodge from the notion of a centre. Interstices are webs of thinking through and alongside each other, tugging and influencing."[64] This use of the word "interstitial" recalls particularly strongly the work of Chávez-Silverman, who, as we saw in chapter 1, mobilizes the aspects of her writing that move between conventional categories of thinking in order to create a fragmentary, nonlinear style and genre indeterminacy, and to disrupt established disciplinary and linguistic conventions in academic scholarship. Much the same might be said of Bueno's and Moure's (and indeed Bergvall's) work, which also operates in the interstices between languages, genres, institutional frameworks, and textual versions.

The many similarities between Moure's work and that of Bueno mean that her translation of *Paraguayan Sea* is a natural extension of her previous oeuvre. In it, she makes use of strategies and techniques that appear elsewhere in her writing and translation, and which are themselves amply evident in *Mar Paraguayo*.

From *Mar Paraguayo* to *Paraguayan Sea*

With *Paraguayan Sea*, Moure aimed strategically to open up Bueno's novel to a North American readership by translating it into a mixture of French and English, while leaving the Guarani. Take the first line of her translation:

"Make no mistake: Guarani is as essential to this story as the flight of the birrd, the speck on the window, the cooing of French or the cascade of Nerudaesque outpourings in a single seule suicide of capacious English words" (*PS*, 6). It is no longer Portuguese that "coos" in this version, but rather French; and "Nerudaesque outpourings" no longer refer synecdochically to the Spanish language, but to the English, in a move that perhaps acknowledges the size of the Chilean writer's reputation and influence in the Anglophone world. Guarani, as she states here, remains essential in this new version.

Moure has said to have aimed for "a northern version of [Bueno's] *Paraguayan Sea* that would be trilingual/admixture but still readable in English" (*PS*, 109). In this sense, Moure's version differs in one important way from Bueno's: Moure's is quite readable in English but not as readable in French, while the closer syntactic, grammatical, and lexical proximity of Spanish and Portuguese mean that Bueno's version is fairly readable in both those languages.[65] This is evident if we compare the two versions of the book's opening sentence. As I discussed in the previous section, Bueno's version includes many words in both Spanish and Portuguese as well as a number of hybrid words officially belonging to neither language. Meanwhile, the only definitively French word in Moure's opening sentence is "seule." Other words might belong to either language: "suicide" and "cascade." In Moure's version the syntax is entirely English; in Bueno's the syntax could be either Spanish or Portuguese.

However, even as early as this first line we find evidence of Moure's ability to replicate the linguistic strategies at work in Bueno's text. For instance, she translates "párraro" as "birrd," a spelling that approximates a French accent in the same way that "párraro" approximates an Argentine accent. She also takes advantage, not just here but throughout the narrative, of many words that are homographs in English and French. This was particularly evident when, at a launch event for the book in Canada, Moure read aloud from the beginning of her translation. In the first few paragraphs there is a long list of words that many would assume to be English: *scorpion, macabre, obsession, survive, divine, minute, pure, divination, solitude, desperations, moment, distraction, solitude, abrupt, silence.* Yet all these words were pronounced by Moure according to French rules, reminding us that they also exist in that language and that the text we hear in our head when reading differs depending on the languages with which we are familiar.⁶⁶ By making extensive use of homographs, Moure is able to maintain a degree of multilingualism without abandoning readability entirely.

When she was first approached by Cecilia Vicuña to translate some passages for an anthology of Latin American poetry, Moure tried to give *Paraguayan Sea* an entirely North American linguistic context by translating the Guarani into a native North American language, Mohawk.⁶⁷ Later, when she began planning her translation of the book in its entirety, she decided she preferred to work with an Indigenous language from the part of Canada where she grew up, Tsuu Tina. However, finding a creative collaborator from the Tsuu Tina community—there were only about sixty fluent speakers left and they had their own concerns to deal with—proved difficult, and in the end she decided to cede to Wilson Bueno's insistence that Guarani was essential to the text, and "avoid having to deal with the crazy creative problems that would arise by using another language instead of the Guarani."⁶⁸ By choosing to retain Guarani despite the book's new Canadian context, Moure acknowledges its importance in the work, accepting Bueno's assertion in the book's first line.

Like the work examined in previous chapters, *Mar Paraguayo* has been called "untranslatable."⁶⁹ But as we saw above, Bueno's multilingualism already involves, demands, and invites translation, through its connection to the work of concrete poets, through various forms of intertextual and paratextual translation between Bueno's three languages, and in the "elucidário" or glossary appended to the book. Moure engages with translation in many of the same ways in her own writing; *Paraguayan Sea* continues, complements, and often extends Bueno's translational processes, opening the work up to new readers and keeping it in motion.

Like another multilingual poet and translator, Augusto de Campos, who, as Gonzalo Aguilar points out, "looks for and chooses texts [for translation] with an interdict hanging over them: they are the untranslatables,"⁷⁰ Erín Moure admits that she tends "to choose to translate poets with 'untranslatable' practices, difficulties of language, impossibilities of transferability,"⁷¹ because within those impossibilities she finds "the freedom to work."⁷² Her comments reveal that this supposed "impossibility" is nothing of the kind, but rather a creative opportunity for a translator. They recall, of course, Barbara Cassin's use of the term "untranslatable" to refer to what is difficult rather than impossible, to refer to that which inspires repeated, continued, unfinishable translation.

This section argues that Moure's version is as rich in polysemy and ambiguity as Bueno's, and as open to further reinscription. As we have seen in previous chapters, translation from multiple languages into a single language does not necessarily have to diminish the subversive potential of multilingualism or dull its rich textures. Rather, translators can find creative ways of conveying the previous existence of multiple languages and the particular relationships between them, extending and complementing the linguistic and textual strategies used in the texts from which they are working. In the case of *Paraguayan Sea*, the translation is from multiple languages into multiple other languages, allowing Moure even more creative space.

This assertion is borne out extensively in *Paraguayan Sea* itself. The opening pages are rich in rhyme, rhythm, and cross-lingual repetition that showcase Moure's attention to sound, and which in many instances are more patterned than Bueno's own versions: "Merde la vie que yo llevo en las costas como una señora digna cerca de ser executada en la guillotina" (*MP*, 19) ("Merde la vie that je porte on my back like a madam très digne strut-tutt to the guillotine" [*PS*, 8]); "Desde sus ombros, mi destino igual quel hecho de uno punhal en la clave derecha del corazón" (*MP*, 20) ("From his shoulders, my destiny like a fate faite with a dagger in the right chambre of the heart" [*PS*, 8]). In the first of these examples Moure finds rhymes between *digne* and *guillotine* and turns Bueno's straight description of the woman as "cerca de ser executada" into the much more evocative and colorful "strut-tutt to the guillotine," which gives the sentence a rhythm and energy it lacks in Bueno's version. In the second, she creates repetition out of cross-lingual homonyms ("fate faite") where no such patterning exists in Bueno's sentence. Elsewhere Moure echoes and recreates Bueno's familiar strategies: "Observo: acá uno se llega para supuesta alegría, a lá ô a cá la siempre inalcanzable felicidad, e se pone de risas contra las chicas, levanta-lhes las saias, mete los dedos en la cava de sus corpetes oferecidos" (*MP*, 23) ("I observe: here one arrives at supposed happiness, here or là, that toujours inachèvable félicité, and starts teasing girls, pulling up their jupes and skirts, putting fingers in the recesses of their proffered bodies" [*PS*, 11]). Here Moure turns "las saias" into "jupes and skirts," two words in different languages with basically the same referent. Through this combination, Moure suggests that the same object, named in different languages, becomes a different object altogether. There are no easy equivalences between languages, we are reminded. Each word's range of denotations and connotations differs in some way, even if they overlap to a large extent. We also see Moure mirroring Bueno's habit of creating words that reflect the aural life of one language via the orthography of another (*párraro*, for instance). In this example "inachèvable" uses French orthography to transcribe the English word "unachievable."

Although some passages of *Paraguayan Sea*, like the first line, are less multilingual than they are in *Mar Paraguayo* in order to retain their readability, Moure uses strategies of compensation to mitigate this, creating ambiguity and wordplay where it does not exist in Bueno's version. For instance, near the beginning of the book, the marafona describes her birth in deepest Paraguay and her first trip to the sea as an adult. Bueno tells us she "no tuv[o] miedo del gran abismo de agua e espuma" (*MP*, 20). Meanwhile, Moure's marafona is said to have "had no fear of the huge abyss of eau d'sea et foam" (*PS*, 9). In French, "eau d'sea" means literally "water of the sea" but it is also a riff on the names of luxury fragrances (one such famous example being Issey Miyake's L'eau d'Issey—*eau d'sea*). Readers with knowledge of English, however, might read "eau d'sea" as a playful spelling of *odyssey*, a long and adventurous journey famously made by ship. Thus Moure overlays "agua," an uncharged word in Bueno's version, with references both to contemporary beauty culture and to classical literature.

But Moure's translational creativity is perhaps most impressively demonstrated by the passage already cited above:

Como um juego de jugar: pimpirrota, piribela floral, loculho sierva, cincinati, abrolhos, carmencinda, madressilva, pirilampos, antanas bástitas, casa-marilha, locos complutos, boludo lorgo, lacalheseda, amarelinhas, esconde-atrás, noclins ereiras, marcha adelante, los cantantes jugos de ruedas, teresinas-de-jesus, las teresinas, entrançada gaucha, guapa glauchas, catatéicos, constreros, filíciquis, rosaes, oscuro mistério de fábula original, las tranças, las troupas, helicáreos rans, duncans, vitrinas, duendes, vagaus, pilvos conscentes, broquílides silfos, lunfens de lérias, lunfens vivaces, como un juego-de-jugar.
(*MP*, 29)

Like a game of make-believe: pimpimbaristas, slenderpretty flower, doe-crazy, Sinsinhatty, thwhistle, cinderbella, honeysucker, fireflyes, basting

antennae, housemarvel, completely crazies, bumballs, silksilly, yellowbellies, hideinseek, zinzibabwes, walkabyllies, wheels o'fortune whistles, teresa bejeeza, cowgirl tracings, cute blindsdown, catatonicks, consternators, fillysillies, roseygoos, dark mystère of fabulous origin, trances, troupes, helicopterous silligigs, cancans, glass cabinets, duendes, vagueries, consenting abdominals, bronchious sylphs, festivating lumpens, perennial lumpens, tout comme un jeu of make-believe.
(*PS*, 29)

Here Moure makes extensive use of orthography based on pronunciation in order to defamiliarize common words or phrases (Cincinnati, fireflies, hide-and-seek, vagaries). She creates patterns of sound that swing from one word to the next (especially here: "bumballs, silksilly, yellowbellies, hideinseek, zinzibabwes, walkabyllies"). She creates a multilingual version of a famous fairy-tale character, Cinderella, highlighting her beauty by incorporating the Spanish word "bella." And she showcases the flexibility afforded by the etymologies romance languages share, translating "oscuro misterio de fábula original" (*MP*, 39) as "dark mystère of fabulous origin," turning "fábula" from noun to adjective and "original" from adjective to noun. Moure's creative multilingualism here is equally as rich and evocative as Bueno's.

Moure also takes care to demonstrate to readers the extra layers of meaning that result from the transposition of Bueno's text into English and French. She lays them out for readers in her translation of the book's final lines: "Mi mar? Mi mar soy yo. Iyá" (*MP*, 77) ("My mer? My mere sea? All sea ici, en soi, c'est moi, merci. It's me. Iyá" [*PS*, 67]). That Moure's line is twice the length of Bueno's makes clear the extent to which she has drawn out extra connotations afforded by the introduction of French and English here. Whereas in Spanish and Portuguese the word for "mar" is the same, Moure must use two words: "mer" and "sea." Rather than seeing this as a drawback, she makes the most of the multiple homonyms for that combination of terms ("mere sea," "merci"), creating a more patterned version that incorporates rhyme and repetition and is readable in both English and French, just as Bueno's version is readable in both Portuguese and Spanish.

Moure's version of Bueno's "elucidário," which she calls an "eluci**di**ctionary" (emphasis in original), is also more multifaceted and multilingual than Bueno's. Moure offers translations mainly into English, but sometimes also into French and occasionally Portuguese and Spanish. In contrast, Bueno translates exclusively into Portuguese, with just one example of a Spanish word included. These examples from Moure's "eluci**di**ctionary" demonstrate its more complex linguistic fabric:

AYVU: the human word, le mot

BRINKS'IMI: Brinkski-baby. In Portuguese: Brinksizinho.

CUÑAMBATARÁ: prostitute, fallen woman, marafona floozy, catin, trollop, poufiasse

ĪGUASU: sea, mer, mar

TECOVÉ: life, vie, person, persona, personne
(*PS,* 71, 73, 77)

Unlike the Iluminuras edition, which italicizes the only Spanish word (*persona*) in the "elucidário," Moure's "eluci**di**ctionary" lists words from all her languages in regular roman script, giving them equal status and refusing to signal their difference from one another. Like Obejas's translation of *Oscar Wao*, and like my own translation of Chávez-Silverman's crónica, this is a book that aims to elucidate only to a certain extent. By including multiple languages in the glossary, it is able to retain some mysteries of its own.

In understanding the translational strategies at work in *Paraguayan Sea*, it is important to recognize that Moure is working within a long-standing tradition of feminist translation studies in Canada. As I discussed in chapter 3, Canadian translators developed strategies such as wordplay, nonstandard typography, and graphics to make themselves—and the female subject—visible in translation, especially translations of highly experimental, avant-garde, feminist writing. This "womanhandling" of the source text by translators, as Barbara Godard calls it, often involves buttressing a translation with a preface, postface, or notes, in which the translator willingly advertises their interventionism.[73] These strategies have also been appropriated by translators wishing to undermine heteronormativity and draw attention to queer perspectives in a translation, and who see in translation an apt metaphor for queer identity. Moure herself has described translation work as an embodied, performative gesture that recalls how queer studies scholars understand the connection between translation and queerness:[74] "It is clear to me that translation, and particularly translation of poetry, is a set of performative gestures, a performance, because it involves the body of the translator. Each of us translates differently because we have different bodies, with different cultures and histories, different pains and capacities."[75] Since she is a writer whose whole oeuvre shows a commitment to queer feminist analysis, it makes sense that Moure's translation is responsive to the queer concerns of its source, a book that is quite clearly in large part about bodies and desire. Moure's translatorly body produces a version of *Mar Paraguayo* that maintains and, occasionally, gently heightens its queer connotations, as in these lines where the speaker describes her sexual relationship with the "viejo":

> Colava su grande boca como se fuera aspirarme toda para su caliente interior. Si, havia sangre de la vena aorta por todos los porocs del viejo. Ainda que yo, quando me satisfazia ciertos caprichos, de lojas y jóias, de regalos y reparos, yo costumbrava devolver-lhe en cuspo todo o que su língua ávida me ofertava en saliva con uno indecifrable saber a semen.
> (*MP*, 40)

> He stuck his bouche beante on me as if to suck me totalmente into his hot insides. Yes, aortan blood pulse in every pore of the oldster. Even though I, once certain caprices were satisfied, for magasins et jewels, cadeaux and grabbags, I'd spit back all that his avid tongue had proferred me in saliva with an undecipherable goût of semen.
> (*PS*, 30–31)

In Moure's French/English lines, the act of spitting takes on new, double meaning. The word "goût" is both the French for "taste," through which we understand the speaker to have performed oral sex, and also the English "gout," meaning an eruption of liquid, usually of blood but here of semen. The word's cross-lingual connotations mean that the speaker's act of spitting itself takes on the semblance of ejaculation, reminding readers that her gender is in doubt. In this instance, the target text is queerer than the source.

More extensively, Moure adopts a number of interventionist translation strategies proposed by feminist translators, one of which is footnoting.[76] Her translation includes twelve footnotes that do not appear in any edition of *Mar Paraguayo*, much like the footnotes included by Achy Obejas in her Spanish translation of *Oscar Wao*. Moure's footnotes are playful, not only in the way that they mediate readers' access to the main text, but also in the way that they subtly appropriate Bueno's authorial voice, blurring it with her own. Two footnotes appear right at the beginning of the text, on the first page of the main narrative. In this way Moure advertises her presence as translator early, by following up her paratexual comments with her own initials in parentheses. The first footnote, appended to the words "marafona floozy," reads: "Doll and not doll, faceless and facing, hey Dolly! (EM)." The second footnote appears four lines later, appended to the words "the sea." It reads: "A-fluent sea, a fluency. (EM)." Neither of these footnotes purports to explicate the text in any straightforward way. Rather, they comprise wordplay that draws out obliquely some of the possible contradictory meanings in the words to which they are attached. The first reminds readers that the protagonist and speaker of the novel is both "doll and not doll": both woman and not woman. It also tells us that she is "faceless" (the word "marafona" can refer to a type of a rag doll with a blank face), suggesting that she lacks an easily categorized identity (we might recall Macunáima, Andrade's "héroe sem nenhum caráter" [hero without a character]). And yet she is also defined, contradictorily, as "facing": she faces up to all parts of her own hybrid self. The second footnote describes the sea as both fluent and not fluent. Given that the marafona repeatedly identifies with the sea (here she refers to "my sea"), the suggestion is that she herself—or her language—is both fluent and not fluent. Fluent in the sense of free flowing, moving fluidly from one language to another; and not fluent in the sense that it is not necessarily easily comprehensible, nor does it conform to conventional ideas about what linguistic mastery looks like—I discussed in the introduction how the mixing of two or more languages is often assumed to be the result of insufficient education. In an essay by Christian Kent appended to Moure's translation, it is pointed out that the word "marafona" itself can be read similarly: as "mar afona," an aphonic sea, a silent sea, thus strengthening the connection between the protagonist and water. She is not only doll and not doll, faceless and facing, but also silent and—as the narrative itself proves—voluble. Moure's two footnotes do not attempt to explain a translational choice or expound on a particular complexity in the original, as is common among translators' footnotes. Rather, they flag Moure's presence in the text and signal her approach to the translation to come: an approach that will extend Bueno's polysemy and use of contradiction, and will accommodate the ambiguous, open-ended aspects of his text.

The other ten footnotes included in *Paraguayan Sea* differ from the first two in a number of ways. First, they do not include Moure's initials in parentheses, which has the effect of suggesting to the reader that they are Bueno's footnotes rather than hers. Second, they are informative instead of punning, appended to literary or cultural references in the text. For instance, we find: "A phrase from the Catholic prayer 'Salve Regina': 'in this vale of tears'" (*PS*, 63), and "Refers to Lorca's poem 'Lament for Ignacio Sánchez Mejías'" (*PS*, 40). These footnotes *do* purport to explain, to fill in certain potential blanks in readers' cultural knowledge. They suggest a commitment on Moure's part to assuring the readability of her translation, in much the same way as Achy Obejas commits to a degree of readability in her translation of *Oscar Wao*. And yet, with only twelve footnotes appended to a book as densely intertextual as *Paraguayan Sea*, the partiality of this effort is starkly obvious. The few footnotes that are included seem designed rather to highlight the futility of any such attempt to explain and inform.

So, as in *Oscar Wao*, we have two distinct kinds of footnotes in *Mar Paraguayo*: some that appear to be an integral part of the fiction itself, extending and mirroring its style and linguistic play, and others which depart entirely from the register of the main text, affecting a degree of scholarly rigor. But unlike in *Oscar Wao*, both these sets of footnotes belong to the translator. Moure thus divides her translatorly subjectivity in two, highlighting the degree to which it can resemble that of the author. She strikes a balance between the compulsion to "fill in" blanks produced by the texts, and to create blanks of her own. Once again, Moure's translation proves to be a *strategic* opening out to new readers rather than a full-scale exposition. She challenges our expectations about readability but does not abandon it entirely.

Another translation strategy Moure has in common with the Canadian feminist translation tradition is the inclusion of a preface to advertise her role as translator. In fact, *Paraguayan Sea* includes a large number of paratexts both preceding and following the main narrative, which occupies only 60 pages of a 115-page volume—just a little over half. The original publication was already supplemented by an introductory essay by Néstor Perlongher and the "elucidário," both of which are included in the Nightboat Books edition in Moure's translation. *Paraguayan Sea* also includes further essays by Andrés Sjens and Christian Kent, an interview with the author, a commentary by the translator, and a list of acknowledgments, credits, and biographies. This is in keeping with much of Moure's other work; *O Cidadán*, for instance, includes a long series of epigraphs and extensive acknowledgments before the main text begins. These many paratexts are undoubtedly an attempt to mitigate some of the text's difficulty by offering readers multiple points of access. However, they also highlight the degree to which *Paraguayan Sea* is in conversation with other texts and interlocutors, drawing attention to its open and seemingly unfinishable nature, as the main narrative seems to overspill its conventional boundaries.

A TEXT IN CONTINUED MOTION

I have argued throughout this book that multilingualism and translational strategies give texts a shifting, unfinishable quality and an openness to further reinscriptions in different versions. I have also argued that translation, with its infinite potential for revision and reworking, can contribute to the continued life and growth of a work in unexpected ways. *Mar Paraguayo* is already conspicuously in motion, its multiple languages engendering multiple possible readings. As one perceptive reviewer puts it, this book "no se digiere con la primera lectura, ni con la segunda, ni con la tercera ... Es de ese tipo de literatura que nunca se termina de leer" (cannot be digested at the first reading, nor the second, nor the third. ... It's that kind of literature that you never finish reading).[77] Moure herself remarked that "it just goes on and on."[78]

Moure's translation succeeds in perpetuating that motion by projecting the work into circulation in the Anglophone and Francophone world, where it engenders different, newly challenging readings. What is very clear is that *Paraguayan Sea* is not a translation that "flattens" or homogenizes the original's stylistic, linguistic, and conceptual complexity. Rather, the multilingual, multigenre, multicultural fabric of Bueno's text is transformed, extended and recreated in different circumstances, for different readers. Moure shows that translation, far from being an annihilation of the complexities of multilingual writing, can open up a work to new readerships while allowing meaning to proliferate.

The point is made emphatically by a further rewriting inspired by Moure's translation: a public art installation in downtown Montreal by Canadian artist Andrew Forster in collaboration with Moure herself. Forster, who has long been a creator of mixed-genre, public-access art, titled the exhibition *Mer paraguayenne/Paraguayan Sea*, thereby doubling (or tripling?) the title of the work and acknowledging its existence in multiple versions and multiple languages. This new rewriting gives Bueno's text, transplanted into the northern city of Montreal, fresh meanings and resonances for readers there.

The exhibition, which saw large banners printed with lines from Moure's translation wrapped around a university building, turns a complex and cerebral textual practice out toward public space, where it becomes part of Montreal's hybrid urban fabric. Its visual appearance allows it to compete for our attention with the ubiquitous advertising and branding on the street: the banners are printed in bright yellow, a loud color that's difficult to ignore, and in a "hyperserif" font designed by Forster. This font is the opposite of the more commonly known sans serif typefaces, which are specifically designed for easy reading. A hyperserif font has an excess of serifs—spikes, growths, or hooks on the typeface—which Forster describes as burrs. They needle us, sticking to us, making us get caught on the letters. The result is a font that is not as smooth or readable as a regular serif font, but rather seems to resemble barbed wire. Whereas most fonts are designed to facilitate a smooth reading experience, in contrast, this prickly font forces readers to slow down, accentuating the strangeness of the language used on the banners. It even resembles the ñanduti it describes, the "burrs" spidering outward from each word like embroidery. The additional layer of meaning provided by typography in this version of *Paraguayan Sea* complements Bueno's own attention to the visual appearance of language via his engagement with concrete poetry and is in line with both Bueno's and Moure's commitment to keeping their readers active and challenged.

The exhibition also demonstrates the degree to which the text used is shifting and unfixed. For the purposes of this exhibition, Moure "revised [her] own translation to include even more French."[79] While the printed edition of *Paraguayan Sea* was published in the United States, which meant Moure had to produce a translation that was more readable in English than in French, Forster's exhibition is based on a version of the text that instead prioritizes the largely French-speaking population of Montreal. Like Chávez-Silverman's writing, which contains more or less Spanish depending on the audience for which she is giving a public reading, the multilingualism of Moure's work means it can coexist in multiple versions depending on the audience.

This new version of Bueno's text, which crosses even more borders in addition to those traversed in *Mar Paraguayo* and *Paraguayan Sea*—the border between inside and outside, between institutional and public spaces, between textual and visual art—emphasizes the extent to which it is a still-evolving entity that continues to engender new creative versions. The different versions of *Mar Paraguayo* examined in this chapter are yet more evidence that multilingualism, and the translational processes it entails, coexist and interact with other forms of textual and conceptual hybridity, fluidity, and disruption.

CODA

Beyond America: Multilingualism, Translation, and *Asymptote*

By way of conclusion to this volume, I will spend a few pages discussing two special features on multilingual writing and translation that I edited for *Asymptote*, a quarterly online journal of international literature in translation, in July of 2015 and 2016, back at the very inception of this project. I touched on this briefly in chapter 1, because it was in *Asymptote* that Susana Chávez-Silverman's "Todo verdor perdurará Crónica" was published (the same journal also published early extracts from Moure's *Paraguayan Sea* in 2015), but it merits further discussion because the process of compiling those two special features facilitated the development of this research in numerous ways. In both years, the journal held open submissions for "original poetry and prose, as well as translations, which combine English with one or more other languages."[1] The sheer number of submissions (this remains the journal's most popular special feature since its launch in 2011) is a testament to the wealth of new writers who are experimenting with multilingualism and translational techniques. Each feature published seven pieces of work, and, although we asked that each contribution be at least partially comprehensible to speakers of English, between them they incorporated as many as twenty-five different languages, ranging from major European and Asian languages to smaller languages like Romanian, Greenlandic, and Nahuatl. Some also documented spoken varieties that, like "Spanglish," "Portunhol," and "Frenglish," have only recently started to become languages of literature. All used forms that are ontologically inconsistent with the notion of languages as hermetically sealed units.

Although these features showcased poetry as well as prose, and although they ranged across many more languages than those discussed in this book, it is worth surveying them here because they share many of the qualities I have identified in the work of Chávez-Silverman, Junot Díaz, Achy Obejas, Giannina Braschi, Tess O'Dwyer, Wilson Bueno, and Erín Moure. "Spanglish" literature might be the best studied of all multilingual literatures, largely because of the dominance of the United States in international scholarship, but that does not mean that similar trends cannot be traced across other contemporary literatures and geographies. I want to focus briefly on a number of the contributions to *Asymptote* in order to illustrate that the same preoccupations and strategies are at work in other language communities, especially those where bi- or multilingualism is often the norm rather than the exception (which is, in fact, a majority of global communities). Like the four writers already discussed, the contributors to these features value difficulty, strategically managing the accessibility of their work and slowing down the pace of reading. They demonstrate a debt to oral, conversational forms. They imbricate linguistic ambiguity with genre and gender ambiguity, exploring how multilingualism might represent queer desire or queer bodies, and conversely how the notion of queer might be a useful way of reading multilingualism. They showcase the possibilities afforded by publishing in a digital format, confirming Rebecca Walkowitz's contention that much "born-translated" literature is emerging alongside "born-digital" or "post-digital" literature and is first championed by small online publishers.[2] Many of the contributions were published in two versions, "original" and "translation," but, as with Obejas's version of *Oscar Wao*, O'Dwyer's version of *Yo-Yo Boing!*, and Moure's *Paraguayan Sea*, they reveal the proximity of source and target where multilingual writing is concerned, demonstrating the way translational processes straddle multiple different language versions, keeping them in motion.

It was no easy task to publish this kind of writing. The limitations of my own language skills made reading many of the submissions difficult, although I did frequently have the thematically relevant experience of partial incomprehension. Reading submissions involved the same time, attention, and research demanded of any reader of writing by Chávez-Silverman, Braschi, Díaz, Obejas, Bueno, or Moure. For these reasons, compiling each feature was far from a solo endeavor, and I relied on many colleagues and other valued readers to lend me their competence in other languages as well as their literary acumen. The conversations leading to publication were in themselves a palimpsestuous process, continuing the dialogue that is apparent in much of the writing itself, which, like Chávez-Silverman's crónicas or *Yo-Yo Boing!*'s translation, is often the result of interaction between multiple interlocutors.

Greg Nissan's highly allusive and intertextual poem "For Whom the -R Rolls," published in 2016, employs many of the same strategies used by the writers discussed in this book.[3] The poem is an experiment with "Kiezdeutsch," a little-documented German youth dialect spoken in multiethnic and multilingual neighborhoods of Berlin. Written in a combination of English and "Kiezdeutsch," the poem centers on the rolled "r" of the title, which is often vilified as a threatening incursion into German from Turkish, despite a different kind of rolled "r" having long been recognized as a marker of Bavarian identity. The poem explores how the use of this emergent, mixed variety is often highly politicized. Nissan points out that "Kiezdeutsch" is "a creative and malleable slang for those who use it and a vessel of xenophobic anxieties for those who don't . . . in the right context, it's a sign of belonging; in the wrong one, an impetus for exclusion."[4]

Readers of "For Whom the -R Rolls" are expected to acquire both cultural and linguistic knowledge as they make their way through the poem. Nissan uses hyperlinks to direct readers to online documents that help contextualize his use of "Kiezdeutsch," including articles about language change, linguistic "purity," and immigration, as well as a concordance of "Kiezdeutsch" compiled by the University of Potsdam. Meanwhile, pop-up notes offer translations of certain German words, and etymologies for phrases deriving from Turkish and Arabic, as in the following lines:

> An Isch for an Ich the <u>Zeit</u>
> <u>-(z)ungen</u> pan
> -ic: thast you speak in
> Zungen or tongues—
> <u>Ey man, ey nutte, killer, krass</u>—
> Ey bud, ey slut, that's so badass—
> But they penned the script
> they're 'fraid of.[5]

CODA

When a reader hovers their mouse over the word "Zeit/-(z)ungen," a pop-up note with a translation appears, explaining that the word "Zeitung" means "newspaper" in German. This is helpful, to be sure, for those like myself who do not read much German, allowing us to understand that the media is causing some hysteria over the new pronunciation of the first-person pronoun "Ich" as "Isch" (a pronunciation that leaks into Nissan's English, too: "thast"). However, the use of parentheses in "(z)ungen" (a technique reminiscent of Chávez-Silverman's textual palimpsesting), which is a play on the word "Zunge," meaning "tongue," is left to readers to work out for themselves—at least until two lines further on, when a translation is unexpectedly proffered: "Zungen or tongues." We find translational processes in the following lines, too, in which rhyme links the mainly German "*Ey man, ey nutte, killer, krass*" with the English "*Ey bud, ey slut, that's so badass*," hinting that the one is likely a translation of the other. These lines might appear impenetrable to a reader who knows no German, but it only takes slowing down and paying attention to the clues left by the poet for them to begin to have meaning. Translational strategies are everywhere in this hectic-looking, difficult, multilingual poem; it turns the processes of translation themselves into a work of art, making an aesthetic virtue of foreignization, instability, and seeming opacity. For readers with better language skills than mine, there is even more work to be done, because, despite the poem comprising fewer than a hundred short lines, readers are encouraged to read much, much more than this. A hyperlink on "*Ey man, ey nutte, killer, krass*," for instance, reveals it to be a quotation from an article in *Der Spiegel*, which associates the "sch" sound in "Isch" with immigrant communities, sexist behavior, and poor education.[6] This gives greater clarity to the stanza's final lines ("But they penned the script / they're 'fraid of"), which blame precisely that kind of media outlet for alienating "Kiezdeutsch"-speaking communities in the first place.

Like Nissan, Klara du Plessis also uses pop-up notes to provide English translations of the Afrikaans words and phrases in her three poems in the 2016 feature exploring "the unstable ontology of a polyglot."[7] Sometimes these translations are multiple (like some of Obejas's footnoted translations in her Spanish version of *Oscar Wao*, or Moure's in her "eluci**di**ctionary"), as when "spel" is given a double gloss as "to spell/game"; sometimes they include literal translations, as when the word "tydskrif" is glossed as "magazine (literally, time/writing)." This latter decision allows readers to connect "tydskrif" with other compounds that include the word "skrif," such as "handskrif" and the neologism "skryftaal," which is glossed as "written language (not a real word)." Readers are supported in the work of pulling apart the different elements of Afrikaans words and connecting them, via their shared Germanic roots, to words in English.

Both Nissan's and du Plessis's poems have a similar conversational quality to much of the writing previously discussed in this book. We have seen how Díaz and Chávez-Silverman combine spoken discourse with the conventions of scholarly writing, while Braschi relies on dialogue to structure much of her work, and Bueno plays with the orthographic representation of different varieties of Spanish and Portuguese. We can trace a rich oral life, one that differs from a work's life or lives on the page, through many of the multilingual contributions collected in the two *Asymptote* features, where the audio-recording facility is especially valuable. The importance of sound is evident in Șerban Foarță's "Papillonage" ("Butterflyción"), for instance.[8] Writer and translator Chris Tănăsescu (known as MARGENTO) gives an exuberant, musical reading of this poem by the renowned Romanian poet and songwriter, to which readers can listen alongside the poem and its translation. In Kanya Kanchana's sequence of poems from "Grammar of the Goddess," meanwhile, each verse is built around Sanskrit "seed syllables" or mantras that are valuable for their phonic rather than their semantic connotations, and which are read aloud over the sound of a musical accompaniment.[9] Rajiv Mohabir's four "chutney poems," too, are based on a type of folk song called "chutney music" popularized by the Trinidadian musician Sundar Popo, whose poetics and patterns of singing are worked into the poems.[10] Finally, in chapter 3 I discussed how in the 1980s there emerged a performative tradition of Nuyorican writing, which came to be characterized by colloquial bilingual forms and highly publicized slam poetry competitions;[11] we find this tradition continued in Noel Quiñones's poem "Arroz Poetica Battle Rhyme for Kendrick Lamar."[12] Quiñones is an Afro-Boricua spoken-word poet raised in the Bronx who has competed in slam poetry competitions, and the audio-recording facility allows listeners to hear the poem's powerful cadence and rhythm across English and Spanish, underscoring the relationship between poetry, rap, and songwriting to which the title gestures. As in the recordings of Chávez-Silverman's crónicas, the sonic versions of each of these contributions to the journal differ in many small ways from the texts as they appear on the screen, thereby highlighting their impermanence and openness to being rewritten. The relationship between multilingual writing and spoken discourse has emerged repeatedly as an important feature of the writing discussed in this book, although it has remained in the background of my discussions; the features in *Asymptote* confirm that it will deserve fuller attention in future research in this area.

The work published in *Asymptote* also explores the interconnectedness between multilingualism, race, diaspora, and queer aspects of sex and gender. Rajiv Mohabir's four "chutney poems" center on the sexual awakening of a queer, brown, Indo-Caribbean youth in the United States. Mohabir speaks, with varying degrees of fluency, Caribbean Hindi, Bhojpuri, Urdu, English, Guyanese Creole, and French. In these poems, the movement between languages allows him to relate the violence of colonial history (and the associated trauma of language suppression and delegitimization: "They knifed your *ka—kha—ga—gha—nga*, and forked / your tongue into a mimic tongue against your mother") to the violent policing of queer desires and practices. In "Indo-queer I," for instance, we read that "Before Her Majesty's letters spelled out *homo* / you tied saris and danced launda ke nauch." Through this reference to a centuries-old tradition from the Uttar Pradesh and Bihar regions of India, in which men dress up as women to dance at social functions, particularly weddings, Mohabir depicts the policing of sexuality and gender as a colonial act. Meanwhile, his poem "Shame in Mathura" describes a medical procedure aiming to "cure" homosexuality, and in doing so figures queer desire as a fish-like, feathered creature:

> The doctors
> mined your chest; excavated your wild desire, cast
> the queer catch into the sea and it grew a macaw plume.
> The fourth time you drank poison, your father
>
> tied you to the bedpost gagged, dragged you bound
> to the mandap and clipped your flight feathers.

Like Braschi in *Yo-Yo Boing!*, Mohabir draws parallels here between apparently transgressive sexual and language practices and a transgression of the human/nonhuman border. In doing so, he asks which bodies—and, by extension, which kinds of speech—get to be human.

Throughout this book I have argued that layering and open-endedness are a defining feature of contemporary multilingual writing, and that this feature stems in large part from the processes of translation at work therein. Displacing the conventional model by which there is a single "original" and many translations, Chávez-Silverman, Díaz, Obejas, Braschi, O'Dwyer, Bueno, and Moure's work registers the fact that any "original" is itself multiple and shifting. Translation is *intra*textual as well as *inter*textual; in other words, translational processes are at work not only between or among multiple textual versions, but also within a given version. They move both through and among texts, structuring them so that they remain continually in flux. I discussed in chapter 1 how *Asymptote* is particularly well placed to showcase this shifting, serial aspect of multilingual writing, allowing readers to make comparisons across numerous versions of a text. *Asymptote* was conceived for publication on the internet, and continues to operate entirely online, making the most of the opportunities afforded by its digital format. A typical contribution to the journal exists in at least three versions: original language, English translation, and an audio recording. The digital format enables interactivity between these different versions, facilitating a double or triple reading. The versions are layered and bound together in a digital palimpsest that refuses to let readers forget that any given version will always be provisional, just one among a nexus of different iterations. *Asymptote* has also, since its inception, consistently imbricated literary translation with critical and reflective commentary, reminding us, as Sarah Dillon puts it, that "writing about the palimpsest becomes an act of palimpsesting: any new text about the palimpsest erases, superimposes itself upon, and yet is still haunted by, the other texts in the palimpsest's history."[13] Part of that palimpsest involves incorporating reflection about translation into the published work itself. The "Editor's Note" to the first edition of the journal stated that it would "like to be the sort of magazine where literary translation is not only presented but also discussed."[14] Walkowitz points out that this commitment to displaying translation as process means that *Asymptote* "shares with many born-translated novels a commitment to probing translation while also facilitating it."[15]

One of the most conspicuous ways the journal achieves this aim is by including a translator's note with every contribution. Usually between three hundred and five hundred words, these allow a translator to provide greater context for the piece they have translated, especially if it has been excerpted from a longer work, or to highlight their translational goals or approach. Others use the space to talk about a specific challenge and how they overcame it. Klara du Plessis, for her part, uses the note to explain the centrality of translation to her creative process. One poem, she tells us, "started as English translations of Afrikaans phrases," which she translated "back into Afrikaans, but increasingly loosely and even ungrammatically, dismantling meaning, moving back and forth between the languages according to sound more than semantics."[16] In du Plessis's work, translations are crucial not just to the reading experience, via the pop-up translations provided, but also to the writing itself.

In addition, the journal publishes longer essays by translators about their experience translating a recently published or forthcoming title. For instance, accompanying the 2016 multilingualism feature was an essay by translator David Shook. In it, they discuss three Paraguayan writers whose work has appeared in a multilingual magazine called *Hiedra*—writers who, like Wilson Bueno, blend Spanish, Portuguese, and Guarani. Shook's essay focuses in particular on Jorge Canese's poem "Kribir Mäu" and on Shook's process of translating it into a form of English, under the title "Bät Riting." Even for Paraguayan speakers of "Guarañol," as Shook calls it, Canese's work can be difficult to understand. It explores, Shook writes, "the rupture of literary and prescriptivist strictures, a boldly libertarian idiolect, and the impossibility—and unnecessariness—of a complete understanding."[17] Shook's description of their translation process reveals a parallel with Moure's decision to render *Mar Paraguayo* into "Frenglish": they admit that, in their efforts to recreate the mixed language of Canese's poem, they sometimes opted to "drop into German or pseudo-German, which, while nowhere near as mutually intelligible or geographically overlapping as Portuguese and Spanish, seems to me to replicate the effect so masterfully employed by Canese in the original."[18] Their conclusions about Canese's work—that difficulty ought to be embraced and savored rather than avoided—slot it into place beside that of Chávez-Silverman, Díaz, Braschi, Bueno, and Moure. Essays such as Shook's reveal translators to be forensically detailed readers as well as creative writers. By making space for this kind of discussion, the journal reminds us that literary translation is a creative process to be respected in its own right, and that it overlaps on a continuum with the practices of writing and reading.

I began this book with a quotation from Andrés Neuman in the hope of emphasizing the relationship between translation and movement: "La traducción ni traiciona ni sustituye, es una aportación más, un empujón a un texto que ya estaba en movimiento, como cuando alguien se sube a un coche en marcha" (Translation is neither a betrayal nor a substitute, it is another contribution, a further push to something that is already in motion, like when someone jumps into a moving carriage).[19] Throughout the preceding chapters, I have sought to show that translation, both intratextual and intertextual, keeps a text alive and in motion. Translation need not mean a capitulation to commensurability and standardization in accordance with dominant cultural models, nor a loss of particularity; rather, it can help retain and even supplement a text's complexity and indeterminacy. The contributions collected in *Asymptote*, which draw on dozens of different languages and cultures, remind us that (COVID-19 pandemic notwithstanding) there are more people moving around the world today than at any other time in history, not just because of the effects of globalization but also as a result of violent conflicts such as those in Syria and Central America, which are forcing whole communities to flee. It is likely that this kind of writing will become even more widespread in coming years, as migrants and refugees respond to their new linguistic and cultural environments. Increasingly, both writers and readers will also have to be translators—they will have to jump on the already moving train and see where it takes them.

NOTES

INTRODUCTION: TRANSLATION AND MULTILINGUALISM IN CONTEMPORARY AMERICAN LITERATURE

1. Yuri Herrera, *Signs Preceding the End of the World*, trans. Lisa Dillman (High Wycombe: And Other Stories, 2015), 65. Originally published as Yuri Herrera, *Señales que precederán al fin del mundo* (Cáceres: Periférica, 2010).
2. Andrés Neuman, *Traveller of the Century*, trans. Nick Caistor and Lorenza Garcia (London: Pushkin, 2013), 334. Originally published as Andrés Neuman, *El viajero del siglo* (Madrid: Alfaguara, 2009).
3. In the pages that follow, I use the variant "Latinx," a gender-neutral or nonbinary alternative to "Latino" and "Latina," which was first adopted by members of the queer community online in 2004, and which has achieved a rise in popularity in recent years, especially among academics in the United States. It is not, however, without its critics. It is easier to pronounce for speakers of English than it is for speakers of Spanish, where "x" does not usually follow a consonant, and where its pronunciation differs depending on spelling. What is more, the "degendering" of language through the adoption of the "-x" suffix has greater implications for Spanish, which retains grammatical gender, than it does for English, which does not. Guerra and Orbea have gone so far as to describe the term as "a blatant form of linguistic imperialism—the forcing of US ideals upon a language in a way that does not grammatically or orally correspond with it." Gilbert Guerra and Gilbert Orbea, "The Argument Against the Use of the Term 'Latinx,'" *The Phoenix* (blog), November 19, 2015, http://swarthmorephoenix.com/2015/11/19/the-argument-against-the-use-of-the-term-latinx/. While it continues to exist alongside alternatives such as "Latin@" (which excludes those who identify as gender nonbinary), "Latinx" is the

most widely used variant in scholarly writing in English, and for this reason I have adopted it here.
4. "Yo-Yo Boing! (Spanglish)," Amazon, https://www.amazon.com/Yo-Yo-Boing-Spanglish-Giannina-Braschi/dp/161109089X/ref=sr_1_1?dchild=1&keywords=yo-yo+boing&qid=1621783831&sr=8-1; "Killer Crónicas: Bilingual Memories," University of Wisconsin Press, https://uwpress.wisc.edu/books/2616.htm.
5. See, for example, Glenda R. Carpio, "Junot Díaz's Wondrous Spanglish," in *Junot Díaz and the Decolonial Imagination*, ed. Monica Hanna, Jennifer Harford Vargas, and José David Saldívar (Durham, N.C.: Duke University Press, 2016), 257–90; Maria Lauret, *Wanderwords: Language Migration in American Literature* (London: Bloomsbury, 2014), 211–52.
6. "Code-switching" is the term usually preferred by linguists, defined as "the use of words and structures from more than one language or linguistic variety by the same speaker within the same speech situation, conversation or utterance." Laura Callahan, *English-Spanish Codeswitching in a Written Corpus* (Philadelphia: John Benjamins Publishing Company, 2004), 5. For critiques of the term "code-switching," see Lauret, *Wanderwords*, 42–46; Suresh Canagarajah, *Translingual Practice: Global Englishes and Cosmopolitan Relations* (London: Routledge, 2013), 10. Another term that has been used to describe Braschi's writing is "translingualism." See, for instance, Francisco Moreno-Fernández, "Yo-Yo-Boing! Or Literature as a Translingual Practice," in *Poets, Philosophers, Lovers: On the Writings of Giannina Braschi*, ed. Frederick Luis Aldama and Tess O'Dwyer (Pittsburgh, Penn.: Pittsburgh University Press, 2020), 54–62; Maritza Stanchich, "Bilingual Big Bang: Giannina Braschi's Trilogy Levels the Spanish-English Playing Field," in Aldama and O'Dwyer, *Poets, Philosophers, Lovers*, 63–80. Steven G. Kellman uses the term "translingualism" to describe writers who publish in a language that is not their "mother tongue" or "native language." For him, this decision involves a unidirectional movement from one language to another. Steven G. Kellman, *The Translingual Imagination* (Lincoln: University of Nebraska Press, 2000). For a critique of Kellman's understanding of "translingualism," see Lauret, *Wanderwords*, 13–14. Suresh Canagarajah uses the term in a quite distinct way, to describe communication that "transcends individual languages," in which "the semiotic resources in one's repertoire or in society interact more closely, become part of an integrated resource, and enhance each other . . . mesh in transformative ways, generating new meanings and grammars." Canagarajah, *Translingual Practice*, 8. I find this understanding of the term much more useful in the context of Braschi's writing, although, for the purposes of clarity in my discussion here of the close resemblance between multilingual writing and translation, I prefer to avoid the prefix *trans-*.
7. For further discussion of the official English movement, see Thomas Ricento, "A Brief History of Language Restrictionism in the United States," in *Official English? No!*, ed. S. Dicker, K. Romstedt, and Thomas Ricento (Washington, D.C.: TESOL, 1995), 7–17; Deborah J. Schildkraut, *Press One for English: Language Policy, Public Opinion, and American Identity* (Princeton, N.J.: Princeton University Press, 2005).
8. Schildkraut, *Press One for English*, 2.

INTRODUCTION

9. Brian Lennon, *In Babel's Shadow: Multilingual Literatures, Monolingual States* (Minneapolis: University of Minnesota Press, 2010), 2–3. "Results of the Modern Language Association's Fall 1995 Survey of Foreign Language Enrolments," *MLA Newsletter* 28, no. 4 (1996): 1–2.
10. Emily Apter, *The Translation Zone: A New Comparative Literature* (Princeton, N.J.: Princeton University Press, 2006), 20.
11. R. D. Brecht and W. P. Rivers, Language and National Security in the 21st Century: The Role of Title VI/Fulbright-Hays in Supporting National Language Capacity (Dubuque, Iowa: Kendall/Hunt, 2000); S. Barr, "Looking for People Who Can Talk the Talk—in Other Languages," *Washington Post*, March 12, 2002, https://www.washingtonpost.com/archive/local/2002/03/12/looking-for-people-who-can-talk-the-talk-in-other-languages/ee45fd23-d6a0-48d8-b7f7-65189204f299/.
12. Lennon, *In Babel's Shadow*, 1.
13. Abdelilah Salim Sehlaouai, "Language Learning, Heritage, and Literacy in the USA: The Case of Arabic," *Language, Culture and Curriculum* 21, no. 3 (2008): 281.
14. Mary Louise Pratt, "Building a New Public Idea About Language," *Profession* (2003): 112. For further similar calls, see, for example, Domna C. Stanton, "On Linguistic Human Rights and the United States Foreign Language Crisis," *Profession* (2005): 64–75; Michael Geisler, "To Understand a Culture, Learn Its Language," *Chronicle of Higher Education* 52, no. 29 (2006): B11–12.
15. See for example Azade Seyhan, *Writing Outside the Nation* (Princeton, N.J.: Princeton University Press, 2001); Martha Cutter, *Lost and Found in Translation: Contemporary Ethnic American Writing and the Politics of Language Diversity* (Chapel Hill: University of North Carolina Press, 2005); Debra A. Castillo, *Re-Dreaming America: Toward a Bilingual American Culture* (Albany: State University of New York Press, 2005); Lawrence Alan Rosenwald, *Multilingual America: Language and the Making of American Literature* (Cambridge: Cambridge University Press, 2008); Joshua Miller, *Accented America: The Cultural Politics of Multilingual Modernism* (New York: Oxford University Press, 2011); Lauret, *Wanderwords*.
16. Werner Sollors, *Multilingual America: Transnationalism, Ethnicity and the Languages of American Literature* (New York: New York University Press, 1998), 3. For more information about this project spearheaded by Sollors and Shell, see http://www.fas.harvard.edu/~lowinus/.
17. Sollors, *Multilingual America*, 5.
18. Doris Sommer, *Bilingual Aesthetics: A New Sentimental Education* (Durham, N.C.: Duke University Press, 2004), xiv; 85.
19. Ilan Stavans, "Trump, the Wall and the Spanish Language," *New York Times*, January 30, 2017, https://www.nytimes.com/2017/01/30/opinion/trump-the-wall-and-the-spanish-language.html; Matthew Boyle, "Exclusive—Donald Trump Fires Back at Jeb Bush: He Should Lead by 'Speaking English' While in the United States," *Breitbart News*, September 2, 2015, http://www.breitbart.com/big-government/2015/09/02/exclusive-donald-trump-fires-back-at-jeb-bush-he-should-lead-by-speaking-english-while-in-the-united-states/; "Trump: 'This Is a Country Where We Speak English,'" *CNN Politics*, September 16, 2015, https://edition.cnn.com/videos/politics/2015/09/16/gop-debate-cnn-debate-8p-12.cnn.

INTRODUCTION

20. Francesca Orsini, "The Multilingual Local in World Literature," *Comparative Literature* 67, no. 4 (2015): 345–74; Tim Parks, "The Dull New Global Novel," *New York Review of Books*, February 2010, http://www.nybooks.com/blogs/nyrblog/2010/feb/09/the-dull-new-global-novel/.
21. David Damrosch, *What Is World Literature?* (Princeton, N.J.: Princeton University Press, 2003), 4.
22. Américo Paredes, *George Washington Gómez* (Houston: Arte Público Press, 1990), 12. All parenthetical translations are my own, unless otherwise stated.
23. Paredes, *George Washington Gómez*, 22; 138.
24. Lourdes Torres, "In the Contact Zone: Code-Switching Strategies by Latino/a Writers," *MELUS* 32, no. 1 (2007): 79.
25. Linguists have shown that in literature, as in oral discourse, Spanish often falls into specific lexical categories such as tags, exclamations, vocatives, directives, expletives, quotations, and common nouns. See, for example, Laura Callahan, *English-Spanish Codeswitching in a Written Corpus* (Philadelphia: John Benjamins Publishing Company, 2004). For further sociolinguistic approaches to the mixing of English and Spanish in literary prose, see Gary Keller, "How Chicano Authors Use Bilingual Techniques for Literary Effect," in *Chicano Studies: A Multidisciplinary Approach*, ed. Eugene García, Francisco Lomeli, and Isidro Ortíz (New York: Teacher's College Press, 1984), 171–89; Ernst Rudin, *Tender Accents of Sound: Spanish in the Chicano Novel in English* (Tempe, Ariz.: Bilingual Press/Editorial Bilingüe, 1996); Cecilia Montes-Alcalá, "Code-Switching in U.S. Latino Novels," in *Language Mixing and Code-Switching in Writing*, ed. Mark Sebba, Shahrzad Mahootian, and Carla Johnson (New York: Routledge, 2012), 68–88.
26. Paredes, *George Washington Gómez*, 29.
27. Bill Ashcroft, Gareth Griffiths, and Helen Tiffin, *The Empire Writes Back*, 2nd ed. (London: Routledge, 2002), 16.
28. New scholarly programs that addressed the histories and cultures of Latinxs, African Americans, Native Americans, and Asian Americans were established at leading U.S. universities in response to the demands in 1969 of the Third World Liberation Front, a coalition of minority student protestors. Some of the earliest Latinx departments were the Chicanx Studies departments at San Francisco State University and at California State University, Northridge, established in the autumn of 1969.
29. Gloria Anzaldúa, *Borderlands/La Frontera: The New Mestiza*, 4th ed. (San Francisco: Aunt Lute Books, 2012), 20.
30. Anzaldúa, *Borderlands/La Frontera*, 80.
31. Anzaldúa, *Borderlands/La Frontera*, 77. Despite efforts by Anzaldúa, Chávez-Silverman (whom I discuss in chapter 1), and others, academic exchange remains largely monolingual, and in many disciplines it remains standard practice to translate all quotations from other languages.
32. Anzaldúa, *Borderlands/La Frontera*, 78.
33. *Oxford English Dictionary Online*, s.v. "Spanglish," accessed May 23, 2021, https://www.oed.com/view/Entry/185565?redirectedFrom=spanglish; Anzaldúa, *Borderlands/La Frontera*, 78.
34. E. Acosta-Belén, "Spanglish: A Case of Languages in Contact," in *New Directions in Second Language Learning, Teaching and Bilingual Education*, ed. Marina Burt and Helen Dulay (Washington, D.C.: TESOL, 1975), 151.

INTRODUCTION

35. Roberto González Echevarría, "Is 'Spanglish' a Language?," *New York Times*, March 27, 1997.
36. Urban Dictionary, s.v. "Spanglish," accessed May 23, 2021, http://www.urbandictionary.com/define.php?term=Spanglish.
37. John M. Lipski, *Varieties of Spanish in the United States* (Washington, D.C.: Georgetown University Press, 2008), 71. For a different critique of the term "Spanglish," see Ricardo Otheguy and Nancy Stern, who dispute the suggestion that "Spanglish" is a fixed, third language, and use empirical methods to argue that it is simply one of many popular varieties of Spanish, which should instead be known as "Spanish in the USA." Ricardo Otheguy and Nancy Stern, "On So-Called Spanglish," *International Journal of Bilingualism* 15, no. 1 (2010): 85–100.
38. Anzaldúa, *Borderlands/La Frontera*, 81.
39. Anzaldúa, *Borderlands/La Frontera*, 163.
40. Anzaldúa, *Borderlands/La Frontera*, 216.
41. "We the American Hispanics" (Ethnic and Hispanic Statistics Branch, Bureau of the Census, September 1993), https://www.census.gov/prod/cen1990/wepeople/we-2r.pdf.
42. Puerto Rico has had the status of associated free state since the end of the Spanish-American War in 1898, meaning that its citizens have free movement between the island and the U.S. mainland.
43. Miguel Algarín and Miguel Piñero, *Nuyorican Poetry: An Anthology of Puerto Rican Words and Feelings* (New York: William Morrow, 1975), 9.
44. Ed Morales, *Living in Spanglish* (New York: St Martin's Press, 2002).
45. Ana Celia Zentella, "Preface," in *Bilingualism and Identity: Spanish at the Crossroads with Other Languages*, ed. M. Niño-Murcia and J. Rothman (Philadelphia: John Benjamins Publishing Company, 2008), 3–10; Ana Celia Zentella and Ricardo Otheguy, "Discussion on the Use of the Term 'Spanglish'" (conference paper, Spanish in the U.S. and Spanish in Contact with Other Languages, Florida International University, 2009), http://potowski.org/sites/potowski.org/files/articles/attachments/Summary_debate_Spanglish_Zentella%20_Otheguy.pdf.
46. Giannina Braschi, *Yo-Yo Boing!* (Las Vegas: AmazonCrossing, 2011).
47. U.S. Census Bureau, "Annual Estimates of the Resident Population by Sex, Age, Race, and Hispanic Origin for the United States and States: April 1, 2010 to July 1, 2015," July 2016, https://factfinder.census.gov/faces/tableservices/jsf/pages/productview.xhtml?src=bkmk.
48. Gustavo Pérez Firmat, *Tongue Ties: Logo-Eroticism in Anglo-Hispanic Literature* (New York: Palgrave Macmillan, 2003), 139–41.
49. The term "latinidad" recalls Simón Bolívar's vision of a strong and united Latin America in the face of European colonialism and the emerging dominance of the United States in the early nineteenth century. It also harks back to Cuban writer and activist José Martí's important 1891 essay "Nuestra América," which argued for the nurturing of a unified Latin American culture in the face of growing U.S. expansionism. For further discussion of latinidad as a unifying identity concept, see Marta Caminero-Santangelo, "Latinidad," in *The Routledge Companion to Latino/a Literature*, 2nd ed., ed. Suzanne Bost and Frances R. Aparicio, 13–24 (Abingdon, UK: Routledge, 2014).
50. Anzaldúa, *Borderlands/La Frontera*, 216.

51. Marlene Hansen Esplin, "Self-Translation and Accommodation: Strategies of Multilingualism in Gloria Anzaldúa's *Borderlands/La Frontera: The New Mestiza* and Margarita Cota-Cárdenas's *Puppet*," *MELUS* 41, no. 2 (2016): 176–201.
52. Graham Huggan, *The Postcolonial Exotic: Marketing the Margins* (London: Routledge, 2001), xi; 87.
53. Ellen McCracken, *Paratexts and Performance in the Novels of Junot Díaz and Sandra Cisneros* (New York: Palgrave Macmillan, 2015); see also Sarah Brouillette, *Postcolonial Writers in the Global Literary Marketplace* (New York: Palgrave Macmillan, 2007). On the commodification and marketing of literary prestige, see further Luke Strongman, *The Booker Prize and the Legacy of Empire* (Amsterdam: Rodopi, 2002); James English, *The Economy of Prestige: Prizes, Awards, and the Circulation of Cultural Value* (Cambridge, Mass.: Harvard University Press, 2005); Sarah Brouillette, *Literature and the Creative Economy* (Stanford, Calif.: Stanford University Press, 2014).
54. McCracken, *Paratexts and Performance*.
55. Rachael Gilmour and Tamar Steinitz, eds., *Multilingual Currents in Literature, Translation, and Culture* (New York: Routledge, 2017), 7.
56. Ilan Stavans, *Spanglish: The Making of a New American Language* (New York: HarperCollins, 2003); Ilan Stavans, "Hamlet, Translated into Spanglish," *Literary Hub*, April 2016, https://lithub.com/hamlet-translated-into-spanglish/; Antoine de Saint-Exupéry, *El Little Príncipe*, trans. Ilan Stavans (Neckarsteinach: Edition Tintenfass, 2016).
57. Lipski, *Varieties of Spanish in the United States*, 53; Marta Caminero-Santangelo, *On Latinidad: U.S. Latino Literature and the Construction of Ethnicity* (Gainsville: University Press of Florida, 2007); Elena Machado Sáez, "Reconquista: Ilan Stavans and the Indigenous Other in Multiculturalist Latino Discourse," *Latino Studies* 7, no. 4 (Winter 2009): 410–34. For further critiques of Stavans's project, see Juan Flores, *From Bomba to Hip-Hop: Puerto Rican Culture and Latino Identity* (New York: Columbia University Press, 2000); Paul Allatson, "Ilan Stavans's Latino USA: A Cartoon History (of a Cosmopolitan Intellectual)," *Chasqui* 35, no. 1 (2006): 21–41. For a comprehensive overview of Stavans's career, see Steven G. Kellman, *The Restless Ilan Stavans: Outsider on the Inside* (Pittsburgh, Penn.: University of Pittsburgh Press, 2019).
58. Daniel Alarcón, *El rey siempre está por encima del pueblo* (Mexico City: Sexto Piso, 2009).
59. Ariel Dorfman, for instance, wrote his memoir in English before translating it into Spanish. Ariel Dorfman, *Heading South, Looking North: A Bilingual Journey* (New York: Farrar, Straus and Giroux, 1998); Ariel Dorfman, *Rumbo al sur, deseando al norte: Un romance bilingue* (Barcelona: Planeta, 1998).
60. See, for instance, Aura Xilonen, *Campeón gabacho* (Mexico City: Penguin Random House, 2015).
61. These include spontaneous contact vernaculars in border regions, errors produced by speakers attempting to speak the L2 (the second language) correctly, and idiosyncratic invented speech designed to facilitate communication, as Lipski has demonstrated at some length. John M. Lipski, "Too Close for Comfort? The Genesis of 'Portuñol/Portunhol,'" in *Selected Proceedings of the 8th Hispanic*

INTRODUCTION

Linguistics Symposium, ed. Timothy L. Face and Carol A. Klee (Somerville, Mass.: Cascadilla Proceedings Project, 2006), 1–22. For a study of "Portunhol" in the border region between Spain and Portugal, see María Jesús Fernández García, "Portuñol y literatura," *Revista de Estudios Extremeños* 62 (2006): 555–76.

62. Lipski, "Too Close for Comfort?," 3.
63. See the examples cited in Lipski, "Too Close for Comfort?," 3.
64. Gladis Massini-Cagliari, "Language Policy in Brazil: Monolingualism and Linguistic Prejudice," *Language Policy* 3, no. 1 (2004): 3–23.
65. Shaw N. Gynan, "Language Planning and Policy in Paraguay," *Current Issues in Language Planning* 2, no. 1 (November 2001): 53–118, https://doi.org/10.1080/14664200108668019.
66. Lipski, "Too Close for Comfort?," 14. For more on the matrix language frame model, see Carol Myers-Scotton, *Social Motivations for Code-Switching* (Oxford: Oxford University Press, 1993).
67. Fernández García, "Portuñol y literatura"; See also Luis Ernesto Behares and Carlos Ernesto Diaz, eds., *Os som de nossa terra: Productos artístico-verbales fronterizos* (Montevideo: Asociación de Universidades Grupo Montevideo, Universidad de la República, 1998); Brenda V. de López, *Lenguaje fronterizo en obras de autores uruguayos*, 2nd ed. (Montevideo: Editorial Nordan-Comunidad, 1993).
68. Fernández García, "Portuñol y literatura," 578.
69. Douglas Diegues, *Dá gusto andar desnudo por estas selvas: Sonetos salvajes* (Curitiba: Travessa dos Editores, 2003).
70. Douglas Diegues, "Karta manifesto Del amor amor em portunhol selvagem" [Manifesto letter of love love in portunhol selvagem], *Portal O Globo Cultura*, August 17, 2008, http://oglobo.globo.com/cultura/confira-manifesto-em-defesa-do-portunhol-selvagem-3607777.
71. Diegues, "Karta manifesto."
72. See, for example, the work of Paraguayan poet Jorge Canese (who also publishes as Xorxe Kanexe, Jorge Kanese, and just the initial K). Jorge Canese, *Las palabras K* (Asunción: Arandurã Editorial, 2011).
73. Fábio Aristimunho Vargas, "Fronteiras literárias: As línguas ibéricas e o portunhol" (conference paper, VI Congresso Internacional Roa Bastos, Foz do Iguaçu, 2011), http://www.nelool.ufsc.br/simposio2011/fronteiras_literarias.pdf.
74. It is worth noting that, much like Ilan Stavans has done with "Spanglish," Diegues has gone to some effort to codify "portunhol selvagem" and encourage its use, as is evident from the work posted on his blog: *Portunhol selvagem: El blog de Douglas Diegues*, http://portunholselvagem.blogspot.com. Here one can read Diegues's efforts to translate excerpts from canonical works of English literature into "portunhol selvagem," including parts of Shakespeare's *King Lear* and Edgar Allan Poe's *The Raven*. His choice of the sonnet form for his *Dá gusto andar desnudo por estas selvas: Sonetos salvajes* also suggests a desire to demonstrate the suitability of this hybrid language to established poetic form.
75. Antonio Marques and Leonardo Rocha, "Bolsonaro diz que OAB só defende bandido e reserva indígena é um crime," *Campo Grande News*, April 22, 2015, https://www.campograndenews.com.br/politica/bolsonaro-diz-que-oab-so-defende-bandido-e-reserva-indigena-e-um-crime.

76. René Etiemble, *Parlez-vous franglais?* (Paris: Gallimard, 1991).
77. Philip Thody, *Le Franglais: Forbidden English, Forbidden American: Law, Politics and Language in Contemporary France: A Study in Loan Words and National Identity* (London: Bloomsbury, 2000).
78. Eva Valenti, "'Nous Autres c'est Toujours Bilingue Anyways': Code-Switching and Linguistic Displacement Among Bilingual Montréal Students," *American Review of Canadian Studies* 44 (2014): 279–329.
79. "Census in Brief: English-French Bilingualism Reaches New Heights," *Statistics Canada*, 2017, https://www12.statcan.gc.ca/census-recensement/2016/as-sa/98-200-x/2016009/98-200-x2016009-eng.cfm.
80. Nicole Brossard, "Reconfiguration, from *SeaMother, or the Bitteroded Chapter*," trans. Erín Moure and Robert Mazjels, *Asymptote*, July 2019, https://www.asymptotejournal.com/poetry/nicole-brossard-reconfiguration-seamother-or-the-bitteroded-chapter/.
81. Nicole Brossard, *Picture Theory*, trans. Barbara Godard (Toronto: Guernica, 2006), 11.
82. Brossard, *Picture Theory*, 11.
83. Nancy Huston, *Plainsong* (Toronto: HarperCollins, 1993); Nancy Huston, *Cantique des plaines: Roman* (Montréal: Leméac, 1993).
84. Erín Moure, "Polylingual Writers: The Joyous Sea of Words," *Quebec Writers' Federation*, December 7, 2017, https://qwfwrites.wordpress.com/2017/12/07/the-joyous-sea-of-words-by-erin-moure/.
85. Yasemin Yildiz, *Beyond the Mother Tongue: The Postmonolingual Condition* (New York: Fordham University Press, 2011), 4.
86. Miller, *Accented America*; Juliette Taylor-Batty, *Multilingualism in Modernist Fiction* (Basingstoke, UK: Palgrave Macmillan, 2013); Laura Lonsdale, *Multilingualism and Modernity: Barbarisms in Spanish and American Literature* (Basingstoke, UK: Palgrave Macmillan, 2018).
87. Viktor Shklovsky, *Theory of Prose*, trans. Benjamin Sher (London: Dalkey Archive Press, 2009), 13.
88. Parks, "The Dull New Global Novel"; Emily Apter, *Against World Literature: On the Politics of Untranslatability* (London: Verso, 2013); Minae Mizumura, *The Fall of Language in the Age of English*, trans. Mari Yoshihara and Juliet Winters Carpenter (New York: Columbia University Press, 2008); Lennon, *In Babel's Shadow*; see also Nikil Saval and Dayna Tortorici, "World Lite: What Is Global Literature," *n+1* 17, "The Evil Issue" (Fall 2013), https://nplusonemag.com/issue-17/the-intellectual-situation/world-lite/.
89. Damrosch, *What Is World Literature?*, 25.
90. Lennon, *In Babel's Shadow*, 2; Apter, *Against World Literature*, 4.
91. Fiona J. Doloughan, *Contemporary Narrative: Textual Production, Multimodality and Multiliteracies* (London: Continuum, 2011); Fiona J. Doloughan, *English as a Language in Translation* (London: Bloomsbury, 2016).
92. Rebecca L. Walkowitz, *Born Translated: The Contemporary Novel in an Age of World Literature* (New York: Columbia University Press, 2015), 3–4, emphasis in original. For another approach to "translational" writing, see Waïl S. Hassan, "Agency and Translational Literature: Ahdaf Soueif's *The Map of Love*," *PMLA* 121, no. 3 (2015): 753–68.

INTRODUCTION

93. For instance, Yolanda Martínez San-Miguel describes some of the bilingual poems in Tato Laviera's *AmeRícan* as "untranslatable." Yolanda Martínez-San Miguel, "Boricua (Between) Borders: On the Possibility of Translating Bilingual Narratives," in *Spanglish*, ed. Ilan Stavans (Westport, Conn.: Greenwood Press, 2008), 75; 76. See also Lennon, *In Babel's Shadow*, where he argues that "strong plurilingual writing" is to all intents and purposes "untranslatable" because large trade publishers who rely on the sale of translation rights are unwilling to publish it.
94. For an example of the former tendency, see Lauret, *Wanderwords*, 17–18; for an example of the latter tendency, see Hassan, "Agency and Translational Literature"; Walkowitz, *Born Translated*; Cutter, *Lost and Found in Translation*.
95. For instance, Kathy Mezei, "Bilingualism and Translation in/of Michèle Lalonde's *Speak White*," *The Translator* 4, no. 2 (1998): 229–47; Rosenwald, *Multilingual America*; Michael Boyden and Patrick Goethals, "Translating the Watcher's Voice: Junot Díaz's *The Brief Wondrous Life of Oscar Wao* into Spanish," *Meta: Journal Des Traducteurs/Meta: Translators' Journal* 56, no. 1 (2011): 20–41; Anne-Marie Wheeler, "Issues of Translation in the Work of Nicole Brossard," *Yale Journal of Criticism* 16, no. 2 (2003): 425–54; Françoise Lionnet, "Creole Vernacular Translations in Mauritius," *MLN* 118 (2003): 911–32. See also a number of functionalist descriptive studies in the special issue of *Target* on "heterolingualism." Reine Meylaerts, "Heterolingualism in/and Translation." Special issue, *Target* 18, no. 1 (2006).
96. Reine Meylaerts, "Literary Heteroglossia in Translation: When the Language of Translation Is the Locus of Ideological Struggle," in *Translation Studies at the Interface of Disciplines*, ed. João Ferreira Duarte, Alejandra Assis Rosa, and Teresa Seruya (Amsterdam: John Benjamins Publishing Company, 2006); Rainier Grutman, "Multilingualism and Translation," in *Routledge Encyclopedia of Translation Studies*, ed. Mona Baker (London: Routledge, 2004), 157–60; Rainier Grutman, "Refraction and Recognition" Literary Multilingualism in Translation," *Target* 18, no. 1 (2006), 17–47; Meir Sternberg, "Polylingualism as Reality and Translation as Mimesis," *Poetics Today* 2, no. 4 (1981): 221–39.
97. Barbara Cassin, ed., *Dictionary of Untranslatables: A Philosophical Lexicon*, trans. Emily Apter, Jacques Lezra, and Michael Wood (Princeton, N.J.: Princeton University Press, 2014), xvii; originally published as Barbara Cassin, ed., *Vocabulaire européen des philosophes: Dictionnaire des intraduisibles* (Paris: Éditions de Seuil; Le Robert, 2004).
98. Rebecca L. Walkowitz, "Translating the Untranslatable: An Interview with Barbara Cassin," *Public Books*, June 2014, http://www.publicbooks.org/interviews/translating-the-untranslatable-an-interview-with-barbara-cassin.
99. Rebecca L. Walkowitz, "Close Reading in an Age of Global Writing," *Modern Language Quarterly* 74, no. 2 (2013): 171–95.
100. Frost defines poetry as "that which tends to evaporate from both prose and verse when translated." Robert Frost, unpublished notebook, 1950–1955, Robert Frost Collection, MS 001728 (Dartmouth College, Hanover, N.H.).
101. Abdelfattah Kilito, "Thou Shalt Not Translate Me," 2010, https://vimeo.com/17363157.
102. Anzaldúa, *Borderlands/La Frontera*, 20.
103. Anzaldúa, *Borderlands/La Frontera*, 222.
104. Anzaldúa, *Borderlands/La Frontera*, 224.

INTRODUCTION

105. Anzaldúa, *Borderlands/La Frontera*, 224.
106. Lawrence Venuti, *The Translator's Invisibility: A History of Translation*, 2nd ed. (London: Routledge, 2002).
107. Venuti, *The Translator's Invisibility*, 16.
108. Walkowitz, *Born Translated*, 6.
109. Susan Bassnett and Peter Bush, eds., *The Translator as Writer* (London: Continuum, 2006); Manuela Perteghella and Eugenia Loffredo, eds., *Translation and Creativity: Perspectives on Creative Writing and Translation Studies* (London: Continuum, 2006).
110. Cecilia Rossi, "Literary Translation and Disciplinary Boundaries: Creative Writing and Interdisciplinarity," in *The Routledge Handbook of Literary Translation*, ed. Kelly Washbourne and Ben van Wyke, 42–57 (London: Routledge, 2018); Cecilia Rossi, "Translation as a Creative Force," in *The Routledge Handbook of Translation and Culture*, ed. Sue-Ann Harding and Ovidi Carbonell Cortés (London: Routledge, 2018), 381–97.
111. Damrosch, *What Is World Literature?*, 6; Franco Moretti, "Conjectures on World Literature," *New Left Review* (January–February 2000): 67.
112. For a materialist approach to literary comparatism, see Warwick Research Collective, *Combined and Uneven Development: Towards a New Theory of World-Literature* (Liverpool: Liverpool University Press, 2015).
113. In addition to those I have already discussed, see Roberto Ignacio Díaz, *Unhomely Rooms: Foreign Tongues and Spanish American Literature* (Lewisburg, Penn.: Bucknell University Press, 2002). On Chicanx writing in particular, see Keller, "How Chicano Authors Use Bilingual Techniques for Literary Effect"; Alfred Arteaga, ed., *An Other Tongue: Nation and Ethnicity in the Linguistic Borderlands* (Durham, N.C.: Duke University Press, 1994); Rudin, *Tender Accents of Sound*. See also Callahan, *English-Spanish Codeswitching*, for a comprehensive corpus linguistic approach to English-Spanish literary "code-switching."
114. Yildiz, *Beyond the Mother Tongue*, 4.

1. "MI LENGUA ES UN PALIMPSESTO": SUSANA CHÁVEZ-SILVERMAN'S PALIMPSESTUOUS WRITING

1. Susana Chávez-Silverman, *Killer Crónicas: Bilingual Memories* (Madison: University of Wisconsin Press, 2004). Hereafter references to this volume will appear in the main body of the text as *KC*.
2. *Oxford English Dictionary Online*, s.v. "palimpsest," accessed May 25, 2021, https://www.oed.com/view/Entry/136319?rskey=akaoe3&result=1&isAdvanced=false.
3. Ania Spyra, "Language, Geography, Globalisation: Susana Chávez-Silverman's Rejection of Translation in *Killer Crónicas: Bilingual Memories*," in *Literature, Geography, Translation: Studies in World Writing*, ed. Cecilia Alvstad, Stefan Helgesson, and David Watson (Newcastle: Cambridge Scholars Publishing, 2011), 201.
4. Susana Chávez-Silverman, *Scenes from la Cuenca de Los Angeles y otros Natural Disasters* (Madison: University of Wisconsin Press, 2010). Hereafter references to this volume will appear in the main body of the text as *SC*.

1. "MI LENGUA ES UN PALIMPSESTO"

5. Roshawnda A. Derrick, "Radical Bilingualism in *Killer Crónicas*," *Hispania* 97, no. 3 (2014): 366–67.
6. Spyra, "Language, Geography, Globalisation."
7. AnaLouise Keating, *The Gloria Anzaldúa Reader* (Durham, N.C.: Duke University Press, 2009), 10.
8. Sarah Dillon, *The Palimpsest* (London: Continuum, 2007), 3.
9. Gérard Genette, *Palimpsests: Literature in the Second Degree*, trans. Channa Newman and Claude Doubinsky (Lincoln: University of Nebraska Press, 1982), 1.
10. Susana Chávez-Silverman, interview with author, May 25, 2015.
11. Franco Moretti, *Distant Reading* (London: Verso, 2013).
12. Susana Chávez-Silverman, interview with author, May 25, 2015.
13. Susana Chávez-Silverman, interview with author, May 25, 2015.
14. *Oxford English Dictionary Online*, s.v. "glossary," accessed May 25, 2021, https://www.oed.com/view/Entry/79143?rskey=Nmv55Q&result=1&isAdvanced=false.
15. Doris Sommer, *Bilingual Aesthetics: A New Sentimental Education* (Durham, N.C.: Duke University Press, 2004), 129.
16. Mikhail Bakhtin, *The Dialogic Imagination: Four Essays*, trans. Vadim Liapunov (Austin: University of Texas Press, 1981), 294.
17. Bakhtin, *The Dialogic Imagination*, 354.
18. The *Diccionario panhispánico de dudas* describes this linguistic phenomenon thus: "También es extremadamente débil la pronunciación de la /d/ final de palabra, que en el habla poco esmerada de algunas zonas de España tiende a perderse: [madrí, usté, berdá], por *Madrid, usted, verdad;* en realidad, en la pronunciación normal se articula una /d/ final muy relajada, apenas perceptible. En zonas del centro de España, algunos hablantes cambian por /z/ el sonido /d/ en final de sílaba o de palabra, pronunciación que debe evitarse en el habla esmerada: [azkirír] por *adquirir*, [birtúz] por *virtud*" (The pronunciation of the /d/ at the end of the word is also extremely weak, and in careless speech in some parts of Spain it tends to be lost: [madrí, usté, berdá], for *Madrid, usted, verdad*; in reality, normal pronunciation involves a very relaxed final /d/, almost imperceptible. In parts of central Spain, some speakers replace the /d/ sound with /z/ at the end of a syllable or word, a pronunciation that should be avoided in careful speech: [azkirir] for *adquirir*, [birtúz] for *virtud*). *Diccionario panhispánico de dudas*, s.v. "d," accessed May 25, 2021, https://www.rae.es/dpd/d.
19. Jacques Derrida, *Monolingualism of the Other; Or, the Prosthesis of Origin*, trans. Patrick Mensah (Stanford, Calif.: Stanford University Press, 1996); Rey Chow, *Not Like a Native Speaker: On Languaging as a Postcolonial Experience* (New York: Columbia University Press, 2014), 14.
20. Bakhtin describes novelistic discourse as being characterized by the interaction and conflict between different types of speech, including "social dialects, characteristic group behaviour, professional jargons, generic languages, languages of generations and age groups, tendentious languages, languages of the authorities, of various circles and of passing fashions." Bakhtin, *The Dialogic Imagination*, 262.
21. Susana Chávez-Silverman, "Todo verdor perdurará Crónica," *Asymptote*, July 2015, https://www.asymptotejournal.com/special-feature/susana-chavezsilverman-all-green-will-endure-chronicle/spanish/.

1. "MI LENGUA ES UN PALIMPSESTO"

22. Garrett Stewart, *Reading Voices: Literature and the Phonotext* (Berkeley: University of California Press, 1990), 4.
23. Susana Chávez-Silverman, "Vivir (con) la pregunta: Mis crónicas del Sur, y otras hierbas" (presentation, XX Congreso Internacional de Literatura Hispánica, Santiago de Compostela, June 21–23, 2017).
24. Stewart, *Reading Voices: Literature and the Phonotext*, 10.
25. Susana Chávez-Silverman, "Susana Chávez-Silverman Reading from *Killer Crónicas*," University of Wisconsin Press, http://uwpress.wisc.edu/books/2616-audio.html.
26. Sam McManis, "Author Mixes Spanish, English in Her 'Cronicas,'" *Sacramento Bee*, May 2007.
27. For a discussion of the controversy over the Spanish "Star-Spangled Banner," see Joshua Miller, *Accented America: The Cultural Politics of Multilingual Modernism* (New York: Oxford University Press, 2011), 4.
28. Genette, *Palimpsests*.
29. Genette, *Palimpsests*, 5.
30. Genette, *Palimpsests*, 395.
31. Susana Chávez-Silverman, interview with author, May 25, 2015.
32. Susana Chávez-Silverman, interview with author, May 25, 2015.
33. Susana Chávez-Silverman, interview with author, May 25, 2015.
34. Mary Louise Pratt, *Imperial Eyes* (London: Routledge, 1992), 2.
35. "Tropicalization" is the term Chávez-Silverman and Frances Aparicio have used to refer to the construction of "latinidad" through images of sexuality, passion, and "spice," by others but also from within, thus rendering Latinxs as objectified, exotic foreigners. Frances R. Aparicio and Susana Chávez-Silverman, eds., *Tropicalizations: Transcultural Representations of Latinidad* (Hanover, N.H.: University Press of New England, 1997).
36. Maggie Nelson, *The Argonauts* (Minneapolis, Minn.: Graywolf Press, 2015); Alison Bechdel, *Are You My Mother? A Comic Drama* (Boston: Mariner Books, 2013); Paul B. Preciado, *Testo Junkie: Sex, Drugs, and Biopolitics in the Pharmacopornographic Era* (New York: Feminist Press, 2013). Stacey Young first used the English term "autotheory" in 1997, when she argued that autotheoretical texts "differ from straightforwardly autobiographical accounts . . . in that they not only place personal experience within political contexts, but they also conceive of those contexts as multiple and shifting." Stacey Young, *Changing the Wor(l)d: Discourse, Politics, and the Feminist Movement* (New York: Routledge, 1997), 14.
37. Sara Ahmed, *Living a Feminist Life* (Durham, N.C.: Duke University Press, 2017).
38. Lorde described her book *Zami: A New Spelling of My Name*, as a "biomythography." Audre Lorde, *Zami: A New Spelling of My Name* (Trumansburg, N.Y.: Crossing Press, 1982); Gloria Anzaldúa and AnaLouise Keating, "Now Let Us Shift . . . the Path of Conocimiento . . . Inner Work, Public Acts," in *This Bridge We Call Home: Radical Visions for Transformation*, ed. Anzaldúa and Keating (New York: Routledge, 2002), 540–78.
39. Jacques Derrida, *Speech and Phenomena and Other Essays on Husserl's Theory of Signs* (Evanston, Ill.: Northwestern University Press, 1973), 89.
40. The rhizome "has neither beginning nor end, but always a middle (*milieu*) from which it grows and which it overspills . . . the rhizome is an acentered,

1. "MI LENGUA ES UN PALIMPSESTO"

nonhierarchical, nonsignifying system." Gilles Deleuze and Félix Guattari, *A Thousand Plateaus: Capitalism and Schizophrenia* (London: Athlone Press, 1988), 21.

41. "Like in my last book, *Killer Crónicas*, like *The Mix Tapes*, que digamos, *The Mixquiahuala Letters* de la Ann Castle, or *Hopscotch*, de Julio Cortázar, estas crónicas constan de vignettes" (Like in my last book, *Killer Crónicas*, like *The Mix Tapes*, which is to say, *The Mixquiahuala Letters* by Ana Castillo, or *Hopscotch*, by Julio Cortázar, these crónicas are made up of vignettes) (SC, 8).
42. In a recent challenge to this monograph-centered model, Eric Hayot highlights the financial, psychological, and familial strain placed on scholars by requiring them to publish a book early in their careers. See Eric Hayot, "The Profession Does Not Need the Monograph Dissertation," *Profession*, May 26, 2017, https://profession.mla.hcommons.org/2017/05/26/the-profession-does-not-need-the-monograph-dissertation/.
43. Walter Mignolo, *Local Histories/Global Designs: Coloniality, Subaltern Knowledges, and Border Thinking* (Princeton, N.J.: Princeton University Press, 2000), 261.
44. Julio Cortázar, *Final del juego*, 5th ed. (Buenos Aires: Editorial Sudamericana, 1966), 161–68.
45. Cortázar, *Final del juego*, 161–68.
46. Cortázar, *Final del juego*, 164.
47. Julio Cortázar, *Rayuela*, ed. Julio Ortega and Saúl Yurkievich (Madrid: Colección Archivos, 1991), 263, 361.
48. Cortázar, *Rayuela*, 367.
49. Susana Chávez-Silverman and Librada Hernández, eds., *Reading and Writing the Ambiente: Queer Sexualities in Latino, Latin American, and Spanish Culture* (Madison: University of Wisconsin Press, 2000).
50. Hélène Cixous advocated a feminine mode of writing that would free women from men's dominance of intellectual culture. See Hélène Cixous, "The Laugh of the Medusa," trans. Keith Cohen and Paula Cohen, *Signs* 1, no. 4 (1976): 875–93.
51. Susana Chávez-Silverman, "Tropicalizing the Liberal Arts College Classroom," in *Power, Race, and Gender in Academe: Strangers in The Tower?*, ed. Shirley Geok-lin Lim, María Herrera-Sobek, and Genaro M. Padilla (New York: Modern Language Association, 2000), 132.
52. Chavez-Silverman, "Tropicalizing the Liberal Arts College Classroom," 133, 134.
53. Susana Chávez-Silverman, *Heartthrob: Del Balboa Café al Apartheid and Back* (Madison: Wisconsin University Press, 2019), locs. 1099, 1076 of 5907, Kindle.
54. Chávez-Silverman, *Heartthrob: Del Balboa Café al Apartheid and Back*, loc. 1352 of 5907.
55. Chávez-Silverman, *Heartthrob: Del Balboa Café al Apartheid and Back*, loc. 1043 of 5907.
56. Eve Kosofsky Sedgwick, *Tendencies* (Durham, N.C.: Duke University Press, 1993), 8.
57. Susana Chavez-Silverman, "Axolotl/Bichos Raros Crónica," *PORTAL: Journal of Multidisciplinary International Studies* 9, no. 2 (2012): 1. Emphasis in original.
58. Chávez-Silverman, "Vivir (con) la pregunta: Mis crónicas del Sur, y otras hierbas."
59. Brian Lennon, *In Babel's Shadow: Multilingual Literatures, Monolingual States* (Minneapolis: University of Minnesota Press, 2010), 74. Fiona J. Doloughan, too, has argued that contemporary translational writing makes reading into "a form

1. "MI LENGUA ES UN PALIMPSESTO"

of translation." Fiona J. Doloughan, "Translation as a Motor of Critique and Invention in Contemporary Literature," in *Multilingual Currents in Literature, Translation, and Culture*, ed. Rachael Gilmour and Tamar Steinitz (New York: Routledge, 2018), 165.

60. Spyra, "Language, Geography, Globalisation."
61. See further Shklovsky's discussion in "Art as Device." Shklovsky, *Theory of Prose*, trans. Benjamin Sher (London: Dalkey Archive Press, 2009).
62. Haun Saussy, "The Importance of What Doesn't Translate" (George Steiner Lecture, Queen Mary University of London, March 9, 2015).
63. *Oxford English Dictionary Online*, s.v. "calque," accessed May 25, 2021, https://www.oed.com/view/Entry/26536?rskey=2drT3k&result=1&isAdvanced=false.
64. Maria Lauret, *Wanderwords: Language Migration in American Literature* (London: Bloomsbury, 2014), 242.
65. Esteban Echeverría, *El matadero; La cautiva* (Madrid: Ediciones Cátedra, 1997).
66. Esteban Echeverría, *The Slaughteryard*, trans. Norman Thomas di Giovanni and Susan Ashe (London: Friday Project, 2010).
67. Garrett Stewart, "Modernism's Sonic Waiver: Literary Writing and the Filmic Device," in *Sound States: Innovative Poetics and Acoustical Technologies*, ed. Adelaide Morris (Chapel Hill: University of North Carolina Press, 1997), 237.
68. Doris Sommer, *Bilingual Games: Some Literary Investigations* (New York: Palgrave Macmillan, 2003); Sommer, *Bilingual Aesthetics*.
69. Susana Chávez-Silverman, "All Green Will Endure Chrónicle," trans. Ellen Jones, *Asymptote*, July 2015, https://www.asymptotejournal.com/special-feature/susana-chavezsilverman-all-green-will-endure-chronicle/.
70. Umberto Eco, "Introduction," in *Anna Livia Plurabelle Di James Joyce*, ed. Rosa Maria Bollettieri Bosinelli (Turin: Einaudi, 1996), xi; quoted in Lawrence Alan Rosenwald, *Multilingual America: Language and the Making of American Literature* (Cambridge: Cambridge University Press, 2008), 124.
71. See Patrick O'Neill, *Impossible Joyce: Finnegans Wakes* (Toronto: University of Toronto Press, 2013).
72. Rosenwald, *Multilingual America*, 125–26. Barbara Cassin, ed., *Dictionary of Untranslatables: A Philosophical Lexicon*, trans. Emily Apter, Jacques Lezra, and Michael Wood (Princeton, N.J.: Princeton University Press, 2014), xvii.
73. Rebecca L. Walkowitz, "Close Reading in an Age of Global Writing," *Modern Language Quarterly* 74, no. 2 (2013): 173.
74. Ana Maria Shua, "Killer Crónicas: Bilingual Memories," *Letras Femeninas* 31, no. 1 (2005): 261–62.
75. Susana Chávez-Silverman, email to author, May 25, 2015.
76. Susana Chávez-Silverman, email to author, May 25, 2015.
77. See Derrick, "Radical Bilingualism in *Killer Crónicas*."
78. María José García Vizcaíno, "Cisneros' Code-Mixed Narrative and Its Implications for Translation," *Mutatis Mutandis* 1, no. 2 (2008): 212–24.
79. Gloria Anzaldúa, *Borderlands/La Frontera: The New Mestiza*, 4th ed. (San Francisco: Aunt Lute Books, 2012), 222–25.
80. Naja Marie Aidt, "From *Everything Shimmers*," trans. Susanna Nied, *Asymptote*, July 2015, http://www.asymptotejournal.com/special-feature/naja-marie-aidt-everything-shimmers/.

81. *Diccionario de la lengua española Online*, s.v. "checar," accessed May 25, 2021, https://dle.rae.es/checar.
82. *Diccionario de la lengua española Online*, s.v. "pendejo," accessed May 25, 2021, https://dle.rae.es/pendejo?m=form.
83. Compensation occurs "when loss of meaning, sound-effect, metaphor or pragmatic effect in one part of a sentence is compensated in another part, or in a contiguous sentence." Peter Newmark, *A Textbook of Translation* (London: Prentice Hall, 1988), 90.
84. *Diccionario de la lengua española Online*, s.v. "tiro²," accessed May 25, 2021, https://dle.rae.es/tiro?m=form.
85. Isa. 15:6 (KJV), www.kingjamesbibleonline.org.
86. Eduardo Mallea, *All Green Shall Perish*, trans. John B. Hughes (London: Calder and Boyars, 1967).
87. Dillon, *The Palimpsest*, 9.
88. Genette, *Palimpsests*, 214.
89. Sommer, *Bilingual Games*.
90. Genette, *Palimpsests*, 399.
91. Rosenwald, *Multilingual America*, 123.

2. CENSORSHIP AND (PSEUDO-)TRANSLATION IN JUNOT DÍAZ'S *THE BRIEF WONDROUS LIFE OF OSCAR WAO*

1. Junot Díaz, *The Brief Wondrous Life of Oscar Wao* (London: Faber and Faber, 2008), 322. Hereafter references to the novel will be to this edition and will be given in parentheses in the main text.
2. Junot Díaz, *Drown* (London: Faber and Faber, 1996).
3. Patrick Chamoiseau, Jean Bernabé, and Raphaël Confiant, "In Praise of Creoleness," trans. Mohamed B. Taleb Khyar, *Callaloo* 13, no. 4 (1990): 886–909. Originally published as Patrick Chamoiseau, Jean Bernabé, and Raphaël Confiant, *Éloge de La Créolité* (Paris: Gallimard, 1989).
4. Achy Obejas, "A Conversation with Junot Díaz," *Review: Literature and Arts of the Americas* 42, no. 1 (2009): 42–47.
5. Chamoiseau, Bernabé, and Confiant, "In Praise of Creoleness."
6. Chamoiseau, Bernabé, and Confiant, "In Praise of Creoleness," 901.
7. "I've been asked if I got my footnoting from David Foster Wallace—no disrespect to DFW but Jorge Luis Borges and Patrick Chamoiseau and William Vollmann were my inspirations, especially Chamoiseau." Junot Díaz, "The Brief Wondrous Life of Oscar Wao (Excerpt)," Genius, http://genius.com/Junot-diaz-the-brief-wondrous-life-of-oscar-wao-excerpt-annotated.
8. Patrick Chamoiseau, *Texaco* (Paris: Gallimard, 1992). Marie-José NZengou-Tayo, "Literature and Diglossia: The Poetics of French and Creole 'Interlect' in Patrick Chamoiseau's *Texaco*," *Caribbean Quarterly* 43, no. 4 (1997): 87.
9. Domnita Dumitrescu, "'Dude was figureando hard': El cambio y la fusión de códigos en la obra de Junot Díaz," in *Perspectives in the Study of Spanish Language Variation: Papers in Honor of Carmen Silva Corvalán*, ed. Andrés Enrique Arias, Manuel J. Gutiérrez, Alazne Landa, and Francisco Ocampo (Santiago de

Compostela: Verba, 2014); Eugenia Casielles-Suárez, "Radical Code-Switching in *The Brief Wondrous Life of Oscar Wao*," *Bulletin of Hispanic Studies* 90, no. 4 (June 2013): 475–87.
10. Daniel Arrieta Domínguez, "Language and Race in Junot Diaz's Literature," *Kanagawa University Studies in Language* 31 (2008): 109–21; Glenda R. Carpio, "Junot Díaz's Wondrous Spanglish," in *Junot Díaz and the Decolonial Imagination*, ed. Monica Hanna, Jennifer Harford Vargas, and José David Saldívar (Durham, N.C.: Duke University Press, 2016), 257–90; Rachel Norman, "'A Bastard Jargon': Language Politics and Identity in *The Brief Wondrous Life of Oscar Wao*," *South Atlantic Review* 81, no. 1 (2016): 34–50.
11. Milca Esdaille, "Same Trip, Different Ships," *Black Issues Book Review* 3, no. 2 (April 2001): paragraph 18.
12. For more on race in Díaz's writing, see Paula Moya, who has shown Díaz's indebtedness to a feminist tradition of decolonial thinking about identity—the same tradition of women-of-color feminism of which Anzaldúa was a key part—by reading a story from *This Is How You Lose Her* alongside the work of Audre Lorde. Paula Moya, "Dismantling the Master's House: The Decolonial Imagination of Audre Lorde and Junot Díaz," in Hanna, Harford Vargas, and Saldívar, *Junot Díaz and the Decolonial Imagination*, 231–55. See also Sarah Quesada, who has written about the critical race dialectic in "Monstro," a science fiction story published in the *New Yorker* in which a disease known as "La negrura"—the darkness—runs rampant through the Haitian population: "a disease that is both racially selective and racial in and of itself." Sarah Quesada, "A Planetary Warning? The Multilayered Caribbean Zombie in 'Monstro,'" in Hanna, Harford Vargas, and Saldívar, *Junot Díaz and the Decolonial Imagination*, 295.
13. Chamoiseau, Bernabé, and Confiant, "In Praise of Creoleness," 903, 892.
14. Jesús de Galíndez, *La era de Trujillo: Tesis doctoral sobre la brutal tiranía* (Buenos Aires: Americana, 1958).
15. Díaz, *Drown*, 15.
16. Chamoiseau, Bernabé, and Confiant, "In Praise of Creoleness," 903.
17. From the French, "rest avec," "to stay with," a restavek is a child, typically in Haiti, sent to be a domestic servant in a wealthier household because their family does not have the means to support them.
18. Josefina Ludmer has demonstrated, in an essay on Sor Juana Inés de la Cruz, that silence and censorship are not always imposed by those in power but can be a form of resistance effectively employed by those in positions of marginality. Ludmer identifies "tricks of the weak," which include "not to say but to know, or saying that one doesn't know but knowing, or saying the opposite of what one knows." Josefina Ludmer, "Tricks of the Weak," in *Feminist Perspectives on Sor Juana Inés de La Cruz*, ed. Stephanie Merrim (Detroit, Mich.: Wayne State University Press, 1991), 91. In *Oscar Wao*, these "tricks" operate as self-preservation tactics, allowing Dominicans to participate in a voluntary collective "amnesia" (259), as Yunior calls it, as a way of protecting themselves while living under conditions of domination and violence. For instance, when invited by Trujillo to events at the palace, we are told that Abelard "arrived early, left late, smiled endlessly, and *didn't say nothing*" (215), allowing him to avoid attracting attention to himself or his family.

2. CENSORSHIP AND (PSEUDO-)TRANSLATION

19. Lauren H. Derby and Richard Turits point out that the 1937 massacre remains shrouded in myth. After extensive interviews with survivors, they admit that "we will probably never know with any certainty what triggered this genocide." Lauren H. Derby and Richard Turits, "Temwayaj Kout Kouto, 1937: Eyewitnesses to the Genocide," in *Revolutionary Freedoms: A History of Survival, Strength, and Imagination in Haiti*, ed. Cécile Accilien (Pompano Beach, Fla.: Caribbean Studies Press, 2006), 137. The story of soldiers carrying sprigs of parsley and asking people to say its name in Spanish (the trilled "r" and aspirated "j" in "perejil" are often mispronounced by French speakers) is part of that myth surrounding the massacre; whether or not it has any basis in fact, it nevertheless serves as an example of the hearsay and rumor on which Yunior's narrative (and others like it) must rely.
20. Quoted in Elena Machado Sáez, "Dictating Desire, Dictating Diaspora: Junot Díaz's *The Brief Wondrous Life of Oscar Wao* as Foundational Romance," *Contemporary Literature* 52, no. 3 (2011): 522.
21. Judith Butler, "Ruled Out: Vocabularies of the Censor," in *Censorship and Silencing: Practices of Cultural Regulation*, ed. Robert C. Post (Los Angeles: Getty Research Institute, 1998), 248.
22. Wendy Brown, "Freedom's Silences," in Post, *Censorship and Silencing*, 313.
23. Roland Barthes, *S/Z*, trans. Richard Miller (Oxford: Basil Blackwell, 1974), 4.
24. Barthes, *S/Z*, 4.
25. Barthes, *S/Z*, 11.
26. Roland Barthes, *Image, Music, Text*, trans. Stephen Heath (London: Flamingo, 1984), 62.
27. Maria Lauret, *Wanderwords: Language Migration in American Literature* (London: Bloomsbury, 2014), 249.
28. Vagn Steen, *Skriv Selv* (Copenhagen: Borgen, 1965).
29. Sonja S. Burrows, "Beyond the Comfort Zone: Monolingual Ideologies, Bilingual U.S. Latino Texts" (PhD diss., University of Oregon, 2010), emphasis added.
30. Burrows, "Beyond the Comfort Zone," 10, emphasis added.
31. Tim Lanzendörfer, "The Marvellous History of the Dominican Republic in Junot Díaz's *The Brief Wondrous Life of Oscar Wao*," *MELUS* 38, no. 2 (2013): 127, emphasis added.
32. The Annotated Oscar Wao, http://www.annotated-oscar-wao.com/index.html.
33. Ellen McCracken, *Paratexts and Performance in the Novels of Junot Díaz and Sandra Cisneros* (New York: Palgrave Macmillan, 2015); Gérard Genette, *Palimpsests: Literature in the Second Degree*, trans. Channa Newman and Claude Doubinsky (Lincoln: University of Nebraska Press, 1982), 2.
34. McCracken, *Paratexts and Performance*, 32.
35. McCracken, *Paratexts and Performance*, 32.
36. Butler, "Ruled Out," 248, 253.
37. Butler, "Ruled Out," 253.
38. See further Ellen McCracken's comprehensive discussion of how (particularly digital) paratexts shape the way readers interact with *Oscar Wao*, and how Díaz uses them to undermine the marketing of his Latinx ethnicity as an exotic commodity. McCracken, *Paratexts and Performance*.

39. See for instance, Tim Parks, "The Dull New Global Novel," *New York Review of Books*, February 2010, http://www.nybooks.com/blogs/nyrblog/2010/feb/09/the-dull-new-global-novel/; Minae Mizumura, *The Fall of Language in the Age of English*, trans. Mari Yoshihara and Juliet Winters Carpenter (New York: Columbia University Press, 2008); Emily Apter, *Against World Literature: On the Politics of Untranslatability* (London: Verso, 2013); Brian Lennon, *In Babel's Shadow: Multilingual Literatures, Monolingual States* (Minneapolis: University of Minnesota Press, 2010); Nikil Saval and Dayna Tortorici, "World Lite: What Is Global Literature," *n+1* 17, "The Evil Issue" (Fall 2013), https://nplusonemag.com/issue-17/the-intellectual-situation/world-lite/.
40. Sarah Brouillette, *Postcolonial Writers in the Global Literary Marketplace* (New York: Palgrave Macmillan, 2007), viii, 26.
41. The joke is a pun on the word "nigua," which refers to a parasitic insect known as a chigoe or chigger in English.
42. Shari Benstock, "At the Margin of Discourse," *PMLA* 98, no. 2 (1983): 223.
43. Megan O'Rourke, "Questions for Junot Díaz," *Slate*, April 8, 2008, http://www.slate.com/articles/news_and_politics/recycled/2008/04/questions_for_junot_daz.html.
44. "The Search for Decolonial Love: A Conversation Between Junot Díaz and Paula M. L. Moya," in Hanna, Harford Vargas, and Saldívar, *Junot Díaz and the Decolonial Imagination*, 397. This notion is already present in Octavio Paz's 1950 discussion of Mexicans as perpetual "hijos de la chingada." Octavio Paz, *El laberinto de la soledad*, 22nd ed., ed. Enrico Mario Santí (Madrid: Catédra, 2015).
45. "The Search for Decolonial Love," in Hanna, Harford Vargas, and Saldívar, *Junot Díaz and the Decolonial Imagination*, 397–98.
46. In a personal essay published in the *New Yorker* in 2018, in which he described having been raped as an eight-year-old child, Díaz reiterated that his character Yunior is also a survivor of sexual abuse. Junot Díaz, "The Silence: The Legacy of Childhood Trauma," *New Yorker*, April 8, 2018, https://www.newyorker.com/magazine/2018/04/16/the-silence-the-legacy-of-childhood-trauma. A number of women have subsequently made allegations of sexual misconduct and verbal abuse against Díaz. Although neither body ultimately found reason to permanently suspend him from his duties, the multiple allegations suggest a systematic abuse of power in academic and other professional environments. I would like to note that the research for this chapter was conducted before these allegations came to light, and that the space this book devotes to Díaz's work should not be taken to indicate approval of its author's behavior. My main focus here is on multilingualism and translation in (and of) Díaz's writing, rather than gender politics on or off the page, so I will not address the ethics of the decision to allow him to continue in his role as a public intellectual. Many others, however, have engaged in this important debate. See, for instance, Colleen Flaherty, "Junot Díaz, Feminism and Ethnicity," *Inside Higher Education*, May 29, 2018, https://www.insidehighered.com/news/2018/05/29/rift-among-scholars-over-treatment-junot-d%C3%ADaz-he-faces-harassment-and-misconduct; Linda Martín Alcoff, "This Is Not Just About Junot Díaz," *News and Observer*, May 18, 2018, https://www.newsobserver.com/opinion/op-ed/article211414444.html; A. M., "How Much Should Artists' Personal Lives Affect How We Treat Their Work? Judging Junot Díaz's Art, Not Junot Díaz the Artist," *The Economist*, May 25, 2018, https://

www.economist.com/open-future/2018/05/25/how-much-should-artists-personal-lives-affect-how-we-treat-their-work; Mark Shanahan and Stephanie Ebbert, "Junot Díaz Case May Be a #MeToo Turning Point," *Boston Globe*, June 30, 2018, https://www.bostonglobe.com/metro/2018/06/30/junot-diaz-case-may-metoo-turning-point/3TMFseenE4Go1eVsqbFSxM/story.html.

47. "The Search for Decolonial Love," in Hanna, Harford Vargas, and Saldívar, *Junot Díaz and the Decolonial Imagination*, 398.
48. O'Rourke, "Questions for Junot Díaz."
49. "About Genius," Genius, http://genius.com/Genius-about-genius-annotated.
50. Díaz, "The Brief Wondrous Life of Oscar Wao (Excerpt)."
51. Díaz, "The Brief Wondrous Life of Oscar Wao (Excerpt)."
52. Gideon Toury, "Enhancing Cultural Changes by Means of Fictitious Translations," in *Translation and Cultural Change: Studies in History, Norms and Image-Projection*, ed. Eva Hung (Amsterdam: John Benjamins Publishing Company, 2005), 5.
53. Toury, "Enhancing Cultural Changes," 7.
54. Cristina García, "Translation as Restoration," in *Voice-Overs: Translation and Latin American Literature*, ed. Daniel Balderston and Marcy Schwartz (New York: State University of New York Press, 2002), 45–48. Translator Eduardo Lago describes the process of translating *Drown* similarly as "una labor de restauración. El texto de llegada era el resultado de una operación de regreso al español" (a labor of restoration. The target text was the result of a return journey into Spanish). Eduardo Lago, "El idioma de la imaginación," in *Enciclopedia del español en los Estados Unidos* (Madrid: Instituto Cervantes, 2008), 603.
55. Leo Tak-Hung Chan, "Translating Bilinguality: Theorizing in the Post-Babelian Era," *The Translator* 8, no. 1 (2002): 57.
56. Tak-Hung Chan, "Translating Bilinguality," 57.
57. Junot Díaz, "Language, Violence, and Resistance," in Balderston and Schwartz, *Voice-Overs*, 42–44.
58. Junot Díaz, *Los Boys*, trans. Miguel Martínez-Lage (Barcelona: Mondadori, 1996); Karen Lorrain Cresci, "'Call It My Revenge on English': 'Negocios' de Junot Díaz y sus traducciones disonantes," *Literatura: Teoría, historia, crítica* 19, no. 2 (2017): 172.
59. Achy Obejas, "Translating Junot," *Chicago Tribune*, September 14, 2012, http://articles.chicagotribune.com/2012-09-14/features/ct-prj-0916-book-of-the-month-20120914_1_dominican-republic-oscar-wao-spanglish.
60. Quoted in Cresci, "'Call It My Revenge on English,'" 38.
61. Anna María D'Amore, *Translating Contemporary Mexican Literature: Fidelity to Alterity* (New York: Peter Lang, 2009), 201.
62. Junot Díaz, *Negocios*, trans. Eduardo Lago (New York: Vintage Español, 1997).
63. Karen Lorrain Cresci, "Regreso al Español: La Traducción de *Drown* de Junot Díaz: Entrevista a Eduardo Lago," *Argus-a* 6, no. 23 (February 2017), https://www.argus-a.com/archivos-dinamicas/regreso-al-espanol.pdf.
64. Cresci, "'Call It My Revenge on English,'" 164.
65. Gayatri Chakravorty Spivak, *Outside in the Teaching Machine* (New York: Routledge, 1993), 182.
66. Spivak, *Outside in the Teaching Machine*, 189.
67. Achy Obejas, "Sugarcane," in *Wáchale: Poetry and Prose About Growing Up Latino in America*, ed. Ilan Stavans (Chicago: Cricket Books, 2001), 110–12.

68. Annabel Cox, "Achy Obejas's 'Sugarcane' and Cuban-American Bilingual Literature: Language Choices and Cultural Identities," in *Exile, Language, and Identity*, ed. Magda Stroińska and Vittorina Cecchetto (Frankfurt: Peter Lang, 2003), 134; Annabel Cox, "Literature in the Contact Zone: Emily Apter's 'A New Comparative Literature' and Achy Obejas's 'Sugarcane,'" *Crossings: Journal of Migration and Culture* 5, no. 2 & 3 (2014): 233.
69. Achy Obejas, *Aguas y otros cuentos* (Havana: Letras Cubanas, 2009).
70. Achy Obejas, *We Came All the Way from Cuba So You Could Dress Like This?* (Pittsburgh, Penn.: Cleis Press, 1994).
71. María Teresa Ortega is credited thus in the Vintage Español edition: "asistente a Achy Obejas/redacción" (assistant to Achy Obejas/editing). See Karen Lorrain Cresci for a discussion of the two *Drown* translations.
72. Alejandro Gándara, "Junot Díaz," *El Mundo, El Escorpión*, November 27, 2009, http://www.elmundo.es/elmundo/2008/07/08/escorpion/1215510619.html.
73. Obejas, "Translating Junot."
74. Junot Díaz, *La maravillosa vida breve de Óscar Wao*, trans. Achy Obejas (Barcelona: Random House Mondadori, 2007). Hereafter references to this edition will appear in the main body of the text in abbreviated form as (Mondadori). As Boyden and Goethals note, the decision to publish two editions with marginally different titles was likely for the purposes of copyright differentiation only. Michael Boyden and Patrick Goethals, "Translating the Watcher's Voice: Junot Díaz's *The Brief Wondrous Life of Oscar Wao* into Spanish," *Meta: Journal Des Traducteurs/ Meta: Translators' Journal* 56, no. 1 (2011): 31.
75. Junot Díaz, *La breve y maravillosa vida de Óscar Wao*, trans. Achy Obejas (New York: Vintage Español, 2008). Hereafter references to this edition will appear in the main body of the text in abbreviated form as (Vintage Español). Vintage Español is one of a number of imprints within major trade publishing houses in the United States that print books in Spanish (other examples include HarperCollins's Rayo, and Simon and Schuster's Atria), both original and in translation from English.
76. "There are no systematic textual discrepancies [between the two editions] to hint at fundamentally opposed translation strategies." Boyden and Goethals, "Translating the Watcher's Voice," 31.
77. *Eloge de la creolité* emphasizes that creoleness "should not go without its opaqueness." Chamoiseau, Bernabé, and Confiant, "In Praise of Creoleness," 903. Martiniquan writer Edouard Glissant also begins his manifesto for Caribbean cultural self-determination with "Nous reclamons le droit à l'opacité" (We have a right to our opacity). Eduoard Glissant, *Le discours antillais* (Paris: Editions de Seuil, 1981), 11.
78. A good example of this is the translation of a work like Jacques Derrida's *Living On: Border Lines*, which, in its conscious drive toward "untranslatability," consistently uses wordplay and multiple languages; when unable to replicate the polysemy in English to his satisfaction, translator James Hulbert often gives a word or phrase of the original French in square brackets alongside its multiple possible connotations in English. Jacques Derrida, "Living On: Border Lines," in *Deconstruction and Criticism*, ed. Geoffrey H. Hartman, trans. James Hulbert (London: Routledge and Kegan Paul, 1979), 75–176.
79. Obejas, "Translating Junot."

80. Patrick Chamoiseau, *Texaco*, trans. Rose-Myriam Réjouis and Val Vinurokov (London: Granta, 1997).
81. Chamoiseau, *Texaco*, 1997, 393.
82. It is helpful, in conceiving of translation as elucidation or explanation, to recall that, unlike the Latinate metaphor of carrying meaning across (*trans + latus*), in Sanskrit and most modern Indian languages the word for "translation" is temporal rather than spatial: "anuvad" means "saying after or again, repeating by way of explanation, explanatory repetition or reiteration with corroboration or illustration, explanatory reference to anything already said." Monier Monier-Williams, *An English-Sanskrit Dictionary* (Springfield, Va.: Nataraj Books, 2006).
83. Ellen McCracken, "Performance and Linguistic Spectacle in Sandra Cisneros's *Caramelo* and Junot Díaz's *The Brief Wondrous Life of Oscar Wao*," in *Landscapes of Writing in Chicano Literature*, ed. Imelda Martín-Junquera (New York: Palgrave Macmillan, 2013), 39.
84. For example, in order to explain a reference to the "Ritual del Chüd," Obejas adds a note that begins: "Según la escritora Margaret L. Carter, el ritual de Chüd es una tradición del Himalaya que requiere que el chamán se enfrente al taelus, el forma-cambiador, cara a cara" (According to the writer Margaret L. Carter, the ritual of the Chüd is a Himalayan tradition that requires a shaman to confront the taelus—shape-changer—face to face) (Vintage Español, 89).
85. Maria Tymoczko, "Postcolonial Writing and Literary Translation," in *Post-Colonial Translation: Theory and Practice*, ed. Susan Bassnett and Harish Trivedi (London: Routledge, 1999), 23.
86. Butler, "Ruled Out," 253.
87. That being said, the latter of these two examples (and variations on it) is in use in some parts of Latin America. See *Diccionario de americanismos*, s.v. "bróder," accessed May 27, 2021, https://lema.rae.es/damer/?key=broder.
88. "Historia," Real Academia Española, http://www.rae.es/la-institucion/historia.
89. Boyden and Goethals, "Translating the Watcher's Voice," 32.
90. *Diccionario de la lengua española Online*, s.v. "guagua," accessed May 27, 2021, https://dle.rae.es/guagua.
91. Díaz, "The Brief Wondrous Life of Oscar Wao (Excerpt)."

3. "I WANT MY CLOSET BACK": QUEERING AND UNQUEERING LANGUAGE IN GIANNINA BRASCHI'S *YO-YO BOING!*

1. Giannina Braschi, *Yo-Yo Boing!* (Pittsburgh, Penn.: Latin American Literary Review Press, 1998), 14. AmazonCrossing's two editions of *Yo-Yo Boing!* will be cited in abbreviated form, followed by page number. Abbreviations are as follows: Giannina Braschi, *Yo-Yo Boing!* (Las Vegas: AmazonCrossing, 2011): (*YYB*); Giannina Braschi, *Yo-Yo Boing!*, trans. Tess O'Dwyer (Las Vegas: AmazonCrossing, 2011): (*YYB*, TO).
2. Doris Sommer and Alexandra Vega-Merino, "Either And," in Braschi, *Yo-Yo Boing!*, 1998, 14.
3. Persephone Braham, "*Yo-Yo Boing!* Review," *Latin American Literature and Arts Review: New Writing and Arts in the Americas* 60 (2000): 86.

4. Review of *Yo-Yo Boing!*, by Giannina Braschi, *Publishers Weekly*, December 29, 1997, http://www.publishersweekly.com/9780935480979.
5. Sommer and Vega-Merino, "Either And," 17.
6. Rebecca L. Walkowitz, *Born Translated: The Contemporary Novel in an Age of World Literature* (New York: Columbia University Press, 2015), 29.
7. Viktor Shklovsky, "The Resurrection of the Word," in *Russian Formalism: A Collection of Articles and Texts in Translation*, ed. Stephen Bann and John E. Bowlt, trans. Richard Sherwood (Edinburgh: Scottish Academic Press, 1973), 46. For a discussion of the centrality of linguistic plurality to modernist forms of defamiliarization, see Juliette Taylor-Batty, *Multilingualism in Modernist Fiction* (Basingstoke, UK: Palgrave Macmillan, 2013).
8. Braschi's later novel *United States of Banana* has been hailed as "*The Waste Land* of the 21st Century"; Cristina Garrigós, review of *United States of Banana*, by Giannina Braschi, *Evergreen Review*, no. 128 (Spring 2012), https://evergreenreview.com/read/two-reviews-united-states-of-banana-giannina-braschi/.
9. Bronwen Thomas, *Fictional Dialogue, Speech and Conversation in the Postmodern Novel* (Lincoln: University of Nebraska Press, 2012), 75.
10. Matthew Badura, "The Form of Talk: A Study of the Dialogue Novel," unpublished doctoral dissertation (Temple University, 2010), 37.
11. Roland Barthes, *S/Z*, trans. Richard Miller (Oxford: Basil Blackwell, 1974), 11.
12. Roberto R. Ramírez, "The Hispanic Population in the United States: Population Characteristics March 1998," *Current Population Reports*, October 1999, https://www.census.gov/prod/2000pubs/p20-525.pdf. The Bureau uses the terms "Hispanic" and "Latino" interchangeably to refer to people who reported their origin to be "Mexican, Puerto Rican, Cuban, Central or South American, or some other Hispanic origin" (1).
13. Ana Celia Zentella, "Language Policy/Planning and U.S. Colonialism: The Puerto Rican Thorn in English-Only's Side," in *Sociopolitical Perspectives on Language Policy and Planning in the USA*, ed. Thom Huebner and Kathryn A. Davis (Philadelphia: John Benjamins Publishing Company, 1999), 168. The latest referendum on Puerto Rico's political status took place as recently as November 2020. According to official election-night results, the option to pursue statehood won the referendum: 52.52 percent vs. 47.48 percent. "Plebiscite: Island Wide Results," Elecciones 2020, January 28, 2021, https://elecciones2020.ceepur.org/Escrutinio_General_93/index.html#en/default/PLEBISCITO_Resumen.xml.
14. Rosario Ferré, "Puerto Rico, USA," *New York Times*, March 9, 1998, https://www.nytimes.com/1998/03/19/opinion/puerto-rico-usa.html.
15. Ana Lydia Vega, "Carta Abierta a Pandora," *El Nuevo Día*, March 31, 1998. For further discussion of Puerto Rico's role in language policy and planning in the United States in the 1980s and 1990s, see Zentella, "Language Policy/Planning and U.S. Colonialism." For a wider discussion of language politics in the United States and their relevance to literary studies, see the introduction to Joshua Miller, *Accented America: The Cultural Politics of Multilingual Modernism* (New York: Oxford University Press, 2011), 3–33.
16. Maritza Stanchich, "Bilingual Big Bang: Giannina Braschi's Trilogy Levels the Spanish-English Playing Field," in *Poets, Philosophers, Lovers: On the Writings of*

Giannina Braschi, ed. Frederick Luis Aldama and Tess O'Dwyer (Pittsburgh, Penn.: University of Pittsburgh Press, 2020), 70.
17. Stanchich, "Bilingual Big Bang," 66.
18. José Torres-Padilla, "When Hybridity Doesn't Resist: Giannina Braschi's *Yo-Yo Boing!*," in *Complicating Constructions: Race, Ethnicity and Hybridity in American Texts*, ed. David S. Goldstein and Audrey B. Thacker (Seattle: University of Washington Press, 2007), 291.
19. Torres-Padilla, "When Hybridity Doesn't Resist," 292.
20. Frances Aparicio, "La vida es un Spanglish disparatero: Bilingualism in Nuyorican Poetry," in *European Perspectives on Hispanic Literature of the United States*, ed. Genvieve Fabre (Houston: Arte Público Press, 1988), 147.
21. Aparicio, "La vida es un Spanglish disparatero," 147.
22. Aparicio, "La vida es un Spanglish disparatero," 147.
23. Miguel Algarín and Miguel Piñero, *Nuyorican Poetry: An Anthology of Puerto Rican Words and Feelings* (New York: William Morrow, 1975), 9.
24. Miguel Algarín and Bob Holman, *Aloud: Voices from the Nuyorican Poets Cafe* (New York: Henry Holt, 1994); Ed Morales, *Living in Spanglish* (New York: St. Martin's Press, 2002), 108.
25. Debra A. Castillo, *Re-Dreaming America: Toward a Bilingual American Culture* (Albany: State University of New York Press, 2005), 147.
26. As I discussed in the introduction, Lourdes Torres points out that "most of the Spanish in Latino/a prose fiction is easily understood by a monolingual [Anglophone] speaker and is written with the monolingual reader in mind . . . in fact, bilingual knowledge is often unnecessary because of redundancy and explication of the Spanish text for the monolingual reader." Lourdes Torres, "In the Contact Zone: Code-Switching Strategies by Latino/a Writers," *MELUS* 32, no. 1 (2007): 79.
27. Doris Sommer, *Bilingual Aesthetics: A New Sentimental Education* (Durham, N.C.: Duke University Press, 2004).
28. Sommer, *Bilingual Aesthetics*, 29.
29. Sommer and Vega-Merino, "Either And," 16.
30. On the use of nonstandard orthography to depict dialect and language variation in literature, see "Literature and the Literate Speaker," in Lynda Mugglestone, *Talking Proper: The Rise of Accent as Social Symbol* (Oxford: Oxford University Press, 2007), 173–211; Maria Sutor, *Non-Native Speech in English Literature* (Munich: Herbert Utz Verlag, 2013).
31. Cherríe Moraga and Gloria Anzaldúa, *This Bridge Called My Back: Writings by Radical Women of Color*, 2nd ed. (New York: Kitchen Table: Women of Color Press, 1983).
32. Sandra K. Soto, "Queerness," in *The Routledge Companion to Latino/a Literature*, 2nd ed., ed. Suzanne Bost and Frances R. Aparicio (Abingdon, UK: Routledge, 2015), 75; Gloria Anzaldúa, "To(o) Queer the Writer—Loca, escritora y chicana," in *The Gloria Anzaldúa Reader*, ed. AnaLouise Keating (Durham, N.C.: Duke University Press, 2009), 163–75.
33. José Esteban Muñoz, *Disidentifications: Queers of Color and the Performance of Politics* (Minneapolis: University of Minnesota Press, 1999), 22.
34. Eve Kosofsky Sedgwick, *Tendencies* (Durham, N.C.: Duke University Press, 1993), 8, emphasis in original.

35. Sedgwick, *Tendencies*, 9, emphasis in original.
36. Heiko Motschenbacher, *Language, Gender, and Sexual Identity* (Amsterdam: John Benjamins Publishing Company, 2010).
37. Lawrence La Fountain-Stokes, "La política queer del espanglish," *Debate Feminista* 17, no. 33 (2006): 150.
38. Lawrence La Fountain-Stokes, "Pop-Shock: Shifting Representations of Diasporic Puerto Rican Women's Queer Sexualities in US Latina Cultural Texts," *Letras Femeninas* 31, no. 1 (2005): 79.
39. For a discussion of queer subjectivities in Braschi's earlier poetry collection *El imperio de los sueños*, see María M. Carrión, "Geography, (M)Other Tongues and the Role of Translation in Giannina Braschi's *El imperio de los sueños*," *Studies in 20th Century Literature* 20, no. 1 (1996): 167–91. For a discussion of figures of gender ambivalence, dysfunction, and inversion in her more recent novel, *United States of Banana* (Las Vegas: AmazonCrossing, 2011), and the ways they are refunctionalized in order to explore the relationship between the (post)colonial migrant and the metropole, see Arnaldo Manuel Cruz-Malavé, "'Under the Skirt of Liberty': Giannina Braschi Rewrites Empire," *American Quarterly* 66, no. 3 (2014): 801–18.
40. All translations in parentheses are my own unless otherwise specified.
41. "Strange, odd, peculiar, eccentric. Also: of questionable character; suspicious, dubious." *Oxford English Dictionary Online*, s.v. "queer, adj.1," accessed May 31, 2021, https://www.oed.com/view/Entry/156236?rskey=zes9qu&result=2&isAdvanced=false.
42. Braschi is not the first to read queer sexuality into *The Waste Land*. See Harriet Davidson, "Improper Desire: Reading *The Waste Land*," in *The Cambridge Companion to T. S. Eliot*, ed. A. David Moody (Cambridge: Cambridge University Press, 1994), 121–31. See also Andrej Zavrl's discussion of the gender ambiguity of certain of the poem's characters, most obviously the figure of Tiresias, the "old man with wrinkled female breasts" (l. 64) in whom "the two sexes meet" (l. 72). Andrej Zavrl, "Sexing the Waste Land: Gender, Desire, and Sexuality in T. S. Eliot's *The Waste Land*," *Acta Neophilologica* 38, no. 1–2 (2005): 71–82.
43. "b. *slang* (chiefly *North American*). A sweet or effeminate male; (in later use chiefly) a weakling, a coward, a sissy. Also: a homosexual man." *Oxford English Dictionary Online*, s.v. "pussy, n. and adj.2," accessed May 31, 2021, https://www.oed.com/view/Entry/155161?isAdvanced=false&result=1&rskey=MGrtoh&.
44. La Fountain-Stokes, "Pop-Shock," 93; Monique Wittig, *The Lesbian Body* (New York: William Morrow, 1975).
45. Hélène Cixous, "The Laugh of the Medusa," trans. Keith Cohen and Paula Cohen, *Signs* 1, no. 4 (1976): 875–93; Luce Irigaray, "When Our Lips Speak Together," trans. Carolyn Burke, *Signs* 6, no. 1, "Women: Sex and Sexuality, Part 2" (1980): 69–79.
46. Cixous, "The Laugh of the Medusa," 876.
47. Notably, Toril Moi has argued against the notion of femininity altogether. Toril Moi, "From Femininity to Finitude: Freud, Lacan, and Feminism, Again," *Signs* 29, no. 3 (2004): 844.
48. Cixous, "The Laugh of the Medusa," 881.
49. Giannina Braschi, "Pelos en la lengua," *Hopscotch: A Cultural Review* 2, no. 2 (2001): 50.

50. Recent applications of queer theory to a cross-species continuum have questioned the dominant normative assumption of a natural divide between human and nonhuman animals. For further discussion, see Mel Y. Chen, *Animacies: Biopolitics, Racial Mattering, and Queer Affect* (Durham, N.C.: Duke University Press, 2012); Jennifer Grubbs, ed., "Inquiries and Intersections: Queer Theory and Anti-Speciesist Praxis," special issue, *Journal for Critical Animal Studies* 10, no. 3 (2012); Una Chaudhuri and Holly Hughes, eds., *Animal Acts: Performing Species Today* (Ann Arbor: University of Michigan Press, 2014).
51. For a discussion of Amazon's insatiable expansion, see George Packer, "Cheap Words," *New Yorker*, February 2014, http://www.newyorker.com/magazine/2014/02/17/cheap-words.
52. Giannina Braschi, *Empire of Dreams*, trans. Tess O'Dwyer (New Haven, Conn.: Yale University Press, 1994).
53. Lawrence Venuti, *The Translator's Invisibility: A History of Translation*, 2nd ed. (London: Routledge, 2002).
54. See Gayatri Chakravorty Spivak, *Outside in the Teaching Machine* (New York: Routledge, 1993), 182–91; Venuti, *The Translator's Invisibility*, 20.
55. See, for example, Sherry Simon, *Gender and Translation: Cultural Identity and the Politics of Transmission* (Abingdon, UK: Routledge, 1996), 1–2, in which she demonstrates that the femininity of translation is a long-standing historical trope.
56. Jacques Derrida reminds us that language involves an endless play of signification in the absence or deferral of final meaning. If we look up a word (a signifier) in a dictionary, the definition we find is made up of other words (other signifiers), each of which is defined in the same dictionary by still more words. Although there is a trace of meaning linking these signifiers together, any full, final meaning of the first word we looked up is always already deferred. As Derrida writes, "the signifier first signifies a signifier, and not the thing itself or a directly presented signified." Jacques Derrida, *Of Grammatology*, trans. G. C. Spivak (Baltimore, Md.: Johns Hopkins University Press, 1976), 73. If there is no fixed or transcendental signification but rather a series of continual substitutions and deferrals, then translators are able to question the conventional loyalty to a mythical textual "original."
57. Simon, *Gender and Translation*, viii.
58. Luise von Flotow, "Feminist Translation: Contexts, Practices and Theories," *TTR: Traduction, Terminologie, Rédaction* 4, no. 2 (1991): 74–80.
59. Barbara Godard, "Translating and Sexual Difference," *Resources for Feminist Research* 8, no. 3 (1984): 13–16.
60. Simon, *Gender and Translation*, 16.
61. William M. Burton, "Inverting the Text: A Proposed Queer Translation Praxis," *In Other Words* 36 (Winter 2010): 57.
62. Elizabeth Sara Lewis, "'This Is My Girlfriend, Linda': Translating Queer Relationships in Film: A Case Study of the Subtitles for Gia and a Proposal for Developing the Field of Queer Studies," *In Other Words*, no. 36 (Winter 2010): 11.
63. Lewis, "'This Is My Girlfriend, Linda.'"
64. B. J. Epstein and Robert Gillett, eds., *Queer in Translation* (Abingdon, UK: Routledge, 2017); Christopher Larkosh, *Re-Engendering Translation: Transcultural Practice, Gender/Sexuality and the Politics of Alterity* (Manchester: St. Jerome Pub., 2011).

65. Epstein and Gillett, "Introduction," in *Queer in Translation*, 1.
66. William Spurlin, "Queering Translation," in *A Companion to Translation Studies* (Chichester: Wiley Blackwell, 2014), 302.
67. Larkosh, *Re-Engendering Translation*, 4–5; see also Brian James Baer and Klaus Kaindl, eds., *Queering Translation, Translating the Queer: Theory, Practice, Activism* (London: Routledge, 2020).
68. Von Flotow, "Feminist Translation," 76.
69. Meir Sternberg, "Polylingualism as Reality and Translation as Mimesis," *Poetics Today* 2, no. 4 (1981): 221–39.
70. Sternberg, "Polylingualism as Reality and Translation as Mimesis," 222.
71. Burton, "Inverting the Text"; Lewis, "'This Is My Girlfriend, Linda.'"
72. The omitted passage reads: "Am I funny? Am I a clown? Who the hell do they think I am? What are they expecting from me? I can't please you. Sorry, but it's not my intention to make you laugh. Sorry, but you laugh, okay, I accept your laughter. Does this mean you are accepting me? Well, let me tell you, you're going to have problems with me because I'm not going to keep up with your laughter, why, just because you want to laugh, do I have to make you do what you want. You're imposing your laughter on me. You're not making me laugh. I'm deadly serious right now. And you think I'm funny. It's really insulting. I don't have a sense of humor. Respect my wishes. Don't laugh just for the sake of laughter. It's just a nervous tick. And I don't like it" (*YYB*, 173).
73. "Yo-Yo Boing! (A Scene from the Bilingual Edition)," Giannina Braschi (blog), October 11, 2011, https://gianninabraschi.wordpress.com/2011/10/11/yo-yo-boing-a-scene-from-the-bilingual-edition/.
74. Junot Díaz, "The Brief Wondrous Life of Oscar Wao (Excerpt)," Genius, http://genius.com/Junot-diaz-the-brief-wondrous-life-of-oscar-wao-excerpt-annotated.
75. Mark Currie, *About Time* (Edinburgh: Edinburgh University Press, 2007), 31.
76. O'Dwyer won the Columbia University Translation Centre Award in 1991 for *Empire of Dreams*, her translation of Braschi's *El imperio de los sueños* (San Juan: Editorial de la Universidad de Puerto Rico, 1988).
77. Tess O'Dwyer, "Translator's Note," in Braschi, *Empire of Dreams*, xix.
78. O'Dwyer, "Translator's Note," xix.
79. Currie explains the logic of supplementarity as "a kind of temporal loop by which things which happen later in a sequence are understood as the origins of things from which they apparently originate." Mark Currie, *Postmodern Narrative Theory*, 2nd ed. (Basingstoke, UK: Macmillan Press, 2011), 42. It is, in Derrida's words, when "a possibility produces that to which it is said to be added on." Jacques Derrida, *Speech and Phenomena and Other Essays on Husserl's Theory of Signs* (Evanston, Ill.: Northwestern University Press, 1973), 89.
80. Simone de Beauvoir, *The Second Sex*, trans. Constance Borde and Sheila Malovany-Chevalier (New York: Alfred A. Knopf, 2010). For a discussion of the construction of homosexuality as secondary, with particular reference to lesbian subjectivities, see Annamarie Jagose, *Inconsequence: Lesbian Representation and the Logic of Sexual Sequence* (Ithaca, N.Y.: Cornell University Press, 2002).
81. Walkowitz, *Born Translated*, 29.
82. Walkowitz, *Born Translated*, 3–4.
83. Sommer and Vega-Merino, "Either And," 12.

4. FLUID TRAJECTORIES IN TWO VERSIONS OF WILSON BUENO'S *MAR PARAGUAYO*

1. Wilson Bueno, "Editorial: Tempo de criar," *Nicolau*, no. 1 (1987): 2. Unless otherwise stated, all translations into English are my own. Translations from Bueno's *Mar Paraguayo* are intended to be functional—to facilitate reading—rather than particularly creative. They should be contrasted with Moure's own translations, which I cite regularly in the second part of this chapter.
2. Wilson Bueno, "Mar Paraguayo," *Nicolau*, no. 6 (1987): 25.
3. Wilson Bueno, *Mar Paraguayo* (São Paulo: Iluminuras, 1992). Unless otherwise stated, all references to *Mar Paraguayo* in this chapter will be to a later edition published in Mexico: Wilson Bueno, *Mar Paraguayo* (Toluca: Bonobos, 2006). All further references to this edition will be given in the main text as *MP*.
4. Wilson Bueno, *Paraguayan Sea*, trans. Erín Moure (New York: Nightboat Books, 2017). All further references to this edition will be given in the main text as *PS*.
5. Fábio Aristimunho Vargas, "Fronteiras literárias: As línguas ibéricas e o portunhol," VI Congresso Internacional Roa Bastos, Foz do Iguaçu, 2011.
6. Wilson Bueno, "Fronteiras: Nos entrecéus da linguagem," ed. Simone Homem de Mello, *Humboldt*, "A outra língua—Edição especial sobre literatura," http://www.goethe.de/wis/bib/prj/hmb/the/das/pt3286146.htm, accessed June 1, 2018.
7. Bueno, *Mar Paraguayo*, 1992, 74–78. The glossary in the Mexican Bonobos edition, to which I refer in this chapter, offers translations into Spanish rather than Portuguese.
8. Gary F. Simons and Charles D. Fenning, eds., *Ethnologue: Languages of the World*, 21st ed. (Dallas, Tex.: SIL International, 2018), http://www.ethnologue.com.
9. Bueno, *Mar Paraguayo*, 1992, 75.
10. Wilson Bueno and Claudio Daniel, "Ñemogueta: An Interview with Wilson Bueno by Claudio Daniel," in *PS*, 96.
11. Bueno, *Mar Paraguayo*, 1992, 77.
12. Rebecca L. Walkowitz, "Translating the Untranslatable: An Interview with Barbara Cassin," *Public Books*, June 2014, http://www.publicbooks.org/interviews/translating-the-untranslatable-an-interview-with-barbara-cassin.
13. Barbara Cassin, ed., *Dictionary of Untranslatables: A Philosophical Lexicon*, trans. Emily Apter, Jacques Lezra, and Michael Wood (Princeton, N.J.: Princeton University Press, 2014), xvii.
14. Augusto de Campos, "Poesia concreta (manifesto)," in *Teoria da poesia concreta: Textos críticos e manifestos 1950–1960*, ed. Augusto de Campos, Décio Pignatari, and Haroldo de Campos (São Paulo: Ateliê, 2006), 72.
15. Cynthia García, "I Already Miss the Future: Augusto de Campos Discusses the Creation of Concrete Poetry on the Occasion of His Retrospective at Sesc Pompeia," *New City Brazil*, June 2016, https://www.newcitybrazil.com/2016/06/11/i-already-miss-the-future/.
16. Bueno, "Fronteiras: Nos entrecéus da linguagem," emphasis in original.
17. James Joyce, *Finnegans Wake* (London: Faber and Faber, 1982), 143.
18. The poem, originally published in 1953, can be viewed on his Instagram account. Augusto de Campos (@Poetamenos), "'Lygia fingers,' 1953, poema de Augusto de

Campos, da série poetamenos." Instagram video, April 2, 2019, https://www.instagram.com/p/Bvv_bBgAtbh/?hl=en.

19. Haroldo de Campos, "A obra de arte aberta," *Diario de São Paulo*, March 7, 1955. English translation: Haroldo de Campos, "The Open Work of Art," in *Novas: Selected Writings*, ed. Odile Cisneros and Antonio Sergio Bessa (Evanston, Ill.: Northwestern University Press, 2007), 220–22.

20. Andrew Forster, Erín Moure, and Sherry Simon, "Discussion and Book Launch/Discussion et Lancement de Livre," University of Concordia, November 9, 2017, http://www.concordia.ca/cuevents/finearts/fofa/2017/08/03/exhibition-andrew-forster-erin-moure.html.

21. Luis d'Antin Van Rooten, *Mots d'heures: Gousses, rames* (New York: Grossman, 1967).

22. The marafona is telling her story to an interlocutor, sometimes identified as "lector," the reader, sometimes as one Doctor Paiva, a character whom we never meet but who has presumably been looking after the old man's failing health. Jens Andermann has highlighted the book's oral nature, arguing that it can be understood as "siete u ocho monólogos" (seven or eight monologues) that scream to be read aloud. Jens Andermann, "Abismos del tercer espacio: Mar paraguayo, portuñol salvaje y el fin de la utopía letrada," *Revista Hispanic Moderna* 16, no. 1 (2011): 13.

23. See further Shklovsky's discussion in "Art as Device." Viktor Shklovsky, *Theory of Prose*, trans. Benjamin Sher (London: Dalkey Archive Press, 2009), 1–14.

24. Nádia Nelziza Lovera de Florentino, "Entre gêneros e fronteiras: Uma leitura de Mar paraguayo, de Wilson Bueno" (PhD diss., Universidade Estadual Paulista, 2016), 50–53.

25. Bueno's writing was, for instance, included in an anthology of neobaroque poets with an introduction by Nestor Perlongher. Robert Echavarren, José Kozer, and Jacobo Sefamí, eds., *Medusario: Muestra de poesía latinoamericana* (Mexico City: Fondo de Cultura Economica, 1996).

26. Severo Sarduy, "The Baroque and the Neobaroque," in *Baroque New Worlds: Representation, Transculturation, Counterconquest*, ed. Lois Parkinson Zamora and Monica Kaup (Durham, N.C.: Duke University Press, 2010), 270–91.

27. Sarduy, "The Baroque and the Neobaroque," 282.

28. Monica Kaup, *Neobaroque in the Americas: Alternative Modernities in Literature, Visual Art, and Film* (Charlottesville: University of Virginia Press, 2012), 3.

29. Haroldo de Campos, "Anthropophagous Reason: Dialogue and Difference in Brazilian Culture," trans. Odile Cisneros, in Cisneros and Bessa, *Novas*, 157–77.

30. Oswald de Andrade, "Manifesto antropófago," *Revista de Antropofagia* 1, no. 1 (1928): 3–7; Oswald de Andrade, "Cannibalist Manifesto," trans. Leslie Barry, *Latin American Literary Review* 19, no. 38 (1991): 38–47.

31. Michel de Montaigne, *Des cannibales suivi de la peur de l'autre* (Paris: Gallimard, 2008); Michel de Montaigne, "On the Cannibals," in *The Complete Essays*, ed. and trans. M. A. Screech (London: Penguin, 1992), 1:228–41.

32. Andrade, "Cannibalist Manifesto," 41.

33. Andrade, "Manifesto Antropófago," 3.

34. De Campos, "Anthropophagous Reason," 177.

4. FLUID TRAJECTORIES IN TWO VERSIONS

35. Haroldo de Campos, "The Rule of Anthropophagy: Europe Under the Sign of Devoration," trans. María Tai Wolff, *Latin American Literary Review* 14, no. 27, "Brazilian Literature" (1986): 44.
36. Mario de Andrade, *Macunaíma: O herói sem nenhum caráter*, 2nd ed. (São Paulo: Companhia das Letras in association with Penguin Group, 2017).
37. Haroldo de Campos, "Anthropophagous Reason," 162.
38. "About Nightboat Books," Nightboat Books, https://nightboat.org/about/history/.
39. "About," Erín Moure, http://erinmoure.strikingly.com/.
40. Eli Burley, "Eli Burley on Erín Moure: *Planetary Noise*," *Lemonhound 3.0*, March 15, 2018, https://lemonhound.com/2018/03/15/eli-burley-on-erin-moure-planetary-noise/.
41. Quoted in Kirsty Hooper, *Writing Galicia into the World: New Cartographies, New Poetics* (Liverpool: Liverpool University Press, 2011), 168.
42. Erín Moure, *Planetary Noise: Selected Poetry of Erín Moure*, ed. Shannon Maguire (Middletown, Conn.: Wesleyan University Press, 2017), ix.
43. Patrick Chamoiseau, Jean Bernabé, and Raphaël Confiant, "In Praise of Creoleness," trans. Mohamed B. Taleb Khyar, *Callaloo* 13, no. 4 (1990): 901; Douglas Diegues, "Karta manifesto del amor amor em portunhol selvagem," *Portal O Globo Cultura*, August 17, 2008, http://oglobo.globo.com/cultura/confira-manifesto-em-defesa-do-portunhol-selvagem-3607777.
44. Harriet Staff, "The Multilingual Erín Moure Talks Translation," *Poetry Foundation*, August 29, 2017, https://www.poetryfoundation.org/harriet/2017/08/the-multilingual-erin-moure-talks-translation.
45. Erín Moure, *My Beloved Wager: Essays from a Writing Practice* (Edmonton: NeWest Press, 2009), 247.
46. Zoë Skoulding, *Contemporary Women's Poetry and Urban Space: Experimental Cities* (Basingstoke, UK: Palgrave Macmillan, 2013), 130.
47. Moure, *Planetary Noise*, 53–56.
48. Moure, *Planetary Noise*, 56–57.
49. Skoulding, *Contemporary Women's Poetry and Urban Space*, 129.
50. Moure, *Planetary Noise*, xiv.
51. Moure, *Planetary Noise*, 77.
52. Moure, *Planetary Noise*.
53. "Crossings: An Interview with Erin Mouré," *Mosaic: An Interdisciplinary Critical Journal* 36, no. 4, "PILGRIMAGE" (2003): 7.
54. "Crossings," 9.
55. Moure, *Planetary Noise*, 163.
56. Susana Chávez-Silverman, *Killer Crónicas: Bilingual Memories* (Madison: University of Wisconsin Press, 2004), 143.
57. Moure, *Planetary Noise*, xxi.
58. Forster, Moure, and Simon, "Discussion and Book Launch."
59. Marjorie Perloff, *Unoriginal Genius: Poetry by Other Means in the New Century* (Chicago: University of Chicago Press, 2010).
60. Erín Moure, *O Cidadán* (Toronto: House of Anansi Press, 2002).
61. Moure, *Planetary Noise*, 76.
62. "Crossings," 2.

63. Caroline Bergvall and Erín Moure, "O YES," in *Antiphonies: Essays in Women's Experimental Poetries in Canada*, ed. Nate Dorward (Willowdale: The Gig, 2008), 169.
64. Bergvall and Moure, "O YES," 170.
65. One obvious reason for the decision to make her translation more readable in English than in French is that *Paraguayan Sea* was published in the United States, not Canada. As Moure explains, "Canadian literary small presses rarely publish translations of works by foreigners, even if translated by Canadians, because they are not able to use their Canada Council funding in such cases to offset the cost of publishing and marketing. As a result, it is difficult to invite Canadian-chosen and translated works across borders to join us in book form." Erín Moure, "Polylingual Writers: The Joyous Sea of Words," *Quebec Writers' Federation*, December 7, 2017, https://qwfwrites.wordpress.com/2017/12/07/the-joyous-sea-of-words-by-erin-moure/.
66. Garrett Stewart, *Reading Voices: Literature and the Phonotext* (Berkeley: University of California Press, 1990).
67. Cecilia Vicuña and Ernesto Livon-Grosman, eds., *The Oxford Book of Latin American Poetry: A Bilingual Anthology* (New York: Oxford University Press, 2009).
68. Erín Moure, email to author, May 13, 2015.
69. Florentino, for instance, describes it as "en muitos respetos, intraduzível" (in many respects, untranslatable). Nelziza Lovera de Florentino, "Entre gêneros e fronteiras," 33; Meanwhile, María Jesús Fernández García has said of Bueno's language, "no necesita traducción, ni la soportaría" (it does not need translating, nor would it withstand it). María Jesús Fernández García, "Portuñol y Literatura," *Revista de Estudios Extremeños* 62 (2006): 564.
70. Gonzalo Aguilar, "Augusto de Campos: The Translation of a Name," *Asymptote*, January 2015, https://www.asymptotejournal.com/criticism/gonzalo-aguilar-augusto-de-campos-the-translation-of-a-name/.
71. Erín Moure, "Emit," in *Planetary Noise*, 165.
72. Moure, *My Beloved Wager*, 255.
73. Barbara Godard, "Translating and Sexual Difference," *Resources for Feminist Research* 8, no. 3 (1984): 13–16.
74. See Christopher Larkosh, *Re-Engendering Translation: Transcultural Practice, Gender/Sexuality and the Politics of Alterity* (Manchester: St. Jerome Pub., 2011); B. J. Epstein and Robert Gillett, eds., *Queer in Translation* (Abingdon, UK: Routledge, 2017). For a fuller discussion, see chapter 3 of this volume.
75. Jessie Chaffee, "The Translator Relay: Erín Moure," *Words Without Borders*, August 28, 2017, https://www.wordswithoutborders.org/dispatches/article/the-translator-relay-erin-moure.
76. Von Flotow has identified footnoting, hijacking, and supplementing as key feminist translation strategies. See Luise von Flotow, "Feminist Translation: Contexts, Practices and Theories," *TTR: Traduction, Terminologie, Rédaction* 4, no. 2 (1991): 74–80.
77. "¿Qué es Mar Paraguayo?," *Profética: Casa de la Lectura*, June 13, 2012, http://www.profetica.com.mx/libreria-2/propuestas/que-es-mar-paraguayo.
78. Forster, Moure, and Simon, "Discussion and Book Launch."
79. Chaffee, "The Translator Relay."

CODA: BEYOND AMERICA: MULTILINGUALISM, TRANSLATION, AND *ASYMPTOTE*

1. "Submit," *Asymptote*, http://www.asymptotejournal.com/submit/.
2. See Rebecca L. Walkowitz, *Born Translated: The Contemporary Novel in an Age of World Literature* (New York: Columbia University Press, 2015), 235–45.
3. Greg Nissan, "For Whom the -R Rolls," *Asymptote*, July 2016, http://www.asymptotejournal.com/special-feature/greg-nissan-for-whom-the-r-rolls/.
4. See translator's note in Nissan, "For Whom the -R Rolls."
5. Nissan, "For Whom the -R Rolls." Underlining indicates hyperlinked text.
6. Klaus Brinkbäumer et al., "De verlorene Welt," *Der Spiegel*, April 3, 2006, http://www.spiegel.de/spiegel/print/d-46502879.html.
7. Klara du Plessis, "Three Poems," *Asymptote*, July 2016, https://www.asymptotejournal.com/special-feature/klara-du-plessis-three-poems/.
8. Şerban Foarţă, "Butterflyçión," trans. MARGENTO, *Asymptote*, July 2016, http://www.asymptotejournal.com/special-feature/serban-foarta-butterflycion/.
9. Kanya Kanchana, "Grammar of the Goddess," *Asymptote*, July 2016, http://www.asymptotejournal.com/special-feature/kanya-kanchana-grammar-of-the-goddess/.
10. Rajiv Mohabir, "Four Poems," *Asymptote*, July 2016, http://www.asymptotejournal.com/special-feature/rajiv-mohabir-four-poems/.
11. See Miguel Algarín and Bob Holman, *Aloud: Voices from the Nuyorican Poets Cafe* (New York: Henry Holt, 1994); Miguel Algarín and Miguel Piñero, *Nuyorican Poetry: An Anthology of Puerto Rican Words and Feelings* (New York: William Morrow, 1975).
12. Noel Quiñones, "Arroz Poetica Battle Rhyme for Kendrick Lamar," *Asymptote*, July 2016, http://www.asymptotejournal.com/special-feature/noel-quinones-arroz-poetica-battle-rhyme-for-kendrick-lamar/.
13. Sarah Dillon, *The Palimpsest* (London: Continuum, 2007), 9.
14. "Issue Jan 2011," *Asymptote*, January 2011, http://www.asymptotejournal.com/jan-2011/.
15. Walkowitz, *Born Translated*, 239; 240.
16. Du Plessis, "Three Poems."
17. David Shook, "David Shook on Translating 'Bät Riting' by Jorge Canese," *Asymptote*, July 2016, https://www.asymptotejournal.com/criticism/jorge-canese-bat-riting/.
18. Shook, "David Shook on Translating 'Bät Riting' by Jorge Canese."
19. Andrés Neuman, *El viajero del siglo* (Madrid: Alfaguara, 2009), 319; Andrés Neuman, *Traveller of the Century*, trans. Nick Caistor and Lorenza Garcia (London: Pushkin, 2013), 334.

BIBLIOGRAPHY

"About." Erín Moure. http://erinmoure.strikingly.com/.
"About Genius." Genius. http://genius.com/Genius-about-genius-annotated.
"About Nightboat Books." Nightboat Books. https://nightboat.org/about/history/.
Acosta-Belén, E. "Spanglish: A Case of Languages in Contact." In *New Directions in Second Language Learning, Teaching and Bilingual Education*, ed. Marina Burt and Helen Dulay, 151–58. Washington, D.C.: TESOL, 1975.
Aguilar, Gonzalo. "Augusto de Campos: The Translation of a Name." *Asymptote*, January 2015. https://www.asymptotejournal.com/criticism/gonzalo-aguilar-augusto-de-campos-the-translation-of-a-name/.
Ahmed, Sara. *Living a Feminist Life*. Durham, N.C.: Duke University Press, 2017.
Aidt, Naja Marie. "From *Everything Shimmers*," trans. Susanna Nied. *Asymptote*, July 2015. http://www.asymptotejournal.com/special-feature/naja-marie-aidt-everything-shimmers/.
Alarcón, Daniel. *El rey siempre está por encima del pueblo*. Mexico City: Sexto Piso, 2009.
Alcoff, Linda Martín. "This Is Not Just About Junot Díaz." *News and Observer*, May 18, 2018. https://www.newsobserver.com/opinion/op-ed/article211414444.html.
Algarín, Miguel, and Bob Holman. *Aloud: Voices from the Nuyorican Poets Cafe*. New York: Henry Holt, 1994.
Algarín, Miguel, and Miguel Piñero. *Nuyorican Poetry: An Anthology of Puerto Rican Words and Feelings*. New York: William Morrow, 1975.
Allatson, Paul. "Ilan Stavans's Latino USA: A Cartoon History (of a Cosmopolitan Intellectual)." *Chasqui* 35, no. 1 (2006): 21–41.
A. M. "How Much Should Artists' Personal Lives Affect How We Treat Their Work? Judging Junot Díaz's Art, Not Junot Díaz the Artist." *The Economist*, May 25, 2018. https://www.economist.com/open-future/2018/05/25/how-much-should-artists-personal-lives-affect-how-we-treat-their-work.

Andermann, Jens. "Abismos del tercer espacio: Mar paraguayo, portuñol salvaje y el fin de la utopía letrada." *Revista Hispanic Moderna* 16, no. 1 (2011): 11–22.

Andrade, Mario de. *Macunaíma: O herói sem nenhum caráter*. 2nd ed. São Paulo: Companhia das Letras in association with Penguin Group, 2017.

Andrade, Oswald de. "Cannibalist Manifesto," trans. Leslie Barry. *Latin American Literary Review* 19, no. 38 (1991): 38–47.

——. "Manifesto antropófago." *Revista de Antropofagia* 1, no. 1 (1928): 3–7.

The Annotated Oscar Wao. http://www.annotated-oscar-wao.com/index.html.

Anzaldúa, Gloria. *Borderlands/La Frontera: The New Mestiza*. 4th ed. San Francisco: Aunt Lute Books, 2012.

——. "To(o) Queer the Writer—Loca, escritora y chicana." In *The Gloria Anzaldúa Reader*, ed. AnaLouise Keating, 163–75. Durham, N.C.: Duke University Press, 2009.

Anzaldúa, Gloria, and AnaLouise Keating. "Now Let Us Shift . . . the Path of Conocimiento . . . Inner Work, Public Acts." In *This Bridge We Call Home: Radical Visions for Transformation*, ed. Anzaldúa and Keating, 540–78. New York: Routledge, 2002.

Aparicio, Frances. "La vida es un Spanglish disparatero: Bilingualism in Nuyorican Poetry." In *European Perspectives on Hispanic Literature of the United States*, ed. Genvieve Fabre, 147–60. Houston: Arte Público Press, 1988.

Aparicio, Frances R., and Susana Chávez-Silverman, eds. *Tropicalizations: Transcultural Representations of Latinidad*. Hanover, N.H.: University Press of New England, 1997.

Apter, Emily. *Against World Literature: On the Politics of Untranslatability*. London: Verso, 2013.

——. *The Translation Zone: A New Comparative Literature*. Princeton, N.J.: Princeton University Press, 2006.

Arrieta Domínguez, Daniel. "Language and Race in Junot Diaz's Literature." *Kanagawa University Studies in Language* 31 (2008): 109–21.

Arteaga, Alfred, ed. *An Other Tongue: Nation and Ethnicity in the Linguistic Borderlands*. Durham, N.C.: Duke University Press, 1994.

Ashcroft, Bill, Gareth Griffiths, and Helen Tiffin. *The Empire Writes Back*. 2nd ed. London: Routledge, 2002.

Badura, Matthew. "The Form of Talk: A Study of the Dialogue Novel." Unpublished doctoral dissertation, Temple University, 2010.

Baer, Brian James, and Klaus Kaindl, eds. *Queering Translation, Translating the Queer: Theory, Practice, Activism*. London: Routledge, 2020.

Bakhtin, Mikhail. *The Dialogic Imagination: Four Essays*, trans. Vadim Liapunov. Austin: University of Texas Press, 1981.

Barr, S. "Looking for People Who Can Talk the Talk—in Other Languages." *Washington Post*, March 12, 2002. https://www.washingtonpost.com/archive/local/2002/03/12/looking-for-people-who-can-talk-the-talk-in-other-languages/ee45fd23-d6a0-48d8-b7f7-65189204f299/.

Barthes, Roland. *Image, Music, Text*, trans. Stephen Heath. London: Flamingo, 1984.

——. *S/Z*, trans. Richard Miller. Oxford: Basil Blackwell, 1974.

Bassnett, Susan, and Peter Bush, eds. *The Translator as Writer*. London: Continuum, 2006.

BIBLIOGRAPHY

Beauvoir, Simone de. *The Second Sex*, trans. Constance Borde and Sheila Malovany-Chevalier. New York: Alfred A. Knopf, 2010.
Bechdel, Alison. *Are You My Mother? A Comic Drama*. Boston: Mariner Books, 2013.
Behares, Luis Ernesto, and Carlos Ernesto Diaz, eds. *Os som de nossa terra: Productos artístico-verbales fronterizos*. Montevideo: Asociación de Universidades Grupo Montevideo, Universidad de la República, 1998.
Benstock, Shari. "At the Margin of Discourse." *PMLA* 98, no. 2 (1983): 204–25.
Bergvall, Caroline, and Erín Moure. "O YES." In *Antiphonies: Essays in Women's Experimental Poetries in Canada*, ed. Nate Dorward, 167–76. Willowdale: The Gig, 2008.
Boyden, Michael, and Patrick Goethals. "Translating the Watcher's Voice: Junot Díaz's *The Brief Wondrous Life of Oscar Wao* into Spanish." *Meta: Journal des Traducteurs/ Meta: Translators' Journal* 56, no. 1 (2011): 20–41.
Boyle, Matthew. "Exclusive—Donald Trump Fires Back at Jeb Bush: He Should Lead by 'Speaking English' While in the United States." *Breitbart News*, September 2, 2015. http://www.breitbart.com/big-government/2015/09/02/exclusive-donald-trump-fires-back-at-jeb-bush-he-should-lead-by-speaking-english-while-in-the-united-states/.
Braham, Persephone. "*Yo-Yo Boing!* Review." *Latin American Literature and Arts Review: New Writing and Arts in the Americas* 60 (2000): 86–87.
Braschi, Giannina. *Empire of Dreams*, trans. Tess O'Dwyer. New Haven, Conn.: Yale University Press, 1994.
———. *Imperio de los sueños*. San Juan: Editorial de la Universidad de Puerto Rico, 1988.
———. "Pelos en la lengua." *Hopscotch: A Cultural Review* 2, no. 2 (2001): 50.
———. *United States of Banana*. Las Vegas: AmazonCrossing, 2011.
———. *Yo-Yo Boing!* Las Vegas: AmazonCrossing, 2011.
———. *Yo-Yo Boing!* Pittsburgh, Penn.: Latin American Literary Review Press, 1998.
———. *Yo-Yo Boing!*, trans. Tess O'Dwyer. Las Vegas: AmazonCrossing, 2011.
———. "Yo-Yo Boing! (A Scene from the Bilingual Edition)." *Giannina Braschi* (blog), October 11, 2011. https://gianninabraschi.wordpress.com/category/yo-yo-boing/.
Brecht, R. D., and W. P. Rivers. *Language and National Security in the 21st Century: The Role of Title VI/Fulbright-Hays in Supporting National Language Capacity*. Dubuque, Iowa: Kendall/Hunt, 2000.
Brinkbäumer, Klaus, Peter Wensierski, Stefan Berg, Dominik Cziesche, Barbara Hardinghaus, Udo Ludwig, Sven Röbel, and Markus Verbeet. "De verlorene Welt." *Der Spiegel*, April 3, 2006. http://www.spiegel.de/spiegel/print/d-46502879.html.
Brossard, Nicole. *Picture Theory*, trans. Barbara Godard. Toronto: Guernica, 2006.
———. "Reconfiguration, from *SeaMother, or the Bitteroded Chapter*," trans. Erín Moure and Robert Mazjels. *Asymptote*, July 2019. https://www.asymptotejournal.com/poetry/nicole-brossard-reconfiguration-seamother-or-the-bitteroded-chapter/.
Brouillette, Sarah. *Literature and the Creative Economy*. Stanford, Calif.: Stanford University Press, 2014.
———. *Postcolonial Writers in the Global Literary Marketplace*. New York: Palgrave Macmillan, 2007.
Brown, Wendy. "Freedom's Silences." In *Censorship and Silencing: Practices of Cultural Regulation*, ed. Robert C. Post, 313–27. Los Angeles: Getty Research Institute, 1998.
Bueno, Wilson. "Editorial: Tempo de criar." *Nicolau*, no. 1 (1987): 2.

———. "Fronteiras: Nos entrecéus da linguagem," ed. Simone Homem de Mello. *Humboldt*, "A outra língua—Edição especial sobre literatura." http://www.goethe.de/wis/bib/prj/hmb/the/das/pt3286146.htm.
———. "Mar Paraguayo." *Nicolau*, no. 6 (1987): 25.
———. *Mar Paraguayo*. São Paulo: Iluminuras, 1992.
———. *Mar Paraguayo*. Toluca: Bonobos, 2006.
———. *Paraguayan Sea*, trans. Erín Moure. New York: Nightboat Books, 2017.
Bueno, Wilson, and Claudio Daniel. "Ñemogueta: An Interview with Wilson Bueno by Claudio Daniel." In *Paraguayan Sea*, trans. Erín Moure, 91–103. New York: Nightboat Books, 2017.
Burley, Eli. "Eli Burley on Erín Moure: *Planetary Noise*." *Lemonhound 3.0*, March 15, 2018. https://lemonhound.com/2018/03/15/eli-burley-on-erin-moure-planetary-noise/.
Burrows, Sonja S. "Beyond the Comfort Zone: Monolingual Ideologies, Bilingual U.S. Latino Texts." PhD diss., University of Oregon, 2010.
Burton, William M. "Inverting the Text: A Proposed Queer Translation Praxis." *In Other Words* 36 (Winter 2010): 54–68.
Butler, Judith. "Ruled Out: Vocabularies of the Censor." In *Censorship and Silencing: Practices of Cultural Regulation*, ed. Robert C. Post, 247–59. Los Angeles: Getty Research Institute, 1998.
Callahan, Laura. *English-Spanish Codeswitching in a Written Corpus*. Philadelphia: John Benjamins Publishing Company, 2004.
Caminero-Santangelo, Marta. "Latinidad." In *The Routledge Companion to Latino/a Literature*, 2nd ed., ed. Suzanne Bost and Frances R. Aparicio, 13–24. Abingdon, UK: Routledge, 2014.
———. *On Latinidad: U.S. Latino Literature and the Construction of Ethnicity*. Gainsville: University Press of Florida, 2007.
Campos, Augusto de. (@Poetamenos). "'Lygia fingers,' 1953, poema de Augusto de Campos, da série poetamenos." Instagram video, April 2, 2019. https://www.instagram.com/p/Bvv_bBgAtbh/?hl=en.
———. "Poesia concreta (manifesto)." In *Teoria da poesia concreta: Textos críticos e manifestos 1950–1960*, ed. Augusto de Campos, Décio Pignatari, and Haroldo de Campos, 71–72. São Paulo: Ateliê, 2006.
Campos, Haroldo de. "A obra de arte aberta." *Diario de São Paulo*, March 7, 1955.
———. "Anthropophagous Reason: Dialogue and Difference in Brazilian Culture," trans. Odile Cisneros. In *Novas: Selected Writings*, ed. Odile Cisneros and Antonio Sergio Bessa, 157–77. Evanston, Ill.: Northwestern University Press, 2007.
———. "The Open Work of Art." In *Novas: Selected Writings*, ed. Odile Cisneros and Antonio Sergio Bessa, 220–22. Evanston, Ill.: Northwestern University Press, 2007.
———. "The Rule of Anthropophagy: Europe Under the Sign of Devoration," trans. María Tai Wolff. *Latin American Literary Review* 14, no. 27, "Brazilian Literature" (1986): 42–60.
Canagarajah, Suresh. *Translingual Practice: Global Englishes and Cosmopolitan Relations*. London: Routledge, 2013.
Canese, Jorge. *Las palabras K*. Asunción: Arandurã Editorial, 2011.
Carpio, Glenda R. "Junot Díaz's Wondrous Spanglish." In *Junot Díaz and the Decolonial Imagination*, ed. Monica Hanna, Jennifer Harford Vargas, and José David Saldívar, 257–90. Durham, N.C.: Duke University Press, 2016.

BIBLIOGRAPHY

Carrión, María M. "Geography, (M)Other Tongues and the Role of Translation in Giannina Braschi's *El imperio de los sueños.*" *Studies in 20th Century Literature* 20, no. 1 (1996): 167–91.
Casielles-Suárez, Eugenia. "Radical Code-Switching in *The Brief Wondrous Life of Oscar Wao.*" *Bulletin of Hispanic Studies* 90, no. 4 (June 2013): 475–87.
Cassin, Barbara, ed. *Dictionary of Untranslatables: A Philosophical Lexicon*, trans. Emily Apter, Jacques Lezra, and Michael Wood. Princeton, N.J.: Princeton University Press, 2014.
——, ed. *Vocabulaire européen des philosophies: Dictionnaire des intraduisibles.* Paris: Éditions de Seuil; Le Robert, 2004.
Castillo, Debra A. *Re-Dreaming America: Toward a Bilingual American Culture.* Albany: State University of New York Press, 2005.
"Census in Brief: English-French Bilingualism Reaches New Heights." *Statistics Canada*, 2017. https://www12.statcan.gc.ca/census-recensement/2016/as-sa/98–200-x /2016009/98–200-X2016009-eng.cfm.
Chaffee, Jessie. "The Translator Relay: Erín Moure." *Words Without Borders*, August 28, 2017. https://www.wordswithoutborders.org/dispatches/article/the-translator-relay -erin-moure.
Chamoiseau, Patrick. *Texaco.* Paris: Gallimard, 1992.
——. *Texaco*, trans. Rose-Myriam Réjouis and Val Vinurokov. London: Granta, 1997.
Chamoiseau, Patrick, Jean Bernabé, and Raphaël Confiant. *Éloge de La Créolité.* Paris: Gallimard, 1989.
——. "In Praise of Creoleness," trans. Mohamed B. Taleb Khyar. *Callaloo* 13, no. 4 (1990): 886–909.
Chaudhuri, Una, and Holly Hughes, eds. *Animal Acts: Performing Species Today.* Ann Arbor: University of Michigan Press, 2014.
Chávez-Silverman, Susana. "All Green Will Endure Chrónicle," trans. Ellen Jones. *Asymptote*, July 2015. https://www.asymptotejournal.com/special-feature/susana -chavezsilverman-all-green-will-endure-chronicle/.
——. "Axolotl/Bichos Raros Crónica." *PORTAL: Journal of Multidisciplinary International Studies* 9, no. 2 (2012): 1–4.
——. *Heartthrob: Del Balboa Café al Apartheid and Back.* Madison: Wisconsin University Press, 2019. Kindle.
——. *Killer Crónicas: Bilingual Memories.* Madison: University of Wisconsin Press, 2004.
——. *Scenes from la Cuenca de Los Angeles y otros Natural Disasters.* Madison: University of Wisconsin Press, 2010.
——. "Susana Chávez-Silverman Reading from *Killer Crónicas.*" University of Wisconsin Press. http://uwpress.wisc.edu/books/2616-audio.html.
——. "Todo verdor perdurará Crónica." *Asymptote*, July 2015. https://www.asymptote journal.com/special-feature/susana-chavezsilverman-all-green-will-endure -chronicle/spanish/.
——. "Tropicalizing the Liberal Arts College Classroom." In *Power, Race, and Gender in Academe: Strangers in The Tower?*, ed. Shirley Geok-lin Lim, María Herrera-Sobek, and Genaro M. Padilla, 132–53. New York: Modern Language Association, 2000.

———. "Vivir (con) la pregunta: Mis crónicas del Sur, y otras hierbas." Presentation, XX Congreso Internacional de Literatura Hispánica, Santiago de Compostela, June 21–23, 2017.

Chávez-Silverman, Susana, and Librada Hernández, eds. *Reading and Writing the Ambiente: Queer Sexualities in Latino, Latin American, and Spanish Culture*. Madison: University of Wisconsin Press, 2000.

Chen, Mel Y. *Animacies: Biopolitics, Racial Mattering, and Queer Affect*. Durham, N.C.: Duke University Press, 2012.

Chow, Rey. *Not Like a Native Speaker: On Languaging as a Postcolonial Experience*. New York: Columbia University Press, 2014.

Cixous, Hélène. "The Laugh of the Medusa," trans. Keith Cohen and Paula Cohen. *Signs* 1, no. 4 (1976): 875–93.

Cortázar, Julio. *Final del juego*. 5th ed. Buenos Aires: Editorial Sudamericana, 1966.

———. *Rayuela*, ed. Julio Ortega and Saúl Yurkievich. Madrid: Colección Archivos, 1991.

Cox, Annabel. "Achy Obejas's 'Sugarcane' and Cuban-American Bilingual Literature: Language Choices and Cultural Identities." In *Exile, Language, and Identity*, ed. Magda Stroińska and Vittorina Cecchetto, 125–38. Frankfurt: Peter Lang, 2003.

———. "Literature in the Contact Zone: Emily Apter's 'A New Comparative Literature' and Achy Obejas's 'Sugarcane.'" *Crossings: Journal of Migration and Culture* 5, no. 2 & 3 (2014): 231–43.

Cresci, Karen Lorrain. "Regreso al Español: La Traducción de *Drown* de Junot Díaz: Entrevista a Eduardo Lago." *Argus-a* 6, no. 23 (February 2017). http://www.argus-a.com.ar/archivos-dinamicas/regreso-al-espanol.pdf.

———. "'Call It My Revenge on English': 'Negocios' de Junot Díaz y sus traducciones disonantes." *Literatura: Teoría, historia, crítica* 19, no. 2 (2017): 147–81.

"Crossings: An Interview with Erin Mouré." *Mosaic: An Interdisciplinary Critical Journal* 36, no. 4, "PILGRIMAGE" (2003): 1–16.

Cruz-Malavé, Arnaldo Manuel. "'Under the Skirt of Liberty': Giannina Braschi Rewrites Empire." *American Quarterly* 66, no. 3 (2014): 801–18.

Currie, Mark. *About Time*. Edinburgh: Edinburgh University Press, 2007.

———. *Postmodern Narrative Theory*. 2nd ed. Basingstoke, UK: Macmillan Press, 2011.

Cutter, Martha. *Lost and Found in Translation: Contemporary Ethnic American Writing and the Politics of Language Diversity*. Chapel Hill: University of North Carolina Press, 2005.

D'Amore, Anna María. *Translating Contemporary Mexican Literature: Fidelity to Alterity*. New York: Peter Lang, 2009.

Damrosch, David. *What Is World Literature?* Princeton, N.J.: Princeton University Press, 2003.

Davidson, Harriet. "Improper Desire: Reading *The Waste Land*." In *The Cambridge Companion to T. S. Eliot*, ed. A. David Moody, 121–31. Cambridge: Cambridge University Press, 1994.

Deleuze, Gilles, and Félix Guattari. *A Thousand Plateaus: Capitalism and Schizophrenia*. London: Athlone Press, 1988.

Derby, Lauren H., and Richard Turits. "Temwayaj Kout Kouto, 1937: Eyewitnesses to the Genocide." In *Revolutionary Freedoms: A History of Survival, Strength, and Imagination in Haiti*, ed. Cécile Accilien, 137–43. Pompano Beach, Fla.: Caribbean Studies Press, 2006.

Derrick, Roshawnda A. "Radical Bilingualism in *Killer Crónicas*." *Hispania* 97, no. 3 (2014): 366–67.
Derrida, Jacques. "Living On: Border Lines." In *Deconstruction and Criticism*, ed. Geoffrey H. Hartman, trans. James Hulbert, 75–176. London: Routledge and Kegan Paul, 1979.
———. *Monolingualism of the Other; Or, the Prosthesis of Origin*, trans. Patrick Mensah. Stanford, Calif.: Stanford University Press, 1996.
———. *Of Grammatology*, trans. G. C. Spivak. Baltimore, Md.: Johns Hopkins University Press, 1976.
———. *Speech and Phenomena and Other Essays on Husserl's Theory of Signs*. Evanston, Ill.: Northwestern University Press, 1973.
Díaz, Junot. *The Brief Wondrous Life of Oscar Wao*. London: Faber and Faber, 2008.
———. "The Brief Wondrous Life of Oscar Wao (Excerpt)." Genius. http://genius.com/Junot-diaz-the-brief-wondrous-life-of-oscar-wao-excerpt-annotated.
———. *Drown*. London: Faber and Faber, 1996.
———. *La breve y maravillosa vida de Óscar Wao*, trans. Achy Obejas. New York: Vintage Español, 2008.
———. *La maravillosa vida breve de Óscar Wao*, trans. Achy Obejas. Barcelona: Random House Mondadori, 2007.
———. "Language, Violence, and Resistance." In *Voice-Overs: Translation and Latin American Literature*, ed. Daniel Balderston and Marcy Schwartz, 42–44. New York: State University of New York Press, 2002.
———. *Los Boys*, trans. Miguel Martínez-Lage. Barcelona: Mondadori, 1996.
———. *Negocios*, trans. Eduardo Lago. New York: Vintage, 1997.
———. "The Silence: The Legacy of Childhood Trauma." *New Yorker*, April 8, 2018. https://www.newyorker.com/magazine/2018/04/16/the-silence-the-legacy-of-childhood-trauma.
Díaz, Roberto Ignacio. *Unhomely Rooms: Foreign Tongues and Spanish American Literature*. Lewisburg, Penn.: Bucknell University Press, 2002.
Diegues, Douglas. *Dá gusto andar desnudo por estas selvas: Sonetos salvajes*. Curitiba: Travessa dos Editores, 2003.
———. "Karta manifesto del amor amor em portunhol selvagem." *Portal O Globo Cultura*, August 17, 2008. http://oglobo. globo.com/cultura/confira-manifesto-em-defesa-do-portunhol-selvagem-3607777.
———. *Portunhol selvagem: El blog de Douglas Diegues*. http://portunholselvagem.blogspot.com.
Dillon, Sarah. *The Palimpsest*. London: Continuum, 2007.
Doloughan, Fiona J. *Contemporary Narrative: Textual Production, Multimodality and Multiliteracies*. London: Continuum, 2011.
———. *English as a Language in Translation*. London: Bloomsbury, 2016.
———. "Translation as a Motor of Critique and Invention in Contemporary Literature." In *Multilingual Currents in Literature, Translation, and Culture*, ed. Rachael Gilmour and Tamar Steinitz, 150–67. New York: Routledge, 2018.
Dorfman, Ariel. *Heading South, Looking North: A Bilingual Journey*. New York: Farrar, Straus and Giroux, 1998.
———. *Rumbo al sur, deseando al norte: Un romance bilingüe*. Barcelona: Planeta, 1998.

Dumitrescu, Domnita. "'Dude was figureando hard': El cambio y la fusión de códigos en la obra de Junot Díaz." In *Perspectives in the Study of Spanish Language Variation: Papers in Honor of Carmen Silva Corvalán*, ed. Andrés Enrique Arias, Manuel J. Gutiérrez, Alazne Landa, and Francisco Ocampo. Santiago de Compostela: Verba, 2014.

du Plessis, Klara. "Three Poems." *Asymptote*, July 2016. https://www.asymptotejournal.com/special-feature/klara-du-plessis-three-poems/.

Echavarren, Robert, José Kozer, and Jacobo Sefamí, eds. *Medusario: Muestra de poesía latinoamericana*. Mexico City: Fondo de Cultura Economica, 1996.

Echeverría, Esteban. *El matadero; La cautiva*. Madrid: Ediciones Cátedra, 1997.

———. *The Slaughteryard*, trans. Norman Thomas di Giovanni and Susan Ashe. London: Friday Project, 2010.

Eco, Umberto. "Introduction." In *Anna Livia Plurabelle Di James Joyce*, ed. Rosa Maria Bollettieri Bosinelli. Turin: Einaudi, 1996.

English, James. *The Economy of Prestige: Prizes, Awards, and the Circulation of Cultural Value*. Cambridge, Mass.: Harvard University Press, 2005.

Epstein, B. J., and Robert Gillett, eds. *Queer in Translation*. Abingdon, UK: Routledge, 2017.

Esdaille, Milca. "Same Trip, Different Ships." *Black Issues Book Review* 3, no. 2 (April 2001).

Esplin, Marlene Hansen. "Self-Translation and Accommodation: Strategies of Multilingualism in Gloria Anzaldúa's *Borderlands/La Frontera: The New Mestiza* and Margarita Cota-Cárdenas's *Puppet*." *MELUS* 41, no. 2 (2016): 176–201.

Etiemble, René. *Parlez-vous franglais?* Paris: Gallimard, 1991.

Fernández García, María Jesús. "Portuñol y Literatura." *Revista de Estudios Extremeños* 62 (2006): 555–76.

Ferré, Rosario. "Puerto Rico, USA." *New York Times*, March 9, 1998. http://www.puertorico-herald.org/issues/vol2n06/Ferre-Rosario-PuertoRicoUSA.html.

Flaherty, Colleen. "Junot Díaz, Feminism and Ethnicity." *Inside Higher Education*, May 29, 2018. https://www.insidehighered.com/news/2018/05/29/rift-among-scholars-over-treatment-junot-d%C3%ADaz-he-faces-harassment-and-misconduct.

Flores, Juan. *From Bomba to Hip-Hop: Puerto Rican Culture and Latino Identity*. New York: Columbia University Press, 2000.

Foarță, Șerban. "Butterflyción," trans. MARGENTO. *Asymptote*, July 2016. http://www.asymptotejournal.com/special-feature/serban-foarta-butterflycion/.

Forster, Andrew, Erín Moure, and Sherry Simon. "Discussion and Book Launch/Discussion et Lancement de Livre." University of Concordia, November 9, 2017. http://www.concordia.ca/cuevents/finearts/fofa/2017/08/03/exhibition-andrew-forster-erin-moure.html.

Frost, Robert. Unpublished notebook, 1950–1955. Robert Frost Collection, MS 001728. Dartmouth College, Hanover, N.H.

Galíndez, Jesús de. *La era de Trujillo: Tesis doctoral sobre la brutal tiranía*. Buenos Aires: Americana, 1958.

Gándara, Alejandro. "Junot Díaz." *El Mundo, El Escorpión*, November 27, 2009. http://www.elmundo.es/elmundo/2008/07/08/escorpion/1215510619.html.

García, Cristina. "Translation as Restoration." In *Voice-Overs: Translation and Latin American Literature*, ed. Daniel Balderston and Marcy Schwartz, 45–48. New York: State University of New York Press, 2002.

BIBLIOGRAPHY

García, Cynthia "I Already Miss the Future: Augusto de Campos Discusses the Creation of Concrete Poetry on the Occasion of His Retrospective at Sesc Pompeia." *New City Brazil*, June 2016. https://www.newcitybrazil.com/2016/06/11/i-already-miss-the-future/.

García Vizcaíno, María José. "Cisneros' Code-Mixed Narrative and Its Implications for Translation." *Mutatis Mutandis* 1, no. 2 (2008): 212–24.

Garrigós, Cristina. Review of *United States of Banana*, by Giannina Braschi. *Evergreen Review*, no. 128 (Spring 2012). https://evergreenreview.com/read/two-reviews-united-states-of-banana-giannina-braschi/.

Geisler, Michael. "To Understand a Culture, Learn Its Language." *Chronicle of Higher Education* 52, no. 29 (2006): B11–12.

Genette, Gérard. *Palimpsests: Literature in the Second Degree*, trans. Channa Newman and Claude Doubinsky. Lincoln: University of Nebraska Press, 1982.

Gilmour, Rachael, and Tamar Steinitz, eds. *Multilingual Currents in Literature, Translation, and Culture*. New York: Routledge, 2017.

Glissant, Eduoard. *Le discours antillais*. Paris: Editions de Seuil, 1981.

Godard, Barbara. "Translating and Sexual Difference." *Resources for Feminist Research* 8, no. 3 (1984): 13–16.

González Echevarría, Roberto. "Is 'Spanglish' a Language?" *New York Times*, March 27, 1997.

Grubbs, Jennifer, ed. "Inquiries and Intersections: Queer Theory and Anti-Speciesist Praxis." Special issue, *Journal for Critical Animal Studies* 10, no. 3 (2012).

Grutman, Rainier. "Multilingualism and Translation." In *Routledge Encyclopedia of Translation Studies*, ed. Mona Baker, 157–60. London: Routledge, 2004.

———. "Refraction and Recognition: Literary Multilingualism in Translation." *Target* 18, no. 1 (2006): 17–47.

Guerra, Gilbert, and Gilbert Orbea. "The Argument Against the Use of the Term 'Latinx.'" *The Phoenix* (blog), November 19, 2015. http://swarthmorephoenix.com/2015/11/19/the-argument-against-the-use-of-the-term-latinx/.

Gynan, Shaw N. "Language Planning and Policy in Paraguay." *Current Issues in Language Planning* 2, no. 1 (November 2001): 53–118. https://doi.org/10.1080/14664200108668019.

Hanna, Monica, Jennifer Harford Vargas, and José David Saldívar, eds. *Junot Díaz and the Decolonial Imagination*. Durham, N.C.: Duke University Press, 2016.

Hassan, Waïl S. "Agency and Translational Literature: Ahdaf Soueif's *The Map of Love*." *PMLA* 121, no. 3 (2015): 753–68.

Hayot, Eric. "The Profession Does Not Need the Monograph Dissertation." *Profession*, May 26, 2017. https://profession.mla.hcommons.org/2017/05/26/the-profession-does-not-need-the-monograph-dissertation/.

Herrera, Yuri. *Señales que precederán al fin del mundo*. Cáceres: Periférica, 2010.

———. *Signs Preceding the End of the World*, trans. Lisa Dillman. High Wycombe: And Other Stories, 2015.

"Historia." Real Academia Española. http://www.rae.es/la-institucion/historia.

Hooper, Kirsty. *Writing Galicia into the World: New Cartographies, New Poetics*. Liverpool: Liverpool University Press, 2011.

Huggan, Graham. *The Postcolonial Exotic: Marketing the Margins*. London: Routledge, 2001.

Huston, Nancy. *Cantique des plaines: Roman*. Montréal: Leméac, 1993.
——. *Plainsong*. Toronto: HarperCollins, 1993.
Irigaray, Luce. "When Our Lips Speak Together," trans. Carolyn Burke. *Signs* 6, no. 1, "Women: Sex and Sexuality, Part 2" (1980): 69–79.
"Issue Jan 2011." *Asymptote*. January 2011. http://www.asymptotejournal.com/jan-2011/.
Jagose, Annamarie. *Inconsequence: Lesbian Representation and the Logic of Sexual Sequence*. Ithaca, N.Y.: Cornell University Press, 2002.
Joyce, James. *Finnegans Wake*. London: Faber and Faber, 1982.
Kanchana, Kanya. "Grammar of the Goddess." *Asymptote*, July 2016. http://www.asymptotejournal.com/special-feature/kanya-kanchana-grammar-of-the-goddess/.
Kaup, Monica. *Neobaroque in the Americas: Alternative Modernities in Literature, Visual Art, and Film*. Charlottesville: University of Virginia Press, 2012.
Keating, AnaLouise. *The Gloria Anzaldúa Reader*. Durham, N.C.: Duke University Press, 2009.
Keller, G. "How Chicano Authors Use Bilingual Techniques for Literary Effect." In *Chicano Studies: A Multidisciplinary Approach*, ed. E. García, F. Lomeli, and I. Ortíz, 171–89. New York: Teacher's College Press, 1984.
Kellman, Steven G. *The Restless Ilan Stavans: Outsider on the Inside*. Pittsburgh, Penn.: University of Pittsburgh Press, 2019.
——. *The Translingual Imagination*. Lincoln: University of Nebraska Press, 2000.
Kilito, Abdelfattah. "Thou Shalt Not Translate Me," 2010. https://vimeo.com/17363157.
"Killer Crónicas: Bilingual Memories." University of Wisconsin Press. https://uwpress.wisc.edu/books/2616.htm.
La Fountain-Stokes, Lawrence. "La política queer del espanglish." *Debate Feminista* 17, no. 33 (2006): 141–53.
——. "Pop-Shock: Shifting Representations of Diasporic Puerto Rican Women's Queer Sexualities in US Latina Cultural Texts." *Letras Femeninas* 31, no. 1 (2005): 79–98.
Lago, Eduardo. "El idioma de la imaginación." In *Enciclopedia del español en los Estados Unidos*, 602–3. Madrid: Instituto Cervantes, 2008.
Lanzendörfer, Tim. "The Marvellous History of the Dominican Republic in Junot Díaz's *The Brief Wondrous Life of Oscar Wao*." *MELUS* 38, no. 2 (2013): 127–42.
Larkosh, Christopher. *Re-Engendering Translation: Transcultural Practice, Gender/Sexuality and the Politics of Alterity*. Manchester: St. Jerome Pub., 2011.
Lauret, Maria. *Wanderwords: Language Migration in American Literature*. London: Bloomsbury, 2014.
Lennon, Brian. *In Babel's Shadow: Multilingual Literatures, Monolingual States*. Minneapolis: University of Minnesota Press, 2010.
Lewis, Elizabeth Sara. "'This Is My Girlfriend, Linda': Translating Queer Relationships in Film: A Case Study of the Subtitles for Gia and a Proposal for Developing the Field of Queer Studies." *In Other Words*, no. 36 (Winter 2010): 3–22.
Lionnet, Françoise. "Creole Vernacular Translations in Mauritius." *MLN* 118 (2003): 911–32.
Lipski, John M. "Too Close for Comfort? The Genesis of 'Portuñol/Portunhol.'" In *Selected Proceedings of the 8th Hispanic Linguistics Symposium*, ed. Timothy L. Face and Carol A. Klee, 1–22. Somerville, Mass.: Cascadilla Proceedings Project, 2006.

———. *Varieties of Spanish in the United States*. Washington, D.C.: Georgetown University Press, 2008.
Lonsdale, Laura. *Multilingualism and Modernity: Barbarisms in Spanish and American Literature*. Basingstoke, UK: Palgrave Macmillan, 2018.
López, Brenda V. de. *Lenguaje fronterizo en obras de autores uruguayos*. 2nd ed. Montevideo: Editorial Nordan-Comunidad, 1993.
Lorde, Audre. *Zami: A New Spelling of My Name*. Trumansburg, N.Y.: Crossing Press, 1982.
Ludmer, Josefina. "Tricks of the Weak." In *Feminist Perspectives on Sor Juana Inés de La Cruz*, ed. Stephanie Merrim, 86–93. Detroit, Mich.: Wayne State University Press, 1991.
Machado Sáez, Elena. "Dictating Desire, Dictating Diaspora: Junot Díaz's *The Brief Wondrous Life of Oscar Wao* as Foundational Romance." *Contemporary Literature* 52, no. 3 (2011): 522–55.
———. "Reconquista: Ilan Stavans and the Indigenous Other in Multiculturalist Latino Discourse." *Latino Studies* 7, no. 4 (Winter 2009): 410–34.
Mallea, Eduardo. *All Green Shall Perish*, trans. John B. Hughes. London: Calder and Boyars, 1967.
Marques, Antonio, and Leonardo Rocha. "Bolsonaro diz que OAB só defende bandido e reserva indígena é um crime." *Campo Grande News*, April 22, 2015. https://www.campograndenews.com.br/politica/bolsonaro-diz-que-oab-so-defende-bandido-e-reserva-indigena-e-um-crime.
Martínez-San Miguel, Yolanda. "Boricua (Between) Borders: On the Possibility of Translating Bilingual Narratives." In *Spanglish*, ed. Ilan Stavans, 72–87. Westport, Conn.: Greenwood Press, 2008.
Massini-Cagliari, Gladis. "Language Policy in Brazil: Monolingualism and Linguistic Prejudice." *Language Policy* 3, no. 1 (2004): 3–23.
McCracken, Ellen. *Paratexts and Performance in the Novels of Junot Díaz and Sandra Cisneros*. New York: Palgrave Macmillan, 2015.
———. "Performance and Linguistic Spectacle in Sandra Cisneros's *Caramelo* and Junot Díaz's *The Brief Wondrous Life of Oscar Wao*." In *Landscapes of Writing in Chicano Literature*, ed. Imelda Martín-Junquera, 33–46. New York: Palgrave Macmillan, 2013.
McManis, Sam. "Author Mixes Spanish, English in Her 'Crónicas.'" *Sacramento Bee*, May 2007.
Meylaerts, Reine. "Heterolingualism in/and Translation." Special issue, *Target* 18, no. 1 (2006).
———. "Literary Heteroglossia in Translation: When the Language of Translation Is the Locus of Ideological Struggle." In *Translation Studies at the Interface of Disciplines*, ed. João Ferreira Duarte, Alejandra Assis Rosa, and Teresa Seruya. Amsterdam: John Benjamins Publishing Company, 2006.
Mezei, Kathy. "Bilingualism and Translation in/of Michèle Lalonde's *Speak White*." *The Translator* 4, no. 2 (1998): 229–47.
Mignolo, Walter. *Local Histories/Global Designs: Coloniality, Subaltern Knowledges, and Border Thinking*. Princeton, N.J.: Princeton University Press, 2000.
Miller, Joshua. *Accented America: The Cultural Politics of Multilingual Modernism*. New York: Oxford University Press, 2011.

Mizumura, Minae. *The Fall of Language in the Age of English*, trans. Mari Yoshihara and Juliet Winters Carpenter. New York: Columbia University Press, 2008.

Mohabir, Rajiv. "Four Poems." *Asymptote*, July 2016. http://www.asymptotejournal.com/special-feature/rajiv-mohabir-four-poems/.

Moi, Toril. "From Femininity to Finitude: Freud, Lacan, and Feminism, Again." *Signs* 29, no. 3 (2004): 841–76.

Monier-Williams, Monier. *An English-Sanskrit Dictionary*. Springfield, Va.: Nataraj Books, 2006.

Montaigne, Michel de. *Des cannibales suivi de la peur de l'autre*. Paris: Gallimard, 2008.

——. "On the Cannibals." In *The Complete Essays*, ed. and trans. M. A. Screech, vol. 1, 228–41. London: Penguin, 1992.

Montes-Alcalá, Cecilia. "Code-Switching in U.S. Latino Novels." In *Language Mixing and Code-Switching in Writing*, ed. Mark Sebba, Shahrzad Mahootian, and Carla Johnson, 68–88. New York: Routledge, 2012.

Moraga, Cherríe, and Gloria Anzaldúa. *This Bridge Called My Back: Writings by Radical Women of Color*. 2nd ed. New York: Kitchen Table: Women of Color Press, 1983.

Morales, Ed. *Living in Spanglish*. New York: St Martin's Press, 2002.

Moreno-Fernández, Francisco. "*Yo-Yo-Boing!* Or Literature as a Translingual Practice." In *Poets, Philosophers, Lovers: On the Writings of Giannina Braschi*, ed. Frederick Luis Aldama and Tess O'Dwyer, 54–62. Pittsburgh, Penn.: Pittsburgh University Press, 2020.

Moretti, Franco. "Conjectures on World Literature." *New Left Review* (January–February 2000): 54–68.

——. *Distant Reading*. London: Verso, 2013.

Motschenbacher, Heiko. *Language, Gender, and Sexual Identity*. Amsterdam: John Benjamins Publishing Company, 2010.

Moure, Erín. *My Beloved Wager: Essays from a Writing Practice*. Edmonton: NeWest Press, 2009.

——. *O Cidadán*. Toronto: House of Anansi Press, 2002.

——. *Planetary Noise: Selected Poetry of Erín Moure*, ed. Shannon Maguire. Middletown, Conn.: Wesleyan University Press, 2017.

——. "Polylingual Writers: The Joyous Sea of Words." *Quebec Writers' Federation*, December 7, 2017. https://qwfwrites.wordpress.com/2017/12/07/the-joyous-sea-of-words-by-erin-moure/.

Moya, Paula. "Dismantling the Master's House: The Decolonial Imagination of Audre Lorde and Junot Díaz." In *Junot Díaz and the Decolonial Imagination*, ed. Monica Hanna, Jennifer Harford Vargas, and José David Saldívar, 231–55. Durham, N.C.: Duke University Press, 2016.

Mugglestone, Lynda. *Talking Proper: The Rise of Accent as Social Symbol*. Oxford: Oxford University Press, 2007.

Muñoz, José Esteban. *Disidentifications: Queers of Color and the Performance of Politics*. Minneapolis: University of Minnesota Press, 1999.

Myers-Scotton, Carol. *Social Motivations for Code-Switching*. Oxford: Oxford University Press, 1993.

Nelson, Maggie. *The Argonauts*. Minneapolis, Minn.: Graywolf Press, 2015.

BIBLIOGRAPHY

Nelziza Lovera de Florentino, Nádia. "Entre gêneros e fronteiras: Uma leitura de Mar paraguayo, de Wilson Bueno." PhD diss., Universidade Estadual Paulista, 2016.
Neuman, Andrés. *El viajero del siglo*. Madrid: Alfaguara, 2009.
———. *Traveller of the Century*, trans. Nick Caistor and Lorenza Garcia. London: Pushkin, 2013.
Newmark, Peter. *A Textbook of Translation*. London: Prentice Hall, 1988.
Nissan, Greg. "For Whom the -R Rolls." *Asymptote*, July 2016. http://www.asymptote journal.com/special-feature/greg-nissan-for-whom-the-r-rolls/.
Norman, Rachel. "'A Bastard Jargon': Language Politics and Identity in *The Brief Wondrous Life of Oscar Wao*." *South Atlantic Review* 81, no. 1 (2016): 34–50.
NZengou-Tayo, Marie-José. "Literature and Diglossia: The Poetics of French and Creole 'Interlect' in Patrick Chamoiseau's *Texaco*." *Caribbean Quarterly* 43, no. 4 (1997): 81–101.
Obejas, Achy. *Aguas y otros cuentos*. Havana: Letras Cubanas, 2009.
———. "A Conversation with Junot Díaz." *Review: Literature and Arts of the Americas* 42, no. 1 (2009): 42–47.
———. "Sugarcane." In *Wáchale: Poetry and Prose About Growing Up Latino in America*, ed. Ilan Stavans, 110–12. Chicago: Cricket Books, 2001.
———. "Translating Junot." *Chicago Tribune*, September 14, 2012. http://articles .chicagotribune.com/2012-09-14/features/ct-prj-0916-book-of-the-month -20120914_1_dominican-republic-oscar-wao-spanglish.
———. *We Came All the Way from Cuba So You Could Dress Like This?* Pittsburgh, Penn.: Cleis Press, 1994.
O'Neill, Patrick. *Impossible Joyce: Finnegans Wakes*. Toronto: University of Toronto Press, 2013.
O'Rourke, Megan. "Questions for Junot Díaz." *Slate*, April 8, 2008. http://www.slate.com /articles/news_and_politics/recycled/2008/04/questions_for_junot_daz.html.
Orsini, Francesca. "The Multilingual Local in World Literature." *Comparative Literature* 67, no. 4 (2015): 345–74.
Otheguy, Ricardo, and Nancy Stern. "On So-Called Spanglish." *International Journal of Bilingualism* 15, no. 1 (2010): 85–100.
Packer, George. "Cheap Words." *New Yorker*, February 2014. http://www.newyorker .com/magazine/2014/02/17/cheap-words.
Paredes, Américo. *George Washington Gómez*. Houston: Arte Público Press, 1990.
Parks, Tim. "The Dull New Global Novel." *New York Review of Books*, February 2010. http://www.nybooks.com/blogs/nyrblog/2010/feb/09/the-dull-new-global-novel/.
Paz, Octavio. *El laberinto de la soledad*, ed. Enrico Mario Santí. 22nd ed. Madrid: Cátedra, 2015.
Pérez Firmat, Gustavo. *Tongue Ties: Logo-Eroticism in Anglo-Hispanic Literature*. New York: Palgrave Macmillan, 2003.
Perloff, Marjorie. *Unoriginal Genius: Poetry by Other Means in the New Century*. Chicago: University of Chicago Press, 2010.
Perteghella, Manuela, and Eugenia Loffredo, eds. *Translation and Creativity: Perspectives on Creative Writing and Translation Studies*. London: Continuum, 2006.
"Plebiscite: Island Wide Results." Elecciones 2020, January 28, 2021. https://elecciones 2020.ceepur.org/Escrutinio_General_93/index.html#en/default/PLEBISCITO_ Resumen.xml.

Pratt, Mary Louise. "Building a New Public Idea About Language." *Profession* (2003): 110–19.
———. *Imperial Eyes*. London: Routledge, 1992.
Preciado, Paul B. *Testo Junkie: Sex, Drugs, and Biopolitics in the Pharmacopornographic Era*. New York: Feminist Press, 2013.
Publishers Weekly. Review of *Yo-Yo Boing!*. 1998. http://www.publishersweekly.com/9780935480979.
"¿Qué es Mar Paraguayo?" *Profética: Casa de la Lectura*, June 13, 2012. http://www.profetica.com.mx/libreria-2/propuestas/que-es-mar-paraguayo.
Quesada, Sarah. "A Planetary Warning? The Multilayered Caribbean Zombie in 'Monstro.'" In *Junot Díaz and the Decolonial Imagination*, ed. Monica Hanna, Jennifer Harford Vargas, and José David Saldívar, 291–318. Durham, N.C.: Duke University Press, 2016.
Quiñones, Noel. "Arroz Poetica Battle Rhyme for Kendrick Lamar." *Asymptote*, July 2016. http://www.asymptotejournal.com/special-feature/noel-quinones-arroz-poetica-battle-rhyme-for-kendrick-lamar/.
Ramírez, Roberto R. "The Hispanic Population in the United States: Population Characteristics March 1998." *Current Population Reports*, October 1999. https://www.census.gov/prod/2000pubs/p20-525.pdf.
"Results of the Modern Language Association's Fall 1995 Survey of Foreign Language Enrolments." *MLA Newsletter* 28, no. 4 (1996): 1–2.
Ricento, Thomas. "A Brief History of Language Restrictionism in the United States." In *Official English? No!*, ed. S. Dicker, K. Romstedt, and Thomas Ricento, 7–17. Washington, D.C.: TESOL, 1995.
Rosenwald, Lawrence Alan. *Multilingual America: Language and the Making of American Literature*. Cambridge: Cambridge University Press, 2008.
Rossi, Cecilia. "Literary Translation and Disciplinary Boundaries: Creative Writing and Interdisciplinarity." In *The Routledge Handbook of Literary Translation*, ed. Kelly Washbourne and Ben van Wyke, 42–57. London: Routledge, 2018.
———. "Translation as a Creative Force." In *The Routledge Handbook of Translation and Culture*, ed. Sue-Ann Harding and Ovidi Carbonell Cortés, 381–97. London: Routledge, 2018.
Rudin, E. *Tender Accents of Sound: Spanish in the Chicano Novel in English*. Tempe, Ariz.: Bilingual Press/Editorial Bilingüe, 1996.
Saint-Exupéry, Antoine de. *El Little Príncipe*, trans. Ilan Stavans. Neckarsteinach: Edition Tintenfass, 2016.
Sarduy, Severo. "The Baroque and the Neobaroque." In *Baroque New Worlds: Representation, Transculturation, Counterconquest*, ed. Lois Parkinson Zamora and Monica Kaup, 270–91. Durham, N.C.: Duke University Press, 2010.
Saussy, Haun. "The Importance of What Doesn't Translate." George Steiner Lecture, Queen Mary University of London, March 9, 2015.
Saval, Nikil, and Dayna Tortorici. "World Lite: What Is Global Literature." *n+1* 17, "The Evil Issue" (Fall 2013). https://nplusonemag.com/issue-17/the-intellectual-situation/world-lite/.
Schildkraut, Deborah J. *Press One for English: Language Policy, Public Opinion, and American Identity*. Princeton, N.J.: Princeton University Press, 2005.
Sedgwick, Eve Kosofsky. *Tendencies*. Durham, N.C.: Duke University Press, 1993.

BIBLIOGRAPHY

Sehlaouai, Abdelilah Salim. "Language Learning, Heritage, and Literacy in the USA: The Case of Arabic." *Language, Culture and Curriculum* 21, no. 3 (2008): 280–91.

Seyhan, Azade. *Writing Outside the Nation*. Princeton, N.J.: Princeton University Press, 2001.

Shanahan, Mark, and Stephanie Ebbert. "Junot Díaz Case May Be a #MeToo Turning Point." *Boston Globe*, June 30, 2018. https://www.bostonglobe.com/metro/2018/06/30/junot-diaz-case-may-metoo-turning-point/3TMFseenE4Go1eVsqbFSxM/story.html.

Shklovsky, Viktor. "The Resurrection of the Word." In *Russian Formalism: A Collection of Articles and Texts in Translation*, ed. Stephen Bann and John E. Bowlt, trans. Richard Sherwood. Edinburgh: Scottish Academic Press, 1973.

——. *Theory of Prose*, trans. Benjamin Sher. London: Dalkey Archive Press, 2009.

Shook, David. "David Shook on Translating 'Bät Riting' by Jorge Canese." *Asymptote*, July 2016. https://www.asymptotejournal.com/criticism/jorge-canese-bat-riting/.

Shua, Ana Maria. "Killer Crónicas: Bilingual Memories." *Letras Femeninas* 31, no. 1 (2005): 261–62.

Simon, Sherry. *Gender and Translation: Cultural Identity and the Politics of Transmission*. Abingdon, UK: Routledge, 1996.

Simons, Gary F., and Charles D. Fenning, eds. *Ethnologue: Languages of the World*. 21st ed. Dallas, Tex.: SIL International, 2018. http://www.ethnologue.com.

Skoulding, Zoë. *Contemporary Women's Poetry and Urban Space: Experimental Cities*. Basingstoke, UK: Palgrave Macmillan, 2013.

Sollors, Werner. *Multilingual America: Transnationalism, Ethnicity and the Languages of American Literature*. New York: New York University Press, 1998.

Sommer, Doris. *Bilingual Aesthetics: A New Sentimental Education*. Durham, N.C.: Duke University Press, 2004.

——, ed. *Bilingual Games: Some Literary Investigations*. New York: Palgrave Macmillan, 2003.

Soto, Sandra K. "Queerness." In *The Routledge Companion to Latino/a Literature*. 2nd ed., ed. Suzanne Bost and Frances R. Aparicio, 75–83. Abingdon, UK: Routledge, 2015.

Spivak, Gayatri Chakravorty. *Outside in the Teaching Machine*. New York: Routledge, 1993.

Spurlin, William. "Queering Translation." In *A Companion to Translation Studies*, 298–309. Chichester: Wiley Blackwell, 2014.

Spyra, Ania. "Language, Geography, Globalisation: Susana Chávez-Silverman's Rejection of Translation in *Killer Crónicas: Bilingual Memories*." In *Literature, Geography, Translation: Studies in World Writing*, ed. Cecilia Alvstad, Stefan Helgesson, and David Watson, 198–208. Newcastle: Cambridge Scholars Publishing, 2011.

Staff, Harriet. "The Multilingual Erín Moure Talks Translation." *Poetry Foundation*, August 29, 2017. https://www.poetryfoundation.org/harriet/2017/08/the-multilingual-erin-moure-talks-translation.

Stanchich, Maritza. "Bilingual Big Bang: Giannina Braschi's Trilogy Levels the Spanish-English Playing Field." In *Poets, Philosophers, Lovers: On the Writings of Giannina Braschi*, ed. Frederick Luis Aldama and Tess O'Dwyer, 63–78. Pittsburgh, Penn.: University of Pittsburgh Press, 2020.

Stanton, Domna C. "On Linguistic Human Rights and the United States Foreign Language Crisis." *Profession* (2005): 64–75.
Stavans, Ilan. "Hamlet, Translated into Spanglish." *Literary Hub*, April 2016. https://lithub.com/hamlet-translated-into-spanglish/.
———. *Spanglish: The Making of a New American Language*. New York: HarperCollins, 2003.
———. "Trump, the Wall and the Spanish Language." *New York Times*, January 30, 2017. https://www.nytimes.com/2017/01/30/opinion/trump-the-wall-and-the-spanish-language.html.
Steen, Vagn. *Skriv Selv*. Copenhagen: Borgen, 1965.
Sternberg, Meir. "Polylingualism as Reality and Translation as Mimesis." *Poetics Today* 2, no. 4 (1981): 221–39.
Stewart, Garrett. "Modernism's Sonic Waiver: Literary Writing and the Filmic Device." In *Sound States: Innovative Poetics and Acoustical Technologies*, ed. Adelaide Morris, 237–73. Chapel Hill: University of North Carolina Press, 1997.
———. *Reading Voices: Literature and the Phonotext*. Berkeley: University of California Press, 1990.
Strongman, Luke. *The Booker Prize and the Legacy of Empire*. Amsterdam: Rodopi, 2002.
"Submit." *Asymptote*. http://www.asymptotejournal.com/submit/.
Sutor, Maria. *Non-Native Speech in English Literature*. Munich: Herbert Utz Verlag, 2013.
Tak-Hung Chan, Leo. "Translating Bilinguality: Theorizing in the Post-Babelian Era." *The Translator* 8, no. 1 (2002): 49–72.
Taylor-Batty, Juliette. *Multilingualism in Modernist Fiction*. Basingstoke, UK: Palgrave Macmillan, 2013.
Thody, Philip. *Le Franglais: Forbidden English, Forbidden American: Law, Politics and Language in Contemporary France: A Study in Loan Words and National Identity*. London: Bloomsbury, 2000.
Thomas, Bronwen. *Fictional Dialogue, Speech and Conversation in the Postmodern Novel*. Lincoln: University of Nebraska Press, 2012.
Torres, Lourdes. "In the Contact Zone: Code-Switching Strategies by Latino/a Writers." *MELUS* 32, no. 1 (2007): 75–96.
Torres-Padilla, José. "When Hybridity Doesn't Resist: Giannina Braschi's *Yo-Yo Boing!*." In *Complicating Constructions: Race, Ethnicity and Hybridity in American Texts*, ed. David S. Goldstein and Audrey B. Thacker, 290–307. Seattle: University of Washington Press, 2007.
Toury, Gideon. "Enhancing Cultural Changes by Means of Fictitious Translations." In *Translation and Cultural Change: Studies in History, Norms and Image-Projection*, ed. Eva Hung, 3–17. Amsterdam: John Benjamins Publishing Company, 2005.
"Trump: 'This Is a Country Where We Speak English.'" *CNN Politics*, September 16, 2015. https://edition.cnn.com/videos/politics/2015/09/16/gop-debate-cnn-debate-8p-12.cnn.
Tymoczko, Maria. "Postcolonial Writing and Literary Translation." In *Post-Colonial Translation: Theory and Practice*, ed. Susan Bassnett and Harish Trivedi, 19–40. London: Routledge, 1999.

BIBLIOGRAPHY

U.S. Census Bureau. "Annual Estimates of the Resident Population by Sex, Age, Race, and Hispanic Origin for the United States and States: April 1, 2010 to July 1, 2015," July 2016. https://factfinder.census.gov/faces/tableservices/jsf/pages/productview.xhtml?src=bkmk.

Valenti, Eva. "'Nous Autres c'est Toujours Bilingue Anyways': Code-Switching and Linguistic Displacement Among Bilingual Montréal Students." *American Review of Canadian Studies* 44 (2014): 279–329.

Van Rooten, Luis d'Antin. *Mots d'heures: Gousses, rames*. New York: Grossman, 1967.

Vargas, Fábio Aristimunho. "Fronteiras literárias: As línguas ibéricas e o portunhol." Conference paper, VI Congresso Internacional Roa Bastos, Foz do Iguaçu, 2011. http://www.nelool.ufsc.br/simposio2011/fronteiras_literarias.pdf.

Vega, Ana Lydia. "Carta Abierta a Pandora." *El Nuevo Día*, March 31, 1998.

Venuti, Lawrence. *The Translator's Invisibility: A History of Translation*. 2nd ed. London: Routledge, 2002.

Vicuña, Cecilia, and Ernesto Livon-Grosman, eds. *The Oxford Book of Latin American Poetry: A Bilingual Anthology*. New York: Oxford University Press, 2009.

von Flotow, Luise. "Feminist Translation: Contexts, Practices and Theories." *TTR: Traduction, Terminologie, Rédaction* 4, no. 2 (1991): 69–84.

Walkowitz, Rebecca L. *Born Translated: The Contemporary Novel in an Age of World Literature*. New York: Columbia University Press, 2015.

———. "Close Reading in an Age of Global Writing." *Modern Language Quarterly* 74, no. 2 (2013): 171–95.

———. "Translating the Untranslatable: An Interview with Barbara Cassin." *Public Books*, June 2014. http://www.publicbooks.org/interviews/translating-the-untranslatable-an-interview-with-barbara-cassin.

Warwick Research Collective. *Combined and Uneven Development: Towards a New Theory of World-Literature*. Liverpool: Liverpool University Press, 2015.

"We the American Hispanics." Ethnic and Hispanic Statistics Branch, Bureau of the Census, September 1993. https://www.census.gov/prod/cen1990/wepeople/we-2r.pdf.

Wheeler, Anne-Marie. "Issues of Translation in the Work of Nicole Brossard." *Yale Journal of Criticism* 16, no. 2 (2003): 425–54.

Wittig, Monique. *The Lesbian Body*. New York: William Morrow, 1975.

Xilonen, Aura. *Campeón gabacho*. Mexico City: Penguin Random House, 2015.

Yildiz, Yasemin. *Beyond the Mother Tongue: The Postmonolingual Condition*. New York: Fordham University Press, 2011.

Young, Stacey. *Changing the Wor(l)d: Discourse, Politics, and the Feminist Movement*. New York: Routledge, 1997.

"Yo-Yo Boing! (Spanglish)." Amazon. https://www.amazon.com/Yo-Yo-Boing-Spanglish-Giannina-Braschi/dp/161109089X/ref=sr_1_1?dchild=1&keywords=yo-yo+boing&qid=1621783831&sr=8-1.

Zavrl, Andrej. "Sexing the Waste Land: Gender, Desire, and Sexuality in T. S. Eliot's *The Waste Land*." *Acta Neophilologica* 38, no. 1–2 (2005): 71–82.

Zentella, Ana Celia. "Language Policy/Planning and U.S. Colonialism: The Puerto Rican Thorn in English-Only's Side." In *Sociopolitical Perspectives on Language Policy and Planning in the USA*, ed. Thom Huebner and Kathryn A. Davis, 155–71. Philadelphia: John Benjamins Publishing Company, 1999.

———. "Preface." In *Bilingualism and Identity: Spanish at the Crossroads with Other Languages*, ed. M. Niño-Murcia and J. Rothman, 3–10. Philadelphia: John Benjamins Publishing Company, 2008.

Zentella, Ana Celia, and Ricardo Otheguy. "Discussion on the Use of the Term 'Spanglish.'" Conference paper, Spanish in the U.S. and Spanish in Contact with Other Languages, Florida International University, 2009. http://potowski.org/sites/potowski.org/files/articles/attachments/Summary_debate_Spanglish_Zentella%20_Otheguy.pdf.

INDEX

academic publishing, 56, 134
active reading: of Chávez-Silverman's writing, 40, 60; of *Oscar Wao*, 33, 90, 91, 107; of *Yo-Yo Boing!*, 119, 123
African American Vernacular English, 82–83, 103
Ahmed, Sara, 55
Alarcón, Daniel, 15
Algarín, Miguel, 12, 121
Álvarez, Julia, 12, 115
AmazonCrossing, 33, 134, 147
anthropophagy, 163, 164
Anzaldúa, Gloria: *Borderlands/La Frontera*, 9–11, 13, 28, 198n31; "Don't give in, Chicanita," 28–30, 71, 109; "No se raje, Chicanita," 28–30, 71, 109; "To live in the Borderlands means you," 11, 13; "To(o) Queer the Writer—Loca, escritora y chicana," 124
Apter, Emily, 5–6, 24
associated free state, 119
Asymptote (journal), 32, 34–35, 68, 70; features on multilingualism in, 186–94
auto-hypertextuality, 50, 51, 53
autotheory, 54–57, 206n36

Bakhtin, Mikhail, 43–44, 206n20
baroque, 162–63
Barthes, Roland, 33, 79, 89, 90
Bechdel, Alison, 54
Bergvall, Caroline, 173
Biden, Joe, 7
bilingualism, 13, 24; in Anzaldúa, 38, 54, 124; in Braschi, 119–20, 126, 133, 138, 144, 145, 147; in Chávez-Silverman, 38, 51, 53; Chicana, 39; English–French, 21; in "Nuyorican" writing, 122; in Obejas's translation of *Oscar Wao*, 110; translation of Chávez-Silverman's, 71–72
blanks: in *Oscar Wao*, 77–98; in translation of *Oscar Wao*, 104–13
Bolsonaro, Jair, 19
Borges, Jorge Luis, 23, 57, 147, 209n7
Boricua, 13
Borikén. *See* Boricua
borinquen, 103. *See also* Boricua
born translated texts, 25, 146, 187, 192
Braschi, Giannina; 3, 4, 11, 14, 19, 115–147; bilingualism in, 24; collaboration on translation, 31; personal website of, 143; translation of, 27, 134–47;

Braschi, Giannina (*continued*)
untranslatability of, 26; upbringing of, 32. See also "Pelos en la lengua"; *Yo-Yo Boing!*
Brazil: artistic influence between Europe and, 63; border with Paraguay, 150; concrete movement in, 156; Guarani spoken in, 153; Indigenous aspects of culture in, 154; modernist texts in, 63, 164; multiculturalism in, 164–65; national character of, 148
Brazilian Portuguese, 159
Brief Wondrous Life of Oscar Wao, The (Díaz): authorial rewritings of, 92–98; blanks in, 77–98; paratexts of, 79, 80, 91–93, 97, 101, 105, 113, 211n38; as pseudotranslation, 98–101; translation of, 98–114
Brossard, Nicole, 21, 170
Bueno, Wilson, 3, 15, 148–85; murder of, 148; Portunhol in work of, 16–20; translation of, 73–83; translator of, 31 (*see also* Moure, Erín); untranslatability of, 25. See also *Mar Paraguayo*
Butler, Judith, 80, 89, 92, 108, 137, 168

calque, 3, 8; in Chávez-Silverman's writing, 65–66, 68, 74–75; in *Oscar Wao*, 100; in *Yo-Yo Boing!*, 123, 127
Canada, 32, 149, 167, 174; feminist translation studies in, 179; French–English writing in, 20–22; Indigenous languages in, 175;
Canese, Jorge, 93
cannibalist movement, 163–64. See also anthropophagy
Cassin, Barbara, 26–27, 30, 69, 112, 155, 175
Castillo, Ana, 9, 207n41
censorship, 210n18; as a constitutive part of speech, 92; information vacuums produced by, 97; multilingualism as, 3; as productive, 89; typographical signs of, 85. See also blanks; "páginas en blanco"
Chamoiseau, Patrick, 81, 82, 84, 169, 209n7; translation of, 106

Chávez-Silverman, Susana: "(Almost) Milagros Crónica," 56; "Axolotl Crónica," 55, 58–64; "Cartografía Humana/Star Maps Crónica," 42 ; "Diary Inside/Color Local Crónica," 55; "Estragos acuáticos Crónica," 54; "Glossary Crónica," 36, 41–43, 48, 49, 65; "Hawk Call Crónica," 47; "In My Country Crónica," 44; parentheses in, 47, 63; puns in, 38, 47, 48, 57, 68; "San Francisco Transcript/Diary," 52; "Solstice/Shamanic Magia Crónica," 51; "South Coast Plaza Crónica," 46; "Todo verdor perdurará crónica," 68–77; translation in, 65–68; translation of, 68–77; "Un Pico (De) presión Diptych," 47. See also *Killer Crónicas*; *Scenes from la Cuenca de Los Angeles*
Chicanx speech, 9
Chicanx studies, 198n28
Chicanx writing, 8–9
Chow, Rey, 44, 69, 168
Cisneros, Sandra, 9
Cixous, Hélène, 61, 131, 132, 207n50
code-switching, 57, 126, 196n6; intersentential, 4, 17; intrasentential, 4, 38
compensation, 73, 177, 209n83
concrete movement, 34, 149, 155, 156, 162
contact zone, 53, 81
Cortázar, Julio, 23, 58, 63, 90; "Axolotl," 59–60; *Rayuela*, 57, 207 n41. See also "lector cómplice"; "lector hembra"; "lector macho"
creoleness, 81, 84, 169, 214n77. See also creolité
creolité, 81, 84, 87, 214n77. See also creoleness
creolized English, 4, 19, 33, 151; in Obejas's translation of *Oscar Wao*, 109; as producing blanks, 84–86, 91; as restricting access, 97; as writerly, 90

Damrosch, David, 7, 32
de Andrade, Mario. See *Macunaíma*

INDEX

de Andrade, Oswald, 163
de Campos, Augusto, 155, 156, 175. *See also* "Lygia Fingers"
de Campos, Haroldo, 156, 157; on anthropophagy, 163, 164; as founder of *Noigandres*, 155; on *Macunaíma*, 165
Deleuze, Gilles, 31, 39, 55, 94, 140
Derrida, Jacques, 44, 56, 65, 94, 168; on supplementarity, 55, 145, 220n79; trace in, 219n56; translation of, 214n78
dialogue novels, 118
Díaz, Junot: Annotated Oscar Wao website, 91, 93, 95, 96, 107, 108; *Drown*, 81, 86, 94, 102, 104, 108, 111, 213n54; Genius extract, 101, 111, 113, 114, 143, 207n7; *Los boys*, 102; *Negocios*, 102; racial categories in, 82–83, 84, 210n12; sexual misconduct of, 212n46; translation in, 98–101; translation of, 101–13; use of footnotes by, 78, 85, 93, 94, 96, 97, 209n7. See also *Brief Wondrous Life of Oscar Wao, The*
dictatorship, 78, 79, 87, 111
Diegues, Douglas, 18–20, 150–51, 153, 169, 201n74
Dillon, Sarah, 39, 75, 192
Doloughan, Fiona, 25, 207n59
Don Quixote, Spanglish translation of, 14
du Plessis, Klara, 189–90, 193

écriture feminine, 61
Eliot, T. S., 42, 23, 16, 118, 129–30. See also *Waste Land, The*
"elucidário," 152, 175, 178–79, 183
"elucidictionary," 178–79, 189
English First, 5
exoticization, 12, 54. *See also* self-exoticization

false cognate, 65, 67, 68, 123, 127, 172
faux translations, 67, 172
Ferré, Rosario, 120
First Nations cultures, 20

Foarță, Șerban, 190
footnotes, as interventionist translation strategy, 136–37, 138, 181. *See also* Díaz, Junot; Moure, Erín; Obejas, Achy
foreignizing, 29, 70, 72, 74, 99, 101, 109, 138; in feminist translation, 136–37; in postcolonial translation, 135
Forster, Andrew, 184–85
"Franglais," 20
"Frenglish," 20–22

García, Cristina, 101
Geisdorfer Feal, Rosemary, 61
gender fluidity: in "Axolotl Crónica," 59–64; in *Mar Paraguayo*, 159–62; in *Yo-Yo Boing!*, 126–34
Genette, Gérard, 39, 50, 76, 91
genocide, Haitian. *See* parsley massacre
George Washington Gómez (Paredes), 8, 9, 13
glossary: in *Drown*, 81; in the English translation of *Texaco*, 107; in *Killer Crónicas*, 41–42, 53; in *Mar Paraguayo*, 152–55, 221n7; in *Paraguayan Sea*, 179; in *We Came All the Way from Cuba*, 104
Godard, Barbara, 21, 136, 179
González Echevarría, Roberto, 10
Grutman, Rainier, 26
Guarani culture, 150, 165
Guarani language; 3, 16; 18; in Jorge Canese's work, 193; in *Mar Paraguayo*, 19, 149, 151–56, 161, 173; in *Paraguayan Sea*; 173–75; in "portunhol selvagem," 18
"Guarañol," 193
Guattari, Félix. 31, 39, 55, 94, 140. *See also* rhizome

Hansen Esplin, Marlene, 13
Hassan, Waïl, 203n94
Herrera, Yuri, 1, 2
hijacking, 136, 137, 138, 224n76
Hijuelos, Oscar, 12
Hinojosa, Rolando, 9
homosexuality, 146, 191, 220n80

INDEX

Huston, Nancy, 22
hybrid animals, 219n50; in *Mar Paraguayo*, 162, 166; in "Pelos en la lengua," 133; in *Yo-Yo Boing!*, 133, 162
hypertextuality, 50, 53, 58. *See also* auto-hypertextuality

Ibargoyen, Saúl, 17
Indigenous cultures, 153, 163–66
Indigenous languages, 16, 19, 20, 103, 53, 175. *See also* Guarani; Mohawk; Nahuatl; Tsuu Tina
Indigenous peoples, 53, 82, 163, 165
interlingual variation, 139
intersectionality, 11, 39, 55, 124, 126
intertextuality, 168, 50, 117. *See also* Genette, Gerard; hypertextuality
intralingual variation, 32, 44, 110, 139
Irigaray, Luce, 61, 131

jabuti, 163
Joyce, James, 23; *Ulysses*, 118; *Finnegans Wake*, 69, 94, 156

Kanchana, Kanya, 190
Kiezdeutsch, 188–89
Killer Crónicas (Chávez-Silverman), 36–38, 207n41; creative-critical palimpsests in, 54–58; linguistic palimpsests in, 43–45; palimpsests in, 40–42; as rejecting translation, 64; sonic palimpsests in, 45–50; textual palimpsests in, 53–54; title of, 65–66
Kilito, Abdelfattah, 28
Kosofsky Sedgwick, Eve, 63, 125, 133

language politics; English-French, 22; global, 23; in Puerto Rico, 119–21; in the United States, 7, 216n15
language purity, 109, 121, 188
"latinidad," 13–14, 199n49, 206n35
Latinx studies, 14, 56
Latinx writers, 8, 13–15, 80, 83, 120
Lauret, Maria, 65, 90, 196n6
"lector cómplice," 60, 90

"lector hembra," 60, 90
"lector macho," 59, 60
Lennon, Brian, 64, 203n93
Levine, Suzanne Jill, 136
lingua franca: English as, 7; Portuguese as, 16; Spanish as, 15
Lipski, John, 10, 17, 200n61
Lonsdale, Laura, 23
Lorde, Audre, 54, 206n38, 210n12
Los 3 amigos (comic series), 17
Lugo, Fernando, 18
Luiselli, Valeria, 15
Lula da Silva, Luiz Inácio, 18
"Lygia Fingers" (de Campos), 156

Macunaíma (de Andrade), 164–65, 181
male gaze, 59
Mar Paraguayo (Bueno): cultural hybridity in, 162–67; gender and sexual fluidity in, 159–62; linguistic fluidity in, 150–59; "Portunhol" in, 3, 16–20; translation of, 167–85
movimiento antropófago. *See* cannibalist movement
marafona: as character in *Mar Paraguayo*, 150, 152, 157–62, 165, 166, 177, 179, 222n22; as doll, 149, 181; as transvestite or prostitute, 149, 160
MARGENTO. *See* Tănăsescu, Chris
matrix language, 17, 38, 70, 80, 201n66
MERCOSUR, 17–18
metafiction, 117
metalepsis, 24, 144
Meylaerts, Reine, 26
Mignolo, Walter, 57
Miller, Joshua, 23, 206n27, 216n15
Mizumura, Minae, 24
Mohabir, Rajiv, 190–91
Mohawk, 175
monolingualism, 33, 35, 135; English, 5, 6, 41, 58, 61, 120, 135; Portuguese, 16; Spanish, 15
monolingual paradigm, 15, 22, 28, 35
Moretti, Franco, 41
Moure, Erín: Best Translated Poetry Award longlisting, 167; commitment

INDEX

to transnational themes, 167; influence of bilingual Canadian women writers on, 21–22; influence of feminist translation studies on, 179–80; life of, 167; *O Cidadán*, 168, 170, 172, 173, 183; poetry by, 168–73; public art installation by, 184–85; translational creativity of, 177–78; translation of *Paraguayan Sea*, 73–86; use of different names by, 171; use of footnotes by, 181–82. See also *Search Procedures*; *Sheep's Vigil by a Fervent Person*
multilingualism: as American-inflected, 15; in Anzaldúa, 12; in *Asymptote*, 186–87, 191, 193; in Chávez-Silverman, 45, 76; in concrete poetry, 156; in creoleness, 81; in global communities, 187; literary studies of, 2–3, 6, 26; in *Mar Paraguayo*, 149, 159, 166, 175; in modernist literature, 23, 156, 216n7; in Erín Moure's writing, 168; in *Oscar Wao*, 100; in *Paraguayan Sea*, 175, 178, 185; role of in slow reading, 41; as serving dominant paradigms, 14; as translatable, 28; in *The Waste Land*, 129; in *Yo-Yo Boing!*, 147
Muñoz, José Esteban, 124

Nahuatl, 10, 186
Nathanaël, 22
Nelson, Maggie, 54
neobaroque, 34, 149, 162–65, 222n25
Neuman, Andrés, 2, 194
Nicolau (journal), 148
Nissan, Greg, 188–90
Noigandres poets, 155–56
"nonstandard" language, 49, 57, 83, 122, 123, 136, 137, 179, 217n30
Nuyorican Poets Café, 21, 121, 122
"Nuyoricans," 12, 121, 122, 190

Obejas, Achy: translation of *Oscar Wao*, 101–14; upbringing of, 103; as writer, 31, 103–104

O'Dwyer, Tess, 220n76; as character in *Yo-Yo Boing!*, 134; as translator of *Yo-Yo Boing!*, 134–35, 137–45, 147
Official English movement, 119, 120, 196. See also U.S. English
Oscar Wao. See *Brief Wondrous Life of Oscar Wao, The*

"páginas en blanco," 78, 79, 87, 89, 94, 97
palimpsest: in *Asymptote*, 192; in Chávez-Silverman's work, 32, 36, 39, 40, 42, 50, 56, 68, 76; in Díaz's *Oscar Wao*, 97–98, 113–14
Paraguay, 18, 32, 148, 150, 77; languages of, 16, 18, 169, 153; snake indigenous to, 162
paratexts, 32; of Chávez-Silverman's writing, 41, 53, 58; of *Mar Paraguayo*, 175, 182–83; of *Oscar Wao*, 79, 80, 91–93, 97, 101, 105, 113, 211n38
Paredes, Américo, 8, 9, 38, 64, 81, 108
Parks, Tim, 7, 24
parsley massacre, 88, 211n19
"Pelos en la lengua" (Braschi), 133
Peréz Firmat, Gustavo, 13
plurilingual writing, strong, 203n93
"Portunhol," 3, 4, 16–20, 22, 34, 186, 200–201n61
"portunhol selvagem," 18–20; codification of, 201n74
"Portuñol." See "Portunhol"
postmodernism, 24; in *Yo-Yo Boing!*, 33, 116, 118, 134
postmonolingual condition, 35
poststructuralism, 31, 55, 136, 137
Pratt, Mary Louise, 6, 53
prefacing, 136–38
pseudotranslation, 33, 80, 98–101, 114
Puerto Rico, 5, 12, 13, 19, 103; language in, 119–21, 216n15; referenda in, 216n13; relationship to the United States, 32, 123, 119n42

queer practice, 3, 33, 116, 123, 129, 131, 134
queer theory, 31, 55, 58, 219n50
Quiñones, Noel, 190

readability, 24, 93, 103; of *Mar Paraguayo*, 166, 175; of *Oscar Wao*, 94; of *Paraguayan Sea*, 177, 182; of translations of *Oscar Wao*, 182
Real Academia Española, 73, 109
rhizome, 31, 55, 206–7n40
Rosenwald, Lawrence, 69, 75

Saint-Amour, Paul, 46, 49, 64
Salas Rivera, Raquel, 15
Sarduy, Severo, 162–63
Saussy, Haun, 65
Scenes from la Cuenca de Los Angeles (Chávez-Silverman), 37, 38, 40, 42, 43, 46, 173; acknowledgements to, 50; auto-hypertextuality in, 51–54; foreword to, 64; as teaching tool, 56–57; title of, 47
scholarly publishing. *See* academic publishing
Search Procedures (Moure), 169–70
self-exoticization, 54, 59
September 11, 2001, 5
sexuality: and bilingualism, 124–25; as disturbed by queer theory, 31, 63; in *Mar Paraguayo*, 150, 160; in Rajiv Mohabir's poems, 191; and translation, 137; and tropicalization, 206n35; in *The Waste Land*, 218n42; in *Yo-Yo Boing!*, 127–28, 135, 141, 142, 145
Sheep's Vigil by a Fervent Person (Moure), 171
Shell, Marc, 6
Shklovsky, Viktor, 23, 123
Shook, David, 193
Sollors, Werner, 6
Sommer, Doris, 6, 7, 43, 68, 76; on *Yo-Yo Boing!*, 115–16; 118, 123, 147
"Spanglish": as act of resistance, 12; codification of, 14, 201n74; deprecation of, 3, 9, 10, 58, 66; literary uses of, 5–15; origins of, 8–9; as a queer practice, 124–30; as translatable, 69
Spivak, Gayatri, 135, 103, 104
Spyra, Ania, 37, 64

Stavans, Ilan, 14, 200n57, 201n74
Sternberg, Meir, 26, 138
Stewart, Garrett, 47, 67
supplementarity, 55, 145, 220n79
supplementing, 136, 224n76
surface translations, 3, 158–59

Taíno words, 81, 103, 12
Tănăsescu, Chris, 190
Taylor-Batty, Juliette, 23
third-world feminism, 124
Thody, Philip, 20
Tolstoy, Leo, 23
trace, 65, 219n56
transcription, 17, 48, 49, 67, 82, 144, 177
translatability, 24, 69, 93
translation; in colonial America, 112; as creative practice, 31, 136, 167; as feminine, 136, 146, 147; feminist approaches to, 135–37; foreignizing, 29, 70, 135; games, 38, 89; limitations of, 111–12; as palimpsest, 75–76, 113–14; postcolonial approaches to, 135–36, 144; queer approaches to, 135–37; as secondary, 34, 146, 147, 167; as self-commentary, 142–45
translational turn, 25
translingualism, 196n6
triple frontera, 18, 151
tropicalization, 54, 206n35
Trujillato, 78, 87, 94
Trujillo Molina, Rafael Leonidas, 78, 79, 83, 85, 87, 89, 210n18; disappearance of Jesús Galindez by, 85; in footnotes to *Oscar Wao*, 93, 111, 113; Haitian genocide under, 88; sexual predation by, 94
Trump, Donald, 7
Tsuu Tina, 175,
Tupi people, 163–64

untranslatability, 25–27, 155, 214n78
untranslatables, 26–27, 30, 69, 112, 155, 175, 203n93
U.S. English, 5, 14, 120. *See also* Official English movement

INDEX

Vega, Ana Lydia, 20
Venuti, Lawrence, 29–30, 135
von Flotow, Luise, 136, 224n76

Walkowitz, Rebecca, 25, 27, 30, 146, 192
Waste Land, The (Eliot), 116, 118, 129, 143, 218n42. *See also* Eliot, T. S.
world literature, 2, 24, 32, 41, 144; as Anglo-American, 7, 15, 23; as monolingual, 7

writerly text, 89, 94, 115; *Oscar Wao* as, 33, 79, 90; translation of *Oscar Wao* as, 113

Yildiz, Yasemin, 22
Yo-Yo Boing!: bilingualism in, 19–24; gender and sexuality in, 124–34; reception of, 116–19; translation of, 134–47

Zentella, Ana Celia, 12

GPSR Authorized Representative: Easy Access System Europe, Mustamäe tee 50, 10621 Tallinn, Estonia, gpsr.requests@easproject.com